E&G 蓝皮书 BLUE BOOK

2011中国城市
科学发展综合评价报告（中英文版）
——城市与人

2011 Comprehensive evaluation and grading report on china urban scientific development
(Chinese-English Bilingual Edition)
——City and People

编著 Author

中国城市发展研究院
China City Development Academy

中国社会科学出版社

图书在版编目（CIP）数据

2011 中国城市科学发展综合评价报告 / 中国城市发展研究院等联合编著 . —北京：中国社会科学出版社，2011.10
ISBN 978 - 7 - 5161 - 0232 - 9

Ⅰ. ①2… Ⅱ. ①中… Ⅲ. ①城市 - 发展 - 评估 - 调查报告 - 中国 - 2011 Ⅳ. ①F299.2

中国版本图书馆 CIP 数据核字（2011）第 217577 号

出版策划 任　明
特邀编辑 成　树
责任校对 安　全
技术编辑 李　建

出版发行　**中国社会科学出版社**　　出版人　赵剑英
社　　址　北京鼓楼西大街甲 158 号　　邮　编　100720
电　　话　010 - 64040843（编辑）　　64058741（宣传）　　64070619（网站）
　　　　　010 - 64030272（批发）　　64046282（团购）　　84029450（零售）
网　　址　http：//www.csspw.cn（中文域名：中国社科网）
经　　销　新华书店
印　　刷　北京奥隆印刷厂
版　　次　2011 年 10 月第 1 版　　印　次　2011 年 10 月第 1 次印刷
开　　本　710 × 1000　1/16
印　　张　23
字　　数　386 千字
定　　价　280.00 元

《中国城市科学发展综合评级体系(E&G)设计》

著作权声明

　　《中国城市科学发展综合评级体系（E&G）设计》是中国城市发展研究院的重大研究成果之一，已经通过专家论证和中华人民共和国国家版权局的审核，"中华人民共和国国家版权局著作权登记证书"登记号为：2008-A-012255。

　　未经本院书面授权，严禁任何形式盗用、复制或仿造本《综合评级体系设计》，严禁任何形式使用本《综合评级体系设计》进行评价或其他活动。一经发现，本院将依法追究相关者的法律责任。

中国城市发展研究院

2011 年 10 月 9 日

《2011 中国城市科学发展综合评价报告》
编 辑 机 构

编 辑 委 员 会

编 辑 部

目　录

前　言

本着尽力做得更好的原则，到今年的《报告》完成时，已经是 10 月了。

年度《中国城市科学发展综合评价报告》的编写工作进入第四年了。对前三年所取得的成绩和应吸取的经验，我们沉下心来思索、总结，以发展的观念客观、理性地对待自己的成果，最终坚定了在原有基础上加以调整、完善的决心。

自 2011 年 3 月起，我们先后组织了数十位专业学者及行业专家，召开了近十次大小会议，从确立主题、解构框架、设计方法、划分版块等方面进行了充分的探讨和研究，数易其稿，再以 4 个多月的时间完成了大量的数据分析、问卷调查及报告组稿等工作，最终才有了这本《2011 中国城市科学发展综合评价报告》。除了基本构架，不同以往的是，今年的《报告》有了一个明确的主题——"城市与人"，我们下调了评价的视角，关注的焦点逐渐转移至最贴近民生、最反映民声的地方，旗帜鲜明地提出，城市应为人而发展。

这里，我们首先要感谢在今年《报告》编写的前后提供极大帮助的兄弟单位、机构及社会各界的朋友。

感谢中国国际经济交流中心在《报告》筹备及编写过程中的支持，不仅从国家宏观政策与发展战略角度给予了理论指导，使《报告》更具权威性和政策参考价值，还协助组织了一批国内权威专家，多次参与论证研究思路、主题观点、体系框架、数据分类及处理方法等，使《报告》更具科学性和探索性，同时，几位专家还直接参与了文字分析报告的研究、起草和总体修改工作。

感谢中国战略文化促进会在《报告》编写过程中给予的关注和帮助，从历史、文化与战略关系的角度指导我们对方向的把握，深化报告的传承性与前瞻性，还提供了很多可供借鉴的参考资料。

还要感谢其他在不同方面给予我们不同帮助的机构或个人，感谢那些始终关注我们成长的读者们。你们，始终是鼓舞我们继续前行的明灯。

编辑部

2011 年 10 月 10 日

序　言

关于城市

(十一届全国政协副主席　孙家正)

　　伴随着经济的发展、科技的进步，城市化进程明显加快。城市的发展，促进了人类社会现代化进程。目前，城市的数量和规模日益扩大，全世界城市人口在超过农业人口后迅速攀升，全球性的"城市时代"已经来临。

　　城市文明的发展是历史的进步，他广泛而深刻地影响着人们的生活方式和社会心理。城市的发展为人们带来了更多的舒适、便利和机会，也带来一些新的困扰和问题。我们赖以生存的城市家园不同程度地面临着记忆消失、面貌趋同、交通拥挤、环境恶化等诸多问题。城市的发展不断地满足并刺激着人们的物质需求，而精神上、心理上的慰藉和憧憬却在不同程度地失落。人们在为城市日新月异的变化而兴奋的同时，应该保持一种忧患意识，冷静思考城市乃至整个经济社会如何科学发展。

　　我们究竟需要一个什么样的生存空间？我们究竟在追求怎样的生活？当人们试图以全新的、理性的眼光审视扑朔迷离的城市形态时，不约而同地选择了文化的视角。我认为，《中国城市科学发展综合评价报告》出版的意义在于，它的编辑和作者也试图从城市的个性差异，也就是从城市的文化角度去审视和评价每一个城市。

　　文化是什么？文化是一定历史、一定地域、一定人类群体的生存状态和愿望的反映，同时，又对人的生存和发展产生广泛而深刻的影响。城市文化问题，可以说是当代备受关注的世界性话题。

　　城市是市民的安居之所和精神家园，城市建设应秉持以人为本的原则。城市的规划、建设、管理和服务都必须坚持面向最广大的普通民众，同时也要回应不同人群的诉求。创造人与自然友好相处的生态环境，形成亲切无碍的人际关系，构建和谐自然的城市空间，是民众的共同愿望和要求。面对现代生活的迅捷变化和市场经济下的激烈竞争，人们的物质需求需要不断地满足，而心理上的迷茫和困扰尤需抚慰。民众的生存状态、心理感受，需要更多的人文关怀。城市文化形态的变化和发展过程应该同时成为不断满足人们的精神需求、提高人的素质、促进人的全面发展的过程。城市建设和管理呼唤着深切的人文关怀。一个城市是否具有这种人文关怀的精神、环境和氛围，应成为考评城市建设水平高低、管理质量优劣的重要标尺。

形神兼备是文化城市的重要特征。所谓形，就是城市的建筑、街道、景观，表现为城市外在的风貌气度；所谓神，就是蕴含在城市历史和现实当中的文化内涵，闪耀着一个城市独有的内在品格和气质。物态景观和人类活动因共有的文化内涵而和谐统一。一个城市只有形神兼备，浑然一体，才能保持永不衰竭的魅力。一个对城市的科学评价体系，也应当从"形"和"神"两个角度去审视城市。我们感到欣慰的是，《中国城市科学发展综合评价报告》的编辑和作者在这方面做出了不懈的努力。

人创造了有形的城市，城市反过来又以无形的方式陶冶人、塑造人。市民的价值观念、思维方式、道德水准、社会风尚等因素是城市文化建设的综合反映，也是城市文化建设发挥作用的过程与结果。

无论是有形的城市面貌，还是无形的城市精神，都是一定的文化使然。文化如水，滋润万物，悄然无声。文化留存于城市空间的每一个角落，融汇于城市生活的全部过程和每一个细节。文化对城市的营造、演变，对市民的生活、行为都产生着潜移默化的作用，城市是文化的容器。城市中的街区、广场、建筑、雕塑、装置、绿化、小品等等构成了城市有形和外在的物态系统，作用于我们的视觉、听觉、嗅觉、触觉而直抵心灵；同时，它们又承载着在城市空间中发生着的人类活动，正是这些千姿百态、生动有趣的活动使城市富有了充沛的人气和旺盛的活力。

拒绝和防止趋同，保护和彰显个性，是当代城市建设中应该特别注意的问题。现代化、全球化无疑是一把双刃剑，其益处无需赘言，其弊端也显而易见。现代化对于传统的消解，全球化对于个性的抹杀已是不争的事实。正因为如此，近年来，保护文化多样性的声浪日趋高涨。尊重和珍惜城市的历史传统、地域风貌和民族特色，方能保持并彰显一个城市所独有的文化韵味。一个城市区别于另一个城市的，不仅在于它的规划布局、色彩基调、建筑样式，更重要的还在于其内在的气质、情感及其文化底蕴。城市的文化特色将是城市特有风貌和文化精神的完美结合。发现、界定、保护、传承和拓展城市的文化个性与特色，方可构建起轮廓清晰、结构完整、布局合理、神采独具的城市文化形象。

保护历史文化遗产是城市建设中的重大课题。历史文化遗产在城市建设中焕发着穿越时空的悠久魅力。一座城市就是一部历史，我们不能割断历史，割断历史便也撕裂了现在。人类需要前瞻又耽于回忆，我们不能失去记忆，失去记忆也便失去了憧憬。城市中的物质与非物质的文化遗产见证着城市的生命历程，保持和延续着城市文化，并促进着城市肌体的健康发展，同时也赋予了人们真切的归宿感与认同感。我们必须坚守、传承、培育城市的优秀文化传统，尽可能避免盲目开发对文化遗产、文化环境的破坏。精心呵护历史文化遗产，维系历史文脉，留住城市记忆，是人们生存发展的心理需求，也是当代人对祖先和子孙的责任。

城市不是钢筋、混凝土的堆砌物，而是一个有机的生命体。城市的演化和发展是一个生命体的成长发育和有机完善的过程。我们要尊重城市内在的遗传基因，顺应城市生成肌理和发展规律，在改造与完善中，有机更新，有序发展，使其生态环境不断优化、服务功能日趋完备、文化韵味更加浓郁。

城市建设不但要继承传统，同时也要适应时代的发展和生活的需要不断地创造和更新。成功的城市必定是在保持自己文化传统基础上进行再创新的城市。坚守历史传统、适应时代需要的文化创新是城市发展的灵魂和活力。包括城市建设内在的文化创新，需要有坚定的自信和包容的胸怀。对外开放是中国的基本国策，和而不同是中国的哲学思维，追求和谐是中国人的价值取向。

城市从来就不是孤立的存在。追根溯源，是农村、农业和农民孕育并哺乳了城市。这一点，在中国城市化进程中尤为明显。反哺农村，善待农民，促进城乡协调发展是城市发展的应有之义。这不仅是道义上的必须，也是城市自身持续发展的必备条件。

对中国城市按着科学发展观进行综合评级，不但有利于促进中国城市社会经济的健康发展，而且也是对城市文化的总结和肯定。我衷心希望《中国城市科学发展综合评价报告》取得成功，为中国城市发展做出独特的贡献。

第一部分 2011 中国城市发展总报告

城市：如何为人发展
　　　　如何让人幸福

　　我国第六次人口普查数据表明，截至 2010 年底，我国的城镇化率已经达到 49.68％，这一统计主要基于现实的城镇常住人口的规模。如果从户籍管理、社会保障等体制角度出发，这一城镇化率可能具有偏高的"水分"；而如果将全社会的就业结构现状，以及社会生活方式的基本特征，作为城镇化的内容和尺度，实质性的城镇化率或许还不止这些。无论城镇化水平从何角度衡量，如何准确表达，人们正越来越感受到，城市的发展已经关乎到几乎所有人的利益。城镇因为发展用地，必然波及农业、农村和农民；因为规划调整，必然波及市政、企业和市民。在政府和有关专家们围绕城镇化率指标或喜或忧、争论不休的时候，社会各界、城乡居民们则越来越关心：我们究竟为什么要发展城市？发展城市对我们有什么好处？发展快慢与我们有什么关系？这也恰恰是在城镇发展中如何贯彻科学发展观必须回答的核心问题。

　　在这里，我们只是客观地以几年间的数据分析及研究积累为基础，尝试着从民生、民声的角度，折射出中国城市（镇）发展进程中产生的一些现象，无论是正面的，抑或是负面的，"以人为本"地探讨城市究竟为什么而发展，又该如何发展？

一、以民生为本，评价城市发展及其政策体系

　　"城市为人而发展"、"城市让生活美好"等等口号，在越来越多场合的出现，引起了人们普遍的共鸣，逐渐地、必然地成为社会的共识，转为人们的追求。这样的追求无论属于回归还是理想，都要求对城市的发展、更新、完善指导理念和相应的评价体系，将当前对城市物态形象疯狂的、

几乎变态的追求和欣赏，更多地转向对人的生活和自身发展的真切关注，将以人为本的科学发展观，真正落实为城市的发展观，形成新的、系统的发展评价指标，并构建相应的发展体制和路径。

中国城市发展研究院从 2008 年开始，运用年度统计指标数据，研究提出了一套新的系统的城市评价体系，对全国地级及以上城市进行综合分类评价，从科学发展观的角度评价城市发展得失，进行全新的尝试。连续 3 年的坚持与完善，使评价报告在社会上产生了一定的影响，在获得好评的同时，许多人也提出了非常中肯的、完善性的批评和建议。在各界的热情支持、鼓励下，从 2011 年开始，我们在沿袭原有分类的基础上，进一步优化了分类体系，主要是从指标的逻辑关系上更加清晰人与城市的关系，以便在分类更加科学的基础上，完善判断和分析的方法，从年度指标的评价排序上更为清晰、更为直接地发现城市与人关系的趋势、特征和主要矛盾等。

现有的城市统计指标涵盖经济、社会、文化等各个领域，我们将这些指标分为三大类：第一类是经济发展水平，主要反映经济发展的规模、要素效益和外部效应，总体是属于生产类指标；第二类是公共服务水平，主要反映政府投入社会公共服务事业的规模和范围，总体属于社会共享类的财富分配指标；第三类是居民分享水平，主要反映城乡居民在城市发展中分享到的各项实惠和机会，总体属于城市发展成果最终由居民收获的个人受益类指标。除了评价城市在每一类上的表现外，重点将评价分析三类指标之间的关系。其逻辑关系为：一类指标反映的能力决定二类指标的规模和水平；二类、三类指标反映的规模和水平，则是通过一定的分配制度和技术路径决定大小与多少。如果一个城市的三类指标在城市排序中位置差别较小，可视为居民实际分享的成果与城市发展水平比较协调，相反则认为是问题，供大家探究原因。尝试用这一方法，即从居民最终个人受益角度评价城市综合发展的得与失。

由于统计指标只是反映可物化、可量化的指标，本报告的目的，只是努力反映当前中国城市发展中趋势性的表象和特征，各类排序的结果显然有利于每个城市找到不同发展领域的差距，有利于城市间的交流，但无意对其中某个城市的工作性问题做出评价，指标排序也不宜成为考核一个城市管理水平的依据。表露现象背后存在的大量理念性、政策性、体制性、工作性问题，必须通过分解多个专题，通过个案、访谈、实证等多种社会调查方法才能给予系统解答。此外，目前的城市统计指标是结果性的，并不反映城市居民的需求，也无法借此判断居民对城市发展成就的满意程度，因此也不能作为评价城市居民幸福指数的依据。为了弥补统计指标的局限性，我们在北京、深圳两地共做了1600多份问卷调查，将城市人口按户籍、职业等分为若干个群体，了解他们各自对城市发展的关注范围和关注度，这或许可以为我们寻找政府发展目标与居民需求之间的差距提供一定帮助。

二、现阶段，中国城市发展进程中表现出来的总体趋势

1. 发展阶段中普遍面临的问题与挑战

不管是在全球还是在一个国家范围内，城市发展过程中的问题或者说不协调性始终是广泛存在的，只是在不同阶段的表现程度不一、形式不同而已。在中国，现阶段城市发展不协调的问题，体现在经济社会发展的许多方面和不同层次，究其原因，其实是很复杂的一个课题，涉及到自然地理、历史人文、政策体制等等。单从其表现形式来说，可以简单归纳为以下几个方面：

（1）现代市场经济体制尚不完善，盲目投资与低水平扩张的体制性根源导致经济增长速度快、质量低的深层次矛盾不断凸显。

（2）主体功能定位模糊，生产要素无法实现合理地自由流动及优化配置，区域发展极不平衡，且差距仍有扩大趋势。

（3）社会公共事业的发展明显滞后于经济发展，不尽合理的公共服务资源配置、仍欠完善的社会保障体系、尚显薄弱的非政府组织以及其他复杂的社会矛盾都不利于和谐发展的主题。

（4）可持续发展压力日趋严峻。经济总量的扩张伴随着工业化、城市（镇）化的加速推进，而粗放型经济增长方式却导致运行成本的快速增长。人口、资源、环境与经济、社会协调发展的生态经济模式仍处于摸索阶段。

2. 国家采取的相应措施及取得的成效

2006年3月14日，十届全国人大四次会议表决通过了关于国民经济和社会发展第十一个五年规划纲要的决议。面对新起点上的新机遇、新挑战，"十一五"规划突出了六大重点：推进经济增长方式的转变、调整优化产业结构、解决三农问题、推进城市化健康发展、促进区域协调发展、切实加强和谐社会建设。其中，民生建设得到前所未有的重视，22项指标中有8项涉及公共服务和人民生活，有2项更是作为约束性指标首次列入规划。

几年里，面对复杂多变的国内外经济环境，经历了国际金融危机、汶川大地震等一系列历史罕见的严峻挑战，但国民经济总体实现了宏观调控的预期目标，经济平稳较快增长，单项改革有明显成效，人民生活不断改善，经济社会发展态势总体良好。

（1）经济实力和综合国力大幅提升。2009年，我国国内生产总值为

340507 亿元，比 2005 年①的 184937 亿元增长 84.12%，年均增长率达 12.98%。

国内生产总值

（亿元）

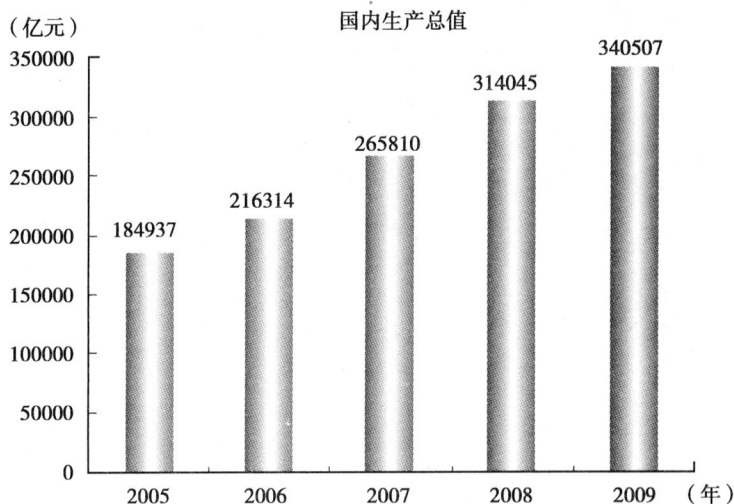

（2）人民生活水平得到明显改善。城镇居民年人均可支配收入从 2005 年的 10493 元增至 2009 年的 17175 元，增长 63.68%，年均增长 10.36%；农民年人均纯收入从 3255 元增至 5153 元，增长 58.31%，年均增长 9.62%。其他如人均绿地面积、人均住宅使用面积、人均城市道路面积、每万人拥有公共汽车数等多项民生指标均逐年递增。

民民收入增长趋势

（元）

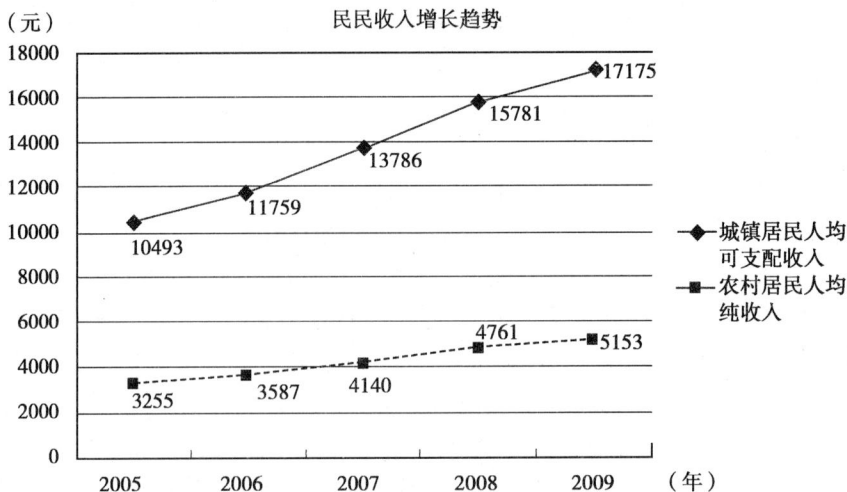

——城镇居民人均可支配收入
——农村居民人均纯收入

---

① "十一五"规划时间为 2006 年至 2010 年，鉴于实际统计数据的取得时限，我们的动态分析一律采用 2005 年至 2009 年的数据进行。

其他民生指标增长情况

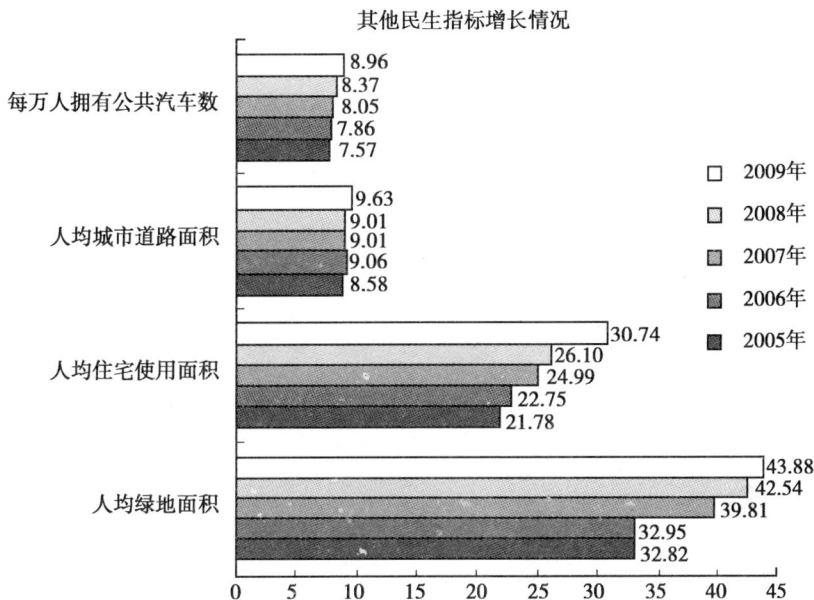

每万人拥有公共汽车数
8.96
8.37
8.05
7.86
7.57

人均城市道路面积
9.63
9.01
9.01
9.06
8.58

人均住宅使用面积
30.74
26.10
24.99
22.75
21.78

人均绿地面积
43.88
42.54
39.81
32.95
32.82

2009年
2008年
2007年
2006年
2005年

0 5 10 15 20 25 30 35 40 45

（3）在一系列区域发展战略和政策的有力推动下，中、西部和东北地区发展速度逐渐加快，区域协调发展取得初步成效。2005—2009年间，东、中、西和东北地区人均国内生产总值年均增速分别为12.34%、13.65%、14.87%和12.64%，中、西部和东北地区增速均高于东部地区，西部地区尤其明显；其他如人均GDP、城镇居民人均可支配收入、农村居民纯收入等指标均呈此趋势。

年平均增长率对比情况

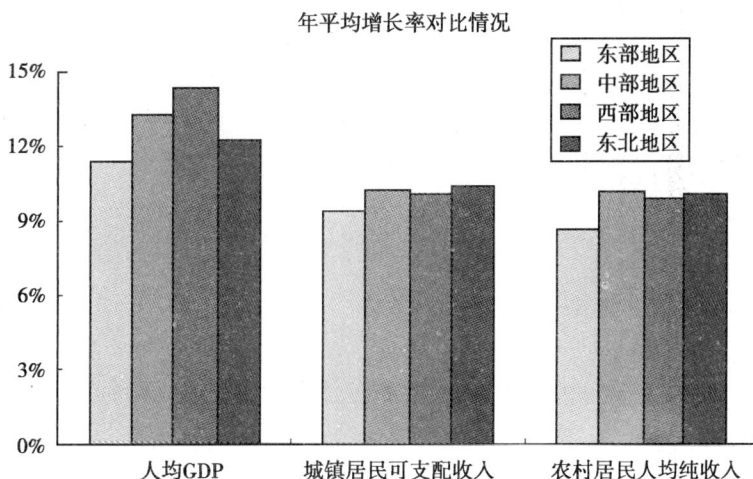

东部地区
中部地区
西部地区
东北地区

15%
12%
9%
6%
3%
0%

人均GDP   城镇居民可支配收入   农村居民人均纯收入

（4）发展要素利用效率不断提升。单位土地面积产出率持续上升，由 2005 年的 85867 万元增至 2009 年的 131560 万元，增幅为53.21%，年均增长率为 8.91%；能源消费总量仍持续增长，由 2005年的 235997 万吨标准煤增至 306647 万吨标准煤，增幅为 29.94%，但万元 GDP 能耗则呈下降趋势，由 2005 年的 1.28 吨降至 0.9 吨，降幅达 29.69%。

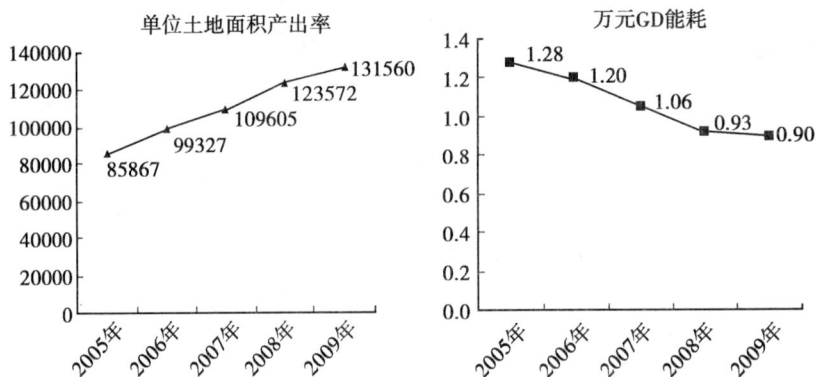

单位土地面积产出率

年份	产出率（万元）
2005年	85867
2006年	99327
2007年	109605
2008年	123572
2009年	131560

万元GD能耗

年份	能耗
2005年	1.28
2006年	1.20
2007年	1.06
2008年	0.93
2009年	0.90

（5）社会状况总体保持和谐稳定。在经历了一系列重大事件的冲击和影响后，全国社会形势在总体上始终保持着平稳、有序的发展态势，社会矛盾趋于缓和。交通事故发生数、死亡人数、直接财产损失均呈明显下降趋势，火灾事故统计数据显示出同样的特点。

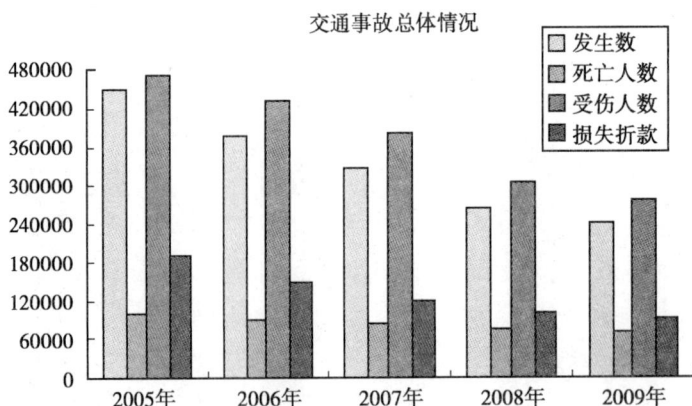

交通事故总体情况

发生数　死亡人数　受伤人数　损失折款

火灾事故发生数

火灾事故死亡、受伤人数

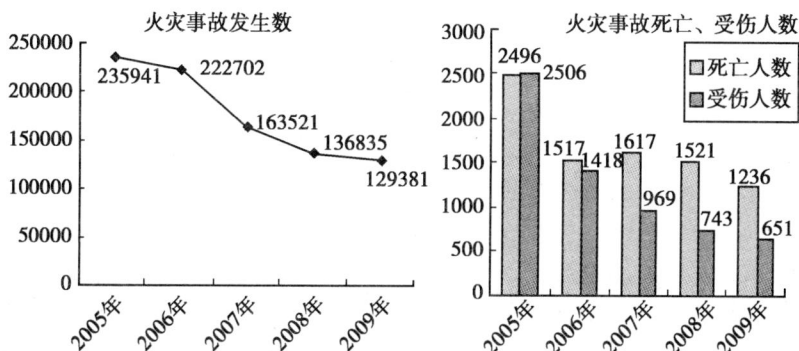

三、中国城市所处经济发展阶段的判断

人均 GDP 是判断经济社会发展阶段的重要指标和主要依据。根据钱纳里等学者的发展阶段理论和世界银行提出的指标体系，把随人均收入增长而发生的结构转变过程划分为三个阶段（如表）。

钱纳里的人均收入阶段（人均 GDP）　　　　　（单位：美元）

	工业化起始阶段	工业化实现阶段			后工业化阶段
		初期阶段	中期阶段	后期阶段	
人均 GDP（1970）	140—280	280—560	560—1120	1120—2100	2100 以上
人均 GDP（1996）	620—1240	1240—2480	2480—4960	4960—9300	9300 以上
人均 GDP（2007）	748—1495	1495—2990	2990—5981	5981—12000	12000 以上

根据 2009 年我国城市统计数据，初步划分出符合上述阶段标准的城市区位，并在其中选择若干典型城市进行了详细地数据处理及分析说明，帮助理解每一阶段的发展特征。

（一）人均 GDP 超过 3000 美元后的发展特征

人均 GDP 达到 3000 美元，这是经济发展过程中所处的一个重要转折时期，经济发展和城镇化均进入活跃、加速发展的重要阶段，也是经济结构调整的关键时期。我国进入人均 GDP3000—6000 美元的城市有 108 个，占全部地级及以上城市总数的 38%。为了准确判断和把握这一阶段城市发展面临的机遇和挑战，我们在排名前 50、前 100、前 150 名中选择人口在 200 万—500 万的特大城市，兼顾地域分布和城市类型，以江门、南昌、株洲、长春等城市为参照。

此一阶段，城市发展特征表现为：

1. 经济平稳快速发展，城乡居民收入稳步提高

与 2005 年相比，营口人均 GDP 增长 1 倍，株洲、肇庆人均 GDP 增长近 90%，各地人均 GDP 年均增速在 15% 左右。与此同时城镇化进程快速推进，南昌市城镇人口由 2005 年的 378 万增加到 2009 年的 391 万，城镇化率上升至 63%，提高近 9 个百分点。随着城镇化的快速推进，城乡居民收入水平稳步提高，株洲、肇庆五年间城镇居民可支配收入增长 1.5 倍，年均增速在 10% 左右。各地城乡收入比值差距相近，基本在 2:1 至 2.5:1 之间，城乡收入差距呈现波动下降的良好态势。株洲城乡收入比从 2005 年的 2.8:1 下降到 2009 年的 2.68:1；江门城乡收入比从 2005 年的 2.57:1 下降到 2.52:1。

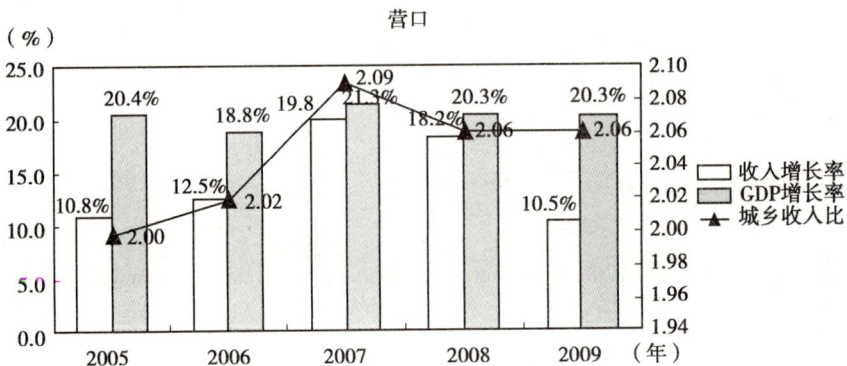

营口

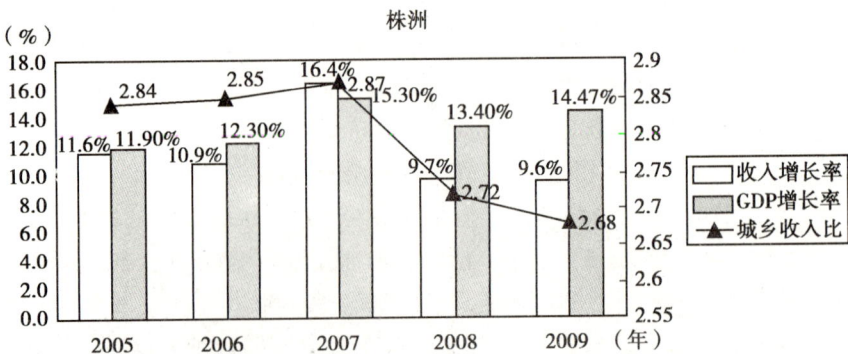

株洲

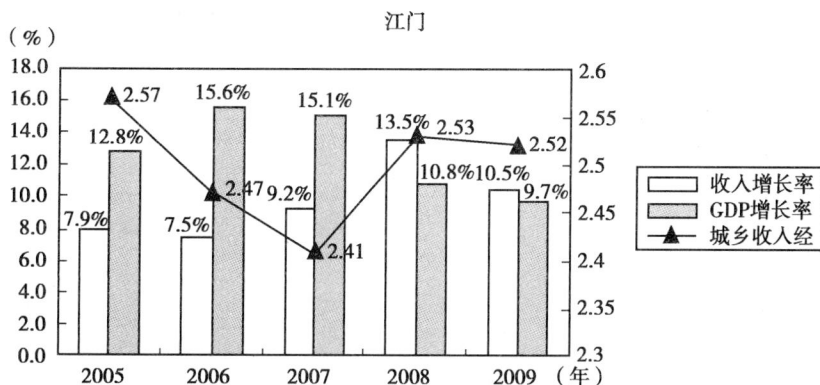

江门

□ 收入增长率		
■ GDP增长率		
▲ 城乡收入经		

2. 以工业为主导，环境污染制约经济发展

按照国际经验，人均 GDP 超过 3000 美元，产业结构中第二产业占据主导地位，第三产业比重上升。结合我国经济发展基本特征、数据可见，由于城市产业优势的差异，成都、肇庆呈现二三产业同步前进；营口、南昌、江门、株洲等大部分地区第二产业比重占 50%以上，五年间第二产业比重继续上升，经济发展仍然处于工业拉动经济增长阶段。

部分城市产业结构变化

城市	时间	三大产业比重
营口	2005 年 2009 年	10.8 : 51.38 : 37.82 8.45 : 55.91 : 35.65
株洲	2005 年 2009 年	13.45 : 50.48 : 36.07 10.52 : 54.67 : 34.81
江门	2005 年 2009 年	9 : 52.82 : 38.18 7.78 : 57.98 : 34.24
肇庆	2005 年 2009 年	31.46 : 25.17 : 43.37 19.18 : 37.08 : 43.73
南昌	2005 年 2009 年	7.2 : 52.81 : 39.99 6.09 : 55.32 : 38.59
成都	2005 年 2009 年	7.68 : 42.45 : 49.87 5.95 : 44.46 : 49.59

但是，经济增长模式仍然是依托资源的粗放式发展，大气污染问题日趋突出。营口二氧化硫和烟尘排放量五年间增加 22%，产出污染处理率下降了 42%；江门二氧化硫和烟尘排放量相比 2005 年分别增加了 29%和27%，产出污染处理率下降了 6%；肇庆废水排放量相比 2005 年增加了22%，烟尘排放量增加了 160%还多，二氧化硫排放量增加 25%，产出污

染处理率下降18%；株洲在产业发展过程中注重节能减排，废水排放量五年间下降15%，二氧化硫和烟尘排放量下降30%左右。

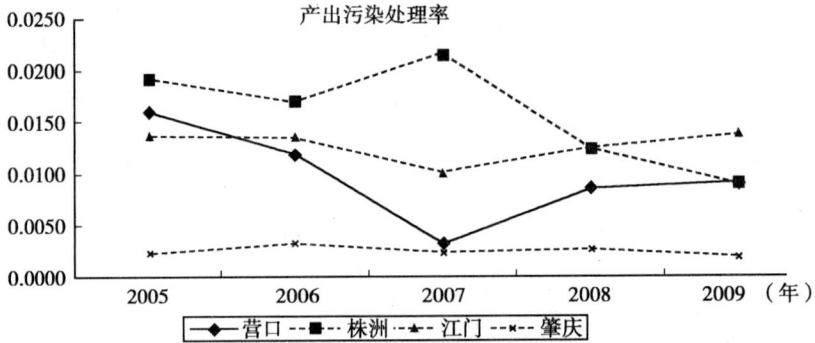

产出污染处理率

环境影响比较

	二氧化硫排放量（吨）		烟尘排放量（吨）		废水排放量（万吨）	
	2005 年	2009 年	2005 年	2009 年	2005 年	2009 年
营口	75597	92007	41936	51074	5400	3319
株洲	93973	65197	47136	33090	9179	7722
江门	37095	48132	16500	20934	11993	10790
肇庆	23337	29093	8510	22433	7231	8846

3. 居民消费支出快速提高，基本消费比重下降，服务性消费比重上升

各地恩格尔系数基本处于0.3—0.4之间，已经进入相对富裕阶段。随着经济增长，居民消费支出也快速增长，相比2005年，南昌、成都、长春和银川人均消费支出分别提高了76%、46%、61%和68%。其中食品消费支出年均增长10%—15%左右，但是大部分城市的食品消费比重较2005年都有所下降，例如南昌食品消费比重从2005年的44.8%降至2009年的35.3%。服务消费支出比重增加主要表现在交通、通讯及医疗保健支出的大幅上升以及教育文化娱乐支出稳步增长，南昌、银川居民交通通讯支出增幅最快，五年间增加1倍多，到2009年分别占消费支出比重的12%和14%；医疗消费支出增加比较显著，相比2005年，长春医疗保健支出增加1倍，南昌、银川、成都增加50%以上；教育文化娱乐支出各地年均增长14%左右，占消费支出的10%—15%。

恩格尔系数

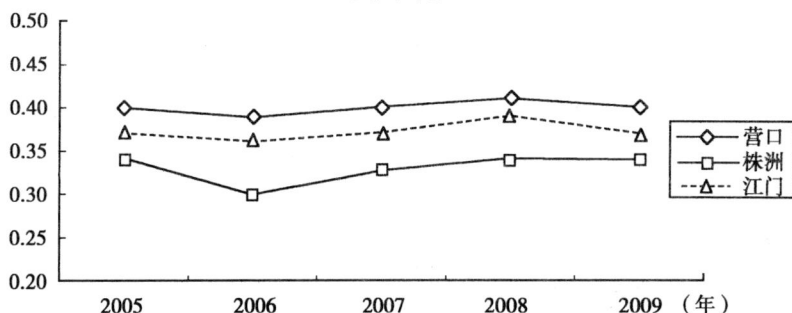

部分城市消费结构比较

	南昌		成都		长春		银川	
	2005 年	2009 年	2005 年	2009 年	2005 年	2009 年	2005 年	2009 年
人均消费性支出	7064 元	12406 元	9642 元	14087 元	8321 元	13409 元	7313 元	12272 元
食品	44.8%	35.3%	35.3%	37.5%	36.1%	32.2%	35.8%	32.8%
医疗保健	7.0%	7.5%	6.2%	6.7%	9.1%	11.7%	8.5%	8.9%
交通通信	8.4%	12.1%	19.5%	16.3%	11.6%	11.6%	11.2%	14.2%
教育文化娱乐	12.5%	11.0%	12.7%	13.5%	14.1%	12.2%	13.1%	11.5%

4. 社会保障水平稳步提高，地区间发展仍不均衡

营口社会保障水平经过五年发展，覆盖率大幅提高。相比 2005 年，营口医疗保险覆盖率增加 2 倍，达到 42%，是株洲医疗保险覆盖率的 3 倍，是肇庆医疗保险覆盖率的 4.7 倍；惠州养老保险五年间增加 1 倍，接近 40%；株洲、肇庆、南昌低于 15%。

部分城市社会保障覆盖率比较

	营口		株洲		江门		肇庆	
	2005 年	2009 年	2005 年	2009 年	2005 年	2009 年	2005 年	2009 年
养老保险	15%	26%	9%	11%	12%	15%	07%	11%
医疗保险	14%	42%	10%	14%	11%	18%	7%	9%
失业保险	9%	9%	10%	7%	9%	12%	6%	7%

（二）人均 GDP 超过 6000 美元后的发展特征

国际经验表明，当人均 GDP 超过 6000 美元后，城市化进程和国民经济发展进入加速阶段，不仅带来经济总量的增长，更带来社会经济成分、分配方式和组织形式的日益多样化。近年来，我国东部部分经济发达城市人均 GDP 先后超过 5000 美元。按照常住人口计算，2009 年经济总量前 23 位的大城市人均 GDP 超过或接近 6000 美元，其中北京、上海、佛山、大连、宁波人均 GDP 在 10000 美元—12000 美元之间，天津、杭州、青岛、沈阳、南京、东莞、长沙人均 GDP 在 8000 美元—9000 美元之间。武汉、唐山、烟台、济南、郑州人均 GDP 在 6000 美元—8000 美元之间。此阶段发展特征表现为：

1. 经济保持快速增长，收入涨幅与经济不同步

五年间，长沙、济南 GDP 年均增长接近 15%，高于全国平均水平；北京、上海年均增长 11%—13%。GDP 增长率经过 2005—2007 年的快速增长，2008、2009 年平稳下降，这主要受国际金融危机和国内周期的影响，促使地方政府淡化经济规模总量目标，强化结构调整。随着经济增长，居民可支配收入稳步增长，但是各地人均收入差距较大，收入增长率呈波动变化，城乡收入差距仍在扩大。北京、上海、天津收入年均增幅与 GDP 增幅相近，接近 12%。其中上海城乡收入比五年间扩大到 2.34；北京城乡收入比波动下降，五年间仅下降 0.6 个百分点。长沙人均可支配收入五年间增长 1.6 倍，年均增幅接近 13%，进入历史最快时期，也是城乡收入差距开始缩小时期，五年间下降 15%，但城乡收入仍略高于 2，差距仍属过大。

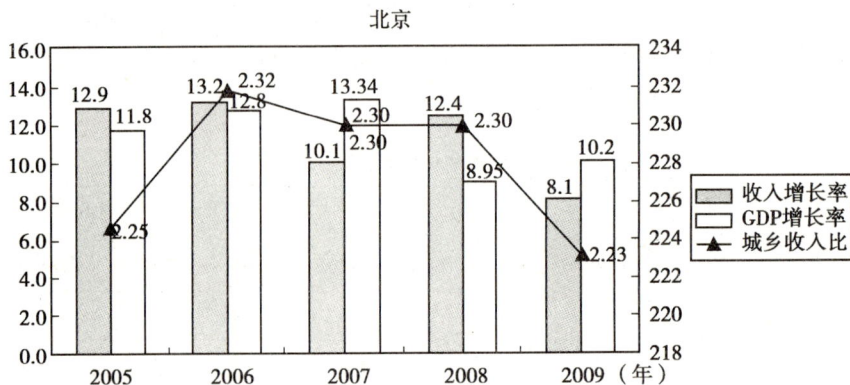

北京

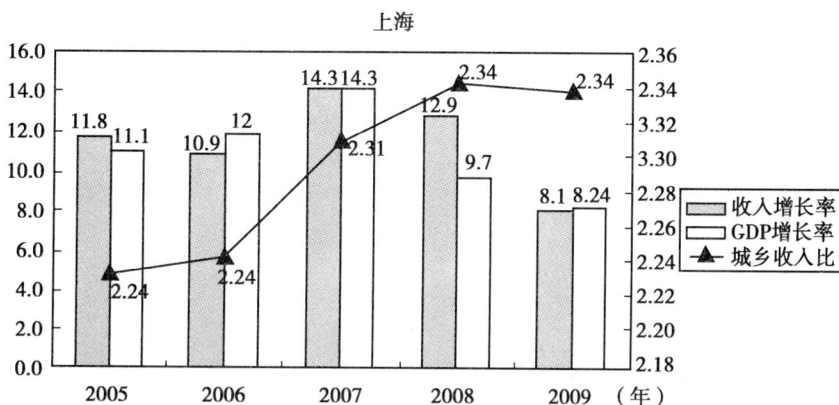

上海

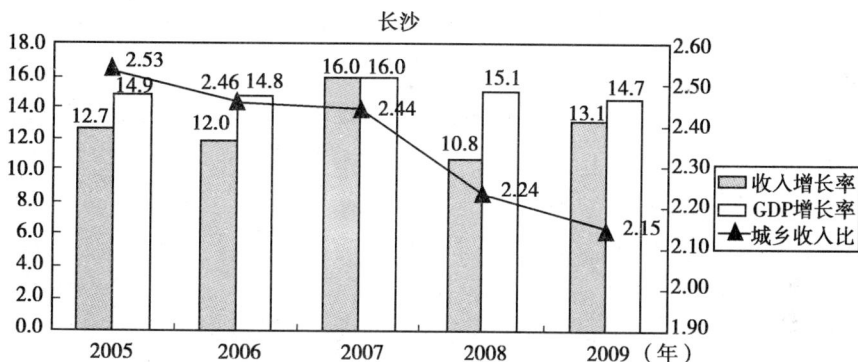

长沙

2. 产业、就业结构以科技引领向现代化转型

从投资主导、第二产业为主的经济结构向消费主导、创新推动的后工业社会转变是人均 GDP 超过 6000 美元后各城市发展的共同特点。从总量看，北京、上海第三产业的增速快于第二产业，科技的创新和信息产业人力资本的积累大大促进了产业结构的优化升级，科技支出比重超过 5%，信息业从业人员比重居于全国前列，但与纽约、巴黎、香港等世界城市相比，第三产业仍有较大上升空间。天津、唐山、长沙等地区，第二产业保持强劲优势，工业重型化特征明显，高新科技带动工业转型效果显著。长沙重工业对规模工业增长的贡献率达 70% 以上，工业内部结构逐渐以高新技术、先进使用技术提升经济效益；济南高新技术产业产值五年间增长 30.7%，占规模以上工业总产值比重为 41.5%，提高了 2 个百分点。

城市	时间	三大产业比重
北京	2005 年 2009 年	1.4 : 29.5 : 69.1 1 : 23.2 : 75.8
上海	2005 年 2009 年	0.9 : 48.6 : 50.5 0.7 : 39.9 : 59.4
天津	2005 年 2009 年	2.7 : 57.1 : 40.2 1.9 : 60.1 : 38
宁波	2005 年 2009 年	5.2 : 63.4 : 31.4 4.4 : 53.3 : 42.3
长沙	2005 年 2009 年	7.4 : 43.1 : 49.5 4.8 : 50.6 : 44.6
唐山	2005 年 2009 年	11.6 : 57.3 : 31.1 9.5 : 55.9 : 34.6

3. 发展要素利用效率提高，经济管理水平开始向集约化、高效化、低污染转变

（1）进入工业化后期，资源对经济发展约束力增强，城市开始从要素投入（土地、资本等）、生产率的提高及节能减排角度挖掘集约内涵潜力，对整体经济效益提升影响突出。上海、宁波单位土地生产总值接近20 亿元，五年间土地产出率提高了 50%；长沙、宁波、大连、青岛、佛山土地利用效率与上海接近，并呈稳步提高趋势；北京、郑州土地利用效率低于上海 50%，年均提高 10% 左右；东莞、佛山土地生产率则是上海的 2 倍。

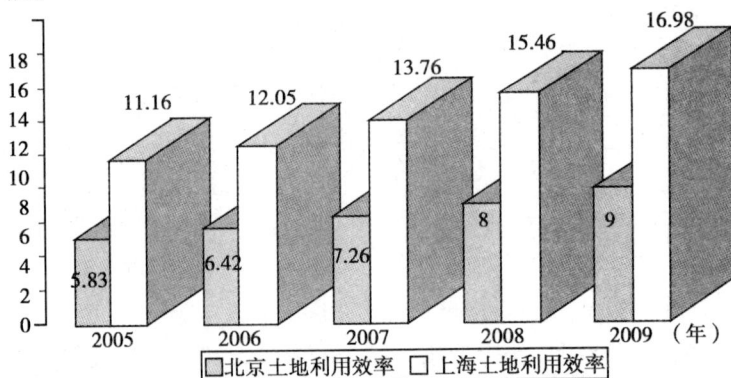

（2）各地劳动生产率的差距逐渐扩大。上海、佛山、大连、青岛优势明显，并得益于经济正处于上升周期，使劳动生产率五年间保持较快增长；佛山、长沙、大连五年间增长 2.5 倍左右；北京与上述城市有一定差

距，主要在于北京市场缺乏足够竞争，劳动力潜能未得到充分发挥。

部分城市劳动生产率变化　　　　　　单位：元/人

时间	北京	上海	佛山	大连	长沙	青岛	郑州
2005 年	156242	456658	268103	355803	203428	143755	975690
2009 年	198878	756516	2214215	747454	394520	793185	251135

（3）能源与环境双重约束下的经济增长低碳式转型。能源消费在经过一轮增长后呈现两种趋势，上海、宁波用电量和单位 GDP 电耗双双大幅度下降，表明经济增长与能源脱钩，转向经济低碳式发展；北京、长沙用电量波动增长，单位 GDP 能耗五年间波动下降 28% 和 35%，表明生产率改善并不稳健，经济增长方式转变依然任重道远。与此同时，主要污染物指标逐年下降，北京、上海、长沙五年间万元 GDP 二氧化硫和废水排放量均下降 60% 左右，产业结构调整，尤其是工业、制造业部分的结构调整成为降低污染的主要途径。

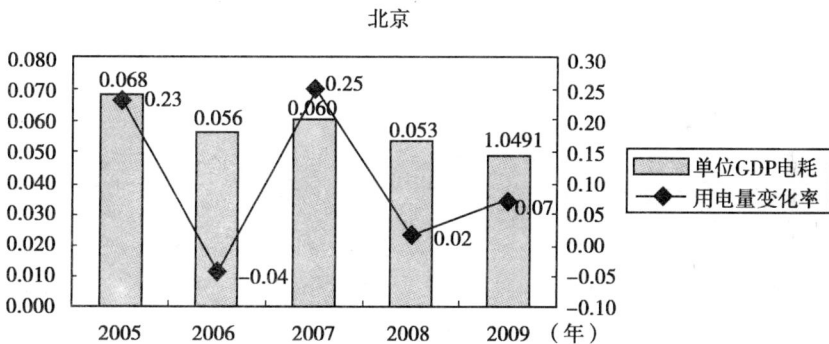

北京

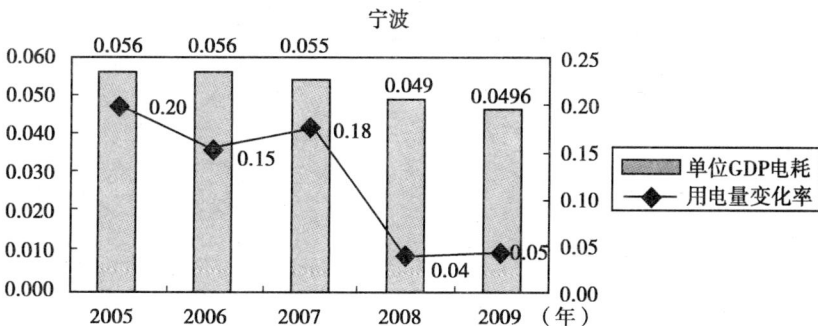

宁波

上海市单位GDP主要污染物排放量

□ 万元GDP废水排放量
□ 万元GDP二氧化硫排放量
■ 万元GDP烟尘排放量

年份		
2009	0.003　0.0016　0.0002	
2008	0.003　0.0022　0.003	
2007	0.004　0.0030　0.003	
2006	0.0005　0.0036　0.0005	
2005	0.0006　0.0041　0.005	

0.0000　0.0010　0.0020　0.0030　0.0040　0.0050　0.0060

长沙市单位GDP主要污染物排放量

□ 万元GDP废水排放量
□ 万无GDP二氧化硫排放量
■ 万元GDP烟尘排放量

年份		
2009	0.0001　0.0014　0.0009	
2008	0.0001　0.0020　0.0013	
2007	0.0002　0.0023　0.0015	
2006	0.0002　0.0027　0.0018	
2005	0.0003　0.0035　0.0028	

0.0000　0.0010　0.0020　0.0030　0.0040　0.0050　0.0060　0.0070

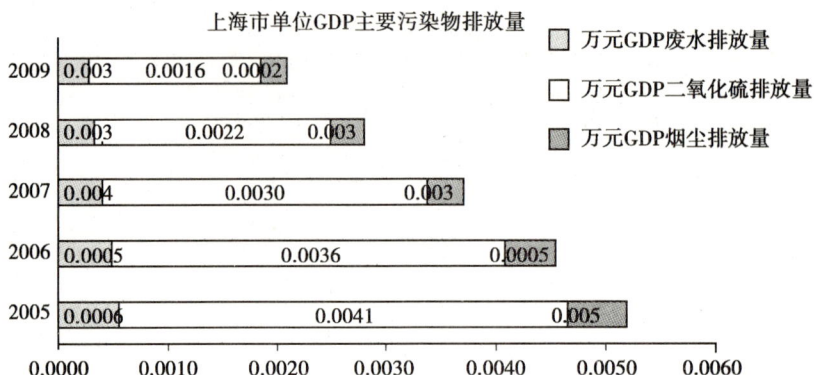

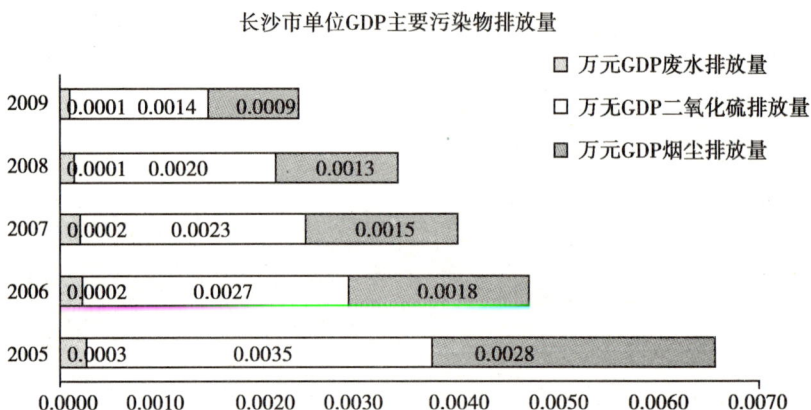

4. 高度重视社会公共服务制度体系建设

经济持续快速发展需要一个稳定的社会环境,各地日益重视社会公共产品与公共服务制度建设,居民医疗保险、养老保险、失业保险覆盖率逐年提高。但各地社会保障水平差距较大,北京、上海养老和医疗保险覆盖率达60%以上,远高于长沙、济南等地;宁波、长沙社会保障五年间发展较为迅速,宁波养老、医疗和失业保险五年间翻了一番,长沙养老、医疗保险五年间增长近1倍;北京养老、医疗和失业保险年均增幅13%左右,唐山社会保障发展速度则相对缓慢。

部分城市社会保障覆盖率比较

	养老保险覆盖率		医疗保险覆盖率		失业保险覆盖率	
	2005 年	2009 年	2005 年	2009 年	2005 年	2009 年
北京	44%	66%	49%	75%	33%	54%
上海	53%	60%	52%	67%	34%	37%
宁波	27%	60%	19%	44%	14%	30%
沈阳	22%	39%	27%	43%	16%	17%
长沙	10%	19%	9%	20%	9%	9%
济南	17%	22%	13%	22%	11%	14%
唐山	14%	18%	11%	13%	9%	10%

5. 居民生活水平快速提高

（1）随着收入水平的提高，人们也提高了对生活便利性和舒适度的要求。经济的高速发展带来交通机动化和绿色化转变，小汽车拥有量随着收入增加而迅速提高，由此带来人均能源消费增长，也随之增加了环境与交通效率的压力。北京、上海、青岛等地发展绿色交通，每万人公交数量超过 10 辆，同时大力发展轨道交通。

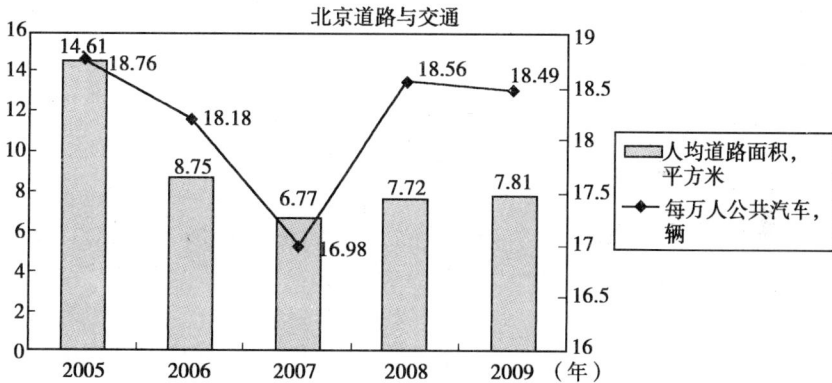

北京道路与交通

人均道路面积，平方米
每万人公共汽车，辆

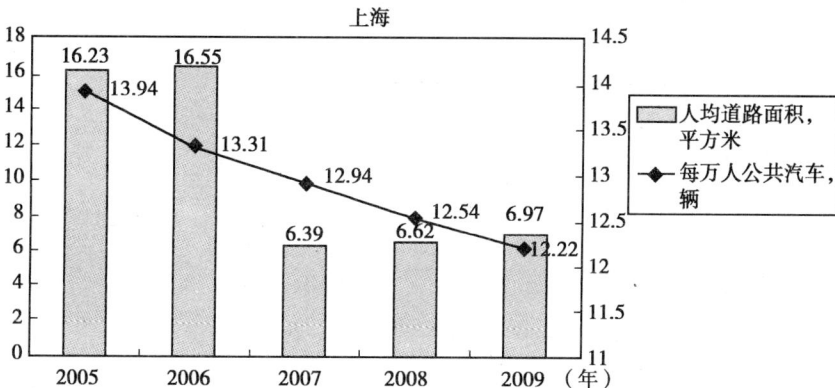

上海

人均道路面积，平方米
每万人公共汽车，辆

（2）住房消费需求快速增加。国际经验表明，人均 GDP5000 美元—8000 美元是房地产的快速上升阶段，只有达到 13000 美元以上时，才能稳步下降。北京、宁波经过住房消费高峰期后，开始趋于缓和；上海、长沙、大连等地住房数量和消费则快速扩张，以长沙为例，居住支出比重五年间增加 1.2 倍，2009 年居住支出占消费支出的 10.83%，人均住房面积同步增长，五年间增加 1.4 倍，2009 年达到人均 29 平方米。

北京

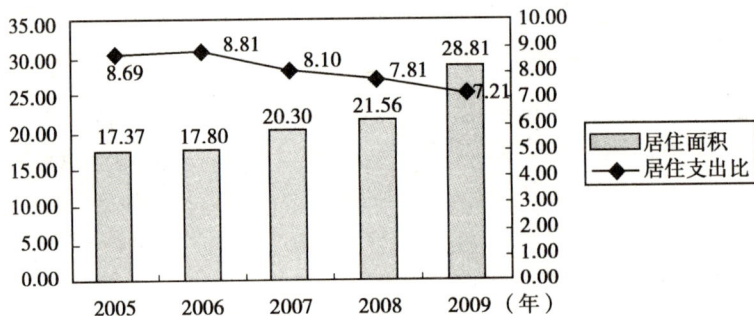

宁波

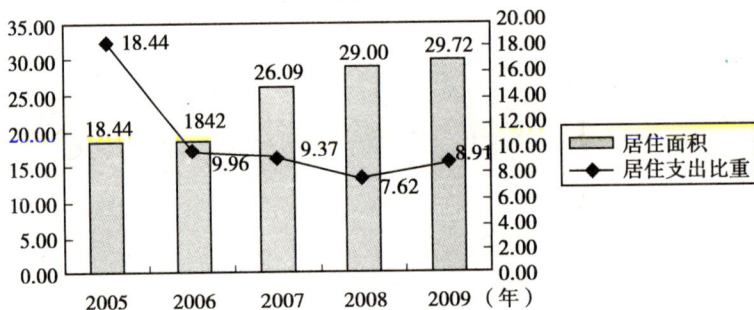

上海

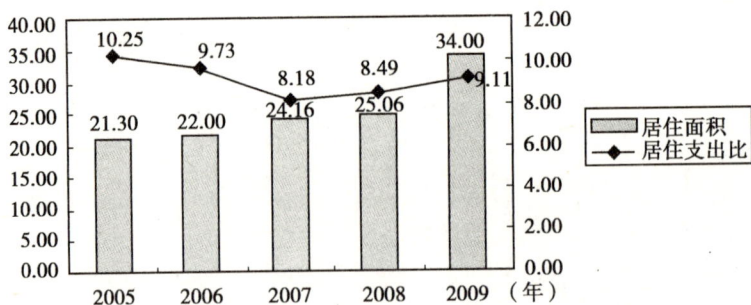

长沙

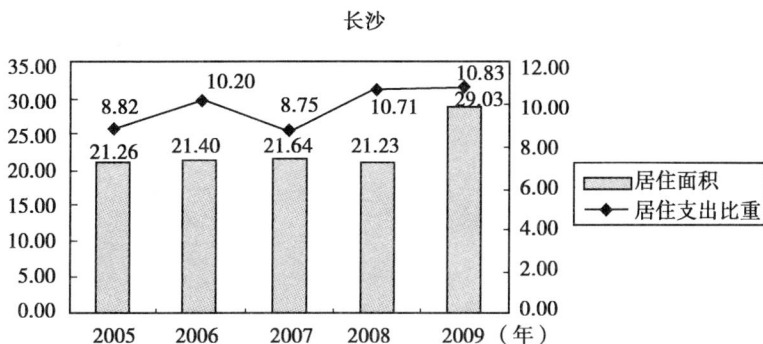

（3）居民基本消费比重提高，服务类消费趋于稳定或略有下降。随着人均GDP的提高，恩格尔系数呈波动下降，上海、长沙、宁波五年间恩格尔系数下降近3个百分点，居民生活质量持续提高。交通通讯支出增速最快，北京、上海、宁波和长沙五年间分别增加52％、76％、66％和87％。医疗、教育支出持续增长，北京、上海每万人拥有医院、卫生院床位数接近50左右，居于全国首位；北京、上海、宁波的教育文化娱乐消费占人均消费性支出的15％。

部分城市消费结构变化情况

	北京		上海		宁波		长沙	
	2005年	2009年	2005年	2009年	2005年	2009年	2005年	2009年
人均消费性支出	13244元	19076元	13773元	20992元	11761元	18202元	9659元	14166元
食品支出	32％	33％	36％	35％	38％	35％	33％	36％
医疗保健	10％	7％	6％	5％	5％	5％	8％	7％
交通通信	15％	15％	14％	17％	16％	17％	13％	16％
教育文化娱乐	17％	15％	16％	15％	16％	15％	17％	12％
居住	9％	7％	10％	9％	8％	9％	9％	11％

（三）人均GDP超过12000美元后的发展特征

人均GDP超过12000美元进入发达状态，经济增长处于从要素驱动为主向效率、创新驱动转化的发展阶段。2009年，鄂尔多斯、苏州、无锡、东营、深圳、广州、克拉玛依和包头达到此标准，其中鄂尔多斯、苏州人均GDP接近20000美元，其他城市在12000美元—16000美元之间。

1. 人均GDP加快增长，城乡收入差距趋于缓和

苏州、无锡、东营GDP年均增幅接近15％，城乡收入差距趋于缓和或逐年下降。无锡、苏州城乡收入比保持在2∶1左右；东营城乡收入差距2009年为2.9∶1，但五年间下降10％。广州城乡收入差距波动下降到

2.5∶1。鄂尔多斯五年间人均 GDP 增长 2.5 倍，年均增幅超过 25%，但城乡收入差距仍逐年扩大，按不变价计算，城乡比从 2005 年的 2.4∶1 扩大到 2009 年的 2.8∶1，说明国民收入分配格局存在失衡现象。

苏州

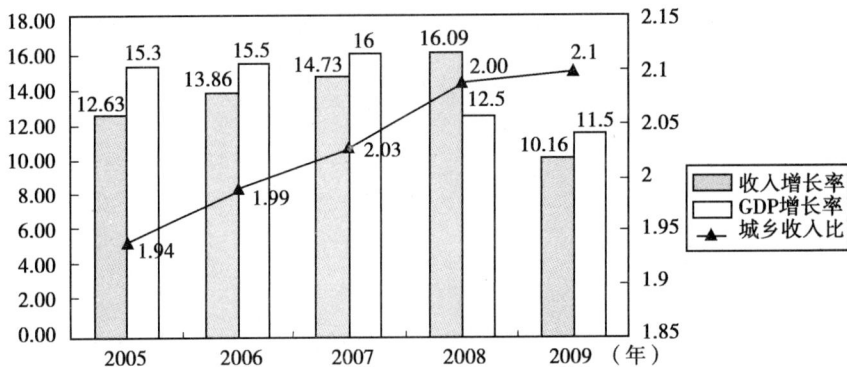

广州

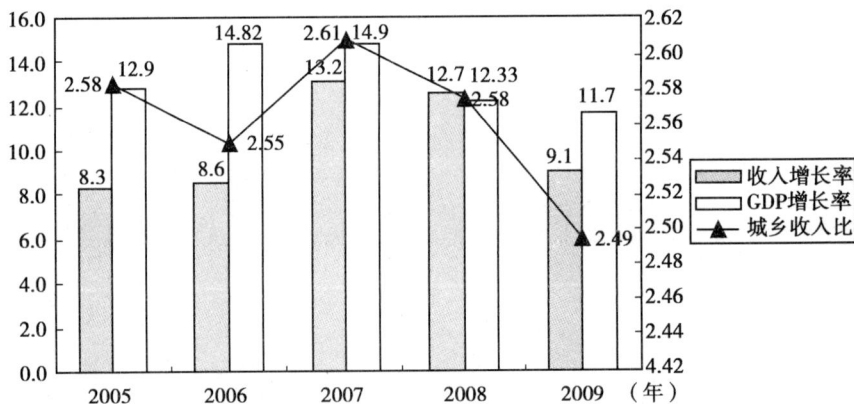

鄂尔多斯

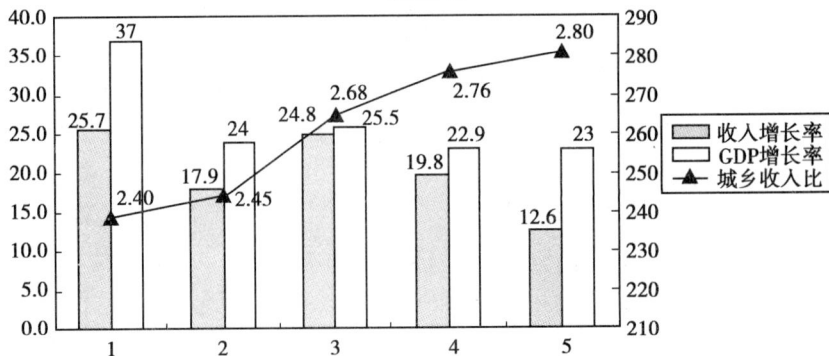

2. 后工业化阶段，产业结构趋向高级化

在人均GDP超过12000美元的城市中，鄂尔多斯、东营、克拉玛依、包头依托资源和产业优势，产业结构形成以装备制造业为主导的增长极，推动经济增长跨越式发展。而苏州、无锡、深圳、广州等东部发达城市，产业结构从生产型服务业向现代服务业转变，第三产业比重达50%以上并成为主导产业，第三产业劳动力数量显著增加，其中无锡第三产业就业比重达53%。服务业类型从最初的商贸、房地产逐步扩展到金融、信息产业、文化创意产业、经营管理咨询等新兴服务业，进入以信息技术、知识发展为主要标志的后工业化时代，科技创新能力的提高为经济发展提供了持续动力。

部分城市三次产业结构

城市	时间	三次产业比重
鄂尔多斯	2005年 2009年	6.83：52.53：40.64 2.80：58.33：38.87
东营	2005年 2009年	4.13：82.28：13.59 3.63：73.92：22.45
包头	2005年 2009年	3.66：53.02：43.32 2.55：54.18：43.26
苏州	2005年 2009年	2.20：66.60：31.20 1.85：58.75：39.41
无锡	2005年 2009年	1.72：60.47：37.81 1.88：56.82：41.30
深圳	2005年 2009年	0.20：53.19：46.61 0.08：46.66：53.25
广州	2005年 2009年	2.53：39.68：57.79 1.89：37.26：60.85

3. 资源环境压力约束经济发展，成为主要制约因素

长期的经济粗放式发展对资源能源依赖过大，环境污染负荷较高，成为加快后现代化城市进程的主要制约因素，这一问题的严重性日渐得到重视。

（1）土地利用效率稳步提高，苏州地均GDP是深圳、广州的近2倍，五年间增加15%；广州、深圳、东营提高40%左右，无锡土地利用率提高近60%。

（2）环境状况稳步改善。鄂尔多斯、东营环境质量改善效果突出，

五年间产出污染处理率翻了一番，烟尘排放量降低了80%左右。但空气污染仍较严重，2009年，鄂尔多斯的二氧化硫排放量是深圳的8倍、东营的3倍、无锡的2.4倍，烟尘排放量是深圳的33倍、东营的5.5倍、广州的3.2倍；无锡、苏州的烟尘排放水平与鄂尔多斯相近，面临同样的烟尘污染压力。

（3）水环境问题引起重视。东太湖流域曾大面积爆发蓝藻污染，通过实施综合整治，总体水质基本达到水域功能类别3类水质标准，无锡五年间废水排放量减少18%，苏州减少26%，但是反映富营养化程度的总磷和总氮指标仍超过3类水质标准。黄河东营段近五年来废水排放量增加26%，COD和氮氧化物超标，且影响到黄河下游河段。广州、深圳的珠江段废水排放量也呈增加趋势，五年间分别增加24%、20%，珠江口水污染仍较重。

环境因子影响比较

城市	地均GDP（万元/平方公里）		产出污染处理率（亿元/吨）		二氧化硫排放量（吨）		烟尘排放量（吨）		废水排放量（万吨）	
	2005年	2009年	2005年	2009年	2005年	2009年	2005年	2009年	2005年	2009年
鄂尔多斯	16.99	19.83	0.57	1.55	283687	225500	213678	37800	3787	1945
东营	13.72	19.99	1.24	2.50	112547	75729	26864	6795	7974	10079
广州	7.01	9.86	0.50	0.57	145009	86100	16106	11900	20249	25116
深圳	6.94	10.08	0.40	0.78	43453	31347	6366	2450	6444	7773
无锡	14.53	23.00	0.64	0.56	149865	93710	48268	41823	50122	41085
苏州	20.65	23.89	0.38	0.33	242362	147286	35804	48054	77682	57315

4. 消费结构明显优化，进入发展享受型消费阶段

居民收入大幅增加，消费水平随之显著提高。鄂尔多斯恩格尔系数从0.28降至0.26，表明居民生活已经进入富裕阶段；广州、深圳、无锡、江苏、东营的恩格尔系数五年间基本稳定在0.3—0.35之间，进入相对富裕阶段。由于服务业快速发展，消费主导——服务业驱动的组合将逐步成为社会经济的增长动力，特别是对于交通、医疗、教育、娱乐等产品的消费。以深圳为例，2009年深圳人均食品支出7535元，比2005年增长41.9%，年均增长9个百分点，恩格尔系数为35%，比2005年略有回升，但五年间总体呈下降趋势，表明居民消费结构不断升级。深圳户籍居民人均医疗、交通通讯、教育文化娱乐服务、居住等项目支出合计10368元，年均增长6.3%，消费支出比重增至48%。

以医疗保健、教育文化娱乐为消费热点持续升温。与2005年相比，

广州教育文化娱乐和医疗保健增幅最大，五年间分别提高了78%和66%，医疗保险消费支出与北京、上海水平相近，教育文化娱乐支出是北京、上海的1.4倍；深圳、鄂尔多斯、东营对公共服务的投入拉动消费增长，每万人剧场和体育场馆数高于北京、上海。

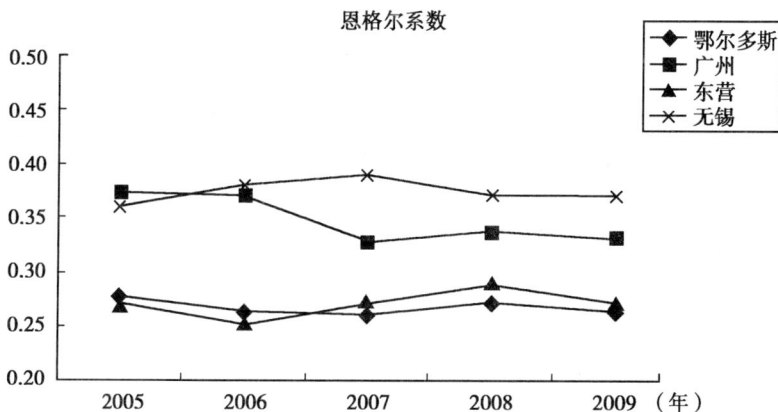

恩格尔系数

5. 城市公共服务支出逐步稳健，城乡公共服务一体化日益紧迫

城市发展重心由经济发展为主转向民生经济发展并重，政府开始探索社会民生新路径，提高居民共享水平。苏州、无锡、广州、深圳具有领先水平的共享型社会保障体系，五大保险参保率达90%以上，养老、医疗保险覆盖率达50%左右，但鄂尔多斯、东营、包头和克拉玛依与上述城市仍存在较大差距。在肯定发达地区社会保障建设取得进展的同时，必须清醒的看到城市中进城务工人员及城镇化进程中的"农转非"的原农村居民没有社会保障，或者仅有水平很低的社会保障，在城乡收入差距难以缩小、城镇化进程加快的形势下，统筹城乡仍任重道远。

2005—2009 年部分城市社会保障水平变化　　　　单位：人

城市	养老保险参保人数		失业保险参保人数		医疗保险参保人数	
	2005 年	2009 年	2005 年	2009 年	2005 年	2009 年
鄂尔多斯	103301	180000	125000	136292	161448	256302
东营	160880	199910	82423	115553	405643	512747
无锡	1280000	1983500	907800	1433300	1508200	2192800
苏州	2269556	2995027	1490143	2343246	1973017	3461794
广州	2049700	2893080	2340700	3121036	2085800	3826813
深圳	3527526	5840900	1431778	2189700	2695830	9113900

四、对本年度的城市评价体系排名情况作出的分析与判断

1. 城市发展差异仍较明显，体现出地区发展的差距

在全部 287 个地级以上城市中，东部 101 个，占 35.2%；中部 101 个，占 35.2%；西部 85 个，占 29.6%。

按照三类指标综合排序分值，在进入前 50 名的城市中，东部有 35 个，占 70%；中部 8 个，占 16%；西部 7 个，占 14%。不同地区发展总水平的差距，明显体现在城市之间。

按照经济发展指标排序，进入前 50 名的城市中，东部有 36 个城市，占 72%；中部 8 个城市，占 16%；西部 6 个城市，占 12%。

按照公共服务投入排序，进入前 50 名的城市中，东部 28 个，占 56%；中部 9 个，占 18%；西部 13 个，占 26%。

按照居民分享水平排序，进入前 50 名的城市中，东部 40 个，占 80%；东部 5 个，西部 5 个，各占 10%。

从前 50 名城市发展综合和专项指标排序中可看出，东部地区的城市综合发展水平要明显好于中西部，而中西部城市之间总体上差距不大；东部地区与中西部地区在城市发展层面的差距，要大于地区发展总水平之间的差距。

改革开放以来，东部尤其是沿海地区依靠区位优势、国外市场等条件，得以大幅度提高发展水平和竞争力，但同时也由于长期的粗放式经济增长方式的影响，过度依赖外部市场，忽视或无视自身产业结构的升级和自主创新能力的改造，使得东部地区在国际产业分工中始终处于产业链末端，较为单一依赖廉价的劳动力和土地要素来维持经济的高速增长。

因此形成的局面是：一方面东部地区的发展受国际经济环境影响极大，经济飞速发展的同时抗风险能力却相对较低，而经济发展的环境、资源成本不可遏制地日益上涨；另一方面，拥有丰富的劳动力和土地资源的中、西部地区，却由于地区之间缺乏合理的分工，东、中、西部地区之间良好互动的发展格局尚未形成，使得东部地区劳动密集型及资源加工型的产业不能合理地向中、西部地区转移，制约了中、西部地区的加速发展进程。以国内生产总值、人均 GDP 为例，我们可以从下图①中清楚地看到这种发展的差异性。

----

① 为了便于集中考量城市发展的区域性差异，我们的文字报告仍然沿用东、中、西部地区的划分方式，但在进行区域数据整理时，只能根据统计数据的取得情况，按照东、中、西、东北地区的划分加以处理。不过，这种划分上的差异不影响我们的整体评价。

按区域划分国内生产总值情况

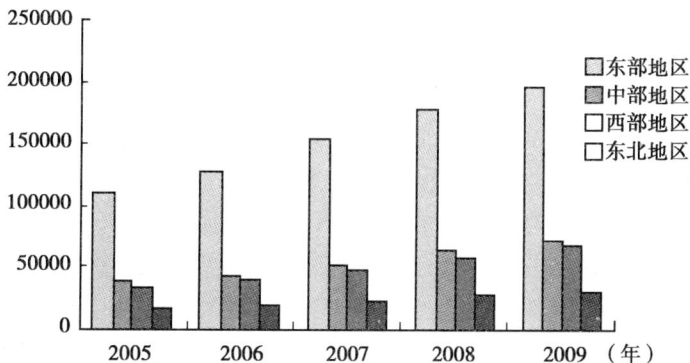

人均GDP

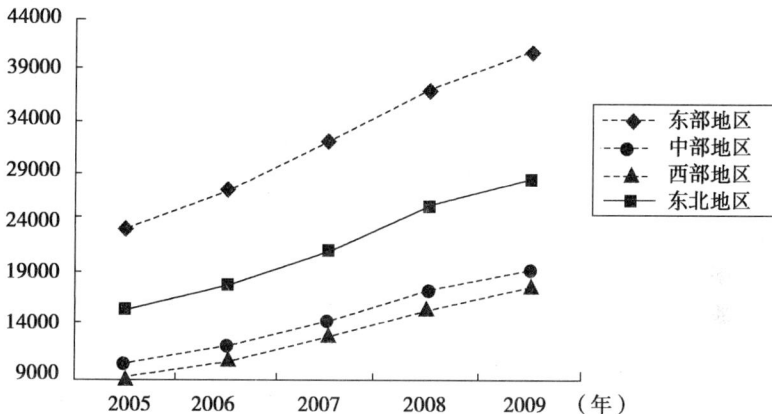

　　下一阶段如何带动中、西部地区又好又快地发展，不断缩小与东部地区的差距。中、西部城市发展面临的任务仍然十分艰巨。

　　2. 城市内部的经济与社会发展水平之间总体上很不协调

　　为了评价三类指标之间的协调性，我们在287个城市按照综合分值排序的基础上，又以前后顺序，每50个城市划为一个区段，如果一个城市三类指标都能进入同一区段，则视为是较为协调的发展城市。

　　在综合水平进入前50名的城市中，三类指标同时进入的有18个，占36%；51—100名中4个，占8%；101—150中4个，占8%；151—200中3个，占6%；201—250中4个，占8%；251—287中2个，占2%。除了第一区段，其余区段的协调程度不超过8%，称得上协调的只占全部城市的11.5%，总体表现可以说是极不协调。

前 50 个城市三类指标协调性较好的 18 个城市中，除了北京、上海以外，中部只有一个长沙，西部只有一个鄂尔多斯，江苏 4 个、浙江 3 个、广东 4 个、福建 1 个、山东 1 个、辽宁 1 个，基本都集中在沿海发达地区。这说明，在目前的城市体制下，只有当经济发展达到相当高的水平时，才有可能实现经济和社会发展的协调。

统观 287 个城市的三类指标关系，总体上可认定为相关性很差，经济发展的高水平并没有相应地带来城市公共服务和居民实际分享成果的高水平。多数城市公共服务和居民分享成果明显滞后于当地的经济发展水平，尤其是一些快速发展的城市表现明显。而经济发展处于低位的城市，虽然就表面看许多地方二、三类指标高于经济发展水平，但无论城市公共服务还是居民的分享水平，都基本处于较低的必需水平，支撑这一水平的包括国家的财政转移支付，并非全靠当地的经济发展水平，因而不会影响上述结论。

城市排名协调性情况

排名区段	相对协调的城市
1—50 名	苏州、宁波、常州、厦门、中山、无锡、上海、青岛、杭州、珠海、深圳、大连、南京、广州、舟山、长沙、鄂尔多斯、北京
51—100 名	芜湖、淄博、秦皇岛、合肥
101—150 名	焦作、黄山、韶关、株洲
151—200 名	南平、鹤壁
201—250 名	池州、滁州、抚州、赣州
251—287 名	商丘、钦州

注：上表中城市排名不分先后。

3. 直辖市、省会城市、计划单列市仍体现出综合优势

以综合指标排序为例，直辖市和省会城市进入前 100 名的城市 26 个，占全部 31 个的 84%，其中进入前 50 名的有 17 个，占 55%；5 个计划单列市全部进入。

以经济发展水平衡量，直辖市、省会城市处于前 100 名的 20 个，占全部 31 个的 64.5%。其中进入前 50 名的 12 个，占 38.7%；5 个计划单列市全部进入。

公共服务投入方面，直辖市、省会城市处于前 100 名有 26 个，占全部 31 个的 84%。其中进入前 50 名的 18 个，占 58%；5 个计划单列市全部进入。

居民分享水平方面，直辖市、省会城市处于前 100 名有 26 个，占全部 31 个的 84。其中进入前 50 名的 12 个，占 38.7%；5 个计划单列市全

部进入。

可见，直辖市、省会城市、计划单列市在集聚经济发展和公共投入资源方面具有绝对的优势，这也说明，目前中国城市的经济社会发展水平在很大程度上依然取决于行政级别和权力的安排。

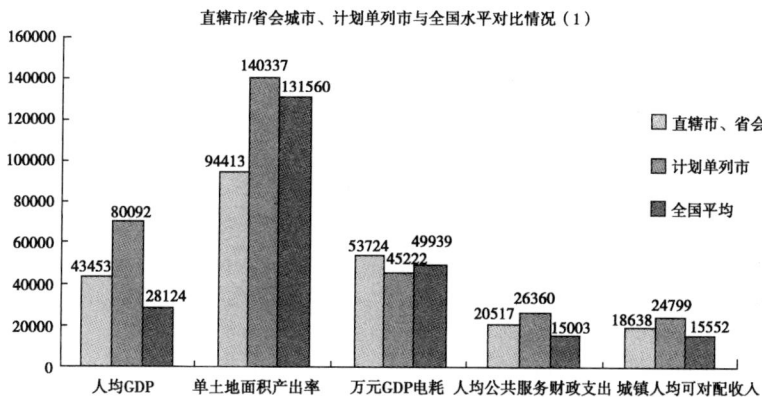

直辖市/省会城市、计划单列市与全国水平对比情况（1）

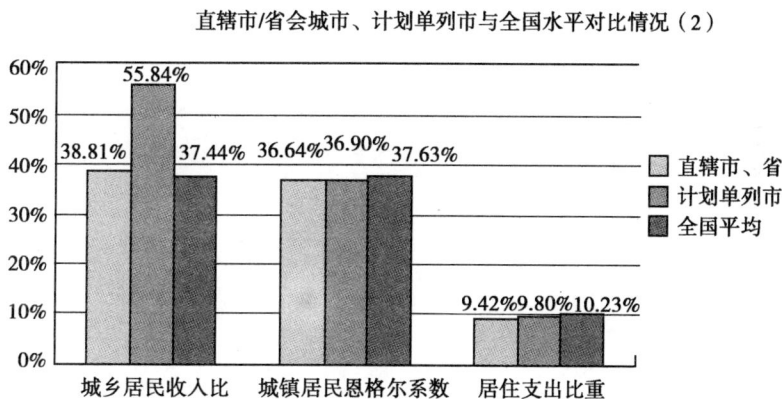

直辖市/省会城市、计划单列市与全国水平对比情况（2）

4. 经济转型还没有取得明显成效

在经济发展类指标系统中，我们利用土地、水、劳动及能源的利用效率，科技信息等技术的投入水平，对外部产生的环境效应等三组指标评价发展的质量。在经济发展水平进入前 50 名的城市中，要素利用效率能够进入前 50 名的有 22 个，占 44%；外部效应较好进入前 50 名的 18 个，占 36%；技术投入水平进入前 50 名的 23 个城市，占 46%。没有一个城市上述三项子系统能够同时进入前 50 名。尽管在经济发展转型的过程中，许多城市加大了技术投入的力度，尤其直辖市和省会城市更为突出，有

80%即25个城市进入技术投入水平前50名，但目前还都没有在提高要素利用水平、降低环境资源污染方面开始呈现出明显的效果。

进一步比较经济增长效率进入前10名的城市中，发展利用效率进入前10名的只有苏州、榆林2个城市，但是经济增长效率进入前10名的城市均没有进入发展外部效应的前10名。这种高速低效的增长将给资源和环境带来巨大压力。虽然高效率经济增长城市将在很长一段时间内仍保持这种宏观经济发展优势，但是资源与环境的"瓶颈"约束已成为更为基础性的新的制约因素。增长短边将向资源与环境需求的转移标志着增长方式的根本性变化。

5. 经济发展水平与居民分享水平不甚协调

城市公共投入水平总体上与经济发展水平并不协调。经济发展总水平进入前50名的城市中，财政公共投入同时进入前50名的只有7个，只占17%，三分之一稍强。

城市发展对居民最直接的影响是收入是否与GDP增长同步。通过城市人均GDP和人均收入增长同步性程度比较可以发现，在经济发展总水平进入前50名的城市中，同步性较好进入前50名的有28个，占56%，刚刚超过一半。

经济发展总水平前50名城市中，个人受益类项目，居民社保覆盖范围及水平进入前50名的24个，占48%；居民生活环境水平进入前50的20个，占40%；居民就业水平进入前50名的14个，占28%。三项都不到一半。

同样，在经济发展总水平前50名城市中，公共服务分享类项目规模进入前50名的有28个，占56%；直辖市、省会城市进入前50名的有23个，占该类城市的74%。

可见，在城市社会服务领域中，由政府组织的各项民生事业，目前发展的总体状态是，公共分享类投入项目相对较好，而居民个人受益类项目实际效果相对稍差。

五、通过城市问卷调查了解居民的实际想法，判断城市公共投入、制度调整和制度建设与居民的实际需求是否存在主要差异

目前，对城市进行评价分级的研究有很多，一般都以采用统计数据计算的客观指标为依据，往往无视或者忽视了作为城市生活主体的居民，即人对城市的主观感受和评价。为了使城市分析评价在更为科学、严谨、全面和符合实际的基础上更加务实，真正贯彻"以人为本"的科学发展观，自今年起，我们将通过问卷调查的方式，尝试将了解城市居民对所处居城市的主观感受，为进一步调整和完善指标体系奠定基础，并将尝试将其纳入到今后的评价体系中来。

2011 年，我们选择了北京、深圳这两个在人口规模构成、地理位置、发展模式速度、管理模式、城市历史等方面都颇极具特点和代表性的城市进行了试点调查，通过系统抽样和随机抽样，回收有效问卷 1629 份。分析结果表明：

1. 居民满意度最高的是城市提供的生活消费和服务，满意度最低的是房价、物价和社会公平，最企盼的是提高收入、稳定物价、解决住房问题、提高政府管理水平、解决社会公平问题、有更多的个人发展机会。这说明，商品和服务的丰富性在城市吸引力中的权重正在下降，吸引力更多的来自于就业、收入、个人发展的机会。这为今后指标体系中相关指标的设定和权重考量提供了研究基础。

2. 以本地户口和外地户口为主要区别的不同身份群体，在收入、居住、社会保障、就业、个人发展机会、教育、医疗等方面都存在明显的不平等，相应的在满意度和城市归属感上有着明显差异。这表明城市社会公平问题日益突出，因此，城市生活各方面的公平度指标，应该成为今后评价体系中的一个重要方面。

3. 如何在现行体制下保留户口身份制度的合理功能，削弱而不是强化其不合理功能，以替代性制度安排进行过渡，打破造成社会不平等的户口身份藩篱，考验着每个城市的管理者的行政智慧和管理能力。在削弱身份壁垒和增强社会公平方面，城市管理者在相应的政策制定、制度调整和制度建设方面的作为，应该成为今后城市评价体系的组成部分。

通过分析两个城市的居民对城市各方面的感受和评价，对比调查项之间、城市之间的关联或差异，帮助我们在客观数据的基础上更为全面、准确地把握"城市发展"与"人民生活"之间的关系。

六、最后的分析

综合今年评价体系分析的结果和问卷调查反映的情况，其实不难得出一个结论：现阶段，中国城市发展中普遍面临的最突出问题，就是经济发展水平、财政支出与公共投入、居民实际享有三者之间未能实现协调、共生式地发展，换句话说，既城市经济的发展并非必然可以有效改善民生，提高居民生活质量。

我们从两个问题入手，探讨一下形成这一现状的主要原因：

1. 民众到底需要什么？

社会发展理论表明，发展是有阶段性的，在不同的发展阶段势必有着不同的发展重点、发展模式和发展理念。经济社会如此，人的需求也是如此。

改革开放以后，飞速发展的经济初步满足了人们对物质、财富的需求，但随着物质层面的需求不断得到满足，人们转而开始更多地关注精神文化层面，以求获得更多、更丰富的幸福感、满足感、成就感等精神上的愉悦。但这一层面的需求更为复杂，不同收入、不同学历甚至不同性别的人这一需求的表现形式都不尽相同，这已经不仅仅是依靠经济手段就可以解决的庞大工程。而目前，众多有关城市发展的课题中，却一直没有从这一方向进行过完整、深入的研究分析，国家现有的统计数据也只是关注于物质成果或者物化的数字。

这就造成无法准确、全面地了解城市发展状况并加以分析研究，国家政策制定者、城市管理执行者无从掌握老百姓的切身需求是什么，他们对城市发展不满意的又是什么。这种单向的、盲目的发展建设，如何及时调整发展思路与规划？如何实现"以人为本"？

2. 为什么经济发展的成果不能直接转化为居民受益？

最实质性的原因就是尚未实现城市管理的制度化和常态化。

大量的数据和实例可以说明，目前，中国城市以 GDP 为核心的发展模式并未得到根本性的触动，民生项目没有成为发展主导，更多的还只限于应急、被迫和小恩小惠，或者说还是问题导向，严重缺乏主动性和针对性，一旦遇到某些发展或管理矛盾时，随时都可能出现侵犯居民利益（交通、菜站、便民商铺、民工学校等）的现象。

缺少制度性的保障，必然导致极其随意的"以人为本"，被动适应中央的发展要求和目标，看财政下单，使得改善民生改出两种极端：既可以极为超前，比如陕西神木开展的全民公费医疗；又可以严重滞后，比如本次排名中，泰安经济水平排名第23，公共服务第167，居民享有第143，朔州三类排名分别为27、110、135，宜宾则为50、171、、164。政府的导向结果或者发展规划与居民需求存在明显的偏差，居高临下安排多，根据需求跟进少。制度路径造成分享类公共服务项目的不均等，将是社会稳定的巨大隐患。

城市发展，始终应以民生为本，尽快促进城市常态发展与管理的科学化、法制化。保障居民享有城市发展成果的权利，首先在制度上保障居民的话语权，畅通居民与城市管理者进行沟通和对话的渠道，让更多的居民切身参与到城市的发展中，起到体验、促进和监督的作用，并最终享受到城市发展的果实。同时，细化民生需求领域、频率和发展趋势，做到有目的、有计划、有针对性地制定各项城市规划；在居民共享项目中实行合理分配，协调效率与公平间的关系；在分享类项目中建立一套合理协调体制，处理好方便百姓和商业获利之间的关系。

这些，也将逐渐成为我们未来研究的重要组成部分。

第二部分　评价体系编制及调整说明

《2011中国城市科学发展综合评价报告》体例编制及调整说明

自2008年首部《中国城市科学发展综合评级报告》（2009年始更名为《中国城市科学发展综合评价报告》）出版以来，每年度的《报告》都会根据当年实际状况，针对编制体例的调整或变化作出必要的说明。

《2011中国城市科学发展综合评价报告》在连续三年的研究探索基础上，综合社会各界，尤其是领域专家、行业学者的反馈与建议，对原有评价体系的架构组合进行了较大幅度的调整，而《报告》本身的版块及内容也作出了相应的设计与变化。为此，我们觉得有必要对本年度《报告》的编制体例做一次全面、完整的梳理与说明，以使广大读者朋友们有一个清晰的脉络。

一、调整原则

《报告》是以中国城市发展研究院的重大成果之一，经多年深入研究设计，拥有自主知识产权的《中国城市科学发展综合评级体系（E&G）设计》为基础编写而成。E&G体系经过专家的多次论证和时间的反复检验，已被证明是科学、有效、务实的城市评价体系。

但是，随着我们关注主题、分析方向的逐渐明晰化和定向化，以及城市发展进程中呈现出来的阶段性特征，必然要对原有的评价体系及其架构进行适应性的调整，这种调整不是颠覆性的，而是在原有基础上作出的延续性的完善与优化。

同时，《报告》依然采用国家统计部门等官方机构公布的权威数据，从公众的角度出发，设计最简单明了的代表指标以体现我们的研究理念，而不创建新的、复杂的模型，便于更多的人理解并接受。

二、指导思想

科学发展观，其核心是"以人为本"。自 2011 年起，《报告》将密切关注民生问题，围绕"城市与人"这一研究主线展开分析与评价。为此，我们在沿袭原有评价系统的分类基础上，进一步优化了分类体系，主要是从指标的逻辑关系上更加清晰化人与城市的关系，更具针对性地完善判断和分析的方法，从年度指标的评价排序上更为清晰、直接地发现城市与人的关系的趋势、特征和主要矛盾等。

三、调整说明

1. 体系结构图

➤ 原有体系结构：

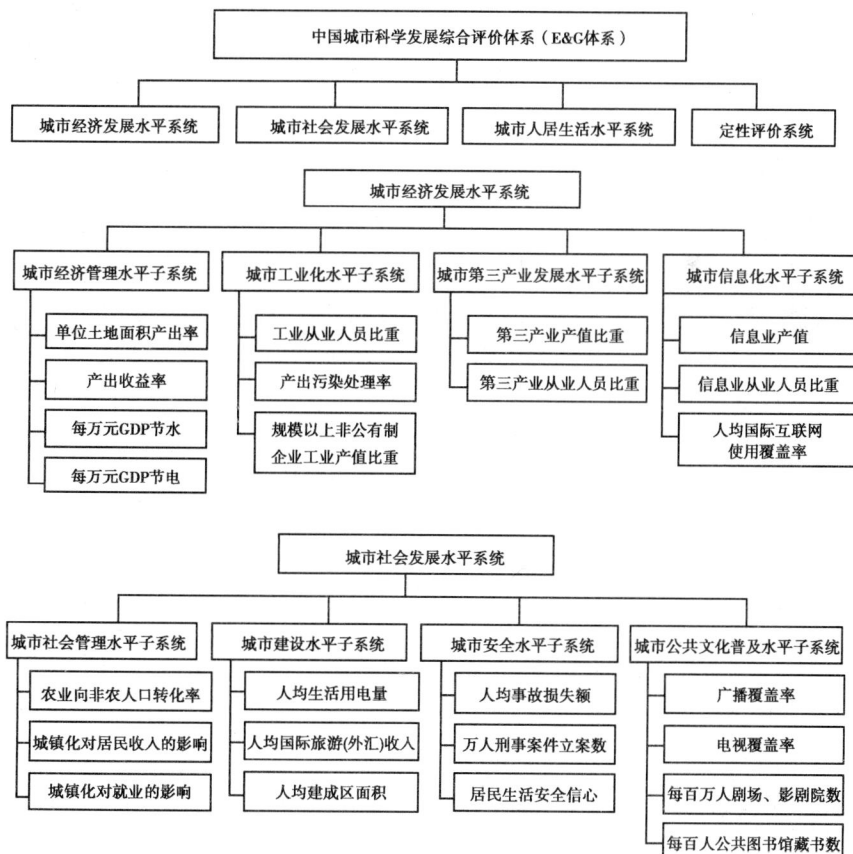

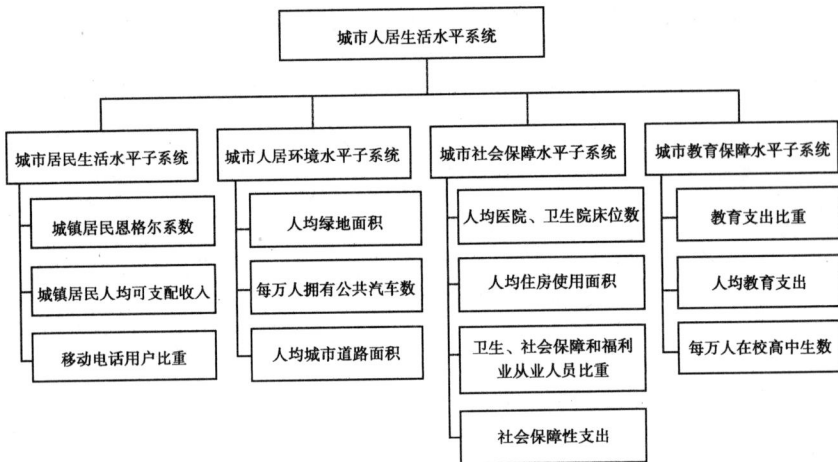

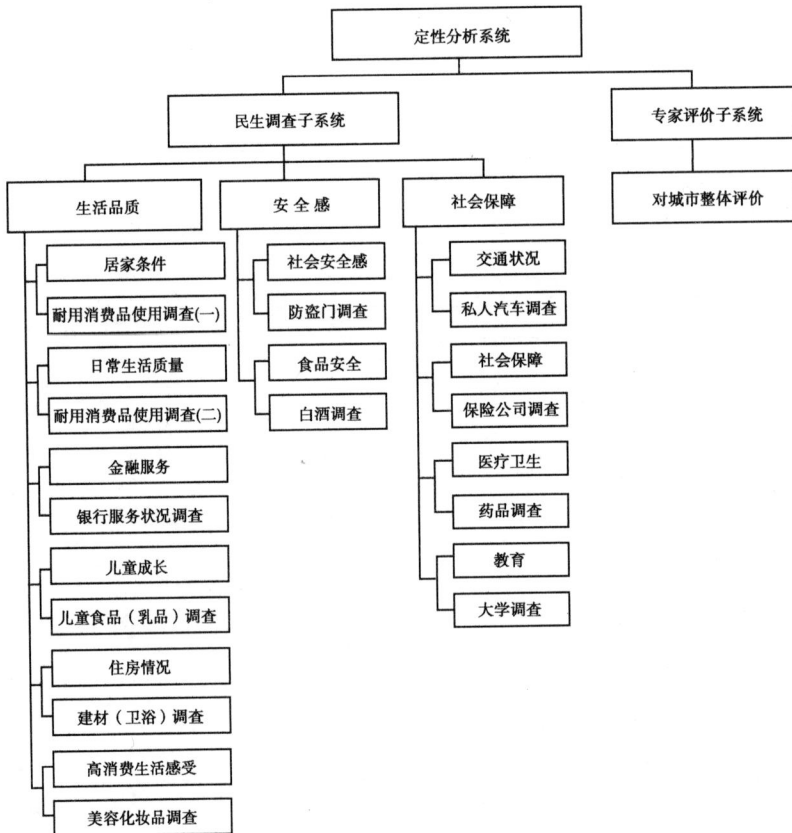

➤ 调整后的架构：

2011 年中国城市科学发展综合评价体系

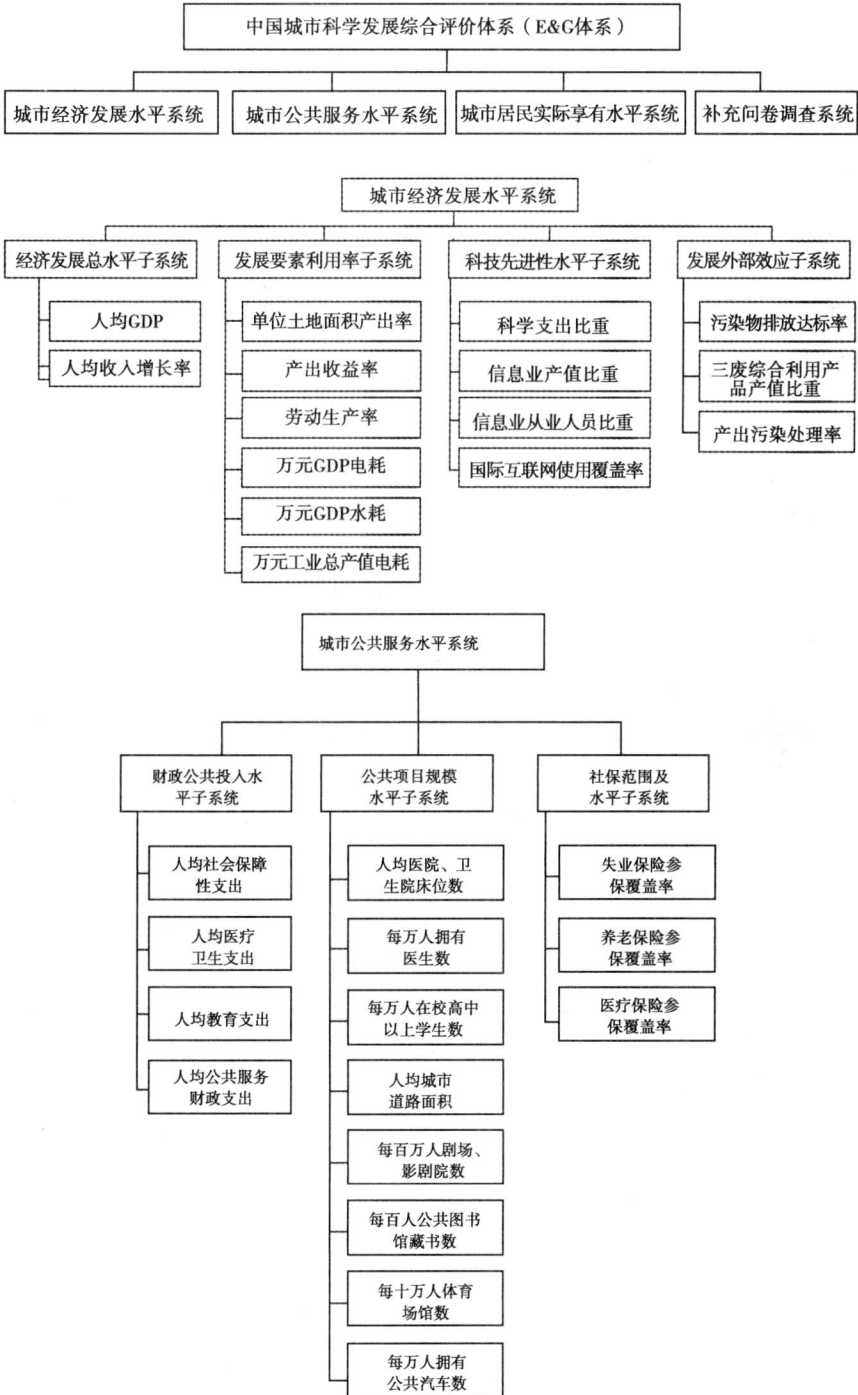

中国城市科学发展综合评价体系（E&G体系）

| 城市经济发展水平系统 | 城市公共服务水平系统 | 城市居民实际享有水平系统 | 补充问卷调查系统 |

城市经济发展水平系统

经济发展总水平子系统
- 人均GDP
- 人均收入增长率

发展要素利用率子系统
- 单位土地面积产出率
- 产出收益率
- 劳动生产率
- 万元GDP电耗
- 万元GDP水耗
- 万元工业总产值电耗

科技先进性水平子系统
- 科学支出比重
- 信息业产值比重
- 信息业从业人员比重
- 国际互联网使用覆盖率

发展外部效应子系统
- 污染物排放达标率
- 三废综合利用产品产值比重
- 产出污染处理率

城市公共服务水平系统

财政公共投入水平子系统
- 人均社会保障性支出
- 人均医疗卫生支出
- 人均教育支出
- 人均公共服务财政支出

公共项目规模水平子系统
- 人均医院、卫生院床位数
- 每万人拥有医生数
- 每万人在校高中以上学生数
- 人均城市道路面积
- 每百万人剧场、影剧院数
- 每百人公共图书馆藏书数
- 每十万人体育场馆数
- 每万人拥有公共汽车数

社保范围及水平子系统
- 失业保险参保覆盖率
- 养老保险参保覆盖率
- 医疗保险参保覆盖率

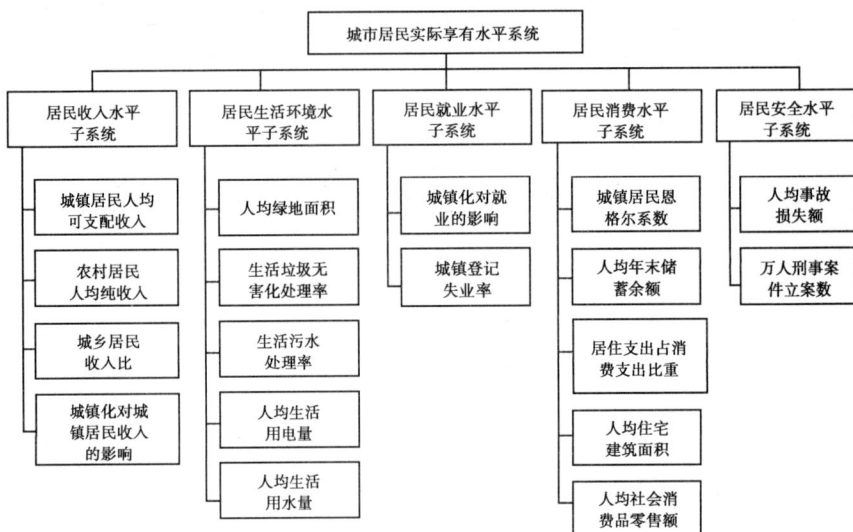

2. 母系统设计

《报告》采用的城市统计指标涵盖经济、社会、文化等各个领域，我们将这些定量的指标分为经济发展、社会发展、人居生活三大母系统。

调整后的评价体系仍分为三大定量母系统：

第一类是经济发展水平，主要反映城市经济发展的规模、要素效益、科技先进性和外部影响效应，总体是属于体现完整性的生产类指标。

第二类是公共服务水平，主要反映政府投入社会公共服务事业的财政、项目规模和范围，总体属于社会共享类的财富分配指标。

第三类是居民享有水平，主要反映城乡居民在城市发展中分享到的各项实惠和机会，总体属于城市发展成果最终由居民收获的个人受益类指标。

三类母系统之间的逻辑关系为：一类指标反映的能力决定二类指标的规模和水平，二类指标的规模和水平则是影响三类指标可实现的基础；而三者间的协调程度就是判断城市是否形成了一套科学、有效的分配制度和技术路径以决定城市居民的受益程度。

由于上述统计指标只是反映可物化、可量化的方面，无法完全地、真实地反映出其背后存在的很多隐蔽性现象与问题。而且，即便是精心设定的第三类母系统，其统计数据仍然是结果性的，不能反映城市居民的实际需求，也就不能以此作为判断居民实际感受的唯一依据。为此，我们设计了一类补充性的、定性类的母系统。

原评价体系中的定性分析系统包括民生调查和专家评价两项，但因为某些缘由尚未执行，调整后的体系取消了原有设定，对城市的定性评价，从 2011 年开始由问卷取代，这类问卷只做总体评价，不做评级排序，是对城市评价报告的有益补充。

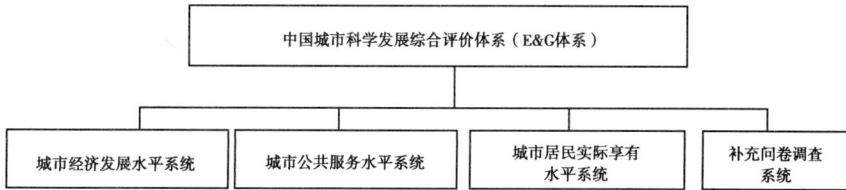

母系统是从分类组合角度告知推演结论的出处、所发现问题的类别属性以及城市综合评价依据，是从城市建设、管理角度，对反映人和城市全面、协调、可持续发展状态，以及相应需求满足程度的各项系统的分类组合，包括了城市发展的主要方面。由它产生的指数，是推演城市科学发展综合指数，也即得出评价结论的基础。

3. 子系统设计

拥有标志性主题的母系统，反映的是整体的价值，其下分别设有相应的各项子系统，反映城市发展中的局部现象。子系统是指标的基础集群，反映出指标设计和选择的走向，是进行科学评价的基础。

我们将各项子系统及其指标在原有基础上重新进行合理调整归类和增减。调整后的 E&G 体系，定量分析部分的三大母系统仍由十二个子系统组成，每个子系统下也包含对应的数个指标，其构成如下：

序号	子系统名称	子系统指标
1	经济发展总水平	人均 GDP
		人均收入增长率（人均收入增长率与 GDP 增长率的协调性）
2	发展要素利用率	单位土地面积产出率（单位建成区面积 GDP 产出）
		产出收益率（地方财政一般预算内收入与 GDP 比值）
		劳动生产率（职工人均工业总产值）
		万元 GDP 电耗
		万元 GDP 水耗
		万元工业总产值电耗
3	科技先进性水平	科学支出比重
		信息业产值比重
		信息业从业人员比重
		国际互联网使用覆盖率

序号	子系统名称	子系统指标
4	发展外部效应	污染物排放达标率（包括工业废水、二氧化硫、烟尘）
		三废综合利用产品产值比重
		产出污染处理率（污染处理率与 GDP 间的比值）
5	财政公共投入水平	人均社会保障性支出
		人均医疗卫生支出
		人均教育支出
		人均公共服务财政支出（上述三项综合）
6	公共项目规模水平	人均医院、卫生院床位数
		每万人拥有医生数
		每万人在校高中以上学生数
		人均城市道路面积
		每百万人剧场、影剧院数
		每百人公共图书馆藏书数
		每十万人体育场馆数
		每万人拥有公共汽车数
7	社会保障范围及水平	养老保险参保覆盖率
		医疗保险参保覆盖率
		失业保险参保覆盖率
8	居民收入水平	城镇居民人均可支配收入
		农村居民人均纯收入
		城乡居民收入比
		城镇化对城镇居民收入的影响（非农人口转化率与收入增长率的协调度）
9	居民生活环境水平	人均绿地面积
		生活垃圾无害化处理率
		生活污水处理率
		人均生活用电量
		人均生活用水量
10	居民就业水平	城镇化对就业的影响（非农人口转化率与失业人口增长率的协调度）
		城镇登记失业率
11	居民消费水平	城镇居民恩格尔系数
		人均年末储蓄余额
		居住支出占消费支出比重
		人均住宅建筑面积
		人均社会消费品零售额
12	居民安全水平	人均事故损失额
		万人刑事案件立案数

4. 权重设计

权重设计即构权，指在解决多指标之间的相互关系和主次程度时，用分解 100% 比例的方式，表现设计者对多指标之间关系或某一指标倾向的态度。

考虑到评价体系中每一项系统，甚至每一项指标，都对评价城市的实际发展状况具有重要的参考价值，因此，调整后的 E&G 体系不再设权重差别，也可以说，实质采取的是均权方式。

5. 综合指数设计

E&G 综合指数由数字构成，每个城市都有不同的综合指数，所有城市综合指数的排序便成为评价活动完成的标志。

综合指数是由指标到子系统，再到母系统推演的最终结果，也是对该城市评价活动的最后结论。不同城市综合指数的对比，实质上构成了城市科学发展的相对标准，即处在发展过程中，线性动态运动选择某一静态时段，对这一时段城市发展所提出的标准。

四、名词释义

1. 中国城市　2011 年度《报告》中评价涉及到了全国 287 个地级及以上城市，因数据可得性等原因，暂未包括港、澳、台地区城市。

2. 科学发展　源于党中央、国务院提出的科学发展观及其内涵和外延。这是因为：科学发展观体现了中国特色社会主义的发展方向、模式和基本特征；体现了中国处于发展中国家和社会主义初级阶段的阶段性特点；体现了中国国情，代表着中国发展追求的目标。

科学发展的基本含义为：以人为中心的发展，包括全面发展，即以经济建设为中心，全面推进经济建设、政治建设、文化建设和社会建设，实现经济发展和社会全面进步；协调发展，即统筹城乡发展、统筹区域发展、统筹经济社会发展、统筹人与自然和谐发展、统筹国内发展和对外开放，推进生产力和生产关系、经济基础和上层建筑相协调，推进经济建设、政治建设、文化建设、社会建设的各个环节、各个方面相协调；以及可持续发展，即促进人与自然的和谐，实现经济发展和人口、资源、环境相协调，坚持走生产发展、生活富裕、生态良好的文明发展道路，保证一代接一代地永续发展。

3. 体系　由指标、子系统、母系统、数据及其计算、定量分析和问卷调查以及综合指数所构成的完整系统。

4. 城市评价　包括对城市的数据分析和综合评价，是建立在指标、子系统、母系统和推演方式基础上的分析与归纳。

五、补充说明

1. 2011 年度《报告》中，除特别说明外，所采用的数据均为国家统计部门等官方机构公布的 2009 年度的统计数据。

2. 数据整理过程中，意外地发现个别城市统计数据存在疑点，在反复核对并参考各类城市年鉴、统计公报等资料后，我们进行了调整，其中包括广元市人均 GDP。

3. 《报告》中除国家统计部门直接公布的人均类指标数据外，我们设定的其他人均性指标均以常住人口为基数加以计算，其中包括国际互联网使用覆盖率，人均社会保障性支出，人均医疗卫生支出，人均教育支出，人均公共服务财政支出，每万人拥有医院、卫生院床位数，人均年末储蓄余额，人均社会消费品零售额等指标。

4. 在获取常住人口数据过程中，因国家统计部门公布的各类统计年鉴中没有或者仅有少量城市的数据，所以我们花费了大量时间，翻阅、查找各类参考资料，包括各地方城市统计年鉴、统计公报、政府工作报告及各类官网等，补齐了大部分城市的常住人口数据，但仍有少部分城市难以查找到来源可靠的数据。为保证每个城市得到尽量公平、客观的比较基础和环境，不因这一重要数据的缺失而大幅度影响评价成绩，我们结合分析过往数年发展趋势，比较其他存在相关关系的指标，参考同一区域内或相似类型城市数据等多种方法，对缺失的数据进行合理的、保守的推测与估算。如与实际情况存在较大出入，还请予以包涵和理解，下年度《报告》中，我们会使用更多的时间，寻找更稳妥的渠道处理可能存在的缺失数据。

5. 与上条所说类似，在处理职工平均工资、三废综合利用产品产值、生活垃圾无害化处理率、二氧化硫去除/排放量、生活污水处理率、人均生活用电量、城镇就业/失业人员、农村居民人均纯收入、城镇居民人均可支配收入、每万人拥有公共汽车数、每百万人剧场影剧院数、每十万人体育场馆数等确实数据的城市时，我们几乎都采用了同样的方法，以求尽可能公正地对待每个城市。

6. 除上述情况外，仍有少量城市确实无此数据，或者无可供推断的数据依据，只能暂记为最低排位，表格中以"/"标示。

第三部分 城市问卷调查分析报告

一、调查设计

● 调查目的

一般城市评级的主要依据是采用统计数据来计算的人均资源拥有量等客观指标，而忽略了城市生活主体（居民）对城市的主观评价。人，才是城市的主体，城市因人而存在，为了使城市评级更加科学和符合实际，中国城市发展研究院试图将城市居民对城市的主观评价纳入到城市评级体系中来。2011 年主要在北京和深圳进行试点调查，了解这两个城市的居民对城市各方面的感受和评价，为今后制定更为完善和科学的城市评级指标体系提供研究基础。

● 调查内容

本次调查试图了解城市生活主体对其所在城市做出的主观评价，内容涵盖生活消费和服务、居住、就业和创业、教育、医疗、社会保障、交通、环境、社会治安、社会公平、社会信任和尊重、政府管理及公共服务等 16 个方面。

● 调查地点

选取北京和深圳作为调查地点。二者都是成熟的大城市，都有 2/3 以上的外来人口，便于了解城市化过程中人们的角色转换和身份变化。其中，北京是古老的传统城市，深圳是新兴的移民城市。

● 调查方法

本次调查采用自编问卷与访谈相结合的调查方法，对北京、深圳两个城市的居民进行抽样调查。根据研究的目的和城市的具体情况，对两个城市先进行系统抽样，然后再在各分层中进行随机抽样。首先通过统计数据查出城市（北京、深圳）各个区的人口数量，确定城市中每个区应该抽取的人数；再根据各个区的不同人群（白领、工人、商业人员、农民工等）分布的具体情况以及区的地理位置①来选取调研地点（区域）（详见

---

① 在一个区中一般选取该区的东、南、西、北、中这五个方位。

图1）；在确定调查区域之后，一般选取各个人群都会去的公共场所进行偶遇抽样，同时考虑到不同公共场所的主要人群有所不同（如公园里面老人比较多，麦当劳、肯德基等处年轻人比较多等），对公共场所的选取进行数量上的平衡。据此，我们选取了胡同/老城区、居民小区、城中村、公园、快餐厅、银行大堂等公共场所进行调查，同时由于有些人群较少到公共场所活动，也选取了一些企业、行政事业单位，并做了一部分入户调查，以确保样本具有代表性。

- **样本状况**

此次调查在北京总共做了 820 份调研问卷，最终回收有效问卷 814 份，调研地区涉及到朝阳、西城（包括原来的宣武区）、东城（包括原来的崇文区）、丰台、海淀、石景山等六个主城区（具体样本分布见表1）；在深圳总共做了 820 份调研问卷，最终回收有效问卷 815 份，调研地区涉及到宝安（其中光明新区归为宝安区）、福田、龙岗（其中坪山新区归为龙岗区）、罗湖、南山、盐田等 6 个主城区（具体样本分布见表1）。

表1　　　　　　　受访者在北京、深圳各区的分布情况

北京	朝阳	西城	东城	丰台	海淀	石景山	合计
	101	209	194	74	172	64	814
深圳	宝安区	福田区	龙岗区	罗湖区	南山区	盐田区	合计
	88	179	111	268	102	67	815

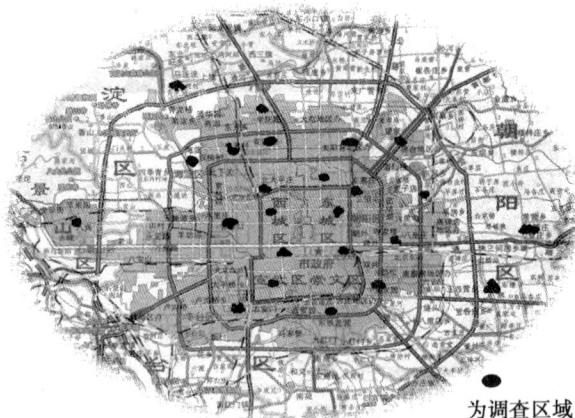

● 为调查区域

图1　北京各区调查地点

二、受访者概况

在北京的受访者中，男性占 48.5%，女性占 51.5%，本市户口占 45.3%，外地户口占 54.7%，非农户口占 69.4%，农业户口占 30.6%，年龄分布从 14 岁到 84 岁，青年和中年人为主体，教育程度分布从小学以下到研究生，受过中等和高等教育的为主体；在深圳的受访者中，男性占 47.2%，女性占 52.8%，本市户口占 32.5%，外地户口占 67.5%，非农户口占 63.7%，农业户口占 36.3%，年龄分布从 18 岁到 64 岁，青年和中年人为主体，教育程度分布从小学以下到研究生，受过中等和高等教育的为主体（详见表2）。

表2　　　　　　　　　　受访者的基本特征

内容		北京		深圳		合计	
		人数	百分比	人数	百分比	人数	百分比
性别	男	395	48.5%	385	47.2%	780	47.9%
	女	419	51.5%	430	52.8%	849	52.1%
年龄	18 周岁及以下	16	2.0%	13	1.6%	29	1.8%
	19—35 周岁	495	60.8%	604	74.3%	1099	67.5%
	36—55 周岁	236	29.0%	184	22.6%	420	25.8%
	56 周岁及以上	67	8.2%	12	1.5%	79	4.9%
户口性质	非农户口	564	69.4%	517	63.7%	1081	66.5%
	农业户口	249	30.6%	295	36.3%	544	33.5%
户口所在地	本市	367	45.3%	261	32.5%	628	38.9%
	外地	444	54.7%	541	67.5%	985	61.1%
	其中：大城市	97	12.0%	92	11.5%	189	11.7%
	中小城市	174	21.5%	195	24.3%	369	22.9%
	乡镇农村	173	21.3%	254	31.7%	427	26.5%
教育程度	小学以下	5	0.6%	2	0.2%	7	0.4%
	小学	21	2.6%	12	1.5%	33	2.0%
	初中	124	15.3%	94	11.6%	218	13.4%
	高中	136	16.7%	165	20.4%	301	18.6%
	中专/技校	66	8.1%	125	15.5%	191	11.8%
	大专	136	16.7%	202	25.0%	338	20.8%
	大学本科	271	33.3%	187	23.1%	458	28.2%
	研究生	54	6.6%	22	2.7%	76	4.7%

表 3 受访者现在（或以前）的职业

职业类型	北京		深圳		合计	
	人数	百分比	人数	百分比	人数	百分比
工人	64	7.9%	56	7.0%	120	7.4%
务农	3	0.4%	3	0.4%	6	0.4%
个体户	124	15.3%	41	5.1%	165	10.2%
商业机构人员	76	9.3%	74	9.2%	150	9.3%
服务业人员	86	10.6%	107	13.3%	193	12.0%
营销人员	46	5.7%	57	7.1%	103	6.4%
企业白领	107	13.2%	185	23.1%	292	18.1%
金融从业者	22	2.7%	21	2.6%	43	2.7%
教育工作者	49	6.0%	24	3.0%	73	4.5%
科研人员和大学教师	11	1.4%	0	0.0%	11	0.7%
律师	2	0.2%	28	3.5%	30	1.9%
医务工作者	18	2.2%	30	3.7%	48	3.0%
工程技术人员	37	4.6%	35	4.4%	72	4.5%
行政事业单位办事人员	69	8.5%	50	6.2%	119	7.4%
无业人员	11	1.4%	16	2.0%	27	1.7%
私营小企业负责人	13	1.6%	33	4.1%	46	2.8%
大中型民营企业高管	1	0.1%	4	0.5%	5	0.3%
大学生	40	4.9%	8	1.0%	48	3.0%
政府、党群组织、事业单位负责人	0	0.0%	3	0.4%	3	0.2%
军人	6	0.7%	0	0.0%	6	0.4%
自由职业者	28	3.4%	27	3.4%	55	3.4%

表 4　　　　　受访者现在（或以前）所在单位的性质

现在（或以前）所在单位的性质	北京		深圳		合计	
	人数	百分比	人数	百分比	人数	百分比
国有企业	157	20.2%	109	13.8%	266	17.0%
集体企业	47	6.0%	53	6.7%	100	6.4%
私营企业	211	27.2%	331	42.0%	542	34.6%
外资企业	59	7.6%	34	4.3%	93	5.9%
个体经营户	153	19.7%	124	15.7%	277	17.7%
合资企业	20	2.6%	30	3.8%	50	3.2%
事业单位	81	10.4%	52	6.6%	133	8.5%
党政机关	30	3.9%	14	1.8%	44	2.8%
其他	19	2.4%	42	5.3%	61	3.9%

表 5

表 5 　　　　　　　　　　　受访者家庭年收入分布状况

家庭年收入	北京		深圳		合计	
	人数	百分比	人数	百分比	人数	百分比
3 万元及以下	121	14.9%	236	29.0%	357	21.9%
3—5 万元	178	21.9%	176	21.6%	354	21.7%
5—7 万元	138	17.0%	100	12.3%	238	14.6%
7—10 万元	148	18.2%	120	14.7%	268	16.5%
10—15 万元	82	10.1%	75	9.2%	157	9.6%
15—20 万元	65	8.0%	42	5.2%	107	6.6%
20—30 万元	40	4.9%	31	3.8%	71	4.4%
30—50 万元	28	3.4%	21	2.6%	49	3.0%
50—100 万元	8	1.0%	12	1.5%	20	1.2%
100 万元以上	6	0.7%	2	0.2%	8	0.5%

表 6 　　　　　　　　　　　　受访者平均家庭年收入

城市	北京	深圳	合计
均值	2.59	2.08	2.33

注：收入区间的等级代码如下：$0 = (0 - 3)$，$1 = (3 - 5)$，$2 = (5 - 7)$，$3 = (7 - 10)$，$4 = (10 - 15)$，$5 = (15 - 20)$，$6 = (20 - 30)$，$7 = (30 - 50)$，$8 = (50 - 100)$，$9 = (100 +)$，单位：万元。均值是每个收入区间的等级代码平均数，并不是货币金额。

三、对城市的总体评价

3.1 对所居城市总体上的满意度

表 7 　　　　　　　　　受访者对所居城市总体上的满意度

城市	很满意	比较满意	一般	不太满意	很不满意	均值
北京	14.8%	48.2%	28.9%	5.5%	2.6%	3.67
深圳	11.2%	50.7%	31.0%	5.0%	2.1%	3.64
合计	13.0%	49.4%	30.0%	5.3%	2.3%	3.65

注：很满意 $=5$，比较满意 $=4$，一般 $=3$，不太满意 $=2$，很不满意 $=1$。显著性 $P = 0.457$，即两城市居民对该问题的评价没有显著差异。

按 5 级满意度评价，中间值为 3，所有受访者的均值为 3.65，大于 3.5，说明人们总体上对所居城市倾向于比较满意。

北京、深圳的受访者对此问题的回答没有显著差异。不仅如此，事实上根据数据处理结果，无论是按年龄、职业、单位性质、收入、户口性质

（农业户口与非农户口）、户口区域（本地与外地）、户口所在地（本市与外地大中小城市和乡镇农村）、本地生活年限分类，还是按这些因素的组合分类，其差异都不具有显著意义。仅在不同学历的人群间存在具有显著差异，表现为受教育程度越高，对城市总体的评价越低，见表8。

表8　　　　　　　　　**不同学历居民对本市总体上的满意度**

教育程度	人数	均值
初等教育（小学及以下、初中）	258	3.77
中等教育（高中、中专、技校）	491	3.69
高等教育（大专、大本、研究生）	869	3.59

显著性 P = 0.007

这说明，在北京和深圳生活的居民，**无论年龄、职业、身份有何不同，其对所居城市总体上的满意度大致相同，处于一般和比较满意之间，接近于比较满意。**而学历与满意度的负相关关系，则有可能是体现了期望值与满意度的负相关关系。

3.2　各群体总体满意度无显著差异的原因：大城市的吸引力

在我们的调查样本中，本市户口和外地户口的比例为 38.9% 和 61.1%，六成多为外地人，考虑到本市户口中还有一部分是外地人在近年内取得本市户口的，实际上的外地人比例还应该更大一些。我们根据受访者在本市的生活年限，将拥有本市户口的人分为两类：生活 11 年以下的为新本地人，11 年及以上的为老本地人，其人数与百分比见表9。

表9　　　　　　　**受访者中老本地人、新本地人与外地人的比例**

身份	人数	百分比
老本地人（在本市生活 11 年及以上）	462	28.7%
新本地人（在本市生活 11 年以下）	160	10.0%
外地人	985	61.3%

老本地人所占比例接近三成，新本地人和外地人共占七成。外地人选择该城市生活和工作，自然是该城市有吸引他之处，否则也不会轻易离乡背井。所以，城市总体评价较高以及各人群无显著差异，合乎常理。

但如果将评价内容具体化和分门别类，满意度的水平和差异就很不同了，后面我们会陆续看到。我们先来看看人们最满意、最不满意和最企盼的是哪些方面。

四、对城市的综合评价及企盼

表10   受访者对所居城市最满意的方面

最满意的方面	位次	人数	百分比
生活便利度	1	805	50.00%
交通	2	643	40.00%
环境	3	590	36.70%
个人发展机会	4	549	34.10%
治安	5	398	24.70%
公共服务	6	380	23.60%
社会保障	7	336	20.90%
医疗	8	287	17.80%
教育	9	266	16.50%
就业	10	194	12.10%
物价	11	96	6.00%
公平度	12	52	3.20%
房价	13	23	1.40%

表11   受访者对所居城市最不满意的方面

最不满意的方面	位次	人数	百分比
房价	1	1216	75.40%
物价	2	1019	63.20%
交通	3	461	28.60%
公平度	4	401	24.90%
治安	5	334	20.70%
医疗	6	328	20.30%
社会保障	7	246	15.30%
就业	8	241	14.90%
教育	9	226	14.00%
环境	10	168	10.40%
个人发展机会	11	160	9.90%
公共服务	12	116	7.20%
生活便利度	13	70	4.30%

表 12　　　　　　　　　　　　受访者对所居城市最企盼的方面

最企盼解决的问题	位次	人数	百分比
提高居民收入	1	916	56.40%
稳定物价	2	832	51.20%
解决住房问题	3	794	48.90%
提高政府管理水平	4	413	25.40%
解决社会公平问题	5	395	24.30%
有更多的发展机会	6	301	18.50%
解决户籍问题	7	284	17.50%
解决医疗问题	8	270	16.60%
解决社会保障问题	9	269	16.60%
解决就业问题	10	246	15.10%
解决社会安全问题	11	235	14.50%
解决环境问题	12	178	11.00%
得到理解和尊重	13	148	9.10%

从百分比看，在最满意的方面，排在前面的是生活便利度、交通、环境、个人发展机会，选择率都在 30% 以上，而选择最少的则是房价、公平度、物价，都在 10% 以下，与其他选择差异明显；在最不满意的方面，房价、物价高高在上，选择率在 60% 以上，其他选择均不到 30%，排在最后的是生活便利度、公共服务、个人发展机会，均低于 10%。

可见，**人们对所居城市最满意的，都是大城市特有的优势**，如生活便利度和个人发展机会。这一点也为前面看到的城市总体评价较高以及各人群无显著差异，提供了注脚。

人们最不满意的，则是房价、物价、公平度，尤其是前二者，选择它们为最不满意方面的居然达到 1216 人和 1019 人，分别占 75.40% 和 63.20%，与其他方面差距巨大（居第 3 位的交通只有 28.60%）。与此对应，**人们最企盼解决的问题**，排在前 5 位的依次为**提高居民收入、稳定物价、解决住房问题**、提高政府管理水平、解决社会公平问题，这 5 项与其它选项差距明显，前 3 项尤甚。

五、身份、职业与收入

提高收入在人们的企盼中排名第一（选择人数多达 916 人），可见其重要性。那么，城市中不同群体的收入水平有何差异？

5.1 户口身份与收入

5.1.1 户口区域、户口性质与收入

按户口划分，本地人收入平均值高于外地人，非农户口收入平均值高于农业户口，差距都很大。将两种户口性质组合，本地非农户口高于本地农业户口，本地农业户口高于外地非农户口，外地非农户口高于外地农业户口，形成递进关系。见表13。

表13   根据户口区域和户口性质区分的平均家庭年收入

身份		人数	家庭年收入均值	显著性
户口区域	本地人	628	3.12	0.000
	外地人	985	1.83	
户口性质	非农户口	1081	2.77	0.000
	农业户口	544	1.47	
户口区域 + 户口性质	本地非农户口	594	3.13	0.000
	本地农业户口	33	2.94	
	外地非农户口	480	2.31	
	外地农业户口	504	1.37	

5.1.2 户口区域、本地生活年限与收入

进一步细分，新本地人又高于老本地人，老本地人高于外地人，差距都十分明显。见表14。

表14   根据户口区域和本地生活年限区分的平均家庭年收入

身份	人数	家庭年收入均值
新本地人	160	3.35
老本地人	462	3.05
外地人	985	1.83

显著性 P = 0.000

5.2 职业与收入

5.2.1 职业类型与收入

为便于分析，对职业进行分类，将21种职业归为工人、商业服务业人员（包括商业机构人员和服务业人员）、个体户和无业人员[①]（因

---

① 因全部样本中无业人员仅27人，同时在现实中，适龄就业人口中完全不做事不挣钱的是极少的，故将其与个体户归为一类。

为受访者中务农的仅有 6 人，也归入此项）、企业主和企业负责人（包括私营小企业负责人、大中型民营企业高管）、企业白领（包括企业白领、营销人员、金融业从业者、工程技术人员、自由职业者、大学生）、专业人员（包括教育工作者、科研人员和大学教师、律师、医务工作者）、行政事业单位人员（包括行政事业单位办事人员、政府和党群组织及事业单位负责人、军人）7 类，不同职业分组的平均家庭年收入见表 15。

表 15   根据职业区分的平均家庭年收入

职业	人数	家庭年收入均值
企业主和企业负责人	51	4.53
专业人员	210	3.26
行政事业单位人员	128	2.43
个体户和无业人员	198	2.40
企业白领	565	2.34
商业服务业人员	343	1.64
工人	120	1.55

显著性 $P = 0.000$

企业主和企业负责人高高在上，其次是专业人员。行政事业单位人员、个体户和无业人员、企业白领相差不多，居中间位置。商业服务业人员和工人落在最后，且与上面的群体差距巨大。

那么，什么人更多地从事较高收入职业，什么人更多地从事较低收入职业？请看表 16。

表 16   不同身份群体的职业分布

身份	企业主和企业负责人	专业人员	行政事业单位人员	个体户和无业人员	企业白领	商业服务业人员	工人
老本地人	2.4%	17.7%	10.0%	8.7%	33.6%	14.2%	13.3%
新本地人	5.0%	22.6%	11.3%	6.3%	40.3%	10.1%	4.4%
外地人	3.1%	9.1%	6.6%	15.1%	34.6%	26.4%	5.1%

老本地人、新本地人中从事专业人员工作的达 17.7% 和 22.6%，而外地人中只有 9.1%，前二者中从事行政事业单位工作的，均在 10% 以上，后者为 6.6%；而前二者中从事商业服务业工作的为 14.2% 和 10.1%，后者中则有 26.4%。个体户和无业人员的比例后者高出很多，工人的比例老本地人最高，企业白领的比例老本地人和外地人差不多，新

本地人最高。可见,户口身份与职业有着一定的联系。

5.2.2 工作单位性质与收入

从受访者工作的单位性质看,收入平均值由高到低分别为:机关事业单位(包括党政机关和事业单位)、外资合资企业、国有企业、集体企业、私营企业、个体,差距十分明显,见表17。

表17　　　　　　　　根据工作单位性质区分的平均家庭年收入

单位性质	人数	家庭年收入均值
机关事业单位	177	3.23
外资合资企业	143	2.94
国有企业	266	2.67
集体企业	100	2.08
私营企业	542	1.97
个体	277	1.71

显著性 $P = 0.000$

那么,什么人更多地在高收入单位工作,什么人更多地在低收入单位工作?见表18可知,老本地人中,22.6%在机关事业单位,而外地人中只有5.6%;32.2%的老本地人在国企,外地人中则是9.5%;老本地人只有6.7%从事个体,而外地人干个体的却高达25.5%。可见户口身份与工作单位性质有着密切的关系。

表18　　　　　　　　不同身份群体的工作单位分布

身份	机关事业单位	外资合资企业	国有企业	集体企业	私营企业	个体
老本地人	22.6%	9.1%	32.2%	8.7%	20.7%	6.7%
新本地人	20.6%	8.5%	28.4%	7.8%	27.0%	7.8%
外地人	5.6%	9.7%	9.5%	5.6%	44.2%	25.5%

5.3 户口身份、职业与收入

我们将户口身份与职业组合,来看它们与收入的关系。根据职业的经济地位和社会地位,将上述7类职业区分为相对高端的职业(行政事业单位人员、专业人员、企业白领、企业主和企业负责人)和相对低端的职业(工人、商业服务业人员、个体户和无业人员),与户口区域组合。从表19可看出,新老本地人的收入均值都高于从事较高端职业的外地人,后者又高于从事较低端职业的外地人,差距同样很明显。

表 19　　　　　　　　根据户口区域和职业区分的平均家庭年收入

身份	人数	家庭年收入均值
新本地人	160	3.35
老本地人	462	3.05
高端职业外地人	521	2.04
低端职业外地人	455	1.60

显著性 P = 0.000

5.4　教育与收入

5.4.1　教育程度与收入

另一个影响收入水平的重要因素，是教育。表 20 是人们的教育程度与家庭年收入的关系，十分明显，学历越高，收入越高，且差距很大。

表 20　　　　　　　　不同学历群体的平均家庭年收入

教育程度	人数	家庭年收入均值
初等教育	258	1.28
中等教育	492	1.71
高等教育	872	2.99

显著性 P = 0.000

5.4.2　教育程度与身份

教育程度与收入成正比，这一点已经和改革开放初期有了很大不同。而各群体收入的高低不同，又和他们的教育程度有关。见表 21 可知，本地人受过高等教育的有 67.0%，外地人只有 20.7%；非农户口有 68.2%，农业户口只有 25.3%；而仅受过初等教育的，本地人只有 8.8%，外地人有 20.7%；非农户口只有 6.7%，而农业户口有 34.1%。从各身份群体的学历均值可以把他们的差别看得更清楚。

表 21　　　　　　　不同户口区域和户口性质群体的教育程度

身份		初等教育	中等教育	高等教育	学历均值	显著性
户口区域	本地人	8.8%	24.2%	67.0%	5.11	0.000
	外地人	20.7%	33.9%	45.4%	4.47	
户口性质	非农户口	6.7%	25.1%	68.2%	5.13	0.000
	农业户口	34.1%	40.6%	25.3%	3.93	
户口区域 + 户口性质	本地非农户口	7.8%	23.9%	68.3%	5.17	0.000
	本地农业户口	27.3%	27.3%	45.5%	4.18	
	外地非农户口	5.5%	26.5%	68.1%	5.08	
	外地农业户口	35.1%	41.0%	23.9%	3.90	

注：小学以下 = 1，小学 = 2，初中 = 3，高中和中专/技校 = 4，大专 = 5，大本 = 6，研究生 = 7

前面看到，新本地人收入高于老本地人，这与新本地人学历较高有很大关系，见表22，老本地人受过高等教育的比例为61.0%，新本地人则为85.0%，老外地人为32.5%，新外地人则为47.3%。仅受过初等教育的，在新本地人中只有1.3%，老本地人中有11.1%，而老外地人中则有29.8%，在新外地人中，则降到了19.4%。这说明**在近十年内进入大城市的非本地居民与之前相比，学历有了很大的提高**。而新本地人鹤立鸡群的学历均值，不仅使他们收入较高，也使他们对城市生活的期望和要求较高，对一些方面的评价偏向于负面。

表22　　　　　　　　不同户口区域和本地生活年限群体的教育程度

身份	初等教育	中等教育	高等教育	学历均值
老本地人	11.1%	28.0%	61.0%	4.92
新本地人	1.3%	13.8%	85.0%	5.69
老外地人（在本市生活11年及以上）	29.8%	37.7%	32.5%	4.12
新外地人（在本市生活11年以下）	19.4%	33.4%	47.3%	4.53

显著性 P = 0.000

同样，高端职业外地人的学历也远高于低端职业的外地人，前者受过高等教育的比例是60.8%，后者只有27.8%；而仅受过初等教育的，前者为10.6%，后者为32.4%，见表23。

表23　　　　　　　　不同户口区域和职业群体的教育程度

身份	初等教育	中等教育	高等教育	学历均值
老本地人	11.1%	28.0%	61.0%	4.92
新本地人	1.3%	13.8%	85.0%	5.69
高端职业外地人	10.6%	28.7%	60.8%	4.87
低端职业外地人	32.4%	39.8%	27.8%	4.02

显著性 P = 0.000

不同身份群体的学历水平有着显著差异。教育程度与收入水平有着直接的相关关系，而一个人的受教育机会却与身份密不可分。这一点我们会在后面的第10部分中看到。

5.4.3　教育、年龄与收入

按一般规律，年龄与收入是倒U形关系。由于此次调查样本中青少年和老年样本数量较少，受访者的年龄也与收入有着正比例关系，请看表24，收入均值由高到低依次为老年、中年、青年、青少年。而前面我们已经看到新本地人的平均收入高于老本地人，可新本地人的平均年龄却比老本地人低了近十岁，见表25，这说明学历对收入的影响更大。

表24　　　　　　　　　　不同年龄组的家庭平均年收入

年龄分组	人数	家庭年收入均值
青少年（18岁及以下）	29	1.90
青年（19—35岁）	1099	2.20
中年（36—55岁）	420	2.62
老年（56岁及以上）	79	2.76

显著性 $P = 0.001$

表25　　　　　　　老本地人、新本地人、外地人的平均年龄

身份	人数	年龄均值	年龄中值
老本地人	462	40.16	40.00
新本地人	160	30.27	30.00
外地人	983	29.44	27.00

显著性 $P = 0.000$

综上所述，**因户口区域、户口性质、职业和单位性质不同而形成的不同身份，是影响收入水平的重大因素**。总的来说，是否拥有本市户口起着重大作用。下面我们还将看到，身份对城市居民生活的各个方面都有影响，也是影响人们对城市各方面评价的重要因素。

值得注意的是，**新本地人的收入均值高于老本地人，当然也高于外地人**。后面我们还将看到，新本地人在很多方面的评价却都低于其他群体，这与他们的学历较高，从而在各方面的期望都比较高有关。

六、居住

在前面表11、12、13人们对城市综合评价的满意方面，房价排在最后一位（选择人数为23），在不满意方面，房价排在第一位（选择人数为1216），在最企盼方面，解决住房问题则排在第三位（选择人数为794），紧随提高收入和稳定物价之后，百分比远高于其后的选项。这说明住房问题是人们最为关心的问题。

6.1　居住状况

所有受访者的全家居住面积均值是65.00平方米，家庭人均居住面积均值为27.20平方米租房者的平均每月房租为1430.98元。

6.1.1　不同收入水平群体的居住状况

见表26，收入越高，居住面积越大，合乎常理。

表 26 不同收入水平群体的居住面积 （单位：平方米）

收入分组	全家居住面积		家庭人均居住面积		显著性	
	人数	均值	人数	均值	全家	家庭人均
低收入（3 万元以下）	339	37.53	338	18.72		
中低收入（3—5 万元）	345	43.29	344	20.34		
中等收入（5—10 万元）	493	62.15	492	27.59	0.000	0.000
中高收入（10—20 万元）	260	78.64	260	29.52		
高收入（20 万元以上）	147	164.59	147	57.32		

6.1.2 不同身份群体的居住状况

从居住面积看，本地人大于外地人，非农户口大于农业户口，且差距巨大。新本地人虽然平均收入高于老本地人，但本地生活年限尚短，平均年龄也小于老本地人 10 岁，财富积累应该稍逊色，故在居住面积上小于老本地人，但即使如此，其均值仍然大大高于高端职业外地人。低端职业外地人照例是叨陪末座。而若按是否在本地购置房产划分，则已购房外地人的居住面积远远大于新本地人，与老本地人也相差不多，未购房外地人则远远落在最后。见表 27。

表 27 不同身份群体的居住面积 （单位：平方米）

身份		全家居住面积均值	家庭人均居住面积均值	显著性	
				全家	家庭人均
户口区域	本地人	99.70	32.67	0.000	0.000
	外地人	42.47	23.51		
户口性质	非农户口	75.97	31.02	0.000	0.000
	农业户口	42.83	19.37		
户口区域 + 本地生活年限	老本地人	109.94	33.51	0.000	0.000
	新本地人	69.80	30.33		
	外地人	42.47	23.51		
户口区域 + 本地生活年限 + 职业	老本地人	109.94	33.51	0.000	0.000
	新本地人	69.80	30.33		
	高端职业外地人	47.30	26.63		
	低端职业外地人	36.94	20.05		
户口区域 + 本地生活年限 + 购房	老本地人	109.94	33.51	0.000	0.000
	新本地人	69.80	30.33		
	已购房外地人	98.41	43.87		
	未购房外地人	33.79	20.32		

从居住方式看，本地人已拥有自己房产的占 63.4%，外地人只有 13.0%，本地人有 9.7% 住公房，外地人只有 0.7%；本地人有 15.6% 租房住，外地人有 65.5%。二者在居住自有房产和租房比例上大致是掉了个个儿。非农户口和农业户口的关系与此类似。新本地人的自有房产比例虽然远高于外地人，但仍然远低于老本地人，他们住自己的房和租房住的比例都是四成上下。见表 28。

表 28　　　　　　　　　　　不同身份群体的居住方式

身份	购买/继承	公房	租房	单位集体宿舍	单位工作房	自建房	建筑工棚
本地人	63.4%	9.7%	15.6%	4.0%	2.7%	4.5%	0.0%
外地人	13.0%	0.7%	65.5%	16.6%	2.7%	0.9%	0.5%
非农户口	45.0%	6.0%	37.1%	6.7%	2.7%	2.2%	0.2%
农业户口	7.6%	0.6%	64.2%	21.8%	2.8%	2.4%	0.6%
老本地人	70.0%	11.7%	7.8%	2.0%	2.6%	5.9%	—
新本地人	43.5%	3.9%	39.6%	9.7%	3.2%	—	—
高端职业外地人	16.6%	0.8%	63.5%	15.8%	2.0%	1.2%	0.2%
低端职业外地人	8.6%	0.7%	68.0%	17.7%	3.5%	0.7%	0.9%

从居住区域看，本地人和非农户口居住在居民小区的比例都远高于外地人和农业户口，而居住在城中村的情况则正好相反，本地人和非农户口只有 7.6% 和 12.1%，外地人和农业户口则高达 23.7% 和 28.3%。见表 29。

表 29　　　　　　　　　　　不同身份群体的居住区域

身份	胡同/老城区	一般小区	高档小区	城中村	工业园区
本地人	7.8%	77.0%	7.0%	7.6%	0.6%
外地人	10.2%	58.2%	4.2%	23.7%	3.7%
非农户口	7.3%	70.7%	7.7%	12.1%	2.2%
农业户口	13.0%	54.8%	0.4%	28.3%	3.5%

6.1.3　不同职业群体的居住状况

从不同职业的居住面积看，企业主和企业负责人高高在上，专业人员次之，行政事业单位人员和企业白领居中，个体户和无业人员、工人和商业服务业人员垫底。见表 30。

表 30	不同职业群体的居住面积			(单位：平方米)
职业	全家居住面积均值	家庭人均居住面积均值	显著性	
			全家	家庭人均
企业主和企业负责人	147.00	61.05		
专业人员	76.64	31.74		
行政事业单位人员	69.21	27.71		
企业白领	65.28	27.66	0.000	0.000
个体户和无业人员	60.10	21.50		
工人	55.51	22.44		
商业服务业人员	46.89	23.34		

从各自工作单位性质看，在机关事业单位工作的面积最大，其次是国有企业、集体企业和外资合资企业，私营企业和个体垫底。见表31。

表 31	根据工作单位性质区分的居住面积			(单位：平方米)
单位性质	全家居住面积均值	家庭人均居住面积均值	显著性	
			全家	家庭人均
机关事业单位	89.72	34.42		
国有企业	79.87	31.59		
集体企业	72.25	25.78		
外资合资企业	68.11	32.09	0.000	0.000
私营企业	54.08	26.06		
个体	43.57	18.84		

综上所述，**不同户口身份和职业类型，居住状况区别很大，无论是居住面积，还是居住方式和居住区域，本地人和相对高端职业的人都占有很大优势。**其表层原因，是与收入水平有关，但根据上一章节的分析，更深刻的原因，还是其与身份的联系。

6.2 对居住状况的满意度

表 32		受访者对目前居住状况的满意度			
很满意	比较满意	一般	不太满意	很不满意	均值
6.5%	29.4%	34.9%	19.4%	9.8%	3.04

注：很满意＝5，比较满意＝4，一般＝3，不太满意＝2，很不满意＝1。

均值接近于3，表明人们的居住满意度居中。

6.3 不同群体的居住满意度

6.3.1 收入与居住满意度

收入与居住满意度成正比，收入越高，对自己目前的居住状况越满意。低收入组和中低收入组的满意度均值都低于3。见表33。

表33　　　　　　　　　　不同收入水平群体的居住满意度

收入分组	人数	居住满意度均值
低收入	313	2.75
中低收入	322	2.85
中等收入	444	3.10
中高收入	233	3.17
高收入	139	3.65

显著性 P = 0.000

6.3.2 身份与居住满意度

本地人的满意度高于外地人，非农户口高于农业户口，两个后者的评价均值都低于3，这与他们各自拥有的居住资源数量相吻合，所以老本地人的满意度鹤立鸡群。而新本地人的满意度不仅低于老本地人，也低于老外地人，甚至低于新外地人，充分显示出他们期望高的特点。在与职业的组合分类中，新本地人与低端职业外地人的评价均值相差无几，都低于3。而评价均值最高的，要数已购房外地人。见表34。

表34　　　　　　　　　　不同身份群体的居住满意度

身份		人数	居住满意度均值	显著性
户口区域	本地人	577	3.15	0.001
	外地人	862	2.96	
户口性质	非农户口	964	3.11	0.000
	农业户口	484	2.89	
户口区域 + 本地生活年限	老本地人	432	3.23	0.000
	新本地人	142	2.91	
	老外地人	102	3.01	
	新外地人	755	2.95	
户口区域 + 本地生活年限 + 职业	老本地人	432	3.23	0.000
	新本地人	142	2.91	
	高端职业外地人	456	3.01	
	低端职业外地人	399	2.89	
户口区域 + 本地生活年限 + 购房	老本地人	432	3.23	0.000
	新本地人	142	2.91	
	已购房外地人	114	3.48	
	未购房外地人	747	2.88	

6.3.3 职业与居住满意度

专业人员、企业主和企业负责人、行政事业单位人员相差无几，高居榜首，企业白领、个体户和无业人员居中，而后者和商业服务业人员、工人的评价都低于中间值3。见表35。

表35　　　　　　　　　　　不同职业群体的居住满意度

职业	人数	居住满意度均值
专业人员	177	3.31
企业主和企业负责人	47	3.30
行政事业单位人员	109	3.29
企业白领	518	3.03
个体户和无业人员	182	2.98
商业服务业人员	305	2.88
工人	101	2.68

显著性 $P = 0.000$

从工作单位性质看，机关事业单位高高在上，外资合资企业和集体企业也都高于3，国有企业、私营企业、个体都低于3，见表36。

表36　　　　　　　　　根据工作单位性质区分的居住满意度

单位性质	人数	居住满意度均值
机关事业单位	146	3.41
外资合资企业	126	3.11
集体企业	91	3.10
国有企业	243	2.97
私营企业	479	2.96
个体	252	2.93

显著性 $P = 0.000$

综上，住房问题关系到人们在城市生活的最基本生活保障。**外地人、新本地人、农业户口、低收入、低社会地位群体的居住状况相对较差，居住满意度呈负面，和与之相反的群体形成鲜明对照。**

七、社会保障

社会保障在人们对城市综合评价的满意方面和不满意方面都排在第7位，前者选择人数为336，后者为246。在最企盼方面，解决社会保障问题排在第9位，选择人数为269。

7.1　社会保障状况

表 37 为所有受访者参加保险状况。参加保险不分所在地，在国内任何地方参加的都算，包括农村的新农保、新农合。

表 37　　　　　　　　受访者参加保险状况

保险类别	人数	百分比
养老保险	1031	63.8%
医疗保险	1163	71.9%
失业保险	553	34.2%
工伤保险	526	32.5%
生育保险	307	19.0%
公费医疗	157	9.7%
商业保险	250	15.5%
住房公积金	506	31.3%
无任何保险	269	16.6%

将上述保险按社保、商业保险等不同性质分类，见表 38。按各自拥有的保险计算，参加社保的有 79.1%，拥有商业保险的有 15.5%，只有公费医疗的占 1.8%，无任何保险的占 16.6%。特别说明一下，这里的有无社保是按最宽泛的算法，即：只要参加了表 37 中的任何一项社保，哪怕仅仅是有工伤保险，或生育保险，都算是有了社保。

表 38　　　　　按保险性质分类的受访者参加保险状况

按保险性质分类	人数	百分比
只有社保	1070	66.2%
既有社保又有商业保险	208	12.9%
只有商业保险	42	2.6%
只有公费医疗	29	1.8%
没有任何保险	268	16.6%
合计	1617	100.0%

注：只有公费医疗指仅有公费医疗而无其他保险的人，拥有公费医疗同时还有社保、商业保险的人都归入了相应的社保、商业保险类别。

7.1.1　不同身份群体参加保险状况

无任何保险的比例，本地人和外地人之间，非农户口和农业户口之间，差距巨大，农业户口中有近三成人无任何保险。而从户口所在地看，来自乡镇农村的人，有三成多无任何保险。见表 39。

表39				不同身份群体参加保险状况		
身份		只有社保	社保+商业保险	只有商业保险	只有公费医疗	无任何保险
户口身份	本地人	69.6%	20.1%	1.9%	2.7%	5.6%
	外地人	64.3%	8.4%	3.0%	1.1%	23.3%
户口性质	非农户口	68.3%	17.2%	2.1%	2.0%	10.2%
	农业户口	61.8%	4.3%	3.5%	1.3%	29.1%
户口所在地	本市	69.6%	20.1%	1.9%	2.7%	5.6%
	外地大城市	65.1%	14.8%	5.8%	0.5%	13.8%
	外地中小城市	65.4%	10.6%	2.7%	1.9%	19.3%
	外地乡镇农村	63.0%	3.5%	1.9%	0.7%	30.9%

从表40可看出，高端职业外地人和低端职业外地人之间也有不小差距，而已购房外地人中无任何保险的，比老本地人还少，新本地人中则是最少的。

表40   **不同身份和职业及有无购房群体参加保险状况**

身份	只有社保	社保+商业保险	只有商业保险	只有公费医疗	无任何保险
本地人	69.6%	20.1%	1.9%	2.7%	5.6%
高端职业外地人	66.9%	9.8%	2.9%	1.3%	19.1%
低端职业外地人	61.3%	6.9%	3.1%	0.9%	27.9%
老本地人	69.6%	19.3%	1.7%	3.5%	5.9%
新本地人	69.9%	21.8%	2.6%	0.6%	5.1%
已购房外地人	66.7%	21.4%	6.3%	—	5.6%
未购房外地人	63.9%	6.4%	2.5%	1.3%	25.9%

7.1.2 不同职业群体参加保险状况

不同职业的保险状况差异十分明显。行政事业单位人员参加社保的比例达到了88.3%。而个体户和无业人员（无业人员在本次调查的全部样本中只有27人）只有64.6%；前者只有7.8%无任何保险，后者中却高达26.8%。见表41。

表41   **不同职业群体参加保险状况**

职业	只有社保	社保+商业保险	只有商业保险	只有公费医疗	无任何保险
行政事业单位人员	78.1%	10.2%	0.8%	3.1%	7.8%
专业人员	71.2%	11.5%	3.8%	4.8%	8.7%

职业	只有社保	社保＋商业保险	只有商业保险	只有公费医疗	无任何保险
工人	78.3%	4.2%	—	2.5%	15.0%
企业白领	66.5%	15.7%	1.8%	0.9%	15.2%
企业主和企业负责人	36.0%	38.0%	8.0%	—	18.0%
商业服务业人员	66.7%	9.7%	1.5%	1.2%	20.9%
个体户和无业人员	51.5%	13.1%	7.1%	1.5%	26.8%

从各自的工作单位看，在国有企业工作的人参加社保的比例达到了 91.4%，无任何保险的只有 5.3%，而从事个体经营的人两个比例数字分别为 55.3% 和 37.4%，可谓泾渭分明。也就是说，从事个体性质工作的人有近四成无任何保险。见表42。

表42　　　　根据工作单位性质区分的参加保险状况

单位性质	只有社保	社保＋商业保险	只有商业保险	只有公费医疗	无任何保险
国有企业	75.6%	15.8%	1.9%	1.5%	5.3%
外资合资企业	70.6%	22.4%	1.4%	—	5.6%
机关事业单位	71.6%	14.2%	1.7%	6.8%	5.7%
集体企业	74.0%	13.0%	2.0%	1.0%	10.0%
私营企业	68.5%	11.0%	1.3%	0.7%	18.4%
个体	48.0%	7.3%	6.2%	1.1%	37.4%

7.2　对社会保障状况的评价

表43　　　　受访者对所居城市社会保障状况的评价

很好	比较好	一般	比较差	很差	均值
5.9%	31.4%	49.8%	10.1%	2.8%	3.27

注：很好 = 5，比较好 = 4，一般 = 3，比较差 = 2，很差 = 1。

评价均值大于3，为正面评价。

7.3　不同群体的社会保障评价

7.3.1　身份与社会保障评价

与各自的社会保障参加度相对应，各群体对社会保障状况的评价与其参加度是一致的。本地人、非农户口的评价明显高于外地人和农业户口，而从户口所在地看，来自本市、外地大城市、外地中小城市、外地乡镇农村的人的评价依次降低。社会保障参加度越高，评价越高，反之亦然。见

表44。

表44 不同身份群体对社会保障状况的评价

身份		人数	社会保障评价均值	显著性
户口区域	本地人	628	3.46	0.000
	外地人	982	3.17	
户口性质	非农户口	1081	3.35	0.000
	农业户口	541	3.13	
户口所在地	本市	628	3.46	0.000
	外地大城市	189	3.28	
	外地中小城市	369	3.20	
	外地乡镇农村	424	3.09	

7.3.2 身份、职业、房产与社会保障评价

表45表明，高端职业外地人的评价与低端职业外地人差不多，都明显低于本地人。说明在社会保障问题上，身份的影响可能比职业要大。而已购房外地人的评价均值与新本地人几乎一样高，也是一个很有意义的现象，后面我们还会看到这个群体对很多方面的评价，"有恒产者有恒心"，即使缺少一个本地户口，已购房外地人对所居城市的认同度也已不亚于本地人。

表45 不同身份和职业及有无购房群体对社会保障状况的评价

身份	人数	社会保障状况评价均值	显著性
本地人	627	3.45	0.000
高端职业外地人	521	3.18	
低端职业外地人	452	3.15	
老本地人	462	3.52	0.000
新本地人	160	3.27	
已购房外地人	127	3.26	
未购房外地人	854	3.15	

综上，社会保障与住房问题一样，是人们在城市生活的基本保障。社会保障也与住房问题一样，呈现出不同身份和职业群体的巨大差异，无论是在现状还是在评价上。**本地人、非农户口、较高端职业或工作单位的人参加社保的比例，都远高于相反的群体，而无任何保险的人数比例则正好倒过来。这说明在社会保障方面，不公平现象十分明显。**

八、就业和创业

前面在人们对城市综合评价最满意、最不满意、最企盼方面，对就业的评价和对解决就业问题的企盼，在 13 个选项中分别居第 8、9、10 位（选择人数分别为 194、241、246），在不满意方面的选择人数还是要多一些，说明就业问题在人们心目中是个问题，但尚不是最紧迫问题。

8.1 工作满意度

表 46　　　　受访者对在自己现在（或以前）工作的满意度

很满意	比较满意	一般	不太满意	很不满意	均值
9.3%	35.8%	40.4%	12.2%	2.2%	3.38

注：很满意 =5，比较满意 =4，一般 =3，不太满意 =2，很不满意 =1。

人们的工作满意度均值高于 3，介于一般和比较满意之间。

8.2 对工作不满意的方面

表 47　　　　　受访者对工作不满意的方面

对工作不满意的方面	频数	百分比
收入	857	57.70%
福利	402	27.10%
发展机会	337	22.70%
工作时间	324	21.80%
劳动强度	320	21.50%
社会地位	304	20.50%
工作稳定	177	11.90%
工作环境	164	11.00%
人际关系	141	9.50%
其他	20	1.30%

表 47 表明，最不满意的是收入，比位居第二、第三的福利和发展机会高出很多，说明收入水平是决定工作满意度的最主要因素。发展机会紧随收入和福利之后。

8.3 不同群体的工作满意度

8.3.1 收入与工作满意度

收入越高，对工作的满意度越高。见表48。

表48　　　　　　　　　　　不同收入水平群体的工作满意度

收入分组	人数	工作满意度均值
低收入	304	3.10
中低收入	311	3.31
中等收入	429	3.45
中高收入	219	3.48
高收入	129	3.78

显著性 P = 0.000

8.3.2 身份与工作满意度

看表49可知，本地人的满意度高于外地人，非农户口高于农业户口，而区分新老本地人之后，新本地人的满意度最低，比外地人还低，再次证明新本地人期望高的特点。

表49　　　　　　　　　　　不同身份群体的工作满意度

身份		人数	工作满意度均值	显著性
户口区域	本地人	545	3.44	0.033
	外地人	835	3.34	
户口性质	非农户口	919	3.44	0.001
	农业户口	470	3.26	
户口区域 + 本地生活年限	老本地人	405	3.50	0.004
	新本地人	137	3.26	
	外地人	835	3.34	

8.3.3 职业与工作满意度

按职业区分，满意度由高到低依次为：企业主和企业负责人、行政事业单位人员、专业人员、企业白领、工人、商业服务业人员、个体户，见表50；按单位性质区分，依次为：机关事业单位、国有企业、外资合资企业、集体企业、私营企业、个体户，见表51。

表50　　　　　　　　　　　不同职业群体的工作满意度

职业	人数	工作满意度均值
企业主和企业负责人	47	3.68
行政事业单位人员	107	3.57
专业人员	140	3.47

职业	人数	工作满意度均值
企业白领	516	3.37
工人	100	3.36
商业服务业人员	305	3.32
个体户和无业人员	166	3.28

显著性 P = 0.016

表 51　　　　　根据工作单位性质区分的工作满意度

单位性质	人数	工作满意度均值
机关事业单位	141	3.65
国有企业	243	3.51
外资合资企业	125	3.46
集体企业	91	3.43
私营企业	476	3.32
个体	249	3.24

显著性 P = 0.000

8.3.4　身份、职业与工作满意度

将户口区域与职业组合，由高到低：老本地人、高端职业外地人、低端职业外地人、新本地人。收入均值最高的新本地人，满意度还不如人们俗称的打工仔和打工妹。见表52。

表 52　　　　　不同身份、职业群体的工作满意度

身份 + 职业	人数	工作满意度均值
老本地人	405	3.50
新本地人	137	3.26
高端职业外地人	438	3.38
低端职业外地人	391	3.29

显著性 P = 0.004

8.4　找工作的途径

从表53可知，本地人中有25.5%是由政府安排工作的，而外地人中

只有2.0%；自己上门找工作的，外地人有28.4%，本地人只有17.5%；网络求职的，外地人有17.1%，本地人只有11.1%；而自己做生意的，外地人有16.7%，本地人只有8.9%。**在身份上不具优势的外地人，就业的主动精神显然要强于本地人。**

表53　　　　　　　　　　不同身份群体的找工作途径

身份	政府安排	政府职介	招聘会	商业职介	招聘广告	亲友介绍	自己上门	网络求职	自己做生意
本地人	25.5%	2.0%	12.5%	1.4%	5.5%	23.2%	17.5%	11.1%	8.9%
外地人	2.0%	1.1%	14.9%	4.0%	8.2%	27.1%	28.4%	17.1%	16.7%

8.5　就业、创业机会

表54　　　　　　　受访者对在所居城市找工作和创业难度的评价

评价的内容	很难	比较难	一般	比较容易	很容易	均值
您觉得在本市找工作难吗	12.7%	29.2%	37.4%	16.2%	4.6%	3.29
您觉得在本市创业难吗	30.6%	40.6%	22.6%	5.2%	0.9%	3.95

注：很难=5，比较难=4，一般=3，比较容易=2，很容易=1。

均值都明显大于3，都是负面评价，而创业难度的评价均值接近于4。就业难度的评价介于一般和比较难之间，创业难度的评价接近于比较难。

8.6　不同群体的就业机会评价

8.6.1　收入与就业机会评价

表55说明，收入越高，越觉得就业难，也就是高收入者反而比低收入者更觉得找工作难。

表55　　　　　　　　不同收入水平群体对就业难度的评价

收入分组	人数	找工作难度均值
低收入	356	3.51
中低收入	354	3.32
中等收入	505	3.26
中高收入	263	3.14
高收入	148	3.11

显著性 P = 0.000

8.6.2　身份与就业机会评价

从表56可知，就业机会多于外地人的本地人，却更加觉得就业难度大。而难度评价最高的，还是收入均值最高的新本地人。

表 56　　　　　　不同身份群体对就业难度的评价

身份	人数	找工作难度均值
老本地人	461	3.39
新本地人	160	3.42
外地人	983	3.23

显著性 $P = 0.005$

8.6.3　职业与就业机会评价

从表 57 可看出，在公认较好单位工作的人，如机关事业单位、国企，觉得难度挺大，而在公认较差单位工作的人，如私企、集体企业，反而觉得难度没那么大。

表 57　　　　　　根据不同单位性质区分的对就业难度的评价

单位性质	人数	找工作难度均值
机关事业单位	177	3.47
国有企业	266	3.33
个体户	277	3.30
私营企业	540	3.25
集体企业	100	3.24
外资合资企业	143	3.05

显著性 $P = 0.012$

上述数据，说明不同人群对就业的要求是不一样的，**拥有较高收入、较好身份和工作单位的人，对就业的标准就会高一些，反之就会低一些。**标准的不同，也会导致评价的不同，这再次说明个人期望与个人评价成反比，期望值越高，评价越低。此外，公认为较好的就业岗位，必然是"僧多粥少"，竞争者众，这也是原因之一。

综上所述，就业问题尚不是人们心目中最迫切的问题，**但要注意到外地人就业渠道少于本地人这一事实，同时注意区分不同群体对工作的不同要求，重视对城市发展非常重要的高收入高学历群体的就业要求。**

九、个人发展机会

在前面人们对所居城市综合评价的 13 个选项中，个人发展机会在最满意方面排名第 4（选择人数为 549），在最不满意方面排名第 11（选择人数为160），说明人们对大城市的个人发展机会还是比较满意的，但在最企盼方面却排名第6（选择人数为301），相当靠前，显示出人们对更多发展机会的渴望。

9.1 对个人发展机会的评价

表58 　　　　　受访者对所居城市个人发展机会多少的评价

城市	很多	比较多	一般	比较少	很少	均值
合计	14.6%	42.9%	29.7%	9.5%	3.4%	3.56

注：很多 = 5，比较多 = 4，一般 = 3，比较少 = 2，很少 = 1。

对发展机会的评价颇令人欣慰，介于一般和比较多之间。

9.2 不同群体的个人发展机会评价

9.2.1 收入与个人发展机会评价

收入越高，对个人发展机会的评价越高，成正比，区别明显。见表59。

表59 　　　　　不同收入水平群体对个人发展机会的评价

收入分组	人数	个人发展机会评价均值
低收入	356	3.20
中低收入	354	3.45
中等收入	506	3.71
中高收入	264	3.74
高收入	148	3.83

显著性 P = 0.000

9.2.2 身份与个人发展机会评价

从户口区域看，本地人和外地人的评价无具显著意义的差别。结合职业，高端职业外地人对本市发展机会的评价最高，低端职业外地人评价最低，本地人居中，但差距不是很大。从户口性质看，非农户口高于农业户口，差距明显。从户口所在地看，依次为：外地大城市、外地中小城市、本市、外地乡镇农村。见表60。说明户口区域差别对个人发展机会评价差异的影响力不大，而户口性质和户口所在地有影响力，拥有非农户口和来自外地城市的人评价较高，农业户口和来自外地乡镇农村的人评价较低，本地人居中。**这体现了不同身份群体在寻求个人发展方面，自身条件、适应能力和进取性的差别。**拥有得天独厚条件的本地人评价居中，是个很耐人寻味的现象。来自外地的低端职业群体和来自外地乡镇农村的人评价相对较低，有可能是受自身条件所限，而来自外地的高端职业群体和来自外地城市的人评价相对较高，除自身条件和适应能力较好外，去发达大城市闯天下，努力干出一番事业的进取精神可能也是一个因素。

表60 不同身份群体对个人发展机会的评价

身份		人数	均值	显著性
户口区域+职业	本地人	627	3.56	0.000
	高端职业外地人	521	3.64	
	低端职业外地人	454	3.47	
户口性质	非农户口	1081	3.64	0.033
	农业户口	543	3.39	
户口所在地	本市	628	3.56	0.000
	外地大城市	189	3.83	
	外地中小城市	369	3.64	
	外地乡镇农村	426	3.36	

9.2.3 职业与个人发展机会评价

表61表明，专业人员的评价高高在上，其次是个体户和无业人员、企业主和企业负责人、企业白领，彼此的评价很接近，而行政事业单位人员、商业服务业人员、工人也很接近，叨陪末座。没有单位荫庇，全凭自己个人奋斗的个体户评价较高，也是一个耐人寻味的现象。

表61 不同职业群体对个人发展机会的评价

职业	人数	个人发展机会评价均值
专业人员	210	3.77
个体户和无业人员	198	3.64
企业主和企业负责人	51	3.63
企业白领	565	3.59
行政事业单位人员	128	3.44
商业服务业人员	342	3.43
工人	120	3.42

显著性 $P = 0.001$

9.2.4 教育与个人发展机会评价

学历越高，评价越高，二者成正比，差距很明显。见表62。显然，自身条件是获得和发现更多个人发展机会的重要因素。

表62　　　　　　　　　　不同学历群体对个人发展机会的评价

学历	人数	个人发展机会评价均值
初等教育	258	3.27
中等教育	491	3.47
高等教育	872	3.69

显著性 P = 0.000

综上，**不同群体在把握、发现个人发展机会方面有差异，这首先是来自于学历、见识、适应能力等自身条件，而期望值、进取性也是重要因素。拥有得天独厚条件的本地人评价居中，没有单位荫庇的个体户评价较高，颇耐人寻味。**而从整体上说，在城市能有更多的发展机会，则是所有受访者的共同愿望。上一章节中，工作不满意方面的排序，发展机会排名靠前，也印证了这一点。

十、教育

教育在人们对城市综合评价的 13 个最满意和最不满意方面中，均位居第9，在满意方面的选择人数（266）略多于不满意方面的（226）。说明人们对所居城市的教育评价，大致持中。

10.1　家庭人口在所居城市上学状况

教育对人们的收入和社会地位影响很大，子女教育也成为时下很多家庭的重中之重，我们特意对此进行了调查，1617 个受访者中，家中有人在本市上学的有534 人，占 33.0%。534 人中，本地人占 60.5%，外地人占 39.5%。基本情况见表63。

表63　　　　　　　有人在本市上学的家庭中，学生上学的基本情况

	内容	人数	百分比
学校性质	公办学校	395	74.8%
	民办学校	114	21.6%
	贵族/国际学校	4	0.8%
	打工子弟学校	15	2.8%
上什么学	幼儿园	115	21.7%
	小学	120	22.6%
	初中	67	12.6%
	高中	44	8.3%
	中专/技校	17	3.2%
	大专	38	7.2%
	大学本科	108	20.4%
	研究生	21	4.0%

大多数是在公办学校上学。从表64可看出，小学到高中，以及大本和研究生，绝大多数是在公办学校，上民办学校比较多的是中专中技和大专，最多的是幼儿园。上打工子弟学校的寥寥无几，也多是在幼儿园阶段。表65表明，在上公办学校的人中，31.3%是外地人（列百分比），而从表66可得知，即使是在高中，也有11.6%是外地人（列百分比）。这说明从小学到高中，公办学校已在一定程度上打破了户口的藩篱。但从表65的行百分比可知，本地人中上公办学校的有85.2%，外地人中只有59.4%，从列百分比可知，公办学校学生中，本地人的比例是外地人的2倍，而在民办学校中，正好相反。这也许说明，外地人进本市公办学校仍然要比本地人困难一些。

表64 学习阶段与学校性质的关系

上什么学	学校性质			
	公办学校	民办学校	贵族/国际学校	打工子弟学校
幼儿园	39.3%	50.9%	1.8%	8.0%
小学	80.0%	17.5%	—	2.5%
初中	87.9%	10.6%	—	1.5%
高中	86.0%	11.6%	2.3%	—
中专/技校	62.5%	37.5%	—	—
大专	75.0%	25.0%	—	—
大学本科	91.6%	7.5%	0.9%	—
研究生	95.2%	4.8%	—	—
合计	74.9%	21.9%	0.8%	2.5%

表65 本地人、外地人的学校性质分布

户口区域		学校性质			
		公办学校	民办学校	贵族/国际学校	打工子弟学校
本地人	行百分比	85.2%	12.6%	0.9%	1.3%
	列百分比	68.7%	35.1%	75.0%	30.8%
外地人	行百分比	59.4%	35.7%	0.5%	4.3%
	列百分比	31.3%	64.9%	25.0%	69.2%

表66 本地人、外地人的学习阶段分布

户口区域		上什么学							
		幼儿园	小学	初中	高中	中专/技校	大专	大本	研究生
本地人	行百分比	19.2%	20.5%	12.9%	12.0%	1.9%	6.9%	22.7%	3.8%
	列百分比	53.0%	54.2%	62.1%	88.4%	37.5%	59.5%	67.3%	57.1%
外地人	行百分比	26.0%	26.4%	12.0%	2.4%	4.8%	7.2%	16.8%	4.3%
	列百分比	47.0%	45.8%	37.9%	11.6%	62.5%	40.5%	32.7%	42.9%

10.2 学费和赞助费

在我们的调查中，534 人中有 352 人交了学费，更有 50 人交了大额赞助费。如果上的是非公办学校，发生学费和赞助费是正常的。如果上的是小学和初中阶段的公办学校，就不应该发生学费，而上任何阶段的公办学校，都不应该发生赞助费，因为在 9 年义务教育阶段，是不用交学费的，入学赞助费更是国家明文规定严禁公办学校收取的。

从表 67 可得知，学习阶段在幼儿园以及高中以上的，交学费的人比例很高，但在免除学费的小学和初中，仍有 35.8% 和 31.8% 的人交了学费。这其中有多少是在公办学校呢？看表 68，上小学的 120 人中，有 96 人在公办学校，而这 96 人中有 22 人交了学费，占 22.9%，其中，本地人有 9 人，占所有上公办小学本地人中的 15.3%，外地人有 11 人，占所有上公办小学外地人中的 35.1%。上初中的 67 人中，有 58 人在公办学校，其中 14 人交了学费，占 24.1%，这里面有 8 人为本地人，占所有上公办初中本地人中的 21.1%，有 4 人为外地人，占所有上公办初中外地人中的 30.0%。这说明，**义务教育阶段违规收学费的现象依然存在，而且发生在外地学生中的比例要大大超过本地学生。**

表 67　　　　　　　学习阶段与是否交学费、赞助费的关系

学习阶段		是否交学费		是否交赞助费	
		不交	交	不交	交
幼儿园	行百分比	6.1%	93.9%	80.0%	20.0%
	列百分比	4.0%	30.8%	19.3%	46.0%
小学	行百分比	64.2%	35.8%	87.5%	12.5%
	列百分比	44.0%	12.3%	22.1%	30.0%
初中	行百分比	68.2%	31.8%	92.4%	7.6%
	列百分比	25.7%	6.0%	12.8%	10.0%
高中	行百分比	34.9%	65.1%	90.7%	9.3%
	列百分比	8.6%	8.0%	8.2%	8.0%
中专/技校	行百分比	—	100.0%	93.8%	6.3%
	列百分比	—	4.6%	3.2%	2.0%
大专	行百分比	18.9%	81.1%	97.3%	2.7%
	列百分比	4.0%	8.5%	7.6%	2.0%
大学本科	行百分比	15.7%	84.3%	99.1%	0.9%
	列百分比	9.7%	25.9%	22.5%	2.0%
研究生	行百分比	33.3%	66.7%	100.0%	—
	列百分比	4.0%	4.0%	4.4%	—
合计		33.3%	66.7%	90.5%	9.5%

表 68　　　　　　　公办小学和初中学生缴纳学费情况

公办学校	身份		不交学费	交学费	合计
小学	本地人	人数	50	9	59
		百分比	84.7%	15.3%	100.0%
	外地人	人数	24	13	37
		百分比	64.9%	35.1%	100.0%
	合计	人数	74	22	96
		百分比	77.1%	22.9%	100.0%
初中	本地人	人数	30	8	38
		百分比	78.9%	21.1%	100.0%
	外地人	人数	14	6	20
		百分比	70.0%	30.0%	100.0%
	合计	人数	44	14	58
		百分比	75.9%	24.1%	100.0%

　　赞助费的情况则更为严重，表 67 表明，从幼儿园到大本，均有赞助费支出，唯有研究生逃脱了这一命运。缴纳比例最高的是幼儿园，其余依次是小学、高中、初中、中专/技校、大专、大本。而从表 69 可看出，赞助费的大头是公办学校，在所有交了赞助费的人中，83.7%的人是交给了公办学校（列百分比），而在公办学校上学的人中，有 10.4%交了赞助费（行百分比）。这说明**国家三令五申禁止公办学校收取的入学赞助费，依然是照收不误的。**

表 69　　　　　　学校性质与是否交学费、赞助费的关系

学校性质		是否交学费		是否交赞助费	
		不交	交	不交	交
公办学校	行百分比	42.9%	57.1%	89.6%	10.4%
	列百分比	94.9%	64.8%	74.2%	83.7%
民办学校	行百分比	5.3%	94.7%	93.9%	6.1%
	列百分比	3.4%	31.1%	22.5%	14.3%
贵族/国际学校	行百分比	25.0%	75.0%	75.0%	25.0%
	列百分比	0.6%	0.9%	0.6%	2.0%
打工子弟学校	行百分比	15.4%	84.6%	100.0%	0.0%
	列百分比	1.1%	3.2%	2.7%	0.0%
合计		33.9%	66.1%	90.7%	9.3%

赞助费和每年学费的平均缴纳数量见表 72。表中数据不限于公办学校，包括了可以收取学费和赞助费的其他类型学校。

表 70　　　交纳了本市学费、入学赞助费的家庭平均交纳的
每年学费和入学赞助费（元）

	北京	深圳	合计	显著性
每年学费均值	7612.35	9715.32	8442.78	0.000
入学赞助费均值	17861.11	4025.00	15647.33	0.020

10.3　对教学质量和教育政策的评价

表 71　　　家中有孩子在本市上学的人对所居城市教学质量的评价

很好	比较好	一般	比较差	很差	均值
11.9%	38.1%	42.5%	5.8%	1.7%	3.54

注：很好=5，比较好=4，一般=3，比较差=2，很差=1。

表 72　　　　受访者对所居城市教育政策的满意度

很满意	比较满意	一般	不太满意	很不满意	均值
5.9%	26.6%	40.0%	20.5%	7.0%	3.01

注：很满意=5，比较满意=4，一般=3，不太满意=2，很不满意=1。

对教学质量的评价均值高于 3.5，为正面评价，位居一般和比较好之间。对教育政策的满意度在中间值上下。

10.4　中小学校的教育机会与公平

能否让自己的孩子上理想的学校，是子女培养教育的核心环节。我们特意设计了这样的问题：您认为您有能力让孩子上理想的中小学校吗？受访者对此的回答见表 73。

表 73　　　受访者对送子女进理想中小学校能力的自我认定

完全有	有一些	一般	不太有	完全没有	均值
14.8%	25.2%	22.8%	24.1%	13.1%	3.05

注：完全有=5，有一些=4，一般=3，不太有=2，完全没有=1。

均值为 3.05，处于中间水平。在不同的社会群体中，这种信心有无差异？哪些群体更有这方面的信心？

10.4.1　收入与教育机会

表 74 表明，受访者的家庭年收入越高，这方面的信心越强，各组的

差距非常大，低收入组和中低收入组的均值都低于3，而高收入组却高达4.06。这说明，经济能力在这方面的作用很大。

表74　　不同收入水平群体对送子女进理想中小学校能力的自我认定

收入分组	人数	能力自我认定均值
低收入	356	2.45
中低收入	347	2.82
中等收入	501	3.11
中高收入	262	3.46
高收入	146	4.06

显著性 P = 0.000

10.4.2　身份与教育机会

经济能力是重要因素，而受访者的身份地位和社会关系则是另一重要因素。从表75可看出，这方面的自信，本地人高于外地人，非农户口高于农业户口，差距很大，两个后者的均值都小于3 。

在本地的生活年限是积累人脉的重要因素，将此与户口身份结合，老本地人高于新本地人，新本地人又高于老外地人，后者又高于新外地人，十分鲜明。有两点很有意思：**有了本地户口，即使在本地生活的年头没有老外地人长，新本地人也比老外地人有更多的自信；而收入均值高于老本地人的新本地人，这方面的信心却明显小于老本地人。**

城市生活经验也是建立社会关系能力的重要基础，自幼长大的生活环境同样对人们在这方面的自信起着潜移默化的作用，从户口所在地看，本市高于外地大城市，外地大城市高于外地中小城市，后者又高于外地乡镇农村，后二者的均值都小于3 。

表75　　不同身份群体对送子女进理想中小学校能力的自我认定

身份		人数	能力自我认定均值	显著性
户口区域	本地人	621	3.31	0.000
	外地人	975	2.88	
户口性质	非农户口	1070	3.18	0.000
	农业户口	538	2.78	
户口区域 + 本地生活年限	老本地人	456	3.38	0.000
	新本地人	159	3.08	
	老外地人	113	2.96	
	新外地人	854	2.87	

身份		人数	能力自我认定均值	显著性
户口所在地	本市	621	3.31	0.000
	外地大城市	186	3.29	
	外地中小城市	369	2.87	
	外地乡镇农村	420	2.70	

10.4.3 职业、身份与教育机会

职业不仅是收入来源，也是社会关系的来源，将身份与职业组合，表76表明，本地人高于高端职业外地人，后者又高于低端职业外地人。即使加进了职业因素，按职业高低进行了区分，高端职业外地人的自我认定均值也还是小于3。而从工作单位性质看，自信由高到低依次为：机关事业单位、国有企业、外资合资企业、集体企业、私营企业、个体户，后三者的均值都小于3。由此可见，户口身份对此问题有着强大的影响力。

表76 　　　　　不同职业和身份群体对送子女进
理想中小学校能力的自我认定

职业和身份		人数	能力自我认定均值	显著性
户口区域 + 职业	本地人	620	3.30	0.000
	高端职业外地人	516	2.97	
	低端职业外地人	450	2.78	
工作单位性质	机关事业单位	176	3.40	0.000
	国有企业	264	3.24	
	外资合资企业	141	3.18	
	集体企业	100	3.13	
	私营企业	535	2.89	
	个体	273	2.78	

根据上面的分析可看出，自己是否有能力让子女上理想的中小学校，主要是取决于经济能力、身份地位和社会关系，是否拥有本地户口至关重要。

综上所述，子女教育是每个城市居民都极为关心的问题，如何让孩子收到良好的教育，是很多家庭花费很大精力倾注很多心血的重要生活内容。而在现行体制下，就中小学教育而言，**无论是在入学、择校，还是在学费、赞助费方面，不同户口身份和收入水平家庭之间的不平等现象都很严重。**

十一、生活消费和服务

在受访者对城市综合评价最满意和最不满意的 13 个选项中，生活便利度分别居首位和末位（选择人数分别为 805 和 70），可见人们对大城市的生活便利度非常满意，认为不是什么重要问题。

11.1 对生活消费和服务的满意度评价

表77   受访者对所居城市生活消费和服务的满意度

很满意	比较满意	一般	不太满意	很不满意	均值
6.8%	34.6%	36.9%	16.3%	5.4%	3.21

注：很满意 = 5，比较满意 = 4，一般 = 3，不太满意 = 2，很不满意 = 1。

均值高于 3，是正面评价。

11.2 对生活消费和服务满意和不满意的方面

最满意的是购物，最不满意的是金融服务。见表 78 和表 79。

表78   受访者对所居城市生活消费和服务中满意的方面

对生活消费和服务中满意的方面	位次	人数	百分比
购物	1	723	46.10%
休闲娱乐	2	435	27.70%
通讯服务	3	421	26.80%
日常生活服务	4	352	22.40%
文化体育	5	238	15.20%
金融服务	6	229	14.60%

表79   受访者对所居城市生活消费和服务中不满意的方面

对生活消费和服务中不满意的方面	位次	人数	百分比
金融服务	1	454	29.80%
日常生活服务	2	400	26.30%
通讯服务	3	371	24.40%
购物	4	358	23.50%
文化体育	5	296	19.40%
休闲娱乐	6	247	16.20%

11.3 不同群体的生活消费和服务满意度

对此问题，按本地人和外地人区分，满意度无具显著意义的区别，说明在这个问题上本外地人感觉都差不多。非农户口的满意度高于农业户口，应该是与二者在收入、居住条件和环境上的差别有关。已购房外地人的满意度远远高于本地人和未购房外地人，也印证了这一点。而满意度很低的，又是期望值很高而自有房产比例只有43.5%的新本地人，与未购房外地人接近。见表80。

表80　　　　　　　　　不同身份群体的生活消费和服务满意度

身份	人数	生活消费和服务满意度均值	显著性
非农户口	1080	3.28	0.000
农业户口	544	3.07	
老本地人	432	3.23	0.003
新本地人	142	2.91	
已购房外地人	114	3.48	
未购房外地人	747	2.88	

过去，城市最大的吸引力曾经就是商品和服务的丰富以及生活便利度。随着社会经济的巨大发展和城市建设的同质化，**目前，在城市生活中，生活消费和服务是人们评价相对稳定和比较满意的方面，这也预示着，它在城市吸引力的构成中，权重将日益下降。**

十二、医疗

医疗在受访者对城市综合评价的满意方面，居第8位（选择人数为287），在不满意方面，居第6位（选择人数为328），后者选择人数多于前者。在人们的企盼中，解决医疗问题居第8位（选择人数为270）。在13个选项的满意度中，大致处于中间靠后的位置。

12.1　城市医疗资源状况：看病便利度

根据本次调查，受访者患病就诊，从出发到看上病，所花时间的平均值是2.9小时。

表81　　　　　　　　　受访者对所居城市看病方便程度的评价

很方便	比较方便	一般	不太方便	很不方便	均值
10.7%	28.2%	25.4%	22.4%	13.2%	3.01

注：很方便=5，比较方便=4，一般=3，不太方便=2，很不方便=1。

对看病便利度的评价均值居中，属中性评价。

12.2 对医疗水平和医疗政策的评价

表82 受访者对所居城市医疗水平的评价

很好	比较好	一般	比较差	很差	均值
15.3%	42.5%	33.7%	5.5%	3.1%	3.61

注：很好=5，比较好=4，一般=3，比较差=2，很差=1。

评价均值高于3.5，在一般和比较好之间，更接近于比较好。

表83 受访者对所居城市医疗政策的满意度

很满意	比较满意	一般	不太满意	很不满意	均值
5.7%	28.5%	41.8%	18.5%	5.5%	3.10

注：很满意=5，比较满意=4，一般=3，不太满意=2，很不满意=1。

均值大于3，属正面评价。

12.3 不同群体的医疗政策满意度

12.3.1 身份与医疗政策满意度

新本地人的满意度最低，不仅与老本地人有很大差距，而且比未购房外地人还要低。已购房外地人的满意度居于新老本地人之间。见表84。

表84 不同身份群体的医疗政策满意度

身份	人数	医疗政策满意度均值
老本地人	459	3.27
新本地人	160	2.98
已购房外地人	127	3.10
未购房外地人	846	3.04

显著性 P=0.000

12.3.2 职业与医疗政策满意度

机关事业单位和国有企业居首，个体和私营企业垫底，后者评价均值低于3。见表85。

表85 根据工作单位性质区分的医疗政策满意度

单位性质	人数	医疗政策满意度均值
机关事业单位	177	3.26
国有企业	265	3.24
集体企业	97	3.18
外资合资企业	142	3.11
个体	274	3.09
私营企业	537	2.99

显著性 P=0.003

综上，对于大城市来说，医疗资源不是问题，问题是医疗服务的公平性。公平性问题将集中在第 16 部分讨论。

十三、交通

交通在受访者对城市综合评价的满意方面，居第 2 位，在不满意方面居第 3 位，但在满意方面的选择人数（643）还是多于不满意方面的（461）。

13.1　城市交通状况

根据我们的调查，受访者每天用在上班路上的平均单程时间，是39.03 分钟。常用交通工具分布见表 86。

表 86　　　　　　　　　受访者最常用的交通工具

私家车/公车	的士	公交/地铁	摩托/电动车	自行车
18.9%	3.1%	68.6%	3.2%	6.2%

13.2　对城市交通状况的评价

表 87　　　　　　受访者对所居城市公共交通便捷程度的评价

很便捷	比较便捷	一般	不太便捷	很不便捷	均值
21.6%	48.5%	19.6%	7.8%	2.6%	3.79

注：很便捷 =5，比较便捷 =4，一般 =3，不太便捷 =2，很不便捷 =1。

评价均值大于 3.5，是较强的正面评价，倾向于比较便捷。

表 88　　　　　　受访者对所居城市交通状况的满意度

很满意	比较满意	一般	不太满意	很不满意	均值
7.6%	24.7%	27.1%	26.7%	14.0%	2.85

注：很满意 =5，比较满意 =4，一般 =3，不太满意 =2，很不满意 =1。

交通状况满意度均值低于 3，是负面评价。

任何大城市，都面临交通拥堵问题，这是城市管理者面临的普遍性问题。

十四、环境

环境在人们对城市综合评价的满意方面，位居第 3（选择人数为590），在不满意方面位居第 10（选择人数为 168），前者远多于后者。在企盼方面，解决环境问题位居第 12 即倒数第二（选择人数为 178）。说明在受访者心目中，环境问题对于自己不是紧要问题。

表89 受访者对所居城市环境状况的满意度

评价的内容	很满意	比较满意	一般	不太满意	很不满意	均值
城市绿化	15.2%	43.5%	32.6%	6.5%	2.2%	3.63
城市空气质量	4.6%	22.0%	42.7%	23.3%	7.5%	2.93
城市环境卫生	5.5%	32.7%	40.0%	16.3%	5.5%	3.16

注：很满意=5，比较满意=4，一般=3，不太满意=2，很不满意=1。

看表89，对空气质量的满意度均值低于3，为负面评价。对城市绿化和环境卫生状况都是正面评价，而且对绿化的评价均值相当高，接近于4。

作为知名大都市，北京和深圳近年来下大力气整治环境，致力于城市绿化，受访者对此是比较满意的。但城市空气质量仍是个严重问题，在受访者对环境问题很不关心的情况下（在排列最企盼问题时几乎把它放到了最后），其评价仍然是负面的。

十五、社会治安

治安在受访者对城市综合评价的满意方面和不满意方面都排在第5位，前者的选择人数是398，后者是334，差不太多，还是满意方面的选择者更多一点。在人们的企盼方面，解决社会安全问题排在第11位，选择人数为225。说明社会治安问题在受访者心目中并不突出。

15.1 城市治安状况

近三年内，三成人自己或亲友被骗过，近四成人自己或亲友被偷被抢过。见表90。

表90 受访者在所居城市遭遇诈骗、偷盗或抢劫抢夺的状况

内容	有	没有
自己或亲友近三年在本市有无被诈骗过	30.3%	69.7%
自己或亲友近三年在本市有无被偷被抢过	39.0%	61.0%

而居住区域和环境要差一些的外地人，被偷被抢的比例要明显高于本地人。见表91。

表91 不同身份群体自己或亲友近三年内
在所居城市遭遇偷盗或抢劫抢夺的状况

身份	有	没有
本地人	36.6%	63.4%
外地人	40.4%	59.6%

15.2 对城市治安状况的评价

表92   受访者对所居城市社会治安状况的满意度

很满意	比较满意	一般	不太满意	很不满意	均值
9.4%	39.3%	34.8%	11.8%	4.8%	3.37

注：很满意=5，比较满意=4，一般=3，不太满意=2，很不满意=1。

均值大于3，为正面评价。

就此次选取的调查城市而言，社会治安问题在受访者关心的问题中并不突出，相对来说也比较满意。

十六、社会公平

社会公平问题是人们关心较多的问题。在受访者对城市综合评价的满意方面中，公平度排在倒数第二位，选择它的只有区区52人，在不满意方面中，排第4位，选择它的人多达401人。在人们的企盼方面中，排在第5位，选择者有395人。

16.1 对社会公平状况的总体评价

表93   受访者对所居城市总体社会公平度的评价

很公平	比较公平	一般	不太公平	很不公平	均值
2.5%	23.8%	39.4%	25.4%	8.9%	2.85

注：很公平=5，比较公平=4，一般=3，不太公平=2，很不公平=1。

均值小于3，为负面评价。说明多数人认为不够公平。

16.2 对社会公平状况的具体评价

表94   受访者对所居城市具体社会公平度的评价

评价的内容	很满意	比较满意	一般	不太满意	很不满意	均值
对收入分配公平的满意度	1.5%	17.2%	33.8%	32.6%	14.8%	2.58
对工作机会公平的满意度	3.5%	22.4%	43.0%	22.7%	8.5%	2.90
对住房制度公平的满意度	1.6%	10.3%	35.3%	33.4%	19.4%	2.41
对教育机会公平的满意度	3.3%	19.3%	39.5%	25.4%	12.6%	2.75
对医疗制度公平的满意度	3.0%	20.9%	45.3%	21.3%	9.5%	2.87

注：很满意=5，比较满意=4，一般=3，不太满意=2，很不满意=1。

对住房制度公平的满意度最低，其次是对收入分配公平的满意度；对工作机会公平的满意度最高，其次是对医疗制度公平的满意度；对教育机会公平的满意度居中。但无一例外，这5个方面的满意度均值都低于3，都是负面评价，其中对住房制度公平的满意度均值低于2.5。

16.3　不同群体的社会公平满意度

在对社会公平的总体评价上，无论是按户口区域、户口性质、户口所在地等身份分类，还是按年龄、本地生活年限、教育程度、工作单位性质区分，都没有具显著意义的差别，只有职业、收入有显著性。这说明人们对社会公平的总体看法趋于一致，多数人认为有欠公平。

具体到对社会某方面制度公平性的评价，情况也有类似之处。某些方面的不同群体评价有显著差异，这里仅举对医疗制度的评价为例。请看表95。本地人的评价高于外地人，而如果将新本地人区分出来，他们的评价比外地人还低。

表95　　　　　　　　　　不同身份群体对医疗制度公平状况的满意度

身份	人数	医疗制度公状况满意度均值	显著性
本地人	627	2.99	0.000
外地人	983	2.79	
老本地人	461	3.10	0.000
新本地人	160	2.67	
外地人	983	2.79	

从职业看，专业人员、企业主和企业负责人评价最高，企业白领和工人最低，其余3个职业相差无几，居中。除了专业人员、企业主和企业负责人外，其余5个职业评价都是负面的。见表96。

表96　　　　　　　　　　不同职业群体对医疗制度公平状况的满意度

职业	人数	医疗制度公平状况满意度均值
专业人员	210	3.06
企业主和企业负责人	51	3.04
商业服务业人员	343	2.92
行政事业单位人员	128	2.91
个体户和无业人员	197	2.90
工人	120	2.80
企业白领	563	2.74

显著性 P = 0.001

从单位性质看，在机关事业单位工作的人评价最高，其次是在国有企业工作的人，评价均值很接近。在私营企业工作的人垫底。除排名第一的外，其余的评价都是负面的。还是在公认较好单位工作的人的评价较高。见表97。

表97   根据工作单位性质区分的对医疗制度公平状况的满意度

单位性质	人数	医疗制度公平状况满意度
机关事业单位	177	3.02
国有企业	266	2.98
个体	276	2.89
集体企业	100	2.88
外资合资企业	143	2.82
私营企业	540	2.76

显著性 $P = 0.005$

社会公平是人们最为关心的问题之一，也是城市管理中的核心问题之一。它不仅关系到社会和谐稳定，更关系到城市吸引力和持续性发展。**有关社会公平方面的评价，是本次调查中总体偏低的评价，不管怎么区分人群，多数群体的评价都是负面的。这一点值得关注。**

十七、社会信任和尊重

在受访者对城市综合评价的最企盼方面，得到理解和尊重排名最后，但选择的人数不算很少，有148人。

17.1 对社会信任和尊重的评价

表98   受访者对所居城市的社会信任度评价

评价的内容	很信任	比较信任	一般	不太信任	很不信任	均值
对政府的信任度	7.2%	27.5%	37.5%	17.8%	10.0%	3.04
对广播电视报刊的信任度	3.9%	22.6%	44.6%	22.2%	6.7%	2.95
对网络内容的信任度	1.4%	10.9%	45.6%	33.0%	9.1%	2.63
社会上人们之间的相互信任度	0.9%	13.6%	49.0%	29.2%	7.4%	2.71

注：很信任 =5，比较信任 =4，一般 =3，不太信任 =2，很不信任 =1。

表98表明，除了对所居城市政府的信任度外，其余信任度评价都是负面的。其中，对社会上人们之间的相互信任度的评价最低，这显示出了多年来社会诚信日益缺失的深刻影响。相应地，对网络内容的信任度也很低。

然而，对社会相互尊重的评价较高，为正面评价。见表99。

表 99   受访者对所居城市社会上人们之间相互尊重程度的评价

很尊重	比较尊重	一般	不太尊重	很不尊重	均值
3.2%	31.8%	50.4%	12.2%	2.5%	3.21

注：很尊重 = 5，比较尊重 = 4，一般 = 3，不太尊重 = 2，很不尊重 = 1。

17.2   不同群体的社会信任度评价

上述四个方面的信任度评价，多数在不同群体间无显著意义区别，只有在对政府的信任度评价上例外。

17.2.1   身份与政府信任度

农业户口对所居城市政府的信任度高于非农户口，低端职业外地人高于老本地人也高于高端职业外地人，新本地人的信任度最低，后两者都呈负面评价。见表 100。

表 100   不同身份群体对所居城市政府的信任度

身份	人数	政府信任度均值	显著性
非农户口	1076	2.99	0.007
农业户口	540	3.14	
老本地人	460	3.08	
新本地人	160	2.79	0.004
高端职业本地人	517	2.99	
低端职业本地人	452	3.12	

17.2.2   职业与政府信任度

行政事业单位人员的信任度最高，他们和随后的个体户和无业人员、商业服务业人员、专业人员的评价都高于 3，是正面评价。企业主和企业负责人最低，他们和工人、企业白领都是负面评价。见表 101。

表 101   不同职业群体对所居城市政府的信任度

职业	人数	政府信任度均值
行政事业单位人员	128	3.36
个体户和无业人员	197	3.28
商业服务业人员	341	3.09
专业人员	208	3.04
企业白领	562	2.91
工人	119	2.88
企业主和企业负责人	51	2.82

显著性 P = 0.000

17.2.3 教育程度与政府信任度

学历越高，对所居城市政府的信任度评价越低，十分鲜明。见表102。

表 102   不同学历群体对所居城市政府的信任度

教育程度	人数	政府信任度均值
初等教育	255	3.27
中等教育	491	3.05
高等教育	867	2.96

显著性 P = 0.000

综上，**教育程度、见识、阅历都对人们的政府信任度有影响。各职业中，企业主和企业负责人的政府信任度最低，是很有意思的。**

十八、城市管理和公共服务

在受访者对城市综合评价的满意方面，公共服务位居第6（选择人数为380），在不满意方面，位居第12（选择人数为116）。在人们的企盼方面，提高政府管理水平位居第4（选择人数为413）。可见，受访者对公共服务是比较满意的，而对提高政府管理水平企盼甚殷。

18.1 对城市管理和公共服务的评价

18.1.1 对行政机关办事效率和管理水平的评价

表 103   受访者对所居城市行政机关办事效率和管理水平的评价

评价的内容	很高	比较高	一般	比较低	很低	均值
对本市行政机关办事效率的评价	2.3%	16.2%	46.6%	24.1%	10.8%	2.75
对本市行政机关管理水平的评价	2.7%	17.4%	51.9%	18.6%	9.4%	2.85

注：很高 =5，比较高 =4，一般 =3，比较低 =2，很低 =1。

均值都小于3，都是负面评价。对办事效率的评价要更低一些。说明受访者中多数人对行政机关的管理水平和办事效率不满意，尤其是后者。

18.1.2 对行政机关服务态度的评价

表 104   受访者对所居城市行政机关服务态度的评价

很好	比较好	一般	比较差	很差	均值
3.1%	23.4%	44.4%	19.4%	9.7%	2.91

注：很好 =5，比较好 =4，一般 =3，比较差 =2，很差 =1。

也是负面评价，但接近于中间值。说明多数人认为所居城市行政机关服务态度一般，但不满意的比满意的多一些。

18.1.3 对政府机关人员和执法人员廉洁度的评价

表105 受访者对所居城市政府机关人员和执法人员廉洁度的评价

很廉洁	比较廉洁	一般	不太廉洁	很不廉洁	均值
2.2%	10.6%	39.1%	29.6%	18.5%	2.48

注：很廉洁＝5，比较廉洁＝4，一般＝3，不太廉洁＝2，很不廉洁＝1。

均值低于2.5，是较强的负面评价。值得一提的是，在以不同方式区分社会群体度量不同群体对廉洁度的评价差异时，多数区分方式都无具显著意义的差异，这说明，对廉洁度的负面评价是社会共识，不同群体的评价几乎无差异。

18.2 不同群体的城市管理和公共服务评价

18.2.1 身份与行政机关管理水平评价

外地人的评价高于本地人，农业户口高于非农户口，差距都很大。从户口所在地看，由高到低：外地乡镇农村、外地中小城市、外地大城市、本市，区别明显。见表106。

表106 不同户口身份群体对所居城市行政机关管理水平的评价

身份		人数	行政机关管理水平评价均值	显著性
户口区域	本地人	625	2.73	0.000
	外地人	981	2.92	
户口性质	非农户口	1080	3.28	0.000
	农业户口	544	3.07	
户口所在地	本市	625	2.73	0.000
	外地大城市	189	2.84	
	外地中小城市	367	2.90	
	外地乡镇农村	425	2.98	

加入本地生活年限、职业和是否已在本地购房等因素，低端职业外地人和未购房外地人的评价最高，已购房外地人和高端职业外地人的评价均值一样，居其次，再次是新本地人，而老本地人的评价最低。见表107。

表 107　　　　　按户口、本地生活年限、职业、房产区分的群体对

所居城市行政机关管理水平的评价

身份	人数	行政机关管理水平评价均值	显著性
老本地人	459	2.71	
新本地人	160	2.78	
高端职业外地人	518	2.90	0.000
低端职业外地人	454	2.94	
老本地人	459	2.71	
新本地人	160	2.78	
已购房外地人	127	2.90	0.000
未购房外地人	853	2.92	

18.2.2　教育程度与行政机关管理水平评价

与政府信任度类似，学历越高，评价越低。见表108。

表 108　　　　不同学历群体对所居城市行政机关管理水平的评价

教育程度	人数	行政机关管理水平评价均值
初等教育	258	3.02
中等教育	488	2.89
高等教育	869	2.78

显著性 P = 0.001

18.3　对城市基础设施状况的评价

表 109　　　　　　受访者对所居城市基础设施状况的评价

很好	比较好	一般	比较差	很差	均值
9.0%	43.8%	35.1%	8.0%	4.1%	3.46

注：很好＝5，比较好＝4，一般＝3，比较差＝2，很差＝1。

均值高出3很多，说明受访者对所居城市的基础设施建设比较满意。

综上所述，**受访者对城市的基础设施状况是比较满意的，这体现出大城市的优势**，而对所居城市行政机关的管理水平、办事效率、服务态度、廉洁度的评价都是负面评价，在不同群体的评价差异方面，外地人、农业户口、来自乡村、低收入、低学历群体的评价相对较高，再次显示出教育程度、见识、阅历对人们公共事务参与兴趣和程度的影响。

十九、城市生活压力

上面的分析涉及了城市生活的多个方面，而归结到一点，是城市居民面临的生活压力状况。无论是收入、住房、就业，还是社会保障、教育、医疗，最终的生活压力都实实在在地落在每一个受访者身上。

19.1 对城市生活压力的评价

表 110　　　　　　受访者对自己在所居城市生活压力的评价

很大	比较大	一般	比较小	很小	均值
29.4%	43.0%	21.6%	4.4%	1.7%	3.94

注：很大 = 5，比较大 = 4，一般 = 3，比较小 = 2，很小 = 1。

均值接近于4，受访者觉得生活压力相当大。

19.2 不同群体的城市生活压力评价

19.2.1 身份与生活压力评价

外地人的生活压力大于老本地人，而新本地人的生活压力自我感觉是最大的，均值超过了4，差距明显。已购房外地人的压力比未购房外地人小了很多，比老本地人还小，说明了住房问题在城市居民生活中的重要地位。见表111。

表 111　　　　　　不同身份群体的生活压力评价

身份	人数	生活压力评价均值	显著性
老本地人	461	3.86	
新本地人	160	4.09	0.016
外地人	981	3.95	
老本地人	461	3.86	
新本地人	160	4.09	
已购房外地人	127	3.72	0.000
未购房外地人	853	3.99	

19.2.2 职业与生活压力评价

从职业类型看，各职业间没有具显著性的差异。

从工作单位性质看，在私营企业工作的人和个体经营者觉得压力最大，评价均值都超过了4；在集体企业和行政事业单位工作的人压力评价最小，但也都在3.5以上；在国有企业和外资合资企业工作的人评价居中。见表112。

表 112　　　　　　　　　根据工作单位性质区分的生活压力评价

单位性质	人数	生活压力评价均值
私营企业	540	4.02
个体	276	4.00
国有企业	265	3.93
外资合资企业	143	3.90
机关事业单位	176	3.79
集体企业	100	3.68

显著性 P = 0.002

综上，对于自己在所居城市感受到的生活压力，受访者整体的评价是压力比较大。而住房问题构成生活压力的重要组成部分，**解决了住房问题，就有了基本的安全感，没解决住房问题，就缺乏基本的安全感。**已购房外地人自我感觉的生活压力比其他群体都低，比拥有本地户口的新老本地人还低，说明了这一点。

这就不难理解为何受访者把房价列在了最不满意方面的首位，把解决住房问题列在了最企盼方面的第3位；也就不难理解为何在户口身份和收入水平上都占有优势的新本地人在很多方面的不满反而比其他群体还要高。

二十、归属感与城市吸引力

城市是人们的生活共同体，城市与人，是共存共荣的关系。城市的居民有无归属感，城市对人有多大的吸引力，是城市发展的核心问题。

20.1　本地归属感

我们问了所有受访者一个问题，您觉得在北京/深圳有家的感觉吗？回答结果如表113所示。

表 113　　　　　　　　受访者对所居城市的归属感

城市	非常有	有一些	一般	不太有	完全没有	均值
北京	29.7%	29.6%	19.0%	13.9%	7.7%	3.60
深圳	7.4%	29.7%	28.7%	22.9%	11.3%	2.99
合计	18.6%	29.6%	23.9%	18.4%	9.5%	3.29

注：非常有＝5，有一些＝4，一般＝3，不太有＝2，完全没有＝1。

合计均值在3以上，说明多数人有一定的归属感。北京高于深圳是可以理解的，因为后者是一个由渔村飞速发展起来的新兴移民城市，市龄才31年，真正的土生土长本地人是极少的。

在外来人口占2/3左右的这两个城市，归属感有这样高的均值，已属不易。说明两个城市的政府都做出了相当的努力，尽量让城市成为所有人共同的家。

20.2 不同群体的本地归属感

在现行体制下，什么人更容易对所居城市产生认同，形成归属感？

20.2.1 身份与归属感

不同身份间的归属感差异十分明显。本地人高于外地人，非农户口高于农业户口，而在外地人中，来自大城市的高于来自中小城市的，后者又高于来自乡镇农村的。各群体间的均值差距都很大，外地人、农业户口的均值都低于3，而本地人接近于4。见表114。

表114 不同身份群体的本地归属感

身份		人数	本地归属感均值	显著性
户口区域	本地人	627	3.95	0.000
	外地人	983	2.87	
户口性质	非农户口	1079	3.50	0.000
	农业户口	543	2.87	
户口所在地	本市	627	3.95	0.000
	外地大城市	189	3.10	
	外地中小城市	368	2.89	
	外地乡镇农村	426	2.76	

20.2.2 本地生活年限与归属感

无疑，在所居城市的生活年限会对人们的本地归属感起作用，见表115。在该市生活的时间越长，归属感越强，生活18年以上的，归属感均值超过了4。而新本地人虽有所居城市的户口，但归属感均值也远低于老本地人，甚至比老外地人还低了不少。

表115 根据本地生活年限区分的本地归属感

本市生活年限和户口区域		人数	本地归属感均值	显著性
本市生活年限	2年及以下	302	2.64	0.000
	2—7年	503	2.89	
	8—17年	373	3.27	
	18年及以上	433	4.24	
户口区域 + 本市生活年限	老本地人	461	4.24	0.000
	新本地人	160	3.11	
	老外地人	114	3.34	
	新外地人	861	2.81	

20.2.3　身份、职业、房产与归属感

表 116 表明，高端职业外地人和低端职业外地人的归属感均值几乎一样，还略低一点点，远低于新老本地人，这说明**职业对归属感的影响很有限，不如户口身份的影响力。而是否在本地购房，却影响很大，**已购房外地人的归属感均值远高于新本地人，再次证明"有恒产者有恒心"。

表 116　　　　　　　　　不同身份群体的本地归属感

身份	人数	本地归属感均值	显著性
老本地人	461	4.24	
新本地人	160	3.11	
高端职业外地人	520	2.87	0.000
低端职业外地人	454	2.88	
老本地人	461	4.24	
新本地人	160	3.11	
已购房外地人	127	3.57	0.000
未购房外地人	855	2.77	

20.2.4　工作单位性质与归属感

职业影响力不明显，单位性质的影响力却很大。在机关事业单位、国有企业工作的人，归属感均值高高在上，其次是在集体企业、外资合资企业工作的人，位居中游，个体经营者和在私营企业就职的人垫底。这说明改革开放到今天，**计划体制下特有的单位所有制和身份制度的影响依然强大。见表 117。**

表 117　　　　　　　　根据单位性质限区分的本地归属感

单位性质	人数	本地归属感均值
机关事业单位	176	3.79
国有企业	266	3.69
集体企业	100	3.45
外资合资企业	143	3.34
个体	276	3.08
私营企业	541	3.00

显著性 P = 0.000

综上，**现行体制下的户口身份制度和行政事业单位及国企的单位所有制遗留特点，对人们的本地归属感有着强大影响力。**户口身份制度限制和

延缓了人们本地归属感的形成。政府在宏观调控（如房产限购）和城市管理（如汽车限购）时有意无意使用的按户口身份设置壁垒的手段，无疑将增强身份制度对归属感的影响力。

二十一、结语：人与城市

21.1　**人是城市的主体，城市因人而存在。**我们不是为了建设城市而建设城市，是为了让人活得更好而建设和发展城市。

21.2　**城市的核心竞争力是人。**只有让在这个城市生活、工作的人能够安居乐业各尽其能，只有不断提升人的素质，只有不断引进并留住高素质的人，这个城市才有生命力，才有持续发展力。这就需要这个城市有吸引力，并能让在这个城市生活的人有较强的归属感。

21.3　**城市吸引力首先来自于更多的就业、提高收入和个人发展机会。**调查数据表明，人们对城市生活消费和服务的满意度在各方面的评价中是最高的，而在最企盼的各选项中生活便利度排在倒数第一。人们最企盼的是提高收入，有更多的发展机会也排名靠前。这说明与改革开放之前相比，情况已经有了很大变化。人们不再是仅仅因为向往大都会的繁华而涌入城市，而是因为城市提供了更多的就业和个人发展机会。

曾几何时，城市最大的吸引力就是商品和服务的丰富以及生活便利度。随着社会经济的巨大发展和各地城市建设的同质化，生活消费和服务在城市吸引力的构成中，权重将日益下降。

因此，城市吸引力不能再仅仅停留在商品的丰富和一味的硬件建设上，而应该着力于增加就业和个人发展机会，着眼于社会生活的多样化。

21.4　**城市吸引力更来自于社会公平。**增加机会是一方面，机会均等是另一方面，这是一枚硬币的两面。如果一个城市存在较多的歧视性政策，不仅妨害人尽其才各尽所能，造成巨大的人力资源浪费，也必将妨害它的吸引力和人们对它的归属感，影响持续发展。

现行体制的户口身份制度，对社会公平和机会均等构成极大影响。从前面的分析可以看出，是否拥有本市户口，影响到城市居民生活的各个方面，而另一个户口壁垒——非农户口与农业户口，虽然影响力有所下降，但余威还在。户口制度对人们的居住、就业、社会保障、医疗、子女教育形成壁垒，造成严重的不公平。宏观调控下的住房限购和城市管理中的汽车限购，又增加了居住和出行的不平等，衣食住行，限购占了一半，都是以户口壁垒为调控手段。所以，户口坚冰不是在被打破，而是冻得更坚硬了。

调查表明，城市中的高学历者和高收入者，有不少是新本地人，更多的是连本地户口都没有的外地人，而他们正是城市建设和发展的生力军。外地人中的已经在本市购房者，对所居城市的认同度很高，缺少的仅仅是一张纸——本地户口，但就是这张纸，对他的生活和工作带来诸多不便，尤其是子女教育问题。应该把已购房外地人视作准本地人，他们中的绝大多数已经把自己的命运与这座城市的命运拴在了一起。孟子说，有恒产者有恒心，着眼于长远，应该鼓励外地人在本地购房。一刀切限制外地人购房，往轻了说，是不得已的临时性措施，往重了说，是短视的政策，弊大于利。

户口制度施行已久，盘根错节，牵一发动全身，需要谋定而后动。但这并不等于可以因循守旧，不进行制度变革的准备和探索，更不等于不仅不去弱化它的不合理作用，反而为了行政的短期需要而强化它的不合理功能。

21.5　**城市化过程，就是一个制度变革的过程**。社会结构变了，制度也就需要变化。城市原有的制度，应该在外来人口不断增加的情况下进行适应性调整。事实上也是如此，在北京，若干年前非本市户口是无法进入本市高中上学的，现在这个藩篱已被打破。城市管理者应该以此为例，探讨如何进一步增加中小学教育、就业、居住、医疗、社会保障的公平度，避免歧视性政策，努力营造拥有更多个人发展机会的城市制度空间。

尤其是中小学义务教育。35 岁左右的人，事业有成，多是单位的业务骨干，或创业已经步入正轨，他们是城市建设的重要力量，而此时他们的子女也到了学龄。如果一个城市能够在中小学义务教育上做到本地人外地人一视同仁，会使这些生力军免除很多后顾之忧，这无疑会大大增加城市的吸引力。

21.6　**城市化过程，也是一个本地人和外来者的融合过程**。在这个过程中，所有的群体都有一个角色转换和身份变化问题，这不仅仅是对外地人的，也是对本地人的。城市管理者应该通过制度的调整和宣传引导，努力让城市成为所有人共同的家。

21.7　**在城市发展中，新本地人和准本地人，是两个很值得重视的群体**。前者学历高收入高期望高，但在所居城市时日尚短，调查表明多数还未在本地购房，对社会的看法和评价比较尖锐，不满足感较强。后者已在所居城市拥有自己的房产，调查表明他们收入也较高，虽无本地户口，对所居城市的归属感却很强。

假以时日，更多的外地人会成为新本地人和准本地人。城市管理者应该在致力于全体居民的公平待遇的同时，关注这两个能力比较强的群体，了解他们的需求和想法，解决他们面临的问题。

21.8 **最后，是对完善城市评价指标体系的几点建议：**

1. 商品和服务的丰富性在城市吸引力中的权重正在下降，吸引力更多的来自于就业、收入、个人发展的机会，这为今后指标体系中相关指标的设定和权重考量提供了研究基础。

2. 以本地户口和外地户口为主要区别的不同身份群体，在收入、居住、社会保障、就业、个人发展机会、教育、医疗等方面都存在明显的不平等，相应的在满意度和城市归属感上有着明显差异。这表明城市社会公平问题日益突出，因此，城市生活各方面的公平度指标，应该成为今后评价体系中的一个重要方面。

3. 如何在现行体制下保留户口身份制度的合理功能，削弱而不是强化其不合理功能，以替代性制度安排进行过渡，打破造成社会不平等的户口身份藩篱，将考验着每个城市的管理者的行政智慧和管理能力。在削弱身份壁垒和增强社会公平方面，城市管理者在相应的政策制定、制度调整和制度建设方面的作为，应该成为今后城市评价体系的组成部分。

（本报告执笔：白南风）

（参加本次问卷调查的主要人员有：调查设计阶段：中国城市发展研究院袁崇法、白南风，中国人民大学陈传波老师、研究生杨龙、吴本健、王瑜、曲囡囡、本科生周翀、喻希、赵彦龙；调查执行阶段：白南风、陈传波、领队杨龙、吴本健、曲囡囡、周翀、喻希、赵彦龙及调查员 19 名中国人民大学本科生，中国城市发展研究院南方分院卢继平、深圳中华职业学校卢和平、凌洁利、苏怡如；数据处理阶段：白南风、陈传波、杨龙、吴本健。描述报告执笔：杨龙、吴本健）

第四部分　中国建制镇发展概况

一、建制镇发展评估的意义

1. 建制镇发展是我国城乡一体化协调发展的"桥头堡"

从 2008 年 1 月 1 日开始执行的《中华人民共和国城乡规划法》，标志着我国城镇化的工作进入到一个全面发展的新阶段。

建制镇是城乡规划中的一个节点，在城乡协调发展中具有非常重要的作用。从我国的新城区化体系来看，建制镇是一个城市赖以依托的，减缓人口过度集中，形成住区、工业区的卫星集散点。它所辖有的行政区域，又往往是市辖区域的一个组成部分。因此，城市的发展离不开建制镇的协调规划与发展。

2. 建制镇有其历史形成的原因，依照其功能的发挥特点，可以分为：行政中心（一定行政区的政治中心，为县、镇政府所在地）、工业镇、渔业镇、工矿镇、旅游镇、交通镇、贸易镇、口岸镇、历史文化名城。依据建制镇历史的成因，保护建制镇的历史风貌，强化其功能特点并服务于城市发展，将成为我国城镇化的一个重要课题。

3. 建制镇又是一个行政管理的级别，与城市的街道有着同样的行政职能。因此，从管理角度看，建制镇又兼有社区管理的行政职能，其设置原则为：

- 凡县级国家机关所在地（又有"城关镇"的提法）；
- 总人口在 2 万人以下的乡、乡政府驻地，非农人口超过 2000 人的居民点；
- 总人口在 2 万人以上的乡、乡政府驻地，非农人口占全乡人口10% 以上的居民点；
- 或少数民族地区、人口稀少的边远地区、山区和小型工矿区、小港口、风景旅游区、边境口岸等地，非农人口虽不足 2000 人，但确有必要设置镇的地区。

从立法的角度看，我国确立的是省、县、乡三级基本行政区，因此，建制镇应属于第三级别基本行政区。改革以来，随着中国经济的迅速发展，原有的行政区划体系也在不断地发生变化。地改市后，以地级城市为中心辖县级市，而县级市不设区，以建制镇为基层行政单位。特别是华东、中南地区，县级市发展很快，形成了"市套市"的结构。

21 世纪开始，我国又逐步试点村民委员会的选举制度，在这个过程中，建制镇作为基层单位的行政职能在逐步削弱，可是，在城乡结合的协调发展中却具有举足轻重的地位。也就是说，城镇化的进程中，建制镇更多的不是从它的行政管理职能考虑，而是从城市发展中的城乡协调一体化的规划地位考虑。

二、建制镇评价和分析的指导思想

为了更好的对建制镇的发展做出评价和分析，有必要对我国城市化、城镇化的含义作重新的阐述。

1. 城市、城镇的概念区分

目前，我国在"城市"和"城镇"的使用上比较混乱：

（1）城市的狭义理解：只含市不含镇。

（2）城市的广义理解：含市又含建制镇。

（3）城镇的狭义理解：含市和建制镇。

（4）城镇的广义理解：含市、建制镇且含集镇。

我们对建制镇的分析与评价是建立在广义城市和狭义城镇的基础上的，旨在研究建制镇与城市关系的城镇化过程。

2. 城市化、城镇化的概念区分

由于城市和城镇概念的混淆，所以出现了"城市化"和"城镇化"两种提法，但在英文中都是"Urbanization"。另外，在日本和我国台湾又有"都市化"的提法，而我国大陆一般把都市理解为特大城市，所以少有都市化的说法。2001 年公布的《中华人民共和国国民经济和社会发展第十个五年计划纲要》中首次提出："要不失时机地实施城镇化战略。"

这里重新阐述概念的目的，是在表明我们对建制镇做出评价的指导思想。从我国城镇化发展的趋势看，未来存在着都市化的可能，也就是如东京、华盛顿、纽约、巴黎的大都市圈的形成和小城镇化人口分散的并存趋势。"城市化"容易产生规模化、集中化、商业化、工业化的误导，所以从城乡协调的角度出发，为避免建制镇的"灭失"和盲目追求"大而全"的倾向，我们认为"城镇化"的提法，更适于我们论证的初衷。

另外，从我们做城镇发展规划的角度理解：

（1）城市化是基于人口集中的一种发展方式，它在工业化时期提供了相对集中的生产制造、流通交易、运输集散的条件，形成集约化的成本效应，但也因此造成了城市资源的巨大负担；城镇化则是在后工业时代，基于解决"城市病"目的所采取的人口疏散、减轻城市资源压力的措施。

（2）城市化造成城乡之间的巨大差异，使社会资源布局的配置失去了平衡，造成城乡之间、地区之间的巨大差别；城镇化则促进了城乡的协调发展，带动乡村的都市化、农产品的商品化和深加工化，传统小镇将成为城市发展的重要依托。

（3）城市化以工业、商业、金融业、运输业为业态基础，成为生产制造、物资流通的集散点，往往具有一种同格化的发展趋势，形成城市间的隔离与竞争；城镇化更注重改变这种同格化的发展模式，可以形成多样化的功能格局，因地制宜地向小城镇建设方向转化，是以服务生活、和谐人与自然、保护历史、宜于人居为目标。

3. 城镇地域范围的界定

不同的人对城镇地域范围的理解也不一样，其中最大的分歧是城镇规划和区域规划工作者把城镇看成是一个"点"，而中国行政区划体系则把城镇看成是个"面"，把城镇所管辖的广大农村也当成了城镇。这种地域范围界定不清，造成统计上的混乱，目前我国的统计资料中几乎所有所谓的"城市"数据都不能代表"城市"。

那么，如何来界定城镇地域范围呢？通常有三种方法：按建成区界定、按城镇功能区界定、按行政区界定。

按行政区界定城镇地域范围虽然不能完全反映城镇化现状，但我们认为综合评价中这是唯一可以采用的数据，对此，我们有如下考虑：

（1）它是我国较为成熟的管理和统计体系，从连续数据的比较分析中可以探讨出必然的规律。

（2）它的地域范围，同时也是它的空间资源，从资源储备的角度考察，空间规模对建制镇的发展无疑是一个客观的基础条件。

（3）建制镇现有指标并不全面，有些需要通过演算和数学推导形成新的数据，这就需要有与之相一致的统计口径的其他统计资料。而我国统计资料都是按行政区划口径得到的。

（4）城镇规划工作者往往拘泥于具体的地块做规划，希望"红线"清晰，但管理者和社会工作者则更着眼于区域空间的发展状况和发展条件。我们所做的评价和分析，不同于城镇规划的具体对象，以综合平均数据为参考，但它所形成的参数，或许在具体规划时可以借鉴。

（5）既然建制镇是在城市所辖范围，那么，我们对建制镇的评价与分析，就成为城市发展评价的必要补充。

（6）城镇化的发展是经济发展的表现，经济发展离不开农业基础。按行政区划，其中包括了农业、林业、牧业等，正是建制镇作为了城乡结合部的发展依托。

（7）从规划学的角度出发，学科本身在发展、在出新。从城市规划扩展到区域规划，已经成为事实，并在发达国家中早已有过实践。

三、建制镇评价与分析的方法

1. 指标体系的建立原则

城镇化的发展并不是由单一因素所决定的，它同时受到地理位置、地理特征、周边环境、本地资源、交通状况等多种因素的影响，其发展速度也必定受到被管辖地、市、县经济发展水平的影响。这就决定了评价与分析建制镇的发展水平以及未来潜力时必须采用多指标的分析方法，同时必须结合所辖地市的状况，也即是把建制镇的发展视为城市协调发展的重要组成部分。

除了发展因素的指标，尚需要做出城镇化现状比较，这包括市政条件、社会服务、公共安全、社会卫生等。

指标体系的建立由于时间及人力的限制，目前只能依据现有收集的统计数据建立指标体系，但其分析方法和指标体系的设计将考虑长久的有效使用，并不断地丰富和完善。

2. 指标体系的设计框架

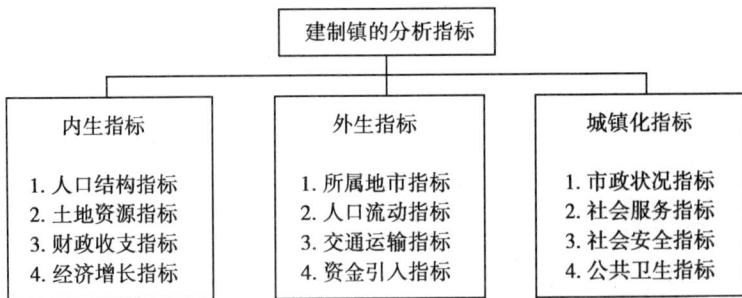

建制镇的分析指标

内生指标	外生指标	城镇化指标
1. 人口结构指标 2. 土地资源指标 3. 财政收支指标 4. 经济增长指标	1. 所属地市指标 2. 人口流动指标 3. 交通运输指标 4. 资金引入指标	1. 市政状况指标 2. 社会服务指标 3. 社会安全指标 4. 公共卫生指标

（1）内生指标，即建制镇自身所具备的条件，这些条件是建制镇历史形成的结果，也是未来发展所依托并无法改变的客观因素。

- 人口结构指标包括：年龄结构、职业结构、流动结构；
- 土地资源指标包括：城域比例、耕地比例、山林比例、人口密度等；
- 财政收支指标包括：收支总额、人均收支总额、人均收入余额；
- 经济增长指标包括：GDP、人均收入、企业利润、居民收入等。

（2）外生指标，即所属地市经济发展的波及影响，包括人口的流动（如果人口流入大于流出，说明该建制镇的城镇化趋势加快，城镇对人口具有吸引力）；物资流通（如果流入大于流出，说明该地区的消费水平高，当地产品的附加价值高）；交通因素（包括客流量、水路、陆路交通状况等）。以上诸因素决定了资金的流入可能性。

- 所属地市指标包括：市辖建制镇数量及分类比较、全市公共设施的平均状况、路网及道路覆盖率、城市规划及相关控规的影响等；
- 人口流动指标包括：流入人口、流出人口、流动人口的年龄结构等；
- 交通运输指标包括：公路、铁路路网密度，水路港口数量，物流吞吐量等；
- 资金引入指标包括：固定资产投资数量、外来企业数量、经济合同数量及金额、银行存款增加额等。

（3）城镇指标（现状指标），即对建制镇城镇化水平的刻画，以反映建制镇社会化服务功能。

- 市政状况指标包括：自来水供应、电力供应、燃气供应、公交状况及运力等；
- 社会服务指标包括：教育设施、文化设施、体育设施、商业网点等；
- 社会安全指标包括：公安机构及安防设施等；
- 公共卫生指标包括：市容环卫、医疗设施、卫生防疫等。

由于建制镇的统计资料尚不完整，暂时未能完全按照上述设想做出系统的分析，仅用可搜集到的资料做初步的比较。

3. 评价分析方法

我国幅员辽阔，地区经济差别很大，做笼统的比较和排序不具有任何的客观解释功能，更难以具有社会说服力。建制镇作为基层行政单位，其权力是有限的，可资利用的条件同样有限，对 19322 个建制镇进行——比较不但工作量浩大，也不可能产生鞭策效应。为此，评价分析中我们采取分地区综合比较的方法，并采取相对指标，即人均指标、比例结构和密度指标做出地区间的比较，以及根据可得到的地理差别做地形因素比较。

另外，城镇化的评价和分析中，对农业耕地的处理也是一个值得探讨的课题。农业始终是经济发展的基础，农业的机械化、现代化、农产品的深加工化、商品化、农副产品的高附加值化等，都可以成为城镇化的契机和战略资源。因此，作为土地资源，我们依然把耕地作为重要的指标来进行比较。

四、建制镇评价和分析的初步结果

（一）内生指标比较

1. 按省级区划进行的数据对比

（1）人口密度

序号	地区	人口密度（人/平方公里）	序号	地区	人口密度（人/平方公里）
1	上海	1966.87	17	广西	249.98
2	江苏	763.96	18	贵州	241.11
3	河南	580.25	19	海南	217.83
4	山东	525.47	20	山西	217.41
5	天津	479.03	21	辽宁	194.25
6	浙江	460.76	22	陕西	173.71
7	安徽	458.05	23	云南	139.84
8	重庆	434.66	24	宁夏	102.51
9	广东	423.54	25	吉林	98.35
10	河北	409.65	26	黑龙江	77.73
11	四川	400.54	27	甘肃	66.11
12	北京	382.74	28	新疆	26.85
13	湖南	357.65	29	内蒙古	21.91
14	福建	320.28	30	青海	9.17
15	江西	276.81	31	西藏	4.32
16	湖北	261.92			

（2）就业人口比例

序号	地区	就业人口比例（%）	序号	地区	就业人口比例（%）
1	浙江	67.28	17	宁夏	51.05
2	河南	57.86	18	河北	49.82
3	山东	56.48	19	西藏	49.80
4	湖南	55.15	20	甘肃	49.80
5	安徽	54.62	21	辽宁	49.76
6	贵州	53.97	22	江西	49.46
7	江苏	53.97	23	内蒙古	49.11
8	重庆	53.94	24	黑龙江	47.76
9	北京	53.85	25	湖北	47.13
10	广西	53.53	26	青海	46.08
11	云南	53.49	27	海南	45.06
12	陕西	52.78	28	天津	44.81
13	四川	52.64	29	吉林	44.43
14	上海	52.29	30	山西	43.27
15	广东	51.97	31	新疆	38.38
16	福建	51.76			

（3）人均财政收入

序号	地区	人均财政收入	序号	地区	人均财政收入
1	上海	5322.39	17	广西	316.45
2	浙江	3225.77	18	吉林	309.31
3	江苏	2674.64	19	四川	305.04
4	北京	2040.16	20	新疆	296.80
5	天津	1551.34	21	安徽	280.19
6	河北	958.54	22	贵州	267.37
7	广东	908.48	23	湖南	266.22
8	辽宁	844.20	24	宁夏	253.88
9	山西	842.45	25	海南	253.18
10	山东	816.86	26	湖北	219.81
11	福建	778.60	27	黑龙江	216.19
12	内蒙古	673.30	28	陕西	183.20
13	江西	415.11	29	甘肃	138.10
14	云南	392.97	30	青海	108.70
15	河南	344.26	31	西藏	97.11
16	重庆	327.23			

（4）人均教育投资

序号	地区	人均教育投资	序号	地区	人均教育投资
1	上海	267.24	17	湖北	42.88
2	浙江	253.96	18	重庆	36.79
3	天津	252.84	19	陕西	33.74
4	江苏	207.40	20	贵州	32.24
5	广东	157.50	21	湖南	29.35
6	辽宁	120.49	22	河南	28.51
7	北京	117.41	23	青海	26.47
8	山东	108.04	24	海南	25.87
9	江西	95.43	25	吉林	25.58
10	山西	86.66	26	安徽	25.16
11	河北	74.22	27	甘肃	24.30
12	新疆	61.21	28	福建	20.46
13	广西	57.96	29	宁夏	15.26
14	云南	57.72	30	黑龙江	6.34
15	四川	57.59	31	西藏	4.03
16	内蒙古	57.08			

（5）人均科技投资

序号	地区	人均科技投资	序号	地区	人均科技投资
1	上海	20.88	17	宁夏	3.08
2	北京	15.81	18	江西	2.97
3	浙江	14.30	19	安徽	2.53
4	广东	11.34	20	广西	2.35
5	江苏	9.26	21	云南	2.30
6	新疆	9.07	22	贵州	2.15
7	河北	7.66	23	吉林	1.78
8	内蒙古	6.68	24	甘肃	1.74
9	山东	6.40	25	重庆	1.54
10	湖南	4.97	26	天津	1.26
11	辽宁	4.17	27	四川	1.10
12	湖北	4.08	28	海南	0.81
13	山西	4.08	29	黑龙江	0.67
14	福建	3.97	30	西藏	0.14
15	河南	3.93	31	青海	0.10
16	陕西	3.25			

(6) 人均社会总投资

序号	地区	人均总投资	序号	地区	人均总投资
1	江苏	11470.70	17	宁夏	2285.61
2	山东	9302.06	18	江西	2039.61
3	浙江	7974.59	19	青海	1789.35
4	上海	7839.90	20	山西	1728.32
5	天津	7353.15	21	湖北	1676.15
6	河北	6513.26	22	陕西	1665.79
7	北京	5948.73	23	湖南	1636.25
8	内蒙古	5921.57	24	新疆	1406.26
9	河南	5627.91	25	甘肃	1195.21
10	重庆	4611.87	26	云南	1004.36
11	福建	4513.17	27	贵州	818.60
12	吉林	4440.50	28	黑龙江	720.74
13	广东	4348.44	29	辽宁	581.72
14	广西	2537.35	30	海南	442.93
15	四川	2326.56	31	西藏	148.74
16	安徽	2292.14			

(7) 人均资产额

序号	地区	人均资产额	序号	地区	人均资产额
1	上海	3062.31	17	四川	268.57
2	北京	2199.72	18	内蒙古	254.49
3	广东	1634.08	19	河北	232.44
4	江苏	1133.80	20	山西	224.11
5	浙江	862.82	21	海南	216.81
6	天津	708.97	22	江西	213.65
7	河南	635.29	23	吉林	208.75
8	山东	594.94	24	宁夏	184.79
9	湖北	538.78	25	贵州	162.38
10	云南	493.96	26	黑龙江	157.23
11	辽宁	487.73	27	陕西	128.20
12	湖南	474.32	28	青海	126.28
13	安徽	359.09	29	广西	125.82
14	重庆	339.61	30	甘肃	122.66
15	福建	313.55	31	西藏	112.78
16	新疆	291.41			

(8) 耕地面积比例

序号	地区	耕地比例（%）	序号	地区	耕地比例（%）
1	江苏	45.20	17	四川	17.73
2	天津	43.95	18	陕西	15.79

序号	地区	耕地比例（%）	序号	地区	耕地比例（%）
3	河南	43.34	19	北京	15.72
4	山东	40.94	20	广西	14.01
5	上海	36.67	21	江西	13.94
6	河北	36.12	22	海南	13.48
7	安徽	32.35	23	广东	11.69
8	黑龙江	26.96	24	贵州	11.22
9	辽宁	25.93	25	福建	9.66
10	山西	22.55	26	甘肃	8.26
11	吉林	22.33	27	云南	7.86
12	重庆	19.18	28	内蒙古	7.26
13	湖南	18.04	29	新疆	4.27
14	湖北	17.84	30	青海	0.94
15	浙江	17.83	31	西藏	0.43
16	宁夏	17.75			

以上可见：按省份排列在前几位的均位于东部地区，尽管其人口密度极高，但人均指标都名列前茅，这是由经济基础和历史条件所决定的。相对集中的人口不仅提供了较多的生产劳动力，同时也形成了巨大的消费人群。但人口的集中必须适度，有效控制城镇规模极为必要。

另外，东、中部地区至今依然是耕地面积比例高的地区。由此证明，农业并非与城镇化相悖，二者具有相辅相成、协调发展的必然结果。

2. 为了更直观的了解地区差异特点，我们进一步按地区进行综合分析和比较：

（1）人口密度地区差别①

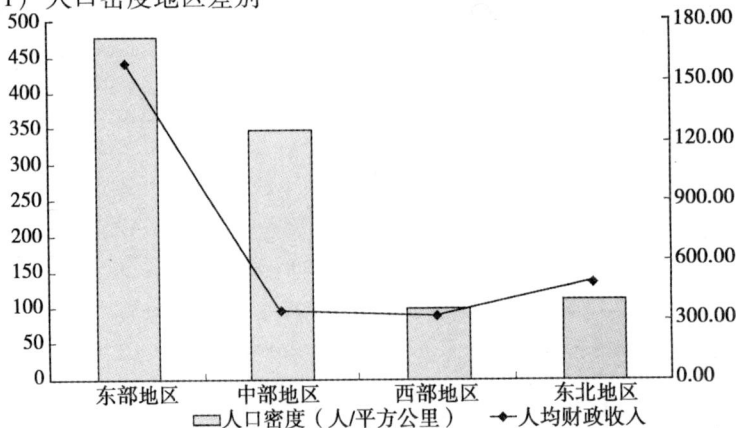

---

① 原设想选用人均GDP的指标，但现有统计资料没有此项指标，故以人均财政收入指标取代。

上图可见，收入与人口密度成正比。我国城镇人口以中、东部最为密集，明显高于西部和东北地区。而东部人均收入奇高，这与改革开放以来，东部沿海地区面向海外市场的出口加工工业发展有关。

这个问题还可以通过建制镇就业人口的统计数据做出理论分析。

（2）地区就业结构

（%）

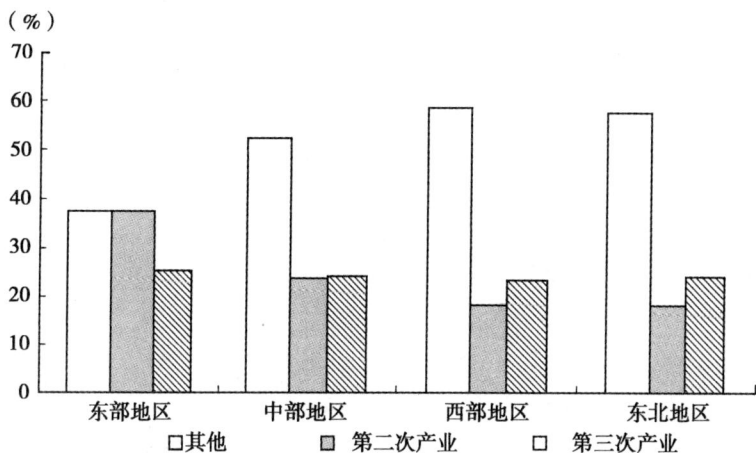

四个地区第三产业的就业比例都差不多，区别主要在第二产业，而图标中的"其他"其实是农业释放出来的冗余劳动力。为此，根据统计指标的解释，进一步的分析：

- 就业人口包括：当地就业总人口＋外地流入人口；
- 第二、三产业就业人口为当地实际就业人口；
- 分析推断外出打工人口状况为：当地外出打工人口＝当地总就业人口＋外来人口－当地第一、二、三次产业已就业人口；
- 就业人口中，第二、三产业有建制镇的统计，应属于当地就业结构。而第二、三产业以外就业人口，由于没有明确归属到农业，但农业就业不可能在建制镇域内有如此高的比例，可以推测，这部分就业人口实际上是冗余外出打工人口。

东部地区的外出打工人口，实际是在东部地区内转移和流动，部分上升到城市，但中、西部包括东北部的劳动力则更多地跨地区寻找工作机会——进入城市。可以想见，就业人口的外流表明当地经济发展缓慢、就业机会少，同时人员的外流进一步影响到当地的消费和生产，造成经济的进一步放缓，逐步拉大了地区间的经济差别。

（3）人均财政结余和人均创税比较①

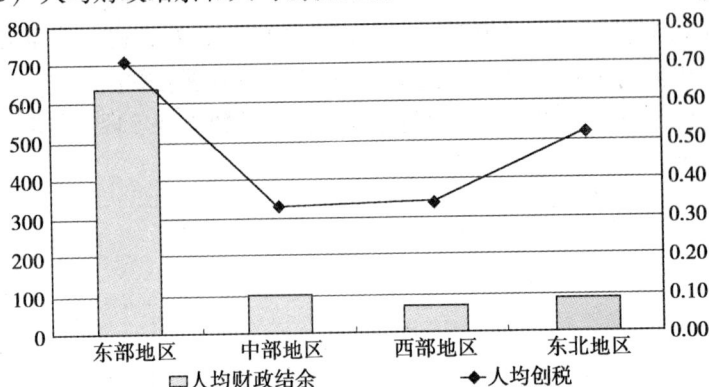

□人均财政结余　◆人均创税

（4）科教投资及比例

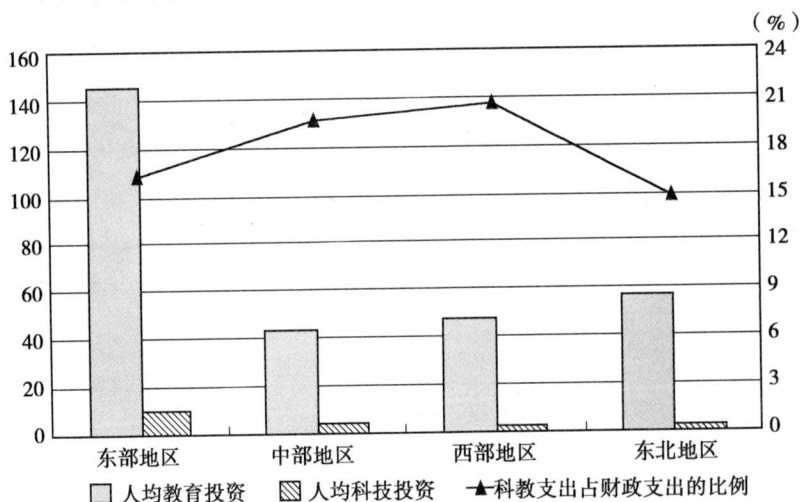

□人均教育投资　▨人均科技投资　▲科教支出占财政支出的比例

从人均角度看，无论教育投资还是科技投资，东部都远远的高于中部、西部，其次是东北部，但财政支出比例上，中、西部却高于东部及东北部。这一方面体现了经济差异所导致的地方财政状况，同时也说明越是偏远地区，其文教事业越依赖于当地的财政力量，而缺少周边教育资源的依托，需要财政拿出更高的支出比例。

2011中国城市科学发展综合评价报告

---

① 暂时使用这一指标，缘于现有资料未有国民收入指标，而地方财政收入或许是地方城镇化的必要资金。

（5）人均投资和资产①

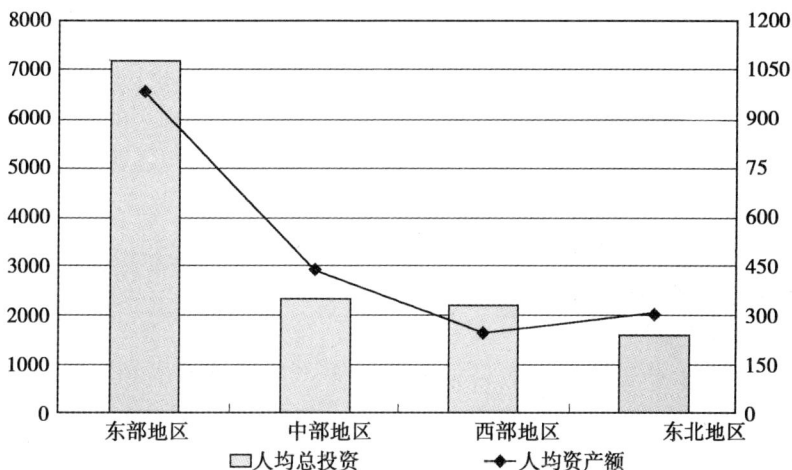

由此可见，中部、西部、东北地区与东部仍有很大的差距。

另外，固定资产投资总额包括新建、扩建和改建，新建、扩建为增加，改建为补偿，所以在资产额上表现得并不一致。为此，我们用资产投资比，权当做一个比较。

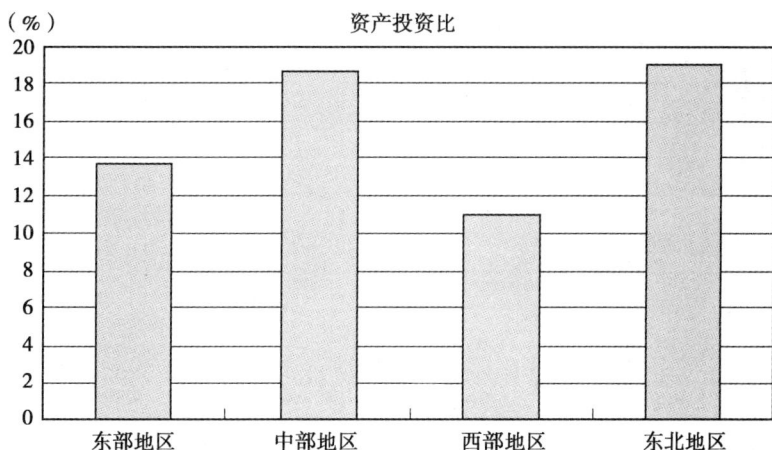

资产投资比的影响因素是资产额和固定资产投资完成额，这个比

① 新形成的资产公式为：新增资产 = 完成的固定资产投资额 – 未结算工程的投资完成额，由于建制镇的统计缺乏历年的连续数据，无法获得上年度数据，也就无法采用此公式，因此，暂用人均额度做地方实力比较。

值实际上既反映了建制镇固定资产投资的规模，也反映了建制镇资产存量的规模。投资完成规模与指标成反比。资产投资比越低，说明当地的投资相对越大；相反，资产规模与指标成正比，资产投资比越高，说明当地的资产存量越大。现在没有一个标准判断什么样的比值是合理的。但如果取平均值＝26.13％，那么，上海、北京、广东、湖北、湖南、黑龙江、新疆七个省市处于平均水平，而辽宁、西藏、云南、海南投资偏少，剩下的省份投资较高。上海、北京、广东尽管资产比例适中，但实际的资产基数大，投资额绝对数并不小，说明这些省市的建制镇已具备一定的资产实力。

从全国建制镇的这一指标计算的平均值仅为15.63％，说明建制镇正处于基本建设的高度投资期及地方资产的积累期，并需要大量外部资金的投入，而实际资金也正逐步地向建制镇倾斜。这是城市发展的必然，建成区不是"摊煎饼"式的向外扩充，就是星状卫星城式的向外连接。建制镇正是在这种城镇化的过程中，成为疏导社会富余资金的方向。

（6）各地区地域耕地面积比例的比较

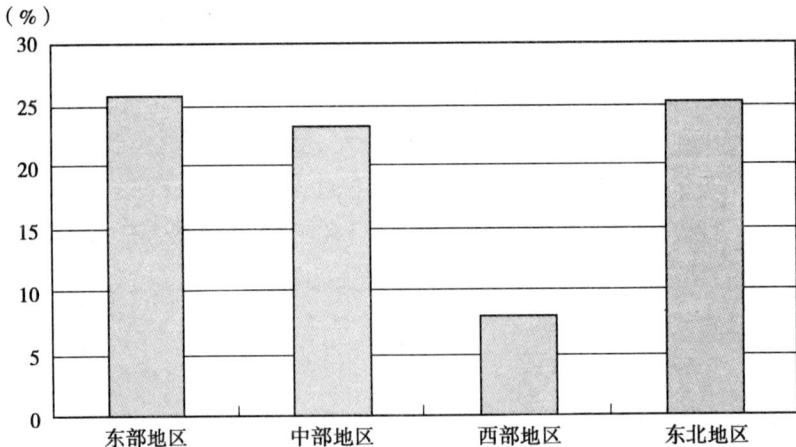

除西部外，各地区耕地比例相差无几。这是因为西部地区行政区域大。为此，做全国总耕地地区分布的比较：

各地区耕地占总耕地比例

东北地区，17.12%　　　　　　　　　东部地区，28.74%

西部地区，30.30%　　　　　　　　　中部地区，23.84%

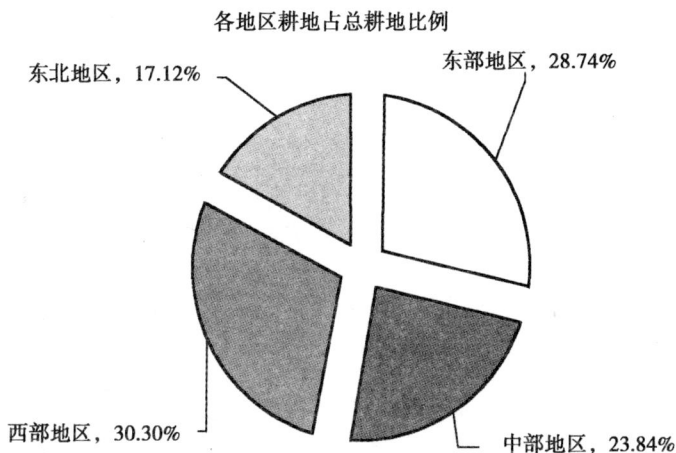

　　比较西部地区行政区域高达57%的比例，西部耕地明显偏少，这主要是西部地形特点所决定的。

　　再比较播种面积和耕地面积的关系：

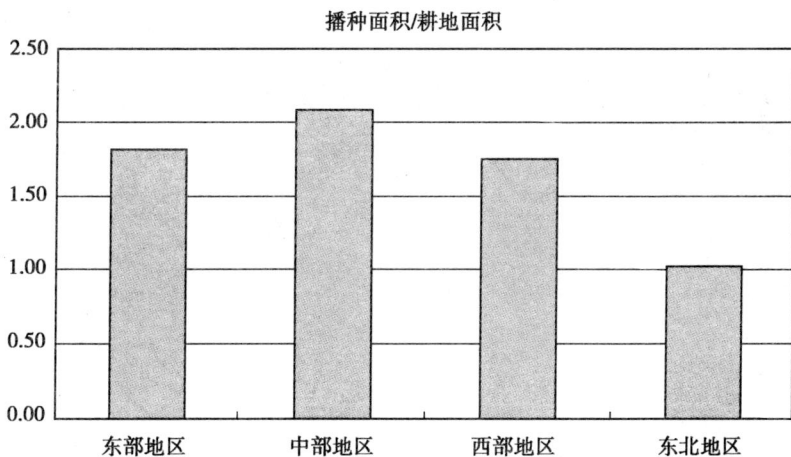

播种面积/耕地面积

　　如果说耕地与行政区域的比值反映了建制镇耕地资源规模的话，那么播种与耕地的比值则反映耕地利用情况。西部地区因为包括了西南三省，所以播种面积比例较高。

　　按全国播种面积来比较，四个地区的比例是：

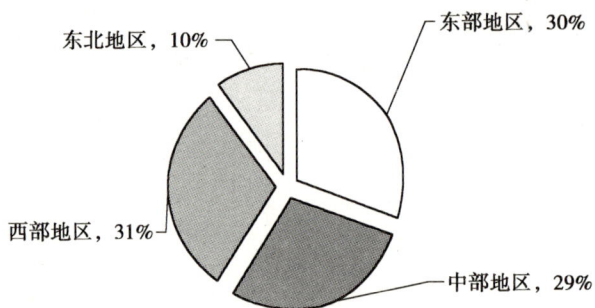

东北地区，10%　　　　　　　　　东部地区，30%

西部地区，31%

中部地区，29%

3. 除了四大块区域的差别比较以外，我们还做了不同地形的比较：

（1）分地形比较的人口密度

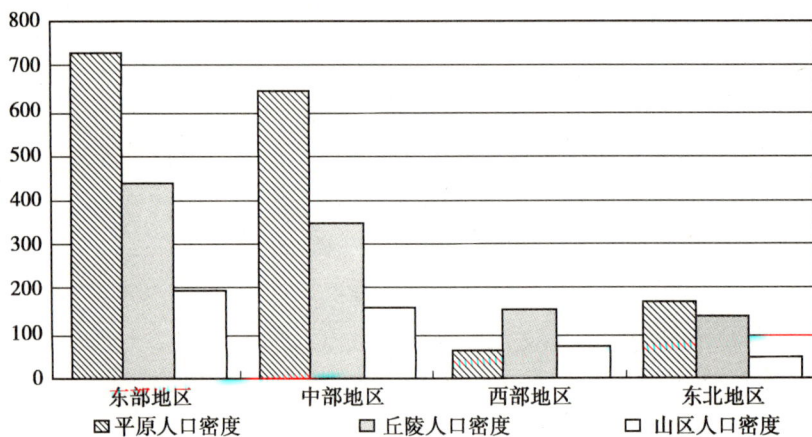

平原人口密度　　　丘陵人口密度　　　山区人口密度

（2）分地形的人均财政收入

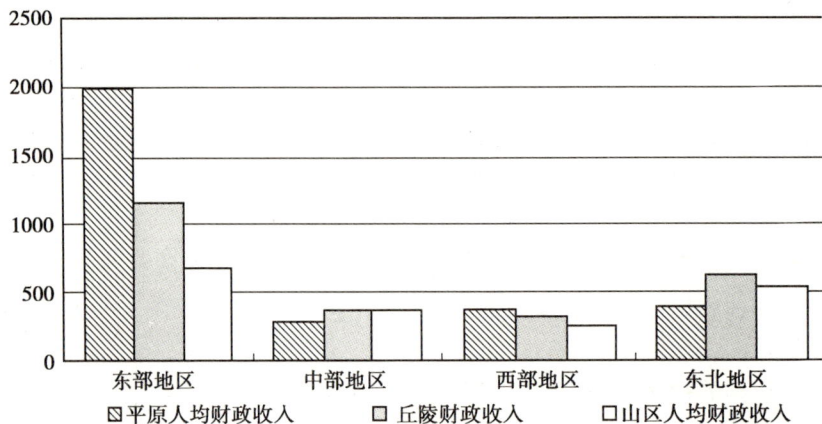

平原人均财政收入　　　丘陵财政收入　　　山区人均财政收入

将上述两项指标叠加作比较：

人口密度与人均财政收入比较

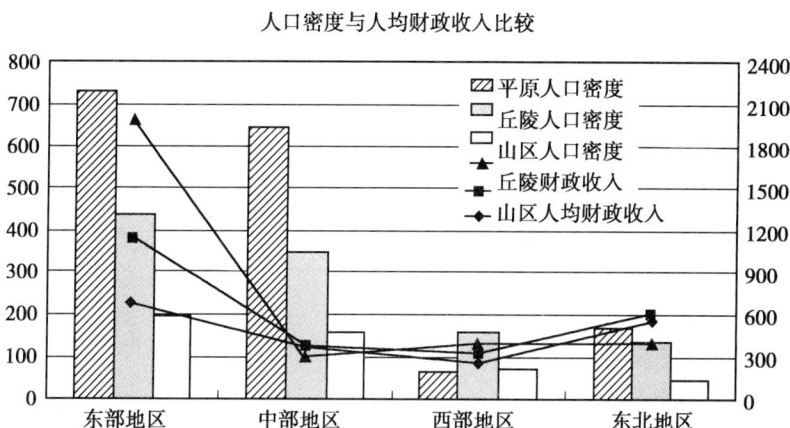

可见，按地形的人口密度，平原高于丘陵、丘陵高于山区（除西部地区为丘陵地带人口密度高），但人均财政收入，在中部、西部和东北部地区，丘陵地带都显示出较高的人均收入水平。进一步做人口比例及财政收入的地区、地形比较来分析原因：

A. 分地区、分地形的人口比例

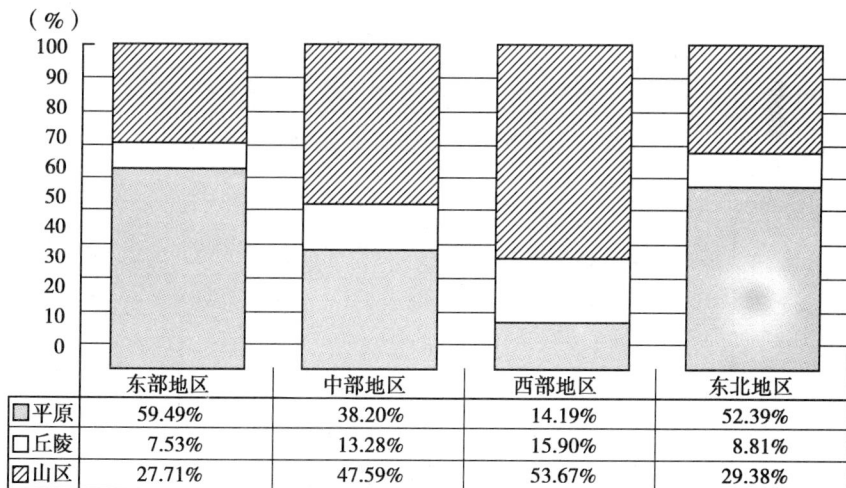

	东部地区	中部地区	西部地区	东北地区
□平原	59.49%	38.20%	14.19%	52.39%
□丘陵	7.53%	13.28%	15.90%	8.81%
▨山区	27.71%	47.59%	53.67%	29.38%

B. 分地区、分地形的财政收入比例

数据比较可见，丘陵地带人口比例低，但财政收入的比例却很高。这或许是一个财政政策的问题，抑或与资源开采有关，例如当地林业、采矿业的发展。

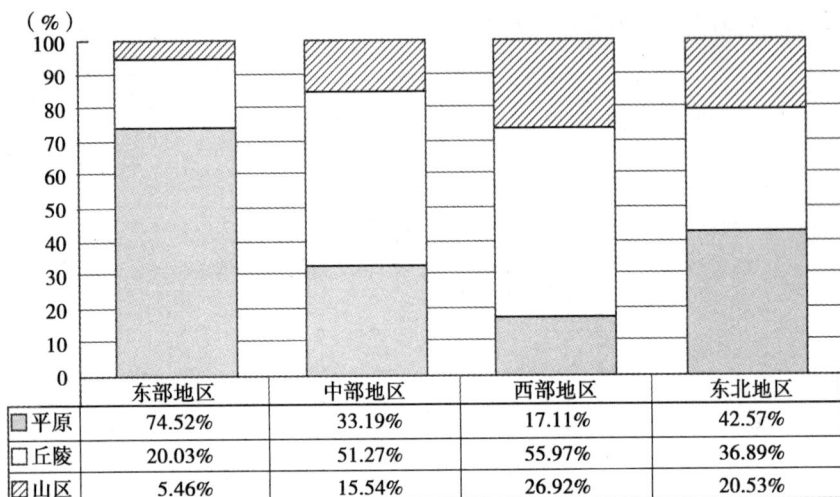

	东部地区	中部地区	西部地区	东北地区
▢ 平原	74.52%	33.19%	17.11%	42.57%
▢ 丘陵	20.03%	51.27%	55.97%	36.89%
▨ 山区	5.46%	15.54%	26.92%	20.53%

（二）外生指标的比较分析

（由于外生因素和所辖省市有关，所以近 2 万个建制镇需要逐一还原到所辖地市。这是一个很大的工作量，在此暂时省略。）

（三）城镇化指标的比较分析

1. 按省级区划进行的数据对比

（1）镇域比例比较

序号	地区	镇域比例（%）	序号	地区	镇域比例（%）
1	上海	10.69	17	陕西	2.26
2	天津	7.95	18	重庆	2.25
3	河北	7.14	19	贵州	2.20
4	浙江	6.55	20	湖北	2.09
5	北京	6.42	21	云南	1.71
6	江苏	6.41	22	海南	1.62
7	河南	4.81	23	吉林	1.44
8	山东	4.26	24	宁夏	1.43
9	广东	3.84	25	山西	1.43
10	安徽	3.28	26	黑龙江	1.40
11	辽宁	3.24	27	广西	1.37
12	西藏	3.13	28	新疆	1.13
13	湖南	3.12	29	甘肃	0.76
14	福建	2.57	30	内蒙古	0.59
15	四川	2.43	31	青海	0.24
16	江西	2.32			

（2）镇域人口比较

序号	地区	镇域人口比例（%）	序号	地区	镇域人口比例（%）
1	西藏	57.90	17	福建	25.29
2	上海	34.59	18	天津	24.87
3	江苏	33.59	19	湖南	24.45
4	黑龙江	33.10	20	江西	24.02
5	浙江	31.78	21	广东	24.01
6	河北	31.70	22	四川	23.60
7	新疆	30.09	23	重庆	23.57
8	山西	28.74	24	青海	23.06
9	内蒙古	28.37	25	云南	21.36
10	北京	28.00	26	湖北	21.10
11	吉林	27.68	27	山东	20.71
12	河南	27.11	28	贵州	19.41
13	宁夏	26.74	29	陕西	19.33
14	甘肃	26.48	30	安徽	17.61
15	海南	26.47	31	广西	16.80
16	辽宁	26.44			

（3）镇域绿化率

序号	地区	镇域绿化率（%）	序号	地区	镇域绿化率（%）
1	江苏	10.79	17	广西	3.30
2	上海	9.41	18	四川	3.14
3	山东	7.38	19	浙江	3.03
4	北京	7.32	20	宁夏	2.90
5	湖南	5.98	21	贵州	2.81
6	重庆	5.17	22	内蒙古	2.74
7	广东	4.98	23	云南	2.67
8	湖北	4.95	24	甘肃	2.24
9	新疆	4.68	25	陕西	1.84
10	江西	4.49	26	河北	1.70
11	安徽	4.39	27	吉林	1.66
12	海南	4.06	28	黑龙江	1.51
13	山西	4.01	29	天津	0.90
14	河南	3.69	30	青海	0.44
15	福建	3.67	31	西藏	0.04
16	辽宁	3.34			

（4）人均年用电量（千瓦）

序号	地区	人均用电量	序号	地区	人均用电量
1	浙江	3064.67	17	宁夏	245.56
2	江苏	2310.59	18	湖南	234.06
3	广东	1788.69	19	安徽	221.84
4	上海	1718.36	20	湖北	221.19
5	天津	1405.22	21	江西	202.81
6	北京	1323.32	22	黑龙江	199.44
7	福建	1117.71	23	四川	182.34
8	辽宁	1007.95	24	重庆	181.06
9	河北	856.98	25	贵州	166.66
10	山东	844.67	26	甘肃	152.88
11	新疆	517.74	27	陕西	144.24
12	河南	513.77	28	①西藏	140.53
13	内蒙古	365.49	29	海南	138.30
14	吉林	314.07	30	广西	115.71
15	山西	305.29	31	青海	89.37
16	云南	288.78			

（5）路网密度（千米/平方千米）

序号	地区	路网密度	序号	地区	路网密度
1	四川	1.57	17	江西	0.51
2	江苏	1.55	18	山西	0.50
3	上海	1.44	19	陕西	0.50
4	河南	1.18	20	云南	0.48
5	北京	1.10	21	辽宁	0.44
6	山东	1.06	22	海南	0.39
7	湖北	0.90	23	广西	0.32
8	浙江	0.85	24	吉林	0.26
9	安徽	0.82	25	宁夏	0.22
10	天津	0.81	26	黑龙江	0.19
11	河北	0.79	27	甘肃	0.15
12	湖南	0.69	28	内蒙古	0.08
13	重庆	0.67	29	新疆	0.06
14	贵州	0.63	30	青海	0.03
15	福建	0.57	31	西藏	0.01
16	广东	0.56			

---

① 数据有误，做了调整。

路网密度排序的规律与人口密度有关，与经济发达程度有关。

（6）教育状况

①小学生人口比例（按丘陵地带排序）

序号	地区	小学生人口比例（%）			序号	地区	小学生人口比例（%）		
		平原	丘陵	山区			平原	丘陵	山区
1	宁夏	11.26	16.87	11.75	16	四川	7.61	7.38	11.73
2	西藏	15.34	14.25	13.61	17	福建	7.64	6.91	6.45
3	海南	11.62	11.85	10.50	18	湖南	6.30	6.42	6.43
4	贵州		11.65	11.61	19	重庆	5.10	6.39	9.06
5	甘肃	10.34	10.49	11.76	20	辽宁	6.17	6.30	5.66
6	广东	10.28	10.18	9.69	21	湖北	5.65	6.20	6.16
7	云南	10.04	9.92	10.66	22	吉林	6.36	6.09	5.10
8	广西	10.78	9.78	8.58	23	浙江	7.17	6.05	6.57
9	江西	8.60	9.73	8.89	24	内蒙古	6.06	5.82	5.14
10	山西	9.35	8.63	8.98	25	江苏	6.06	5.59	4.12
11	河南	10.32	8.32	8.73	26	黑龙江	5.28	5.31	5.82
12	陕西	9.00	8.31	9.10	27	山东	6.73	5.28	5.88
13	河北	6.80	7.68	7.69	28	天津	6.88	4.86	6.32
14	安徽	9.51	7.58	6.67	29	北京	4.11	4.30	5.10
15	新疆	10.36	7.46	7.68	30	上海	3.02		

②小学师资力量（按丘陵地带排序）

序号	地区	每百学生小教数量（人）			序号	地区	每百学生小教数量（人）		
		平原	丘陵	山区			平原	丘陵	山区
1	北京	9.41	11.73	15.61	17	河南	5.24	5.93	6.31
2	吉林	9.72	11.52	13.24	18	海南	5.32	5.92	6.35
3	内蒙古	9.23	10.31	11.30	19	重庆	8.95	5.87	5.33
4	天津	8.36	9.96	8.35	20	甘肃	5.47	5.35	5.15
5	黑龙江	9.35	8.78	9.29	21	浙江	5.02	5.35	5.95
6	新疆	6.97	8.68	9.01	22	云南	5.28	5.32	5.13
7	山东	6.86	7.80	7.36	23	广西	5.33	5.23	6.37
8	辽宁	7.35	7.61	8.70	24	安徽	4.49	5.11	6.33
9	江苏	6.49	7.32	8.66	25	江西	5.24	5.02	5.32
10	山西	6.16	7.21	7.09	26	四川	5.27	4.96	5.48
11	河北	7.69	7.09	7.17	27	贵州		4.52	4.48
12	陕西	6.18	6.67	6.39	28	广东	4.06	4.47	5.19
13	福建	5.44	6.53	8.24	29	宁夏	5.33	3.29	4.97
14	西藏	6.58	6.16	5.95	30	上海	7.37		
15	湖北	5.86	6.05	6.13	31	青海	6.02		5.91
16	湖南	6.67	6.04	7.16					

③中学生人口比例（按丘陵地带排序）

序号	地区	中学生人口比例（%）			序号	地区	中学生人口比例（%）		
		平原	丘陵	山区			平原	丘陵	山区
1	新疆	7.90	8.13	5.82	17	湖北	5.16	5.20	4.97
2	宁夏	7.09	7.78	6.55	18	广东	5.45	5.15	5.50
3	陕西	7.28	7.47	7.31	19	江苏	5.47	5.11	2.94
4	海南	6.72	6.44	4.65	20	重庆	2.61	5.06	6.67
5	河南	6.53	6.42	4.61	21	广西	6.93	4.86	4.92
6	甘肃	6.21	6.35	6.90	22	内蒙古	4.72	4.83	4.28
7	福建	6.18	6.12	5.81	23	浙江	5.25	4.81	4.56
8	云南	6.49	6.11	5.72	24	辽宁	4.43	4.77	3.78
9	四川	10.17	6.06	12.45	25	湖南	4.76	4.55	5.20
10	贵州		5.76	5.97	26	山东	4.50	4.09	3.31
11	天津	4.61	5.71	5.62	27	吉林	3.99	3.66	3.47
12	安徽	5.47	5.67	6.15	28	北京	2.86	3.40	3.68
13	西藏	10.08	5.55	8.74	29	黑龙江	4.04	3.32	4.70
14	江西	6.04	5.40	5.02	30	上海	2.57		
15	山西	7.39	5.28	5.66	31	青海	6.81		6.75
16	河北	5.61	5.27	6.89					

④中学师资力量（按丘陵地带排序）

序号	地区	每百学生中教师数量（人）			序号	地区	每百学生中教师数量（人）		
		平原	丘陵	山区			平原	丘陵	山区
1	新疆	13.54	12.64	14.96	17	河北	6.33	6.69	7.25
2	福建	9.14	9.66	11.00	18	重庆	6.40	6.44	6.73
3	山西	8.86	9.63	9.48	19	内蒙古	8.55	6.37	5.60
4	河南	8.46	9.53	10.12	20	湖北	6.37	6.27	6.60
5	青海	8.30	9.17	9.33	21	安徽	4.93	6.13	6.36
6	宁夏	8.99	8.79	10.42	22	广西	5.78	6.09	5.78
7	云南	8.22	8.27	8.81	23	吉林	6.45	6.03	6.59
8	陕西	6.98	7.97	7.39	24	浙江	6.68	5.96	6.68
9	贵州	7.22	7.95	8.85	25	北京	6.77	5.93	5.91
10	广东	8.26	7.75	7.63	26	辽宁		5.86	5.63
11	甘肃	7.92	7.51	8.54	27	江苏	5.53	5.73	5.87
12	海南	7.28	7.22	7.98	28	上海	6.41	5.53	7.09
13	西藏	6.84	7.06	7.89	29	山东	6.68	5.05	5.95
14	天津	6.82	6.98	6.99	30	四川	10.02		
15	江西	5.97	6.87	7.18	31	黑龙江	7.55		7.30
16	湖南	6.25	6.78	6.24					

（7）社会保障状况（按丘陵地带排序）
①每万人敬老院数量

序号	地区	每万人敬老院数量（座）			序号	地区	每万人敬老院数量（座）		
		平原	丘陵	山区			平原	丘陵	山区
1	广西	0.54	0.61	0.63	17	山东	0.24	0.25	0.25
2	北京	0.28	0.45	0.65	18	山西	0.21	0.24	0.25
3	江苏	0.27	0.43	0.42	19	陕西	0.13	0.24	0.40
4	重庆	0.97	0.42	0.49	20	广东	0.16	0.24	0.32
5	辽宁	0.50	0.40	0.41	21	新疆	0.28	0.22	0.37
6	江西	0.31	0.37	0.50	22	湖南	0.28	0.22	0.31
7	吉林	0.30	0.36	0.52	23	黑龙江	0.27	0.22	0.26
8	湖北	0.26	0.36	0.54	24	甘肃	0.26	0.20	0.18
9	四川	0.15	0.35	0.25	25	贵州		0.20	0.21
10	内蒙古	0.26	0.34	0.31	26	福建	0.08	0.17	0.30
11	海南	0.21	0.34	0.33	27	云南	0.15	0.17	0.17
12	河南	0.27	0.33	0.39	28	宁夏	0.20	0.12	0.18
13	浙江	0.22	0.33	0.41	29	西藏	1.45	0.00	0.56
14	安徽	0.24	0.33	0.42	30	上海	0.21		
15	天津	0.28	0.30	0.54	31	青海	0.26		0.16
16	河北	0.21	0.28	0.31					

②每万人收养人数

序号	地区	每万人收养人口（人）			序号	地区	每万人收养人口（人）		
		平原	丘陵	山区			平原	丘陵	山区
1	湖北	19.67	21.79	92.11	17	新疆	7.92	6.91	20.67
2	吉林	12.68	20.90	47.71	18	广西	6.57	6.90	23.68
3	江苏	12.60	17.08	48.28	19	河北	5.69	4.84	18.61
4	江西	9.36	17.06	71.22	20	广东	5.21	4.80	22.73
5	北京	20.13	15.70	48.72	21	天津	6.48	4.07	21.36
6	浙江	11.43	14.70	45.04	22	海南	1.35	4.02	9.59
7	辽宁	15.64	14.44	63.35	23	陕西	1.52	3.64	24.93
8	山东	11.93	13.20	48.60	24	山西	2.00	2.70	9.12
9	湖南	10.19	11.87	30.22	25	云南	1.98	2.59	7.41
10	河南	10.04	11.40	48.59	26	贵州		1.93	8.40
11	重庆	39.81	11.19	27.90	27	福建	1.68	1.74	12.64
12	四川	6.40	10.06	19.40	28	甘肃	4.02	1.65	7.18
13	黑龙江	12.06	8.57	22.78	29	西藏	16.97	0.00	30.10
14	内蒙古	6.20	8.46	24.32	30	上海	21.63		
15	宁夏	6.35	8.23	15.99	31	青海	5.01		13.94
16	安徽	6.16	7.75	22.25					

（8）文体设施状况（按丘陵地带排序）

①每万人图书馆、文化站数量（仅镇域人口）

序号	地区	每万人图书馆、文化站数量（座）			序号	地区	每万人图书馆、文化站数量（座）		
		平原	丘陵	山区			平原	丘陵	山区
1	北京	0.76	1.35	1.74	17	湖北	0.86	1.04	1.26
2	天津	1.30	4.17	1.83	18	湖南	0.98	1.11	1.46
3	河北	1.55	3.64	1.91	19	广东	0.56	1.02	1.72
4	山西	2.18	2.68	2.61	20	广西	0.80	1.42	1.65
5	内蒙古	1.86	1.48	0.91	21	海南	1.13	1.67	1.74
6	辽宁	2.10	3.37	2.02	22	重庆	7.69	1.05	1.31
7	吉林	1.15	1.37	1.42	23	四川	0.39	1.75	0.82
8	黑龙江	1.03	0.87	0.72	24	贵州		1.05	1.43
9	上海	0.48			25	云南	0.94	1.16	1.59
10	江苏	0.91	1.42	1.18	26	西藏	1.93	0.18	1.87
11	浙江	1.28	1.65	1.87	27	陕西	1.98	1.82	2.38
12	安徽	1.07	1.40	2.41	28	甘肃	2.56	1.86	2.19
13	福建	1.00	1.05	1.51	29	青海	0.49		1.71
14	江西	1.34	1.21	1.88	30	宁夏	1.42	0.00	1.63
15	山东	1.80	2.12	1.69	31	新疆	2.20	2.98	1.78
16	河南	1.26	1.80	1.43					

②每万人影剧院数量（仅镇域人口）

序号	地区	每万人影剧院（座）			序号	地区	每万人影剧院（座）		
		平原	丘陵	山区			平原	丘陵	山区
1	新疆	0.47	1.07	0.43	17	湖南	0.36	0.27	0.34
2	北京	0.48	1.06	0.91	18	辽宁	0.16	0.25	0.16
3	山西	0.25	0.45	0.37	19	河南	0.16	0.21	0.30
4	湖北	0.45	0.42	0.26	20	贵州		0.18	0.12
5	陕西	0.40	0.41	0.26	21	河北	0.13	0.18	0.13
6	甘肃	0.60	0.39	0.27	22	重庆	0.00	0.17	0.07
7	浙江	0.38	0.39	0.49	23	内蒙古	0.15	0.16	0.07
8	云南	0.26	0.35	0.28	24	四川	0.12	0.12	0.24
9	江苏	0.39	0.35	1.18	25	吉林	0.14	0.09	0.21
10	山东	0.24	0.33	0.20	26	黑龙江	0.08	0.07	0.07
11	广东	0.29	0.32	0.42	27	天津	0.12	0.00	0.00
12	福建	0.24	0.32	0.50	28	西藏	0.00	0.00	0.00
13	安徽	0.21	0.32	0.33	29	宁夏	0.26	0.00	0.18
14	海南	0.33	0.30	0.13	30	上海	0.25		
15	广西	0.25	0.30	0.22	31	青海	0.49		0.25
16	江西	0.26	0.28	0.53					

③每万人体育场馆（仅镇域人口）

序号	地区	每万人体育场馆（座）			序号	地区	每万人体育场馆（座）		
		平原	丘陵	山区			平原	丘陵	山区
1	新疆	1.01	1.07	0.57	17	湖南	0.10	0.27	0.21
2	北京	0.18	1.06	0.30	18	辽宁	0.44	0.25	0.24
3	山西	0.79	0.45	1.03	19	河南	0.41	0.21	0.50
4	湖北	0.11	0.42	0.14	20	贵州		0.18	0.13
5	陕西	0.40	0.41	0.33	21	河北	0.16	0.18	0.21
6	甘肃	0.54	0.39	0.30	22	重庆	0.00	0.17	0.07
7	浙江	0.38	0.39	0.56	23	内蒙古	0.15	0.16	0.37
8	云南	0.23	0.35	0.27	24	四川	0.17	0.12	0.46
9	江苏	0.36	0.35	1.78	25	吉林	0.08	0.09	0.16
10	山东	0.39	0.33	0.29	26	黑龙江	0.27	0.07	0.27
11	广东	0.82	0.32	0.38	27	天津	0.17	0.00	0.00
12	福建	0.27	0.32	0.30	28	西藏	0.18	0.00	0.00
13	安徽	0.35	0.32	0.63	29	宁夏	0.35	0.00	0.05
14	海南	0.38	0.30	0.13	30	上海	0.21		
15	广西	0.46	0.30	0.31	31	青海	0.49		0.36
16	江西	0.30	0.28	0.69					

以上8项反映城镇化的指标中，按丘陵地带所作的排序，各指标的顺序有很大的差别，原因何在？

我们知道，人均指标、密度指标都是由对应的两个额度指标计算而来。那么任何一个额度的大小，都会影响到相对值指标的变化。一般来说，人口与人均成反比，镇域面积与密度成反比，甚至不由总量决定。中国人口分布极度失衡，自然环境东西差异极大，这就决定了在采用相对指标时，往往意识中的落后地区却排序在前。

那么能否说明这样的分析不科学，不反映地区发展的真实情况？我们认为，这恰恰说明，城镇化的过程中偏远地区与东部地区并不是按同样目标建设的。西部地区、山区应有自己的城镇化特点，如按城市的要求去配置建制镇公共服务设施，由于人口稀少，其利用率远不如城市。

另外，从城镇化的投资倾向上看，小城镇资源配置比大城市容易，潜在需求的满足额度小，这就可以保证投资风险小、回收快，具有更高的投资效益，对地方经济的带动更具有"四两拨千斤"的作用。这是我们今后更值得研究的问题。

2. 为了更好的了解指标的地区、地形差异，我们把上述主要指标按地区、地形做一个综合比较：

（1）按地区、地形分解的人均年用电量比较

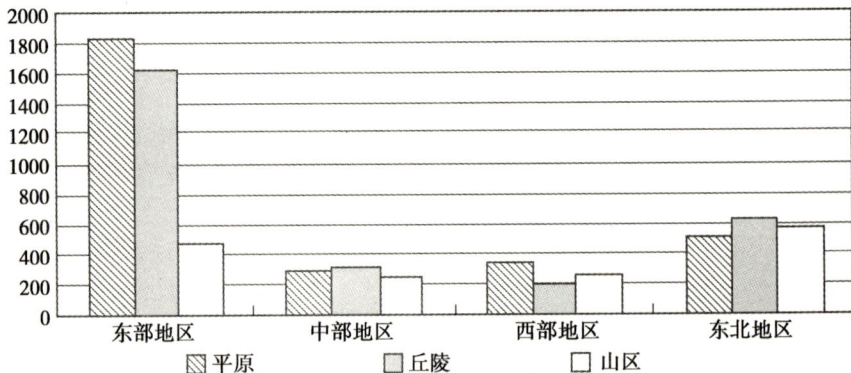

东部偏远地带的丘陵、山区高于其他地区，这是东部总体发达的必然。但中部、东北部的丘陵地带以及东北地区的山区都有较高的人均用电量，说明资源型产业比例较高，与我们前述的财政收入分析相一致。

（2）按地区、地形分解的路网密度比较

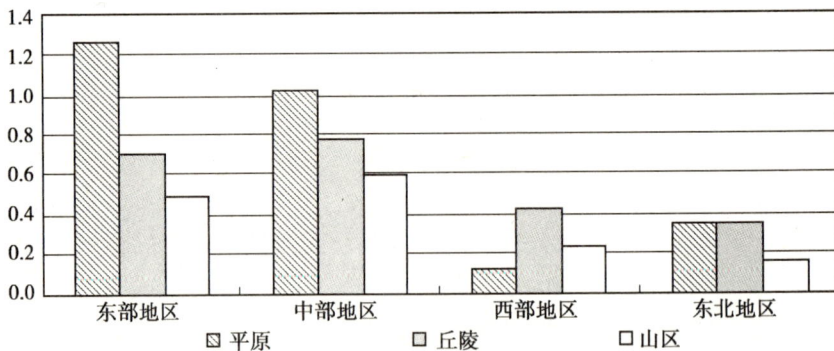

东部地区自古以来交通发达，才有了商贾云集、人口聚集的繁荣。改革开放以来，东部地区利用海上通道的对外贸易得到了更大的发展。这是由得天独厚的地理位置所决定的，但也正是因为有了经济基础，其路网才更加发达。

为此，须进一步分析建制镇行政区域大小的比较：

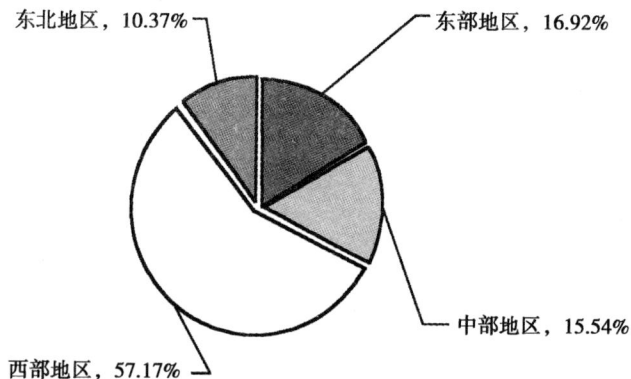

西部地区占有一半以上的建制镇行政区域面积，基数大、密度低。
再比较村镇密度：

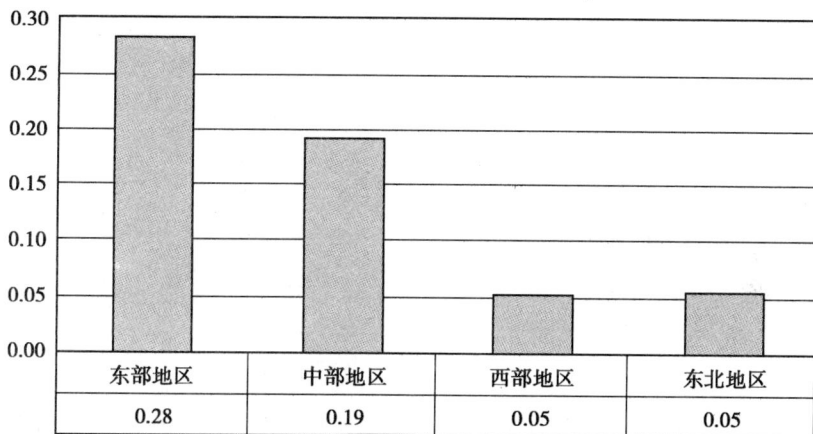

东部地区	中部地区	西部地区	东北地区
0.28	0.19	0.05	0.05

显然，东部省份村镇密度高，西部省份村镇密度低。
进一步比较地区建制镇公路里程比例：

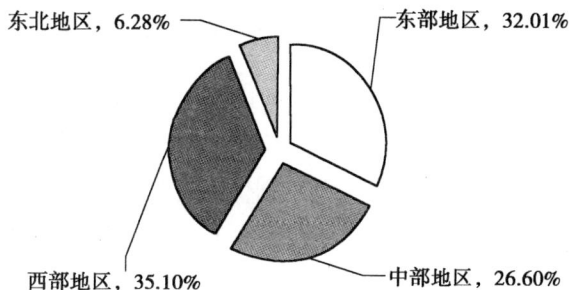

理论上讲，村镇分布稀疏需要更长的公路里程，而不是密集的路网。由于车流量、单里程投资成本等因素，西部公路建设靠过桥费回收资金有一定的困难，而地方财政的拮据，不可能完全依靠地方财政实现，需要"先致富，再建路"。

（3）按地区、地形分解的教育比较

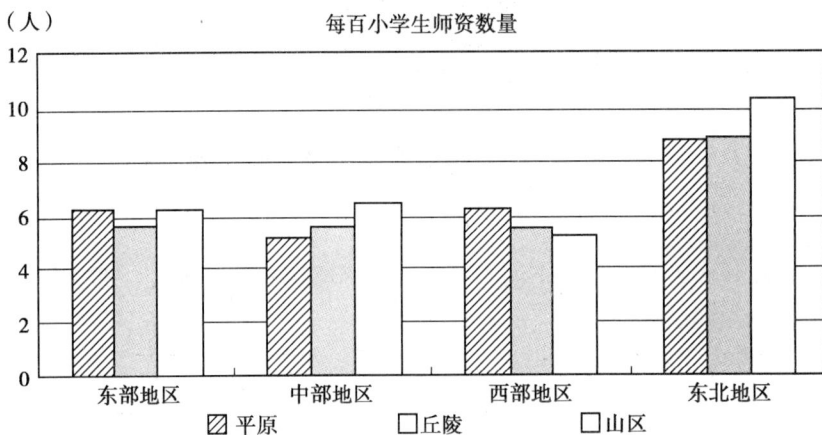

每百小学生师资数量

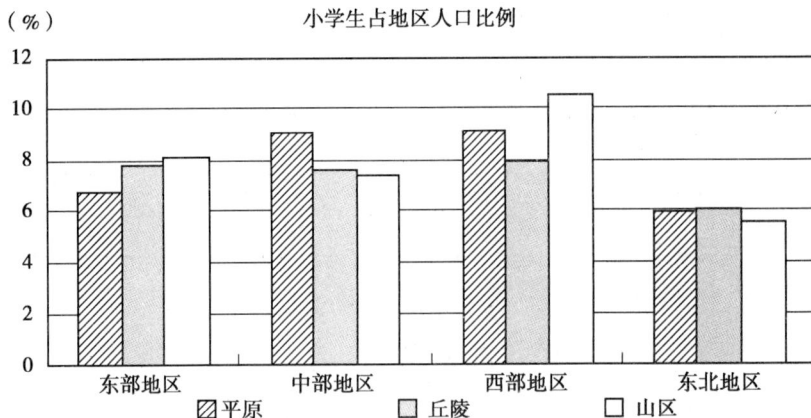

小学生占地区人口比例

以小学生师资指标与小学生人口指标对比，可以看出东北地区小学生人数实际在减少，所以相对百名学生的教师比例就高了。

（4）按地区、地形分解的社会福利保障比较

敬老院、福利院之所以丘陵、山区为多，主要原因在于城乡有着不同的社会保障制度。城市以福利金融制度和辅助的财政补充为社会福利系统，而农村主要靠家庭及家族集群的集体赡养。所以，农村敬老院的建设

每万人敬老院、福利院数量

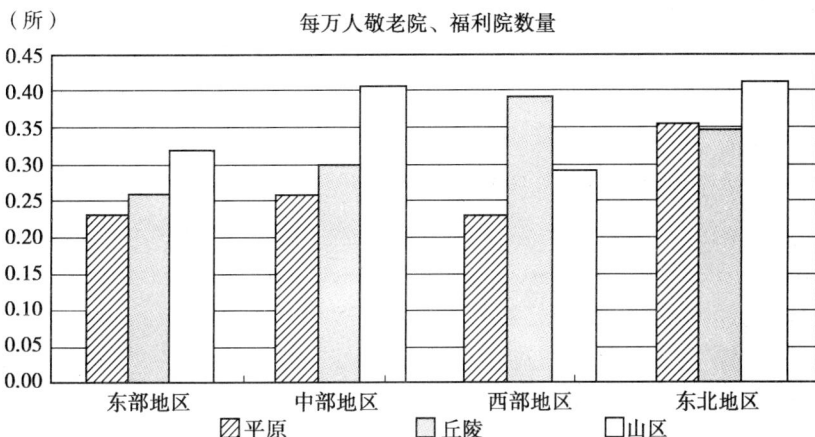

| | 东部地区 | 中部地区 | 西部地区 | 东北地区 |

☑ 平原　　　□ 丘陵　　　□ 山区

（人）　　　　　　每万人收养人口

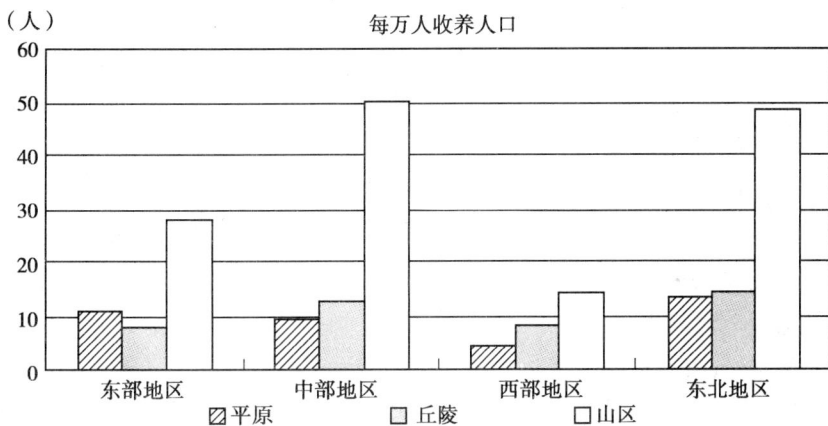

| | 东部地区 | 中部地区 | 西部地区 | 东北地区 |

☑ 平原　　　□ 丘陵　　　□ 山区

更早于城市，农村集中收养的人口也高于城市。由此还可以看出一种现象：越富裕的地方，平均家庭收入也相对高，集中收养的比例就会低。这或许就是山区高于平原的原因。

我国已逐步进入老龄化的社会，城镇化的发展，将必定面临着养老问题的模式设计。农村实现社保基金，按城市福利金融的体制建立农村社保体系，但我们不应忽视集中收养方式的敬老院的建设。在这个问题上，城市要向农村学习——高质量地建立敬老院等社会福利设施。

五、根据以上指标分析得出如下结论

1. 建制镇的发展要坚持科学的发展观

我国幅员辽阔，地区差别极大，先进与落后不是人为的结果，也不是

短期之内可以解决的。客观的地理环境、地方人文、生活的特点，形成了历史演变的必然结果。因此，建制镇的发展及其城镇化的规划，应该充分的分析当地的历史演进因素，把握当地的人文特点，挖掘自身潜力和资源优势，因地制宜的制订发展规划。特别要避免我国城市发展中存在的同格化倾向。另外，保护当地环境和历史人文遗产，也是我国未来城镇化建设发展中，建制镇规划的一项重要原则。从继承和发展的角度规划和建设建制镇。

2. 建制镇的发展要坚持改革开放的方向

在我国，"镇"是因行政管理而确立，并随经济发展而形成的，更多强调管辖，从责权的角度封闭了地区的发展思路。而在西方的概念中，镇是规模更小的"定居点"，通常位于农村或城乡结合部，更多从人居角度考虑。

我国城市建设中普遍存在着贪大求洋的倾向，无序的私搭乱建成为城市管理的死角，甚至形成"城中村"，给治安管理带来很大的隐患，根本原因就在于缺乏前期的规划和对小城镇建设的定位。在城市地界扩大的过程中，镇越来越拥有了定居点的功能，成为城乡协调发展的桥梁与节点。因此，建制镇的发展和规划要与城市的建设及发展相结合，镇与镇形成合理的布局和资源的互补，不盲目的自我发展工业，创造适宜人居的条件。建制镇的规划要有其自身的特点，作为城市的附属卫星城，更应该以宜于人居为目的。这就是一种开放的思路。

3. 建制镇的发展要坚持创造更多的就业机会

"定居点"应成为建制镇发展的一个基本出发点，一个地区对人的吸引力应该成为地区发展的选择目标。人口流失对建制镇来说，特别是贫困地区建制镇的发展来说，已经成为突出的问题，成为当地经济发展的桎梏。我们所作的统计分析虽不深刻、翔实，但已可窥见一斑。这种人口的"蒸发"现象，在工业国家里几乎都曾经出现过，成为城乡人口失衡的重大社会问题，我国现在也正面临着这样的挑战。

4. 建制镇的发展要以地、县两级城市为主体

统计分析中我们已经看到，建制镇的发展还需要投入资金完成基础设施的建设，而依靠镇财政一己之力是根本不可能完成的。因此，应该把建制镇的发展作为城市规划的组成部分，并作为城市发展的一项指标。从服务城市的角度创造农副产品深加工基地、小商品生产基地、旅游度假基地等，以创造更多的就业机会。

我们对东部、中部、北部的 19 个省市做了一个大概的建制镇隶属比较（见《报告》后附光盘）。这 19 个省市的 13011 个建制镇，占了全国的近 70%，除三大直辖市的建制镇外，河北、山西、山东、辽宁、广东、江苏、湖北等省，建制镇几乎 100% 的由省、地、县三级城市所覆盖。这说明中国已经进入全面城镇化的发展时期，建制镇的规划与发展是省、地、县三级城市自身发展不可推卸的责任，并应该成为城市发展的考核指标。而从比例中可以看到，地级市所辖建制镇占到了镇个数的 64.74%、镇人口的 65.61%、镇地域的 77.73%，实际为城市的发展提供了更大的空间。

5. 建制镇的发展要坚持环境优先的原则

多数建制镇的环境依然优于城市，这应该成为建制镇发展的一个优势。尽管从数据分析上我们无从把握建制镇的环境污染问题，但从地方财政的分析中，隐约可见受利益驱使的环境破坏隐忧。建制镇的发展，不能再走城市建设先污染后治理的老路，必须从合理规划、杜绝污染出发。根据资源特点审慎定位，做到先规划后建设，先措施后实施，不仅包括镇区规划，同时也应该包括经济发展规划。为此，国家应该在政策和资金上予以支持，在试点的基础上加以推广，并把建制镇的改造列入经济发展纲要和五年计划。

6. 建制镇的发展要坚持以人为本的原则

传统的城市规划侧重于城市功能，并以工商业发展需要作为城市功能的定位和配套，以形成巨大的城市机器。受辖于城市的建制镇应更多地从人居环境的角度规划自己的小城镇建设。特别是在前已经提到过的敬老院问题，尽管乡镇的设施及服务质量达不到城市的水平，但因乡镇起步早，时间长，数量远远多于城市，并有空气新鲜、环境安宁的优势，更适于老年人居住养生。

7. 建制镇发展要以提高管理水平为核心

建制镇的发展不仅仅是空间规划和物质布局的问题，同时也是社会发展的管理问题。城镇是一个系统，城镇管理是一门科学，需要多学科的知识融合。对管理者进行必要的培训，提高科学管理意识、管理水平，应该形成一种长效机制。

另外，应该有一支城镇建设的专业队伍，长期跟踪、研究乡镇建设问题，为政府决策提供政策依据，为管理培训提供针对性的教育内容。目前，我们对农房制订了相应的建设导则，城镇规划实际上也把建制镇的规划管理纳入了进去，但是，由于依托规划单位，单一从设计角度指导，而又以经济效益为先，实际上，小城镇的发展与规划只是停留在口号上。

8. 建制镇发展要依托地方的农业特色

寿光的大葱、蔬菜造就了当地的脱水蔬菜产业，陕北的苹果吸引了东南亚的果酱商，赣州的脐橙、和田的大枣等成为了城镇的品牌。发展城镇，不是偏废农业，必须将城乡协调一体化，作为建制镇发展的根本原则。结合农业的发展，如内蒙古可在植草固沙的同时建立牧草基地、养殖基地、乳品加工基地等。

9. 提倡从区域规划的角度，整合建制镇规划

区域规划主要是在城市规划和工矿区规划的基础上发展起来的，要对整个规划地区国民经济与社会发展中的建设布局问题作出战略决策，把同区域开发与整治有关的各项重大建设落实到具体地域，进行各部门综合协调的总体布局，为编制中长期部门规划和城市规划提供重要依据。可把区域规划视作介于经济区划与城市规划之间的一个中间环节，经济区划为区域规划指明方向，区域规划为城市规划提供依据。因此，只有贯彻区域规划的思想，才可能将同辖区内的各建制镇协调一致，防止各司其政的盲目发展，及同格化的竞争。这样才能促使城市规划跳出城市建成区、规划控制区的范围，从经济区域范围协调发展建制镇群。

10. 加强和完善建制镇的统计工作

由于建制镇的统计工作尚不完善，并且为每两年公布一次，每次的统计指标也不尽相同，这就给连续分析和研究建制镇问题带来了困难。

建制镇的统计也是作为城镇化发展评价、分析、预测的数据基础，但所不同的是，建制镇的发展是城市发展的组成部分，并且不完全与城市的发展指标相一致。既然国家已经着手进行了建制镇的统计，就应该根据建制镇发展的特点和国家对建制镇发展的定位要求设计建制镇的统计指标，并作为城市统计的子项指标体系，纳入到城市统计之中，同时，不断坚持完善下去。

（本报告执笔：赵昭）

第五部分 城市排行榜及部分城市数据

第一节 中国城市科学发展典范城市

排 名	城 市	排 名	城 市
1	厦门市	11	上海市
2	宁波市	12	嘉兴市
3	苏州市	13	广州市
4	杭州市	14	大连市
5	常州市	15	鄂尔多斯市
6	珠海市	16	镇江市
7	深圳市	17	南京市
7	北京市	18	青岛市
9	中山市	19	威海市
10	无锡市	19	长沙市

上述城市即为"中国城市科学发展综合评价（E&G）体系"综合排名前 20 位的城市。

第二节 中国城市科学发展典型城市

一、综合实力典型城市

排 名	城 市	排 名	城 市
21	天津市	36	济南市
22	绍兴市	37	烟台市
23	舟山市	38	东莞市
24	呼和浩特市	39	包头市
25	佛山市	40	芜湖市
26	金华市	41	台州市
26	东营市	42	福州市
28	成都市	43	南通市
28	银川市	44	扬州市
30	湖州市	45	铜陵市
30	武汉市	46	乌海市
32	太原市	47	昆明市
33	郑州市	48	淄博市
34	马鞍山市	49	温州市
35	沈阳市	50	秦皇岛市

上述城市即为"中国城市科学发展综合评价（E&G）体系"综合排名第 21—50 位的城市。

二、系统发展典型城市（三大母系统排名前 50 名城市）

经济发展水平系统

排　名	城　市	排　名	城　市
1	苏州市	26	泰安市
2	扬州市	27	朔州市
3	宁波市	28	济南市
4	台州市	29	深圳市
5	东营市	30	连云港市
6	常州市	31	泰州市
7	嘉兴市	32	南通市
8	金华市	33	铜陵市
9	厦门市	34	大连市
10	中山市	35	徐州市
11	无锡市	36	广州市
12	呼和浩特市	37	南京市
12	上海市	38	榆林市
14	青岛市	39	天津市
15	晋城市	40	长治市
16	镇江市	41	延安市
17	盐城市	42	太原市
18	潍坊市	42	新余市
19	石家庄市	44	鹰潭市
20	杭州市	45	舟山市
21	烟台市	46	泉州市
22	珠海市	47	长沙市
23	湖州市	48	北京市
23	绍兴市	49	鄂尔多斯市
23	昆明市	50	威海市

公共服务水平系统

排　名	城　市	排　名	城　市
1	北京市	26	鄂尔多斯市
2	厦门市	27	威海市
3	深圳市	28	舟山市
4	上海市	29	呼伦贝尔市
5	珠海市	30	盘锦市
6	杭州市	31	常州市
7	广州市	32	长春市
7	克拉玛依市	33	鞍山市
9	大连市	33	长沙市
10	天津市	35	抚顺市
11	苏州市	36	昆明市
12	宁波市	37	兰州市
13	武汉市	38	大庆市
14	包头市	39	中山市
15	银川市	40	济南市
16	沈阳市	40	佛山市
17	乌海市	42	青岛市
18	南京市	43	郑州市
19	呼和浩特市	44	阳泉市
20	嘉峪关市	45	乌鲁木齐市
21	本溪市	46	马鞍山市
22	太原市	47	三亚市
23	无锡市	48	营口市
24	攀枝花市	48	辽阳市
25	铜陵市	50	石嘴山市

居民实际享有水平系统

排 名	城 市	排 名	城 市
1	常州市	26	马鞍山市
2	北京市	27	无锡市
3	佛山市	28	金华市
4	杭州市	29	江门市
5	镇江市	30	克拉玛依市
5	嘉兴市	31	绍兴市
7	宁波市	32	三亚市
8	中山市	33	沈阳市
9	东莞市	34	舟山市
10	厦门市	35	衢州市
11	湖州市	35	广州市
12	南通市	37	岳阳市
13	珠海市	38	丽水市
14	成都市	39	廊坊市
15	泉州市	40	盐城市
16	苏州市	41	温州市
16	郑州市	42	南京市
18	深圳市	43	青岛市
19	鄂尔多斯市	44	银川市
20	台州市	45	随州市
20	长沙市	46	上海市
20	惠州市	47	徐州市
23	威海市	48	盘锦市
24	嘉峪关市	49	大连市
25	福州市	50	龙岩市

第三节　中国城市特色发展优势城市

一、经济增长效率优势城市

即经济发展总水平子系统排名前 10 名的城市：

城市	城市
珠海市	上海市
东莞市	榆林市
厦门市	嘉兴市
杭州市	苏州市
宁波市	绍兴市

二、居民收入统筹优势城市

即居民收入水平子系统排名前 10 名的城市：

城市	城市
长沙市	中山市
常州市	佛山市
镇江市	宁波市
舟山市	湖州市
天津市	鞍山市

三、要素利用效率优势城市

即发展要素利用效率子系统排名前 10 名的城市：

城市	城市
鄂尔多斯市	金华市
延安市	盐城市
榆林市	苏州市
泰州市	庆阳市
吕梁市	绍兴市

四、人居生活环境优势城市

即居民生活环境子系统排名前 10 名的城市：

城市	城市
无锡市	苏州市
杭州市	银川市
厦门市	岳阳市
青岛市	宁波市
长沙市	合肥市

五、外部效应调控优势城市

即发展外部效应子系统排名前 10 名的城市：

城市	城市
鹰潭市	内江市
铜陵市	曲靖市
昆明市	铜川市
日照市	呼和浩特市
阜阳市	淮南市
黄石市	

六、发展速度提升优势城市

即相较 2008 年排名增幅速度前 10 名的城市：

城市	城市
岳阳市	朔州市
宜宾市	宿迁市
盐城市	新余市
鹰潭市	榆林市
枣庄市	吉林市

第四节　2011年中国城市科学发展综合数据分析表（部分）

（综合指数排名为 1—50 位的城市）

一、城市经济发展水平母系统

1. 城市经济发展总水平子系统

| 二级指标 | 城市经济发展总水平子系统 | | | | | | | | | | |
| 三级指标 | 人均GDP | | | | | 人均收入增长效率 | | | | | 分值小结 |
	数值（万元）	排名	分值	上年度城镇人均可支配收入（元）	本年度城镇人均可支配收入（元）	收入增长率	GDP增长率（%）	比值	排名	分值	
厦门市	68938	17	0.936	23948	26131	0.09116	8.00	0.011394	28	0.892	1.828
宁波市	60720	26	0.900	25196	27237	0.08100	6.70	0.012090	25	0.904	1.804
苏州市	122565	2	0.996	24680	27188	0.10162	11.50	0.008837	75	0.704	1.700
杭州市	63333	21	0.920	23534	26171	0.11205	10.00	0.011205	29	0.888	1.808
常州市	70138	15	0.944	21234	23392	0.10163	11.70	0.008686	83	0.672	1.616
珠海市	69890	16	0.940	20949	22859	0.09117	6.60	0.013814	23	0.912	1.852
深圳市	92772	5	0.984	26729	29245	0.09413	10.70	0.008797	77	0.696	1.680
北京市	70452	14	0.948	24725	26738	0.08142	10.20	0.007982	117	0.536	1.484
中山市	62304	23	0.912	21560	23088	0.07087	10.20	0.006948	181	0.280	1.192
无锡市	107365	3	0.992	23263	25027	0.07583	11.60	0.006537	213	0.152	1.144
上海市	78989	10	0.964	26675	28838	0.08109	8.24	0.009841	42	0.836	1.800
嘉兴市	44898	42	0.836	22481	24693	0.09839	9.31	0.010569	33	0.872	1.708

城市经济发展总水平子系统

二级指标	人均GDP			人均收入增长效率							分值小结
三级指标	数值（万元）	排名	分值	上年度城镇人均可支配收入（元）	本年度城镇人均可支配收入（元）	人均收入增长率	GDP增长率（%）	比值	排名	分值	
广州市	89082	6	0.980	25317	27610	0.09057	11.70	0.007741	128	0.492	1.472
大连市	70781	13	0.952	17500	19014	0.08651	15.00	0.005768	247	0.016	0.968
鄂尔多斯市	134400	1	1.000	19435	21883	0.12596	23.00	0.005476	254	-0.012	0.988
镇江市	62084	24	0.908	19001	21041	0.10736	13.67	0.007854	123	0.512	1.420
南京市	67455	18	0.932	22337	24678	0.10480	11.55	0.009074	64	0.748	1.680
青岛市	57251	27	0.896	20464	22368	0.09304	12.20	0.007626	137	0.456	1.352
威海市	63519	20	0.924	18537	20117	0.08523	12.09	0.007050	172	0.316	1.240
长沙市	56620	28	0.892	17891	20238	0.13118	14.70	0.008924	70	0.724	1.616
天津市	62574	22	0.916	19423	21402	0.10189	16.50	0.006175	228	0.092	1.008
绍兴市	54316	32	0.876	24646	26874	0.09040	9.30	0.009720	46	0.820	1.696
舟山市	55311	30	0.884	22257	24082	0.08200	11.00	0.007454	151	0.400	1.284
呼和浩特市	61108	25	0.904	20267	22397	0.10510	15.90	0.006610	208	0.172	1.076
佛山市	80686	9	0.968	22494	24578	0.09265	13.50	0.006863	189	0.248	1.216

城市经济发展总水平子系统

二级指标	人均GDP			人均收入增长效率							分值小结
三级指标	数值（万元）	排名	分值	上年度城镇人均可支配收入（元）	本年度城镇人均可支配收入（元）	收入增长率	GDP增长率（%）	比值	排名	分值	
金华市	34294	70	0.724	21408	22915	0.07039	9.10	0.007736	131	0.480	1.204
东营市	102370	4	0.988	19487	21313	0.09370	12.40	0.007557	145	0.424	1.412
成都市	35215	67	0.736	15580	17589	0.12895	14.70	0.008772	80	0.684	1.420
银川市	34453	69	0.728	14180	15715	0.10825	13.00	0.008327	103	0.592	1.320
湖州市	38865	54	0.788	21604	23280	0.07758	10.20	0.007606	140	0.444	1.232
武汉市	51144	37	0.856	16712	18385	0.10011	13.70	0.007307	156	0.380	1.236
太原市	44319	43	0.832	15230	15607	0.02475	2.60	0.009521	52	0.796	1.628
郑州市	44231	45	0.824	15732	17117	0.08804	11.40	0.007723	132	0.476	1.300
马鞍山市	51879	35	0.864	18330	20390	0.11238	12.10	0.009288	59	0.768	1.632
沈阳市	54654	31	0.880	17013	18475	0.08593	14.05	0.006116	233	0.072	0.952
济南市	50376	39	0.848	20802	22722	0.09230	12.18	0.007578	144	0.428	1.276
烟台市	52683	34	0.868	19350	21125	0.09173	13.50	0.006795	193	0.232	1.100
东莞市	56601	29	0.888	30275	33045	0.09149	5.30	0.017263	11	0.960	1.848

二级指标	城市经济发展总水平子系统										
三级指标	人均GDP			人均收入增长效率							
	数值（万元）	排名	分值	上年度城镇人均可支配收入（元）	本年度城镇人均可支配收入（元）	收入增长率	GDP增长率（%）	比值	排名	分值	分值小结
包头市	84979	8	0.972	20861	23089	0.10680	17.60	0.006068	237	0.056	1.028
芜湖市	39142	52	0.796	14939	16747	0.12103	15.36	0.007879	120	0.524	1.320
台州市	35489	66	0.740	22738	24429	0.07437	8.52	0.008729	82	0.676	1.416
福州市	38015	56	0.780	19009	20289	0.06734	13.00	0.005180	258	-0.028	0.752
南通市	37642	58	0.772	17540	19469	0.10998	14.00	0.007856	122	0.516	1.288
扬州市	40418	49	0.808	15465	17332	0.12072	13.82	0.008735	81	0.680	1.488
铜陵市	46765	41	0.840	15173	16769	0.10519	13.70	0.007678	134	0.468	1.308
乌海市	64147	19	0.928	15999	17621	0.10138	22.80	0.004447	268	-0.068	0.860
昆明市	25826	113	0.552	14482	16496	0.13907	12.80	0.010865	30	0.884	1.436
淄博市	54229	33	0.872	17629	19284	0.09388	13.20	0.007112	168	0.332	1.204
温州市	32588	76	0.700	22851	24467	0.07072	8.50	0.008320	105	0.584	1.284
秦皇岛市	27110	107	0.576	14081	15961	0.13351	9.50	0.014054	22	0.916	1.492

2. 城市发展要素利用效率子系统

发展要素利用效率子系统

二级指标	单位土地面积产出率			产出收益率			劳动生产率			万元GDP水耗			万元GDP电耗			万元工业总产值电耗			分值小结
三级指标	数值	排名	分值	数值	排名	分值	数值	排名	分值	数值	排序	分值	数值	排序	分值	数值	排序	分值	
厦门市	81945.042	218	0.132	0.1385	4	0.988	377045.938	130	0.484	0.00112	237	0.056	0.0579	205	0.184	0.0248	154	0.388	2.232
宁波市	172482.171	60	0.764	0.1000	16	0.940	689346.471	41	0.840	0.00055	146	0.420	0.0469	184	0.268	0.0207	123	0.512	3.744
苏州市	238895.062	26	0.900	0.0963	21	0.920	1771262.260	4	0.988	0.0040	103	0.592	0.0263	97	0.616	0.0080	41	0.840	4.856
杭州市	129454.275	120	0.524	0.1024	15	0.944	546672.098	71	0.720	0.00081	204	0.188	0.0593	208	0.172	0.0245	148	0.412	2.960
常州市	188054.478	46	0.820	0.0857	36	0.860	1663767.325	5	0.984	0.00098	225	0.104	0.0674	224	0.108	0.0247	151	0.400	3.276
珠海市	88022.263	206	0.180	0.0976	19	0.928	422530.710	108	0.572	0.00208	270	-0.076	0.0765	239	0.048	0.0239	144	0.428	2.080
深圳市	100877.215	175	0.304	0.1074	11	0.960	718036.465	36	0.860	0.00124	243	0.032	0.0618	215	0.144	0.0210	127	0.496	2.796
北京市	90022.222	202	0.196	0.0705	83	0.672	198878.143	233	0.072	0.00076	197	0.216	0.0491	193	0.232	0.0253	159	0.368	2.080
中山市	391602.650	3	0.992	0.1668	2	0.996	1616721.355	6	0.980	0.00009	5	0.984	0.0882	249	0.008	0.0271	170	0.324	3.960
无锡市	230033.180	30	0.884	0.1688	1	1.000	1861206.661	3	0.992	0.00050	133	0.472	0.0389	157	0.376	0.0152	91	0.640	4.204
上海市	169824.492	64	0.748	0.0739	68	0.732	756516.404	31	0.880	0.00162	259	-0.032	0.0665	223	0.112	0.0291	180	0.284	2.992
嘉兴市	233905.878	29	0.888	0.0769	60	0.764	536292.325	76	0.700	0.00023	41	0.840	0.0304	120	0.524	0.0132	79	0.688	4.372
广州市	98578.355	180	0.284	0.0920	27	0.896	507596.685	81	0.680	0.00114	238	0.052	0.0448	180	0.284	0.0238	143	0.432	2.496
大连市	168585.465	67	0.736	0.0750	65	0.744	747454.339	33	0.872	0.00078	198	0.212	0.0365	148	0.412	0.0191	111	0.560	3.688
鄂尔多斯市	198256.881	42	0.836	0.0833	41	0.840	1324091.205	7	0.976	0.00007	2	0.996	0.0054	8	0.972	0.0044	15	0.944	5.468
镇江市	160776.587	77	0.696	0.0607	131	0.480	939419.136	19	0.928	0.00073	190	0.244	0.0433	174	0.308	0.0200	121	0.520	3.176

二级指标	发展要素利用效率子系统																		
三级指标	单位土地面积产出率			产出收益率			劳动生产率			万元GDP水耗			万元GDP电耗			万元工业总产值电耗			分值小结
	数值	排名	分值	数值	排名	分值	数值	排名	分值	数值	排序	分值	数值	排序	分值	数值	排序	分值	
南京市	70740.147	237	0.056	0.1027	14	0.948	622005.598	50	0.804	0.00190	265	-0.056	0.0662	222	0.116	0.0315	188	0.252	2.120
青岛市	177797.333	54	0.788	0.0777	56	0.780	793184.667	25	0.904	0.00044	117	0.536	0.0231	82	0.676	0.0115	67	0.736	4.420
威海市	138011.574	107	0.576	0.0576	156	0.380	1273416.919	8	0.972	0.00023	39	0.848	0.0176	55	0.784	0.0051	19	0.928	4.488
长沙市	150392.133	87	0.656	0.0658	109	0.568	366853.981	137	0.456	0.00050	131	0.480	0.0127	35	0.864	0.0055	20	0.924	3.948
天津市	113623.112	148	0.412	0.1093	9	0.968	716165.707	37	0.856	0.00065	177	0.296	0.0681	225	0.104	0.0316	190	0.244	2.880
绍兴市	255459.720	18	0.932	0.0675	100	0.604	613552.563	53	0.792	0.00035	88	0.652	0.0159	48	0.812	0.0056	22	0.916	4.708
舟山市	104948.255	165	0.344	0.0911	29	0.888	552452.900	69	0.728	0.00050	132	0.476	0.0431	173	0.312	0.0218	134	0.468	3.216
呼和浩特市	106752.760	164	0.348	0.0650	111	0.560	370895.981	134	0.468	0.00061	169	0.328	0.0180	58	0.772	0.0153	93	0.632	3.108
佛山市	319264.715	8	0.972	0.0528	174	0.308	2214215.038	2	0.996	0.00054	144	0.428	0.0775	241	0.040	0.0266	167	0.336	3.080
金华市	250149.958	21	0.920	0.0728	72	0.716	585301.773	59	0.768	0.00018	23	0.912	0.0143	43	0.832	0.0071	32	0.876	5.024
东营市	199900.000	40	0.844	0.0393	240	0.044	1169914.750	11	0.960	0.00033	81	0.680	0.0438	176	0.300	0.0199	120	0.524	3.352
成都市	102564.993	170	0.324	0.0860	34	0.868	309121.950	168	0.332	0.00043	113	0.552	0.0338	136	0.460	0.0183	106	0.580	3.116
银川市	50273.765	269	-0.072	0.0762	62	0.756	239654.577	207	0.176	0.00100	227	0.096	0.0601	212	0.156	0.0396	208	0.172	1.284
湖州市	144977.145	97	0.616	0.0726	73	0.712	698248.443	40	0.844	0.00045	120	0.524	0.0419	169	0.328	0.0176	103	0.592	3.616
武汉市	97281.263	184	0.268	0.0684	95	0.624	364801.208	138	0.452	0.00125	244	0.028	0.0485	189	0.248	0.0262	163	0.352	1.972
太原市	63071.057	250	0.004	0.0761	63	0.752	199086.455	232	0.076	0.00090	216	0.140	0.0913	254	-0.012	0.0754	261	-0.040	0.920
郑州市	98175.231	181	0.280	0.0913	28	0.892	487935.130	89	0.648	0.00069	184	0.268	0.0718	228	0.092	0.0399	210	0.164	2.344

二级指标	发展要素利用效率子系统																			
三级指标	单位土地面积产出率			产出收益率			劳动生产率			万元GDP水耗			万元GDP电耗			万元工业总产值电耗			分值小结
	数值	排名	分值	数值	排名	分值	数值	排名	分值	数值	排序	分值	数值	排序	分值	数值	排序	分值	
马鞍山市	87617.171	208	0.172	0.0957	25	0.904	791682.843	26	0.900	0.00311	282	-0.124	0.1329	274	-0.092	0.0751	260	-0.036	1.724
沈阳市	108063.638	161	0.360	0.0750	64	0.748	774082.688	29	0.888	0.00094	219	0.128	0.0334	134	0.468	0.0121	72	0.716	3.308
济南市	99742.991	177	0.296	0.0627	124	0.508	343156.970	149	0.408	0.00043	114	0.548	0.0415	165	0.344	0.0263	165	0.344	2.448
烟台市	157522.979	79	0.688	0.0511	180	0.284	1110644.659	12	0.956	0.00024	45	0.824	0.0197	63	0.752	0.0065	27	0.896	4.400
东莞市	432633.816	1	1.000	0.0614	128	0.492	2677110.825	1	1.000	0.00319	283	-0.128	0.1172	269	-0.072	0.0634	248	0.012	2.304
包头市	119164.725	129	0.488	0.0601	137	0.456	687996.223	42	0.836	0.00100	226	0.100	0.0700	226	0.100	0.0680	252	-0.004	1.976
芜湖市	69384.592	238	0.052	0.0770	59	0.768	745908.825	34	0.868	0.00105	233	0.072	0.0474	185	0.264	0.0231	142	0.436	2.460
台州市	175901.112	57	0.776	0.0667	102	0.596	496089.023	85	0.664	0.00036	91	0.640	0.0277	102	0.596	0.0167	96	0.620	3.892
福州市	142297.530	102	0.596	0.0750	66	0.740	389942.710	124	0.508	0.00050	134	0.468	0.0289	112	0.556	0.0121	73	0.712	3.580
南通市	305617.426	10	0.964	0.0693	90	0.644	1058692.027	13	0.952	0.00042	110	0.564	0.0296	115	0.544	0.0121	71	0.720	4.388
扬州市	234986.620	28	0.892	0.0690	91	0.640	1209896.202	9	0.968	0.00042	112	0.556	0.0305	121	0.520	0.0010	1	1.000	4.576
铜陵市	73134.043	235	0.064	0.0961	22	0.916	611898.287	54	0.788	0.00049	129	0.488	0.1203	270	-0.076	0.0607	243	0.032	2.212
乌海市	40416.623	278	-0.108	0.0700	87	0.656	388514.947	125	0.504	0.00248	275	-0.096	0.3204	283	-0.128	0.2419	284	-0.132	0.696
昆明市	63461.288	248	0.012	0.1115	8	0.972	206324.311	228	0.092	0.00106	234	0.068	0.0475	186	0.260	0.0456	218	0.132	1.536
淄博市	111656.621	154	0.388	0.0527	176	0.300	1017306.522	14	0.948	0.00085	209	0.168	0.0909	253	-0.008	0.0345	199	0.208	2.004
温州市	148667.341	91	0.640	0.0774	57	0.776	367258.671	136	0.460	0.00095	222	0.116	0.0330	133	0.472	0.0181	105	0.584	3.048
秦皇岛市	90397.989	200	0.204	0.0700	85	0.664	335504.753	153	0.392	0.00091	217	0.136	0.0809	246	0.020	0.0530	230	0.084	1.500

3. 城市科技先进性水平子系统

二级指标	科技先进性水平子系统																
三级指标	科学支出比重					国际互联网使用率					信息业产值比重			信息业从业人员比重			分值小计
	科学支出(万元)	地方财政一般预算内支出(万元)	数值	排序	分值	国际互联网用户数(户)	常住人口(万人)	数值	排序	分值	数值	排序	分值	数值	排序	分值	
厦门市	83952	2680527	0.03132	20	0.924	645200	252.0000	0.2560	11	0.960			0	0.01084	132	0.476	2.360
宁波市	169678	5060788	0.03353	17	0.936	1473000	689.5000	0.2136	15	0.944			0	0.00673	227	0.096	1.976
苏州市	287710	6867778	0.04189	8	0.972	1852094	936.9500	0.1977	18	0.932			0	0.00889	178	0.292	2.196
杭州市	220721	4903983	0.04501	7	0.976	1783282	786.2000	0.2268	13	0.952			0	0.02716	6	0.980	2.908
常州市	57968	2187465	0.02650	30	0.884	820336	445.1800	0.1843	25	0.904			0	0.01100	125	0.504	2.292
珠海市	39795	1212918	0.03281	18	0.932	298000	149.1200	0.1998	16	0.940			0	0.01394	64	0.748	2.620
深圳市	791591	10008394	0.07909	1	1.000	2475800	891.2300	0.2778	7	0.976			0	0.01982	21	0.920	2.896
北京市	1263072	23193658	0.05446	4	0.988	5049323	1755.0000	0.2877	6	0.980			0	0.05846	2	0.996	2.964
中山市	47840	1171169	0.04085	10	0.964	538500	251.7400	0.2139	14	0.948			0	0.00974	155	0.384	2.296
无锡市	146915	4056142	0.03622	14	0.948	1170222	619.5700	0.1889	22	0.916			0	0.00951	159	0.368	2.232
上海市	2153111	29896500	0.07202	2	0.996	12500000	1921.3200	0.6506	2	0.996			0	0.01692	34	0.868	2.860
嘉兴市	59007	1611135	0.03662	13	0.952	646741	418.6000	0.1545	35	0.864			0	0.00566	244	0.028	1.844
广州市	323623	7899155	0.04097	9	0.968	2801900	1033.4500	0.2711	8	0.972			0	0.02126	18	0.932	2.872
大连市	185188	4711648	0.03930	11	0.960	1231956	617.0000	0.1997	17	0.936			0	0.02309	12	0.956	2.852
鄂尔多斯市	32606	2316345	0.01408	94	0.628	71570	162.5400	0.0440	214	0.148			0	0.01757	33	0.872	1.648
镇江市	37078	1213152	0.03056	21	0.920	370800	306.9400	0.1208	61	0.760			0	0.00655	230	0.084	1.764

二级指标		科技先进性水平子系统														
三级指标	科学支出比重					国际互联网使用率					信息业产值比重			信息业从业人员比重			分值小计
	科学支出（万元）	地方财政一般预算内支出（万元）	数值	排序	分值	国际互联网用户数（户）	常住人口（万人）	数值	排序	分值	数值	排序	分值	数值	排序	分值	
南京市	137913	4612662	0.02990	25	0.904	1421028	771.3100	0.1842	26	0.900			0	0.01071	135	0.464	2.268
青岛市	102229	4335754	0.02358	37	0.856	1614347	849.0000	0.1901	21	0.920			0	0.00496	256	-0.020	1.756
威海市	38934	1369102	0.02844	28	0.892	320903	281.6100	0.1140	64	0.748			0	0.00434	267	-0.064	1.576
长沙市	107816	3140820	0.03433	16	0.940	756300	664.2200	0.1139	65	0.744			0	0.01225	102	0.596	2.280
天津市	339953	11242778	0.03024	22	0.916	5333900	1228.1600	0.4343	4	0.988			0	0.01230	97	0.616	2.520
绍兴市	77951	1695366	0.04598	6	0.980	732847	458.1000	0.1600	32	0.876			0	0.00517	253	-0.008	1.848
舟山市	21057	827392	0.02545	33	0.872	197199	103.5000	0.1905	20	0.924			0	0.01394	65	0.744	2.540
呼和浩特市	17595	1651584	0.01065	129	0.488	330765	270.8500	0.1221	60	0.764			0	0.02659	7	0.976	2.228
佛山市	84083	2669355	0.03149	19	0.928	1116493	599.6800	0.1862	23	0.912			0	0.02163	16	0.940	2.780
金华市	62193	1653599	0.03761	12	0.956	758157	510.0000	0.1487	37	0.856			0	0.01226	99	0.608	2.420
东营市	17894	1052619	0.01700	69	0.728	276593	201.7800	0.1371	48	0.812			0	0.01316	78	0.692	2.232
成都市	92646	6009694	0.01542	83	0.672	1230000	1286.6600	0.0956	81	0.680			0	0.00802	201	0.200	1.552
银川市	10554	724989	0.01456	89	0.648	160079	170.1839	0.0941	86	0.660			0	0.01416	60	0.764	2.072
湖州市	32490	1085102	0.02994	24	0.908	394934	280.0000	0.1410	45	0.824			0	0.00736	214	0.148	1.880
武汉市	101520	5036430	0.02016	51	0.800	1660000	910.0000	0.1824	27	0.896			0	0.01269	86	0.660	2.356
太原市	37219	1599051	0.02328	38	0.852	841973	350.1800	0.2404	12	0.956			0	0.01208	106	0.580	2.388
郑州市	55183	3530483	0.01563	79	0.688	1333612	752.0000	0.1773	28	0.892			0	0.01308	80	0.684	2.264

二级指标	科技先进性水平子系统															分值小计
三级指标	科学支出比重					国际互联网使用率					信息业产值比重			信息业从业人员比重			
	科学支出（万元）	地方财政一般预算内支出（万元）	数值	排序	分值	国际互联网用户数（户）	常住人口（万人）	数值	排序	分值	数值	排序	分值	数值	排序	分值	
马鞍山市	18550	800721	0.02317	39	0.848	127658	129.0000	0.0990	76	0.700			0	0.00454	264	-0.052	1.496
沈阳市	136292	4758822	0.02864	26	0.900	1283000	786.0000	0.1632	31	0.880			0	0.01236	95	0.624	2.404
济南市	52625	2599178	0.02025	50	0.804	1059000	667.8500	0.1586	33	0.872			0	0.01290	84	0.668	2.344
烟台市	52757	2480328	0.02127	47	0.816	696200	693.5100	0.1004	74	0.708			0	0.00431	269	-0.072	1.452
东莞市	116821	2259371	0.05171	5	0.984	1180200	635.0000	0.1859	24	0.908			0	0.01102	123	0.512	2.404
包头市	27231	1955634	0.01392	96	0.620	199979	257.2100	0.0777	114	0.548			0	0.01823	29	0.888	2.056
芜湖市	72630	1084741	0.06696	3	0.992	245791	230.0000	0.1069	71	0.720			0	0.00740	212	0.156	1.868
台州市	45914	1759524	0.02609	31	0.880	752645	573.4000	0.1313	50	0.804			0	0.00903	175	0.304	1.988
福州市	33118	2050925	0.01615	75	0.704	840775	687.0000	0.1224	59	0.768			0	0.01064	137	0.456	1.928
南通市	71348	2374668	0.03005	23	0.912	593035	713.3700	0.0831	100	0.604			0	0.00983	150	0.404	1.920
扬州市	40905	1590064	0.02573	32	0.876	569255	449.5500	0.1266	53	0.792			0	0.01345	73	0.712	2.380
铜陵市	8547	486384	0.01757	68	0.732	96040	74.0000	0.1298	52	0.796			0	0.00686	224	0.108	1.636
乌海市	5930	550425	0.01077	125	0.504	69700	48.7600	0.1429	41	0.840			0	0.01388	66	0.740	2.084
昆明市	42412	2707475	0.01566	78	0.692	4550700	628.0000	0.7246	1	1.000			0	0.01969	23	0.912	2.604
淄博市	37019	1619741	0.02285	40	0.844	443125	510.5100	0.0868	92	0.636			0	0.00607	236	0.060	1.540
温州市	56927	2515604	0.02263	42	0.836	4396035	790.1000	0.5564	3	0.992			0	0.00492	257	-0.024	1.804
秦皇岛市	5986	1037192	0.00577	214	0.148	396870	297.8000	0.1333	49	0.808			0	0.00978	152	0.396	1.352

4. 城市发展外部效应子系统

一级指标	发展外部效应子系统																
二级指标									三废综合利用							
三级指标	工业废水排放达标率			工业二氧化硫去除率			工业烟尘去除率			三废综合利用产品产值(万元)	地方生产总值(万元)	三废综合利用产品产值比重			产出污染处理率			分值小计
	数值	排名	分值	数值	排名	分值	数值	排名	分值			数值	排名	分值	数值	排名	分值	
厦门市	1.000	18	0.932	0.486	128	0.492	0.998	2	0.996	76761	17372349	0.004	102	0.596	0.080	25	0.904	3.920
宁波市	0.874	227	0.096	0.847	10	0.964	0.995	11	0.960	278885	43293025	0.006	69	0.728	0.016	141	0.440	3.188
苏州市	0.999	19	0.928	0.763	23	0.912	0.987	89	0.648	494885	77402000	0.006	72	0.716	0.003	233	0.072	3.276
杭州市	0.962	141	0.440	0.465	140	0.444	0.972	160	0.364	1586099	50875530	0.031	5	0.984	0.002	251	0.000	2.232
常州市	1.000	1	1.000	0.464	142	0.436	0.981	125	0.504	346308	25199300	0.014	23	0.912	0.007	205	0.184	3.036
珠海市	0.980	93	0.632	0.704	34	0.868	0.988	70	0.724	9600	10386627	0.001	240	0.044	0.029	83	0.672	2.940
深圳市	0.963	137	0.456	0.609	75	0.704	0.995	13	0.952	38516	82013176	0.000	266	−0.060	0.008	200	0.204	2.256
北京市	0.986	63	0.752	0.653	56	0.780	0.990	61	0.760	71680	121530000	0.001	260	−0.036	0.003	249	0.008	2.264
中山市	0.982	85	0.664	0.130	233	0.072	0.999	1	1.000	25321	15664106	0.002	205	0.184	0.157	6	0.980	2.900
无锡市	0.987	60	0.764	0.655	55	0.784	0.988	75	0.704	163146	49917200	0.003	134	0.468	0.006	218	0.132	2.852
上海市	0.988	58	0.772	0.616	72	0.716	0.993	26	0.900	161409	150464500	0.001	233	0.072	0.003	238	0.052	2.512
嘉兴市	0.985	69	0.728	0.504	117	0.536	0.981	122	0.516	135219	19180282	0.007	59	0.768	0.010	186	0.260	2.808
广州市	0.965	133	0.472	0.803	16	0.940	0.993	24	0.908	38516	91382135	0.000	269	−0.072	0.006	216	0.140	2.388
大连市	0.953	159	0.368	0.748	28	0.892	0.992	33	0.872	31868	43495050	0.001	250	0.004	0.010	181	0.280	2.416
鄂尔多斯市	0.933	185	0.264	0.511	113	0.552	0.990	58	0.772	10459	21610000	0.000	265	−0.056	0.015	142	0.436	1.968

二级指标	发展外部效应子系统																	
三级指标	工业废水排放达标率			工业二氧化硫去除率			工业烟尘去除率			三废综合利用产品产值比重					产出污染处理率			分值小计
	数值	排名	分值	数值	排名	分值	数值	排名	分值	三废综合利用产品产值（万元）	地方生产总值（万元）	数值	排名	分值	数值	排名	分值	
镇江市	0.965	132	0.476	0.670	41	0.840	0.992	37	0.856	45636	16720765	0.003	158	0.372	0.026	93	0.632	3.176
南京市	0.954	156	0.380	0.787	18	0.932	0.987	84	0.668	196510	42302608	0.005	96	0.620	0.007	211	0.160	2.760
青岛市	0.999	20	0.924	0.662	51	0.800	0.988	79	0.688	83646	48538672	0.002	199	0.208	0.006	217	0.136	2.756
威海市	1.000	1	1.000	0.019	265	-0.056	0.974	155	0.384	15333	17803493	0.001	245	0.024	0.007	204	0.188	1.540
长沙市	0.900	215	0.144	0.425	152	0.396	0.743	260	-0.036	53816	37447641	0.001	214	0.148	0.000	272	-0.084	0.568
天津市	1.000	16	0.940	0.597	81	0.680	0.986	94	0.628	187882	75218500	0.002	165	0.344	0.003	236	0.060	2.652
绍兴市	0.983	77	0.696	0.420	156	0.380	0.947	207	0.176	109301	23757754	0.005	97	0.616	0.003	247	0.016	1.884
舟山市	0.967	129	0.488	0.329	188	0.252	0.948	206	0.180	14729	5352361	0.003	157	0.376	0.012	171	0.320	1.616
呼和浩特市	1.000	1	1.000	0.708	33	0.872	0.997	4	0.988	26489	16439925	0.002	206	0.180	0.067	30	0.884	3.924
佛山市	0.937	180	0.284	0.360	175	0.304	0.959	181	0.280	58682	48208972	0.001	225	0.104	0.002	261	-0.040	0.932
金华市	0.966	131	0.480	0.637	64	0.748	0.978	135	0.464	78784	17760647	0.004	100	0.604	0.009	194	0.228	2.524
东营市	1.000	1	1.000	0.531	109	0.568	0.993	23	0.912	86029	20589700	0.004	110	0.564	0.025	97	0.616	3.660
成都市	0.997	27	0.896	0.373	163	0.352	0.974	153	0.392	171696	45026032	0.004	121	0.520	0.003	242	0.036	2.196
银川市	0.994	40	0.844	0.663	50	0.804	0.957	187	0.256	29324	5781483	0.005	84	0.668	0.015	151	0.400	2.972
湖州市	0.952	160	0.364	0.549	98	0.612	0.986	100	0.604	70519	11018263	0.006	71	0.720	0.022	110	0.564	2.864

二级指标	发展外部效应子系统																
三级指标	工业废水排放达标率			工业二氧化硫去除率			工业烟尘去除率			三废综合利用产品产值（万元）	地方生产总值（万元）	三废综合利用产品产值比重			产出污染处理率			分值小计
	数值	排名	分值	数值	排名	分值	数值	排名	分值			数值	排名	分值	数值	排名	分值	
武汉市	0.991	49	0.808	0.484	129	0.488	0.986	98	0.612	211828	46208600	0.005	98	0.612	0.005	223	0.112	2.632
太原市	0.973	113	0.552	0.656	54	0.788	0.988	80	0.684	74284	15452409	0.005	89	0.648	0.018	122	0.516	3.188
郑州市	0.992	45	0.824	0.345	183	0.272	0.982	121	0.520	28949	33085053	0.001	243	0.032	0.006	219	0.128	1.776
马鞍山市	0.973	112	0.556	0.486	126	0.500	0.994	20	0.924	13738	6658905	0.002	183	0.272	0.079	26	0.900	3.152
沈阳市	0.914	205	0.184	0.349	181	0.280	0.969	168	0.332	20004	42685137	0.000	267	-0.064	0.003	250	0.004	0.736
济南市	0.988	57	0.776	0.682	36	0.860	0.988	77	0.696	126297	33513645	0.004	125	0.504	0.008	196	0.220	3.056
烟台市	1.000	1	1.000	0.637	63	0.752	0.994	16	0.940	54003	37017900	0.001	212	0.156	0.016	139	0.448	3.296
东莞市	0.978	98	0.612	0.580	89	0.648	0.956	192	0.236	40379	37639142	0.001	232	0.076	0.002	255	-0.016	1.556
包头市	0.983	79	0.688	0.617	71	0.720	0.991	46	0.820	52656	21687980	0.002	170	0.324	0.018	120	0.524	3.076
芜湖市	0.992	46	0.820	0.404	158	0.372	0.958	185	0.264	74944	9019997	0.008	52	0.796	0.009	191	0.240	2.492
台州市	0.926	194	0.228	0.810	15	0.944	0.995	14	0.948	138422	20404529	0.007	62	0.756	0.031	76	0.700	3.576
福州市	0.900	214	0.148	0.504	118	0.532	0.995	10	0.964	33844	26040448	0.001	221	0.120	0.027	89	0.648	2.412
南通市	0.989	55	0.784	0.585	86	0.660	0.963	177	0.296	69211	28728038	0.002	172	0.316	0.003	235	0.064	2.120
扬州市	0.983	75	0.704	0.536	105	0.584	0.994	21	0.920	21941	18563943	0.001	226	0.100	0.028	84	0.668	2.976
铜陵市	0.991	50	0.804	0.962	2	0.996	0.988	71	0.720	118903	3437300	0.035	3	0.992	0.107	15	0.944	4.456

发展外部效应子系统

二级指标	工业废水排放达标率			工业二氧化硫去除率			工业烟尘去除率			三废综合利用产品产值比重					产出污染处理率			分值小计
三级指标	数值	排名	分值	数值	排名	分值	数值	排名	分值	三废综合利用产品产值（万元）	地方生产总值（万元）	数值	排名	分值	数值	排名	分值	
乌海市	0.996	37	0.856	0.592	83	0.672	0.988	78	0.692	20403	3112080	0.007	67	0.736	0.089	21	0.920	3.876
昆明市	0.998	23	0.912	0.870	7	0.976	0.994	18	0.932	201834	18086467	0.011	31	0.880	0.032	72	0.716	4.416
淄博市	1.000	1	1.000	0.675	38	0.852	0.988	74	0.708	340757	24452800	0.014	21	0.920	0.012	177	0.296	3.776
温州市	0.859	237	0.056	0.550	97	0.616	0.989	67	0.736	20709	25273448	0.001	247	0.016	0.012	173	0.312	1.736
秦皇岛市	0.997	30	0.884	0.516	111	0.560	0.992	44	0.828	35661	8045421	0.004	101	0.600	0.051	48	0.812	3.684

5. 城市经济发展水平系统

城市经济发展水平母系统

一级指标	城市发展总水平子系统			发展要素利用效率水平子系统			科技先进性水平子系统			发展外部效应子系统			分值合计
二级指标	数值	排序	分值	数值	排序	分值	数值	排序	分值	数值	排序	分值	
厦门市	1.828	3	0.992	2.232	170	0.324	2.360	20	0.924	3.920	12	0.956	3.196
宁波市	1.804	5	0.984	3.744	54	0.788	1.976	53	0.792	3.188	47	0.816	3.380
苏州市	1.700	9	0.968	4.856	8	0.972	2.196	36	0.860	3.276	44	0.828	3.628
杭州市	1.808	4	0.988	2.960	102	0.596	2.908	2	0.996	2.232	152	0.396	2.976
常州市	1.616	19	0.928	3.276	83	0.672	2.292	25	0.904	3.036	59	0.768	3.272
珠海市	1.852	1	1.000	2.080	183	0.272	2.620	8	0.972	2.940	73	0.712	2.956

一级指标	城市发展总水平子系统			城市经济发展水平母系统									分值合计
				发展要素利用效率水平子系统			科技先进性水平子系统			发展外部效应子系统			
二级指标	数值	排序	分值	数值	排序	分值	数值	排序	分值	数值	排序	分值	
深圳市	1.680	12	0.956	2.796	117	0.536	2.896	3	0.992	2.256	149	0.408	2.892
北京市	1.484	25	0.900	2.080	183	0.272	2.964	1	1.000	2.264	146	0.420	2.592
中山市	1.192	70	0.724	3.960	42	0.836	2.296	24	0.908	2.900	74	0.708	3.176
无锡市	1.144	78	0.692	4.204	32	0.876	2.232	31	0.880	2.852	83	0.672	3.120
上海市	1.800	6	0.980	2.992	100	0.604	2.860	5	0.984	2.512	114	0.548	3.116
嘉兴市	1.708	8	0.972	4.372	23	0.912	1.844	69	0.728	2.808	89	0.648	3.260
广州市	1.472	27	0.896	2.496	142	0.436	2.872	4	0.988	2.388	133	0.472	2.792
大连市	0.968	111	0.560	3.688	59	0.768	2.852	6	0.980	2.416	127	0.496	2.804
鄂尔多斯市	0.988	107	0.576	5.468	1	1.000	1.648	77	0.696	1.968	174	0.308	2.580
镇江市	1.420	29	0.888	3.176	89	0.648	1.764	74	0.708	3.176	49	0.808	3.052
南京市	1.680	12	0.956	2.120	178	0.292	2.268	27	0.896	2.760	92	0.636	2.780
青岛市	1.352	39	0.848	4.420	19	0.928	1.756	75	0.704	2.756	93	0.632	3.112
威海市	1.240	59	0.768	4.488	17	0.936	1.576	87	0.656	1.540	201	0.200	2.560
长沙市	1.616	19	0.928	3.948	44	0.828	2.280	26	0.900	0.568	259	-0.032	2.624
天津市	1.008	104	0.588	2.880	107	0.576	2.520	11	0.960	2.652	101	0.600	2.724
绍兴市	1.696	10	0.964	4.708	10	0.964	1.848	68	0.732	1.884	179	0.288	2.948
舟山市	1.284	52	0.796	3.216	87	0.656	2.540	10	0.964	1.616	196	0.220	2.636
呼和浩特市	1.076	89	0.648	3.108	93	0.632	2.228	33	0.872	3.924	10	0.964	3.116
佛山市	1.216	66	0.740	3.080	96	0.620	2.780	7	0.976	0.932	240	0.044	2.380

| 一级指标 | 城市经济发展水平母系统 | | | | | | | | | | | | |
| 二级指标 | 城市发展总水平子系统 | | | 发展要素利用效率水平子系统 | | | 科技先进性水平子系统 | | | 发展外部效应子系统 | | | 分值合计 |
	数值	排序	分值	数值	排序	分值	数值	排序	分值	数值	排序	分值	
金华市	1.204	67	0.736	5.024	6	0.980	2.420	12	0.956	2.524	111	0.560	3.232
东营市	1.412	34	0.868	3.352	76	0.700	2.232	31	0.880	3.660	22	0.916	3.364
成都市	1.420	29	0.888	3.116	92	0.636	1.552	92	0.636	2.196	153	0.392	2.552
银川市	1.320	41	0.840	1.284	239	0.048	2.072	46	0.820	2.972	64	0.748	2.456
湖州市	1.232	61	0.760	3.616	63	0.752	1.880	63	0.752	2.864	80	0.684	2.948
武汉市	1.236	60	0.764	1.972	198	0.212	2.356	21	0.920	2.632	102	0.596	2.492
太原市	1.628	17	0.936	0.920	262	-0.044	2.388	17	0.936	3.188	47	0.816	2.644
郑州市	1.300	46	0.820	2.344	158	0.372	2.264	28	0.892	1.776	184	0.268	2.352
马鞍山市	1.632	15	0.944	1.724	220	0.124	1.496	106	0.580	3.152	51	0.800	2.448
沈阳市	0.952	116	0.540	3.308	79	0.688	2.404	14	0.948	0.736	252	-0.004	2.172
济南市	1.276	54	0.788	2.448	146	0.420	2.344	22	0.916	3.056	57	0.776	2.900
烟台市	1.100	84	0.668	4.400	21	0.920	1.452	113	0.552	3.296	43	0.832	2.972
东莞市	1.848	2	0.996	2.304	163	0.352	2.404	14	0.948	1.556	200	0.204	2.500
包头市	1.028	102	0.596	1.976	197	0.216	2.056	48	0.812	3.076	55	0.784	2.408
芜湖市	1.320	41	0.840	2.460	145	0.424	1.868	65	0.744	2.492	115	0.544	2.552
台州市	1.416	33	0.872	3.892	47	0.816	1.988	51	0.800	3.576	29	0.888	3.376
福州市	0.752	166	0.340	3.580	65	0.744	1.928	56	0.780	2.412	129	0.488	2.352
南通市	1.288	51	0.800	4.388	22	0.916	1.920	60	0.764	2.120	162	0.356	2.836
扬州市	1.488	25	0.904	4.576	15	0.944	2.380	18	0.932	2.976	63	0.752	3.532

续表

一级指标	城市经济发展水平母系统												分值合计
二级指标	城市发展总水平子系统			发展要素利用效率水平子系统			科技先进性水平子系统			发展外部效应子系统			
	数值	排序	分值	数值	排序	分值	数值	排序	分值	数值	排序	分值	
铜陵市	1.308	43	0.832	2.212	172	0.316	1.636	79	0.688	4.456	2	0.996	2.832
乌海市	0.860	140	0.444	0.696	272	-0.084	2.084	44	0.828	3.876	13	0.952	2.140
昆明市	1.436	28	0.892	1.536	227	0.096	2.604	9	0.968	4.416	3	0.992	2.948
淄博市	1.204	67	0.736	2.004	194	0.228	1.540	93	0.632	3.776	14	0.948	2.544
温州市	1.284	52	0.796	3.048	99	0.608	1.804	72	0.716	1.736	187	0.256	2.376
秦皇岛市	1.492	24	0.908	1.500	229	0.088	1.352	127	0.496	3.684	20	0.924	2.416

二、城市公共服务水平母系统

1. 城市财政公共投入水平子系统

二级指标	财政公共投入水平子系统												分值小计
三级指标	人均社会保障性支出			人均医疗卫生支出			人均教育支出			人均公共服务财政支出			
	数值（元）	排名	分值	数值（元）	排名	分值	数值（元）	排序	分值	数值（元）	排序	分值	
厦门市	825.00000	40	0.844	496.82540	10	0.964	1496.94444	8	0.972	3151.91270	8	0.972	3.752
宁波市	420.44960	149	0.408	443.94489	14	0.948	1118.32777	14	0.892	2228.81073	28	0.892	3.196
苏州市	652.00918	65	0.744	293.82571	77	0.696	1093.81824	16	0.940	2346.72394	23	0.912	3.292
杭州市	617.52735	73	0.712	411.60010	19	0.928	1097.39125	15	0.944	2407.26278	20	0.924	3.508
常州市	469.92228	129	0.488	261.69190	103	0.592	791.47536	55	0.784	1653.30204	79	0.688	2.552

二级指标	财政公共投入水平子系统												
三级指标	人均社会保障性支出			人均医疗卫生支出			人均教育支出			人均公共服务财政支出			分值小计
	数值（元）	排名	分值	数值（元）	排名	分值	数值（元）	排序	分值	数值（元）	排序	分值	
珠海市	765.82618	49	0.808	322.55901	51	0.800	1558.48981	6	0.980	2913.74061	12	0.956	3.544
深圳市	617.01244	74	0.708	425.14278	17	0.936	1533.01168	7	0.976	3463.36748	7	0.976	3.596
北京市	1334.98575	7	0.976	949.45869	2	0.996	2083.57664	3	0.992	5087.72023	3	0.992	3.956
中山市	358.70342	182	0.276	149.75769	279	-0.112	1170.43378	13	0.952	1868.93223	52	0.796	1.912
无锡市	482.59277	123	0.512	231.45084	155	0.384	1040.91709	19	0.928	1992.08483	40	0.844	2.668
上海市	1749.21408	3	0.992	691.45171	4	0.988	1805.80018	4	0.988	5367.10751	2	0.996	3.964
嘉兴市	179.40755	276	-0.100	212.13569	197	0.216	833.46393	41	0.840	1365.96990	135	0.464	1.420
广州市	1070.10499	18	0.932	521.16697	8	0.972	1067.49141	18	0.932	2971.91156	10	0.964	3.800
大连市	1244.08428	10	0.964	364.01945	27	0.896	949.12804	24	0.908	2857.37439	14	0.948	3.716
鄂尔多斯市	1325.82749	8	0.972	638.61203	5	0.984	1652.77470	5	0.984	3817.81715	6	0.980	3.920
镇江市	223.82225	259	-0.032	211.11618	202	0.196	728.57236	72	0.716	1284.30964	150	0.404	1.284
南京市	479.83301	125	0.504	339.55219	39	0.848	830.66860	43	0.832	1828.85740	54	0.788	2.972
青岛市	351.94346	187	0.256	159.01060	273	-0.088	847.09305	36	0.860	1478.45819	107	0.576	1.604
威海市	784.06307	45	0.824	222.64834	174	0.308	841.67111	38	0.852	1986.63755	43	0.832	2.816
长沙市	594.38138	85	0.664	261.81085	102	0.596	709.52546	78	0.692	1728.03740	66	0.740	2.692
天津市	943.68812	27	0.896	441.47342	15	0.944	1413.54709	9	0.968	3075.50726	9	0.968	3.776
绍兴市	222.87710	261	-0.040	243.83322	126	0.500	834.03405	40	0.844	1470.90592	109	0.568	1.872
舟山市	430.91787	144	0.428	712.07729	3	0.992	1022.19324	20	0.924	2368.63768	21	0.920	3.264
呼和浩特市	671.58944	58	0.772	297.21248	69	0.728	819.11759	47	0.816	1852.88167	53	0.792	3.108

二级指标	财政公共投入水平子系统												
三级指标	人均社会保障性支出			人均医疗卫生支出			人均教育支出			人均公共服务财政支出			分值小计
	数值（元）	排名	分值	数值（元）	排名	分值	数值（元）	排序	分值	数值（元）	排序	分值	
佛山市	340.18143	197	0.216	182.43063	245	0.024	982.96758	23	0.912	1645.79276	80	0.684	1.836
金华市	182.74510	273	-0.088	232.15686	153	0.392	818.19608	49	0.808	1355.04510	140	0.444	1.556
东营市	352.85955	186	0.260	288.92854	82	0.676	1081.34106	17	0.936	1811.80989	55	0.784	2.656
成都市	341.52029	196	0.220	231.15187	156	0.380	619.35800	120	0.524	1264.03855	160	0.364	1.488
银川市	766.81754	48	0.812	337.86980	41	0.840	767.24061	64	0.748	1933.94322	49	0.808	3.208
湖州市	181.42857	274	-0.092	231.07143	157	0.376	768.12857	63	0.752	1296.66429	149	0.408	1.444
武汉市	951.64835	26	0.900	341.42857	37	0.856	730.67802	70	0.724	2135.31538	33	0.872	3.352
太原市	917.81370	30	0.884	293.27774	78	0.692	820.70364	45	0.824	2138.08042	32	0.876	3.276
郑州市	481.11702	124	0.508	288.16489	84	0.668	823.70612	44	0.828	1666.36968	75	0.704	2.708
马鞍山市	764.34109	51	0.800	363.56589	29	0.888	695.26357	87	0.656	1966.96899	46	0.820	3.164
沈阳市	1080.53435	16	0.940	431.93384	16	0.940	844.33969	37	0.856	2530.20738	18	0.932	3.668
济南市	578.42330	89	0.648	238.37688	136	0.460	551.03691	165	0.344	1446.63472	111	0.560	2.012
烟台市	497.32520	118	0.532	202.88100	221	0.120	632.18843	110	0.564	1408.46707	121	0.520	1.736
东莞市	237.63780	256	-0.020	48.66142	287	-0.144	204.21732	287	-0.144	674.48661	286	-0.140	-0.448
包头市	1389.52607	6	0.980	295.08962	75	0.704	932.83698	26	0.900	2723.32335	16	0.940	3.524
芜湖市	857.39130	36	0.860	280.43478	89	0.648	589.26522	140	0.444	2042.87391	38	0.852	2.804
台州市	141.08825	286	-0.140	179.45588	254	-0.012	784.05651	60	0.764	1184.67388	185	0.264	0.876
福州市	342.64920	195	0.224	210.77147	204	0.188	667.65502	93	0.632	1269.28239	156	0.380	1.424
南通市	269.70576	235	0.064	206.06417	212	0.156	708.10099	79	0.688	1283.88634	151	0.400	1.308

二级指标	财政公共投入水平子系统													
三级指标	人均社会保障支出			人均医疗卫生支出			人均教育支出			人均公共服务财政支出			分值小计
	数值（元）	排名	分值	数值（元）	排名	分值	数值（元）	排序	分值	数值（元）	排序	分值	
扬州市	261.15004	241	0.040	183.29441	244	0.028	652.22556	98	0.612	1187.66099	183	0.272	0.952
铜陵市	1055.40541	19	0.928	335.13514	44	0.828	750.77027	66	0.740	2256.81081	26	0.900	3.396
乌海市	2163.65874	1	1.000	525.02051	7	0.976	1189.00738	12	0.956	3999.30271	5	0.984	3.916
昆明市	589.01274	87	0.656	252.54777	112	0.556	615.45223	124	0.508	1524.54777	92	0.636	2.356
淄博市	411.15747	155	0.384	191.76902	235	0.064	690.16082	89	0.648	1365.60107	136	0.460	1.556
温州市	167.44716	281	-0.120	235.91950	144	0.428	868.16226	34	0.868	1343.57929	141	0.440	1.616
秦皇岛市	396.23909	162	0.356	297.85091	68	0.732	599.36870	130	0.484	1313.55944	145	0.424	1.996

2. 城市公共项目规模水平子系统（1）

二级指标	公共项目规模水平子系统（1）														
三级指标	每万人拥有医院、卫生院数			每万人拥有医生数			每万人在校高中以上学生数			人均城市道路面积			每百万人剧场、影剧院数		
	数值	排名	分值	数值（人）	排名	分值	数值（人）	排序	分值	数值（平方米）	排名	分值	数值（座）	排名	分值
厦门市	37.734	73	0.712	39.59	9	0.968	1891.07	13	0.952	16.82	28	0.892	7.34	49	0.808
宁波市	33.130	127	0.496	28.30	31	0.880	1153.77	54	0.788	10.33	108	0.572	11.27	26	0.900
苏州市	37.791	71	0.720	25.24	51	0.800	1189.50	50	0.804	23.92	7	0.976	4.58	101	0.600
杭州市	44.304	38	0.852	33.29	14	0.948	1040.81	70	0.724	10.44	104	0.588	6.29	64	0.748
常州市	33.083	128	0.492	21.11	82	0.676	964.28	83	0.672	12.39	71	0.720	12.79	18	0.932

二级指标	公共项目规模水平子系统（1）														
三级指标	每万人拥有医院、卫生院床位数			每万人拥有医生数			每万人在校高中以上学生数			人均城市道路面积			每百万人剧场、影剧院数		
	数值	排名	分值	数值（人）	排名	分值	数值（人）	排序	分值	数值（平方米）	排名	分值	数值（座）	排名	分值
珠海市	39.344	55	0.784	41.50	7	0.976	1290.09	43	0.832	32.52	3	0.992	6.82	55	0.784
深圳市	22.297	248	0.012	86.96	1	1.000	1349.10	38	0.852	36.04	2	0.996	17.89	7	0.976
北京市	48.374	23	0.912	50.05	4	0.988	996.60	76	0.700	7.81	166	0.340	12.60	19	0.928
中山市	34.587	103	0.592	33.24	15	0.944	592.86	179	0.288	8.70	140	0.444	12.17	22	0.916
无锡市	32.384	134	0.468	24.24	60	0.764	1333.01	39	0.848	22.59	8	0.972	9.66	34	0.868
上海市	50.996	17	0.936	30.26	25	0.904	891.42	102	0.596	6.97	179	0.288	7.81	44	0.828
嘉兴市	30.678	150	0.404	22.16	72	0.716	626.22	165	0.344	10.86	96	0.620	8.42	38	0.852
广州市	50.017	19	0.928	41.44	8	0.972	2260.91	4	0.988	14.51	50	0.804	4.12	118	0.532
大连市	48.361	25	0.904	27.18	39	0.848	1653.00	25	0.904	13.53	58	0.772	1.66	222	0.116
鄂尔多斯市	56.971	8	0.972	31.01	22	0.916	480.24	216	0.140	62.11	1	1.000	7.90	42	0.836
镇江市	27.305	187	0.256	18.82	108	0.572	899.23	99	0.608	16.58	29	0.888	12.57	20	0.924
南京市	33.743	116	0.540	26.35	44	0.828	2061.48	8	0.972	17.06	27	0.896	3.66	134	0.468
青岛市	35.956	90	0.644	21.93	76	0.700	1627.17	26	0.900	20.92	10	0.964	7.26	50	0.804
威海市	57.455	7	0.976	27.85	32	0.876	830.21	113	0.552	27.55	4	0.988	1.55	233	0.072
长沙市	54.062	12	0.956	26.32	46	0.820	1727.74	21	0.920	14.48	51	0.800	2.49	182	0.276

二级指标	公共项目规模水平子系统（1）														
三级指标	每万人拥有医院、卫生院床位数			每万人拥有医生数			每万人在校高中以上学生数			人均城市道路面积			每百万人剧场、影剧院数		
	数值	排名	分值	数值（人）	排名	分值	数值（人）	排序	分值	数值（平方米）	排名	分值	数值（座）	排名	分值
天津市	34.133	108	0.572	27.82	33	0.872	971.32	81	0.680	10.41	106	0.580	4.36	113	0.552
绍兴市	31.766	138	0.452	21.24	80	0.684	707.06	137	0.456	17.49	23	0.912	7.70	45	0.824
舟山市	36.280	86	0.660	24.49	57	0.776	579.44	187	0.256	6.96	181	0.280	4.31	114	0.548
呼和浩特市	49.825	20	0.924	27.32	37	0.856	2062.76	7	0.976	12.80	66	0.740	5.05	88	0.652
佛山市	33.156	125	0.504	30.98	23	0.912	699.00	142	0.436	6.24	197	0.216	13.06	15	0.944
金华市	27.741	182	0.276	21.97	73	0.712	866.38	105	0.584	14.64	48	0.812	4.31	114	0.548
东营市	46.367	32	0.876	21.73	79	0.688	646.58	157	0.376	21.84	9	0.968	16.81	8	0.972
成都市	44.388	37	0.856	28.48	29	0.888	1669.07	24	0.908	12.07	76	0.700	1.73	220	0.124
银川市	47.102	31	0.880	23.95	62	0.756	1811.70	18	0.932	17.44	24	0.908	4.38	112	0.556
湖州市	33.229	124	0.508	21.95	74	0.708	428.38	228	0.092	16.58	29	0.888	1.84	213	0.152
武汉市	47.104	30	0.884	28.72	28	0.892	2421.18	2	0.996	13.21	62	0.756	11.46	25	0.904
太原市	70.649	2	0.996	41.96	6	0.980	2046.95	9	0.968	8.27	148	0.412	4.56	103	0.592
郑州市	53.960	14	0.948	25.18	52	0.796	3534.37	1	1.000	10.71	99	0.608	3.86	125	0.504
马鞍山市	22.434	245	0.024	19.50	96	0.620	629.17	162	0.356	13.69	55	0.784	3.14	156	0.380
沈阳市	46.352	33	0.872	28.33	30	0.884	1522.84	32	0.876	10.27	109	0.568	7.03	52	0.796

公共项目规模水平子系统（1）

二级指标	每万人拥有医院、卫生院床位数			每万人拥有医生数			每万人在校高中以上学生数			人均城市道路面积			每百万人剧场、影剧院数		
三级指标	数值	排名	分值	数值（人）	排名	分值	数值（人）	排序	分值	数值（平方米）	排名	分值	数值（座）	排名	分值
济南市	46.298	34	0.868	27.30	38	0.852	1935.83	12	0.956	18.55	20	0.924	2.58	176	0.300
烟台市	37.430	77	0.696	21.82	78	0.692	920.76	96	0.620	15.31	39	0.848	2.79	171	0.320
东莞市	27.850	180	0.284	72.09	2	0.996	906.00	98	0.612	26.00	5	0.984	35.25	2	0.996
包头市	42.413	44	0.828	30.97	24	0.908	782.98	121	0.520	14.67	47	0.816	9.90	33	0.872
芜湖市	38.122	65	0.744	20.63	87	0.656	764.63	125	0.504	19.86	13	0.952	0.95	265	-0.056
台州市	26.439	196	0.220	19.43	97	0.616	575.20	191	0.240	14.81	43	0.832	4.55	104	0.588
福州市	31.654	139	0.448	21.03	83	0.672	1501.11	35	0.864	11.27	84	0.668	10.68	30	0.884
南通市	34.033	111	0.560	16.71	136	0.460	1504.67	34	0.868	6.86	183	0.272	1.89	208	0.172
扬州市	32.174	135	0.464	17.09	128	0.492	1098.89	61	0.760	11.97	79	0.688	0.82	269	-0.072
铜陵市	48.392	22	0.916	24.54	56	0.780	577.54	189	0.248	10.59	101	0.600	4.45	110	0.564
乌海市	55.906	9	0.968	26.24	47	0.816	313.20	263	-0.048	10.99	91	0.640	4.16	116	0.540
昆明市	47.682	26	0.900	59.08	3	0.992	1041.44	69	0.728	9.96	114	0.548	13.19	14	0.948
淄博市	37.786	72	0.716	18.43	115	0.544	1038.97	71	0.720	8.73	139	0.448	0.72	272	-0.084
温州市	25.794	204	0.188	20.74	84	0.668	767.38	123	0.512	12.05	77	0.696	6.91	53	0.792
秦皇岛市	33.583	120	0.524	20.03	92	0.636	643.30	159	0.368	17.23	26	0.900	1.21	251	0.000

城市公共项目规模水平子系统（2）

二级指标	公共项目规模水平子系统（2）									
三级指标	每百人公共图书馆藏书数			每十万人体育场馆数			每万人拥有公共汽车车数			分值小计
	数值（册）	排名	分值	数值（座）	排名	分值	数值（辆）	排名	分值	
厦门市	168.81	9	0.968	6.78	11	0.960	17.63	9	0.968	7.228
宁波市	110.85	21	0.920	2.57	25	0.904	14.63	20	0.924	6.384
苏州市	112.68	20	0.924	0.96	104	0.588	12.31	38	0.852	6.264
杭州市	178.67	8	0.972	1.70	40	0.844	18.80	7	0.976	6.652
常州市	64.39	50	0.804	0.84	125	0.504	11.03	52	0.796	5.596
珠海市	66.68	48	0.812	0.78	132	0.476	12.60	33	0.872	6.528
深圳市	607.99	1	1.000	4.03	16	0.940	45.86	1	1.000	6.776
北京市	350.61	4	0.988	48.99	5	0.984	18.49	8	0.972	6.812
中山市	62.69	52	0.796	1.42	59	0.768	7.49	113	0.552	5.300
无锡市	63.37	51	0.800	0.67	147	0.416	12.53	35	0.864	6.000
上海市	470.72	2	0.996	4.89	14	0.948	12.22	40	0.844	6.340
嘉兴市	103.67	23	0.912	1.08	89	0.648	11.08	51	0.800	5.296
广州市	212.93	6	0.980	/	279	-0.112	13.42	27	0.896	5.988
大连市	159.94	10	0.964	1.46	55	0.784	15.60	15	0.944	6.236
鄂尔多斯市	42.75	83	0.672	6.72	12	0.956	9.05	77	0.696	6.188
镇江市	68.59	45	0.824	0.97	101	0.600	9.57	70	0.724	5.396
南京市	206.09	7	0.976	56.32	4	0.988	11.14	50	0.804	6.472

公共项目规模水平子系统（2）

二级指标	每百人公共图书馆藏书数			每十万人体育场馆数			每万人拥有公共汽车数			分值小计
三级指标	数值（册）	排名	分值	数值（座）	排名	分值	数值（辆）	排名	分值	
青岛市	55.67	58	0.772	1.27	71	0.720	15.57	16	0.940	6.444
威海市	44.47	78	0.692	1.55	47	0.816	13.70	25	0.904	5.876
长沙市	90.12	27	0.896	6.81	10	0.964	14.75	19	0.928	6.560
天津市	121.69	16	0.940	93.06	2	0.996	9.84	68	0.732	5.924
绍兴市	53.82	60	0.764	2.00	32	0.876	12.87	31	0.880	5.848
舟山市	71.41	41	0.840	1.44	57	0.776	9.29	73	0.712	4.848
呼和浩特市	107.36	22	0.916	1.35	64	0.748	16.99	11	0.960	6.772
佛山市	73.44	38	0.852	2.94	22	0.916	8.97	80	0.684	5.464
金华市	65.02	49	0.808	1.51	52	0.796	8.38	89	0.648	5.184
东营市	34.83	101	0.600	3.00	21	0.920	7.73	104	0.588	5.988
成都市	102.69	24	0.908	35.77	6	0.980	14.50	21	0.920	6.284
银川市	137.45	15	0.944	1.53	51	0.800	14.45	22	0.916	6.692
湖州市	78.29	36	0.860	1.29	67	0.736	6.02	148	0.412	4.356
武汉市	119.43	18	0.932	1.63	46	0.820	14.06	24	0.908	7.092
太原市	102.32	25	0.904	0.95	106	0.580	6.59	131	0.480	5.912
郑州市	71.64	40	0.844	0.70	144	0.428	15.53	17	0.936	6.064
马鞍山市	42.76	82	0.676	1.10	86	0.660	7.48	114	0.548	4.048

二级指标	公共项目规模水平子系统（2）										
三级指标	每百人公共图书馆藏书数			每十万人体育馆数			每万人拥有公共汽车数			分值小计
	数值（册）	排名	分值	数值（座）	排名	分值	数值（辆）	排名	分值	
沈阳市	142.45	13	0.952	0.21	238	0.052	9.92	66	0.740	5.740
济南市	150.58	11	0.960	2.41	26	0.900	12.55	34	0.868	6.628
烟台市	78.65	34	0.868	1.17	77	0.696	9.25	74	0.708	5.448
东莞市	335.14	5	0.984	3.52	18	0.932	7.87	102	0.596	6.384
包头市	138.26	14	0.948	1.20	74	0.708	9.25	74	0.708	6.308
芜湖市	26.51	139	0.448	0.95	106	0.580	13.30	29	0.888	4.716
台州市	29.23	126	0.500	1.04	94	0.628	3.23	219	0.128	3.752
福州市	74.85	37	0.856	2.88	24	0.908	14.17	23	0.912	6.212
南通市	36.28	96	0.620	0.33	206	0.180	3.59	213	0.152	3.284
扬州市	51.37	65	0.744	1.15	79	0.688	8.30	91	0.640	4.404
铜陵市	73.25	39	0.848	0.89	119	0.528	6.03	147	0.416	4.900
乌海市	92.18	26	0.900	1.04	94	0.628	7.91	101	0.600	5.044
昆明市	33.97	105	0.584	1.00	97	0.616	21.12	4	0.988	6.304
淄博市	51.66	64	0.748	0.83	127	0.496	7.77	103	0.592	4.180
温州市	39.07	92	0.636	0.83	127	0.496	13.32	28	0.892	4.880
秦皇岛市	30.64	119	0.528	0.73	138	0.452	12.44	37	0.856	4.264

3. 城市社保范围及水平子系统

二级指标	社保范围及水平子系统															分值小计
三级指标	养老保险参保覆盖率					医疗保险参保覆盖率					失业保险参保覆盖率					
	基本养老保险参保(人)	年末总人口(万人)	数值	排名	分值	基本医疗保险参保(人)	年末总人口(万人)	数值	排名	分值	失业保险参保人数(人)	年末总人口(万人)	数值	排名	分值	
厦门市	1219600	177.00	0.689	5	0.984	1284000	177	0.725	8	0.972	1050700	177.00	0.594	5	0.984	2.940
宁波市	3442759	571.02	0.603	9	0.968	2518378	571.02	0.441	23	0.912	1732132	571.02	0.303	14	0.948	2.828
苏州市	2995027	633.29	0.473	12	0.956	3461794	633.29	0.547	12	0.956	2343246	633.29	0.370	10	0.964	2.876
杭州市	3422359	683.38	0.501	11	0.960	2983138	683.38	0.437	24	0.908	2156773	683.38	0.316	12	0.956	2.824
常州市	995574	359.82	0.277	28	0.892	1208444	359.82	0.336	44	0.828	741025	359.82	0.206	22	0.916	2.636
珠海市	780724	102.65	0.761	4	0.988	846791	102.65	0.825	6	0.980	669637	102.65	0.652	4	0.988	2.956
深圳市	5840900	245.96	2.375	1	1.000	9113900	245.96	3.705	1	1.000	2189700	245.96	0.890	2	0.996	2.996
北京市	8276903	1245.83	0.664	7	0.976	9384100	1245.83	0.753	7	0.976	6757117	1245.83	0.542	6	0.980	2.932
中山市	1288073	147.86	0.871	3	0.992	1255238	147.86	0.849	5	0.984	1134303	147.86	0.767	3	0.992	2.968
无锡市	1983500	465.65	0.426	13	0.952	2192800	465.65	0.471	17	0.936	1433300	465.65	0.308	13	0.952	2.840
上海市	8457100	1400.70	0.604	8	0.972	9512000	1400.7	0.679	9	0.968	5235300	1400.70	0.374	9	0.968	2.908
嘉兴市	1358000	339.60	0.400	15	0.944	1176400	339.6	0.346	41	0.840	700700	339.60	0.206	21	0.920	2.704
广州市	2893080	794.62	0.364	20	0.924	3826813	794.62	0.482	16	0.940	3121036	794.62	0.393	7	0.976	2.840
大连市	1627070	584.80	0.278	27	0.896	3958086	584.8	0.677	10	0.964	1065855	584.80	0.182	30	0.884	2.744
鄂尔多斯市	180000	149.48	0.120	112	0.556	256302	149.48	0.171	115	0.544	136292	149.48	0.091	93	0.632	1.732

二级指标	社保范围及水平子系统															分值小计
三级指标	养老保险参保覆盖率					医疗保险参保覆盖率					失业保险参保覆盖率					
	基本养老保险参保人数(人)	年末总人口(万人)	数值	排名	分值	基本医疗保险参保人数(人)	年末总人口(万人)	数值	排名	分值	失业保险参保人数(人)	年末总人口(万人)	数值	排名	分值	
镇江市	627281	269.88	0.232	41	0.840	713722	269.88	0.264	65	0.744	428904	269.88	0.159	40	0.844	2.428
南京市	1883237	629.77	0.299	23	0.912	2501760	629.77	0.397	32	0.876	1820016	629.77	0.289	15	0.944	2.732
青岛市	2592929	762.92	0.340	22	0.916	2408855	762.92	0.316	50	0.804	1429153	762.92	0.187	29	0.888	2.608
威海市	723108	252.97	0.286	25	0.904	724548	252.97	0.286	56	0.780	387520	252.97	0.153	43	0.832	2.516
长沙市	1225523	651.59	0.188	59	0.768	1315038	651.59	0.202	97	0.616	628288	651.59	0.096	84	0.668	2.052
天津市	4015300	979.84	0.410	14	0.948	4440600	979.84	0.453	18	0.932	2392200	979.84	0.244	17	0.936	2.816
绍兴市	1248200	437.74	0.285	26	0.900	1050500	437.74	0.240	77	0.696	689108	437.74	0.157	41	0.840	2.436
舟山市	280329	96.77	0.290	24	0.908	218880	96.77	0.226	84	0.668	149833	96.77	0.155	42	0.836	2.412
呼和浩特市	547848	227.37	0.241	38	0.852	504392	227.37	0.222	86	0.660	380286	227.37	0.167	36	0.860	2.372
佛山市	2462387	367.63	0.670	6	0.980	4005633	367.63	1.090	3	0.992	1408976	367.63	0.383	8	0.972	2.944
金华市	815579	463.68	0.176	66	0.740	625279	463.68	0.135	146	0.420	518037	463.68	0.112	68	0.732	1.892
东营市	199910	184.59	0.108	134	0.468	512747	184.59	0.278	59	0.768	115553	184.59	0.063	153	0.392	1.628
成都市	3046700	1139.63	0.267	30	0.884	3263200	1139.63	0.286	57	0.776	1586800	1139.63	0.139	48	0.812	2.472
银川市	292529	155.55	0.188	60	0.764	770127	155.55	0.495	15	0.944	252075	155.55	0.162	38	0.852	2.560
湖州市	550332	259.17	0.212	47	0.816	491521	259.17	0.190	103	0.592	346100	259.17	0:134	52	0.796	2.204
武汉市	2102900	835.55	0.252	34	0.868	3091800	835.55	0.370	35	0.864	1180700	835.55	0.141	47	0.816	2.548
太原市	708692	365.12	0.194	55	0.784	961134	365.12	0.263	66	0.740	741136	365.12	0.203	24	0.908	2.432
郑州市	1411000	731.47	0.193	57	0.776	828632	731.47	0.113	176	0.300	877433	731.47	0.120	63	0.752	1.828

续表

二级指标	社保范围及水平子系统															分值小计
三级指标	养老保险参保覆盖率					医疗保险参保覆盖率					失业保险参保覆盖率					
	基本养老保险参保人数（人）	年末总人口（万人）	数值	排名	分值	基本医疗保险参保人数（人）	年末总人口（万人）	数值	排名	分值	失业保险参保人数（人）	年末总人口（万人）	数值	排名	分值	
马鞍山市	292344	128.61	0.227	43	0.832	334804	128.61	0.260	68	0.732	186561	128.61	0.145	45	0.824	2.388
沈阳市	2795029	716.55	0.390	17	0.936	3074746	716.55	0.429	26	0.900	1234965	716.55	0.172	34	0.868	2.704
济南市	1365820	603.27	0.226	44	0.828	1331911	603.27	0.221	87	0.656	830215	603.27	0.138	49	0.808	2.292
烟台市	1342300	652.00	0.206	49	0.808	2073099	652	0.318	49	0.808	840319	652.00	0.129	55	0.784	2.400
东莞市	3158100	178.73	1.767	2	0.996	5365700	178.73	3.002	2	0.996	2591500	178.73	1.450	1	1.000	2.992
包头市	533660	219.59	0.243	37	0.856	719407	219.59	0.328	47	0.816	415068	219.59	0.189	28	0.892	2.564
芜湖市	349246	230.10	0.152	85	0.664	418455	230.1	0.182	109	0.568	245311	230.10	0.107	73	0.712	1.944
台州市	900749	578.47	0.156	80	0.684	530546	578.47	0.092	209	0.168	562033	578.47	0.097	83	0.672	1.524
福州市	1232753	637.92	0.193	56	0.780	889141	637.92	0.139	136	0.460	800200	637.92	0.125	60	0.764	2.004
南通市	1017700	762.66	0.133	98	0.612	1328300	762.66	0.174	113	0.552	792200	762.66	0.104	75	0.704	1.868
扬州市	714220	458.80	0.156	81	0.680	885272	458.8	0.193	101	0.600	539016	458.80	0.117	65	0.744	2.024
铜陵市	149407	73.99	0.202	52	0.796	243057	73.99	0.328	46	0.820	143295	73.99	0.194	27	0.896	2.512
乌海市	122829	48.06	0.256	33	0.872	433258	48.06	0.901	4	0.988	98112	48.06	0.204	23	0.912	2.772
昆明市	864300	533.99	0.162	73	0.712	1979900	533.99	0.371	34	0.868	699500	533.99	0.131	54	0.788	2.368
淄博市	821564	421.41	0.195	54	0.788	1878678	421.41	0.446	22	0.916	605402	421.41	0.144	46	0.820	2.524
温州市	1711695	779.11	0.220	45	0.824	1058614	779.11	0.136	143	0.432	694989	779.11	0.089	97	0.616	1.872
秦皇岛市	487458	287.24	0.170	68	0.732	872497	287.24	0.304	52	0.796	290566	287.24	0.101	78	0.692	2.220

4. 城市公共服务水平母系统

一级指标	城市公共服务水平母系统									
二级指标	财政公共投入比重子系统			公共项目规模子系统			社保范围及水平子系统			分值合计
	数值	排序	分值	数值	排序	分值	数值	排序	分值	
厦门市	3.752	9	0.968	7.228	1	1.000	2.940	6	0.980	2.948
宁波市	3.196	34	0.868	6.384	14	0.948	2.828	12	0.956	2.772
苏州市	3.292	30	0.884	6.264	20	0.924	2.876	9	0.968	2.776
杭州市	3.508	19	0.928	6.652	7	0.976	2.824	13	0.952	2.856
常州市	2.552	81	0.680	5.596	39	0.848	2.636	24	0.908	2.436
珠海市	3.544	17	0.936	6.528	10	0.964	2.956	4	0.988	2.888
深圳市	3.596	14	0.948	6.776	4	0.988	2.996	1	1.000	2.936
北京市	3.956	2	0.996	6.812	3	0.992	2.932	7	0.976	2.964
中山市	1.912	125	0.504	5.300	47	0.816	2.968	3	0.992	2.312
无锡市	2.668	72	0.716	6.000	28	0.892	2.840	10	0.964	2.572
上海市	3.964	1	1.000	6.340	16	0.940	2.908	8	0.972	2.912
嘉兴市	1.420	165	0.344	5.296	48	0.812	2.704	21	0.920	2.076
广州市	3.800	7	0.976	5.988	29	0.888	2.840	10	0.964	2.828
大连市	3.716	12	0.956	6.236	22	0.916	2.744	18	0.932	2.804
鄂尔多斯市	3.920	3	0.992	6.188	24	0.908	1.732	95	0.624	2.524
镇江市	1.284	175	0.304	5.396	45	0.824	2.428	43	0.832	1.960
南京市	2.972	49	0.808	6.472	11	0.960	2.732	20	0.924	2.692

一级指标	城市公共服务水平母系统											分值合计
二级指标	财政公共投入比重子系统			公共项目规模子系统			社保范围及水平子系统					
	数值	排序	分值	数值	排序	分值	数值	排序	分值			
青岛市	1.604	145	0.424	6.444	13	0.952	2.608	25	0.904			2.280
威海市	2.816	61	0.760	5.876	34	0.868	2.516	36	0.860			2.488
长沙市	2.692	71	0.720	6.560	9	0.968	2.052	71	0.720			2.408
天津市	3.776	8	0.972	5.924	31	0.880	2.816	15	0.944			2.796
绍兴市	1.872	126	0.500	5.848	35	0.864	2.436	40	0.844			2.208
舟山市	3.264	32	0.876	4.848	59	0.768	2.412	45	0.824			2.468
呼和浩特市	3.108	38	0.852	6.772	5	0.984	2.372	48	0.812			2.648
佛山市	1.836	131	0.480	5.464	42	0.836	2.944	5	0.984			2.300
金华市	1.556	150	0.404	5.184	49	0.808	1.892	85	0.664			1.876
东营市	2.656	74	0.708	5.988	29	0.888	1.628	108	0.572			2.168
成都市	1.488	158	0.372	6.284	19	0.928	2.472	39	0.848			2.148
银川市	3.208	33	0.872	6.692	6	0.980	2.560	29	0.888			2.740
湖州市	1.444	162	0.356	4.356	88	0.652	2.204	64	0.748			1.756
武汉市	3.352	27	0.896	7.092	2	0.996	2.548	32	0.876			2.768
太原市	3.276	31	0.880	5.912	32	0.876	2.432	42	0.836			2.592
郑州市	2.708	69	0.728	6.064	26	0.900	1.828	90	0.644			2.272
马鞍山市	3.164	36	0.860	4.048	108	0.572	2.388	47	0.816			2.248

| 一级指标 | | | | | | | 城市公共服务水平母系统 | | | | | |
| 二级指标 | 财政公共投入比重子系统 | | | 公共项目规模子系统 | | | 社保范围及水平子系统 | | | 分值合计 |
	数值	排序	分值	数值	排序	分值	数值	排序	分值	
沈阳市	3.668	13	0.952	5.740	36	0.860	2.704	21	0.920	2.732
济南市	2.012	115	0.544	6.628	8	0.972	2.292	55	0.784	2.300
烟台市	1.736	139	0.448	5.448	44	0.828	2.400	46	0.820	2.096
东莞市	-0.448	286	-0.140	6.384	14	0.948	2.992	2	0.996	1.804
包头市	3.524	18	0.932	6.308	17	0.936	2.564	28	0.892	2.760
芜湖市	2.804	62	0.756	4.716	67	0.736	1.944	76	0.700	2.192
台州市	0.876	209	0.168	3.752	123	0.512	1.524	116	0.540	1.220
福州市	1.424	164	0.348	6.212	23	0.912	2.004	75	0.704	1.964
南通市	1.308	173	0.312	3.284	152	0.396	1.868	88	0.652	1.360
扬州市	0.952	203	0.192	4.404	85	0.664	2.024	73	0.712	1.568
铜陵市	3.396	24	0.908	4.900	57	0.776	2.512	37	0.856	2.540
乌海市	3.916	4	0.988	5.044	52	0.796	2.772	16	0.940	2.724
昆明市	2.356	93	0.632	6.304	18	0.932	2.368	49	0.808	2.372
淄博市	1.556	150	0.404	4.180	102	0.596	2.524	35	0.864	1.864
温州市	1.616	144	0.428	4.880	58	0.772	1.872	87	0.656	1.856
秦皇岛市	1.996	119	0.528	4.264	94	0.628	2.220	63	0.752	1.908

三、城市居民实际享有水平母系统

1. 城市居民收入水平子系统

二级指标	城市居民实际享有水平子系统										居民收入水平子系统													
三级指标	城镇居民人均可支配收入			农村居民人均纯收入			城乡居民收入比			本年度城镇居民人均收入（元）	去年人均收入（元）	城镇化对居民收入的影响					分值小计
	数值（元）	排序	分值	数值（元）	排序	分值	数值	排序	分值			本年度非农业人口（万人）	上年度非农业人口（万人）	数值	排名	分值	
厦门市	26131	10	0.964	9153	26	0.900	0.35027	177	0.296	26131	23948	142.0086	118.58	0.9111	222	0.116	2.276
宁波市	27237	5	0.984	12641	6	0.980	0.46411	35	0.864	27237	25196	202.0400	198.49	1.0620	158	0.372	3.200
苏州市	27188	6	0.980	12969	4	0.988	0.47701	28	0.892	27188	24680	/	368.43	/	240	0.044	2.904
杭州市	26171	9	0.968	11822	12	0.956	0.45172	47	0.816	26171	23534	354.4800	340.76	1.0690	145	0.424	3.164
常州市	23392	18	0.932	11198	14	0.948	0.47871	26	0.900	23392	21234	178.3100	177.73	1.0980	72	0.716	3.496
珠海市	22859	24	0.908	8552	32	0.876	0.37412	139	0.448	22859	20949	102.6500	99.48	1.0575	163	0.352	2.584
深圳市	29245	2	0.996	29245	1	1.000	1.00000	1	1.000	29245	26729	245.9600	228.07	1.0145	203	0.192	3.188
北京市	26738	8	0.972	11986	11	0.960	0.44828	49	0.808	26738	24725	973.3234	950.71	1.0563	165	0.344	3.084
中山市	23088	21	0.920	13061	3	0.992	0.56571	4	0.988	23088	21560	78.4300	77.26	1.0549	167	0.336	3.236
无锡市	25027	11	0.960	12403	8	0.972	0.49558	18	0.932	25027	23263	/	325.15	/	240	0.044	2.908
上海市	28838	3	0.992	12324	9	0.968	0.42735	67	0.736	28838	26675	1236.1586	1216.56	1.0639	154	0.388	3.084
嘉兴市	24693	12	0.956	12685	5	0.984	0.51371	13	0.952	24693	22481	139.9200	130.14	1.0216	198	0.212	3.104
广州市	27610	4	0.988	11067	15	0.944	0.40083	96	0.620	27610	25317	714.0000	704.17	1.0756	133	0.472	3.024

二级指标									居民收入水平子系统					城镇化对居民收入的影响					
三级指标	城镇居民人均可支配收入			农村居民人均纯收入			城乡居民收入比			本年度城镇居民人均收入(元)	去年人均收入(元)				本年度非农业人口(万人)	上年度非农业人口(万人)	数值	排名	分值	分值小计
	数值(元)	排序	分值	数值(元)	排序	分值	数值	排序	分值										
大连市	19014	42	0.836	10725	16	0.940	0.56406	5	0.984	19014	17500	357.9000	347.83	1.0559	166	0.340	3.100			
鄂尔多斯市	21883	28	0.892	7803	43	0.832	0.35658	164	0.348	21883	19435	47.5400	46.89	1.1106	43	0.832	2.904			
镇江市	21041	33	0.872	9642	22	0.916	0.45825	41	0.840	21041	19001	120.5900	120.50	1.1065	49	0.808	3.436			
南京市	24678	13	0.952	9858	21	0.920	0.39947	99	0.608	24678	22337	/	517.22	/	240	0.044	2.524			
青岛市	22368	27	0.896	9249	24	0.908	0.41349	80	0.684	22368	20464	/	/	/	240	0.044	2.532			
威海市	20117	37	0.856	9226	25	0.904	0.45862	40	0.844	20117	18537	/	/	/	240	0.044	2.648			
长沙市	20238	36	0.860	9432	23	0.912	0.46605	33	0.872	20238	17891	234.7616	234.45	1.1297	26	0.900	3.544			
天津市	21402	29	0.888	10675	18	0.932	0.49879	17	0.936	21402	19423	599.6991	588.27	1.0809	118	0.532	3.288			
绍兴市	26874	7	0.976	12026	10	0.964	0.44750	50	0.804	26874	24646	143.4600	139.97	1.0639	155	0.384	3.128			
舟山市	24082	17	0.936	12612	7	0.976	0.52371	11	0.960	24082	22257	36.1000	35.79	1.0727	139	0.448	3.320			
呼和浩特市	22397	26	0.900	7802	44	0.828	0.34835	180	0.284	22397	20267	108.0100	105.50	1.0794	123	0.512	2.524			
佛山市	24578	14	0.948	10699	17	0.936	0.43531	59	0.768	24578	22494	367.6300	364.34	1.0829	109	0.568	3.220			
金华市	22915	22	0.916	9001	27	0.896	0.39280	107	0.576	22915	21408	107.0600	105.31	1.0529	173	0.312	2.700			
东营市	21313	30	0.884	7327	57	0.776	0.34378	190	0.244	21313	19487	/	/	/	240	0.044	1.948			
成都市	17589	57	0.776	7010	64	0.748	0.39854	100	0.604	17589	15580	629.4000	612.08	1.0979	73	0.712	2.840			
银川市	15715	94	0.628	5389	145	0.424	0.34292	192	0.236	15715	14180	113.7133	98.13	0.9564	220	0.124	1.412			
湖州市	23280	19	0.928	11745	13	0.952	0.50451	15	0.944	23280	21604	81.8400	80.75	1.0632	157	0.376	3.200			

中国城市科学发展综合评价报告2011   170

一级指标																
二级指标	居民收入水平子系统															
三级指标	城镇居民人均可支配收入			农村居民人均纯收入			城乡居民收入比			本年度城镇居民人均收入（元）	去年人均收入（元）	城镇化对居民收入的影响					分值小计
	数值（元）	排序	分值	数值（元）	排序	分值	数值	排序	分值			本年度非农业人口（万人）	上年度非农业人口（万人）	数值	排名	分值	
武汉市	18385	49	0.808	7161	61	0.760	0.38950	113	0.552	18385	16712	541.0100	537.24	1.0924	83	0.672	2.792
太原市	15607	100	0.604	6828	69	0.728	0.43751	56	0.780	15607	15230	275.8298	260.65	0.9684	216	0.140	2.252
郑州市	17117	64	0.748	8121	36	0.860	0.47441	29	0.888	17117	15732	312.3000	301.77	1.0514	174	0.308	2.804
马鞍山市	20390	34	0.868	7947	39	0.848	0.38975	111	0.560	20390	18330	64.0949	63.06	1.0944	77	0.696	2.972
沈阳市	18475	48	0.812	8753	28	0.892	0.47378	30	0.884	18475	17013	464.2000	460.49	1.0773	127	0.496	3.084
济南市	22722	25	0.904	7805	42	0.836	0.34350	191	0.240	22722	20802	/	/	/	240	0.044	2.024
烟台市	21125	32	0.876	8642	30	0.884	0.40909	88	0.652	21125	19350	/	/	/	240	0.044	2.456
东莞市	33045	1	1.000	13064	2	0.996	0.39534	105	0.584	33045	30275	80.9600	76.80	1.0354	189	0.248	2.828
包头市	23089	20	0.924	7826	41	0.840	0.33895	197	0.216	23089	20861	136.0700	135.58	1.1028	58	0.772	2.752
芜湖市	16747	66	0.740	6738	72	0.716	0.40234	95	0.624	16747	14939	113.0972	113.72	1.1272	28	0.892	2.972
台州市	24429	16	0.940	10006	20	0.924	0.40960	87	0.656	24429	22738	104.3900	103.35	1.0637	156	0.380	2.900
福州市	20289	35	0.864	7669	48	0.812	0.37799	129	0.488	20289	19009	373.6274	262.91	0.7511	230	0.084	2.248
南通市	19469	39	0.848	8696	29	0.888	0.44666	52	0.796	19469	17540	357.6500	321.60	0.9981	210	0.164	2.696
扬州市	17332	60	0.764	8295	34	0.868	0.47859	27	0.896	17332	15465	/	217.03	1.1050	240	0.044	2.572
铜陵市	16769	65	0.744	6194	93	0.632	0.36937	45	0.424	16769	15173	43.4767	43.47	1.1050	51	0.800	2.600
乌海市	17621	56	0.780	7342	54	0.788	0.41666	77	0.696	17621	15999	45.8600	44.53	1.0694	144	0.428	2.692
昆明市	16496	73	0.712	5080	170	0.324	0.30795	223	0.112	16496	14482	257.4000	222.37	0.9841	214	0.148	1.296

居民收入水平子系统

| 二级指标 | | | | | | | | | | | | | |
| 三级指标 | 城镇居民人均可支配收入 | | | 农村居民人均纯收入 | | | 城乡居民收入比 | | | 城镇化对居民收入的影响 | | | | | | | | 分值小计 |
	数值(元)	排序	分值	数值(元)	排序	分值	数值	排序	分值	本年度城镇居民人均收入(元)	去年人均收入(元)	本年度非农业人口(万人)	上年度非农业人口(万人)	数值	排名	分值	
淄博市	19284	40	0.844	8013	38	0.852	0.41553	78	0.692	19284	17629	/	/	/	240	0.044	2.432
温州市	24467	15	0.944	10100	19	0.928	0.41280	83	0.672	24467	22851	167.1200	164.44	1.0535	171	0.320	2.864
秦皇岛市	15961	84	0.668	5516	131	0.480	0.34559	186	0.260	15961	14081	120.2400	120.10	1.1322	25	0.904	2.312

2. 城市居民生活环境水平子系统

居民生活环境水平子系统

| 二级指标 | | | | | | | | | | | | | | | | |
| 三级指标 | 人均绿地面积 | | | 生活垃圾无害化处理率 | | | 生活污水处理率 | | | 人均生活用电量 | | | 人均生活用水量 | | | 分值小计 |
	数值(平方米)	排序	分值	数值	排序	分值	数值	排序	分值	数值	排序	分值	数值(吨/人)	排序	分值	
厦门市	80.81	18	0.932	100.00	1	1.000	90.26	17	0.936	1554.48	8	0.972	41.4	142	0.436	4.276
宁波市	38.90	84	0.668	100.00	1	1.000	68.87	136	0.460	941.70	28	0.892	90.35	10	0.964	3.984
苏州市	54.14	38	0.852	100.00	1	1.000	69.80	133	0.472	1073.39	19	0.928	86.81	12	0.956	4.208
杭州市	36.53	91	0.640	100.00	1	1.000	88.87	29	0.888	1055.14	21	0.920	93.04	7	0.976	4.424
常州市	29.88	134	0.468	100.00	1	1.000	73.00	119	0.528	771.65	43	0.832	63.35	49	0.808	3.636
珠海市	50.82	45	0.824	87.18	148	0.412	69.25	135	0.464	1194.65	15	0.944	66.98	42	0.836	3.480
深圳市	391.83	2	0.996	94.30	110	0.564	80.17	79	0.688	3217.28	1	1.000	40.61	145	0.424	3.672

续表

二级指标	居民生活环境水平子系统															分值
三级指标	人均绿地面积			生活垃圾无害化处理率			生活污水处理率			人均生活用电量			人均生活用水量			小计
	数值（平方米）	排序	分值	数值	排序	分值	数值	排序	分值	数值	排序	分值	数值（吨/人）	排序	分值	
北京市	52.52	42	0.836	98.22	85	0.664	77.85	95	0.624	1069.31	20	0.924	39.52	151	0.400	3.448
中山市	9.53	267	-0.064	87.48	145	0.424	90.90	16	0.940	1588.41	6	0.980	139.3	1	1.000	3.280
无锡市	69.53	23	0.912	100.00	1	1.000	86.51	39	0.848	900.93	31	0.880	61.15	55	0.784	4.424
上海市	87.81	16	0.940	82.30	169	0.328	78.90	87	0.656	1145.31	18	0.932	50.66	95	0.624	3.480
嘉兴市	46.99	56	0.780	100.00	1	1.000	82.51	64	0.748	610.00	75	0.704	30.39	207	0.176	3.408
广州市	190.05	6	0.980	82.35	168	0.332	78.43	90	0.644	1555.98	7	0.976	0.06	287	-0.144	2.788
大连市	40.37	77	0.696	94.02	113	0.552	92.91	10	0.964	709.33	54	0.788	23.06	252	-0.004	2.996
鄂尔多斯市	244.29	4	0.988	87.22	146	0.420	78.32	91	0.640	869.50	35	0.864	12.07	280	-0.116	2.796
镇江市	61.86	29	0.888	100.00	1	1.000	66.91	146	0.420	593.93	80	0.684	48.58	104	0.588	3.580
南京市	141.47	10	0.964	74.88	191	0.240	58.65	174	0.308	780.46	42	0.836	57.5	69	0.728	3.076
青岛市	58.09	33	0.872	100.00	1	1.000	85.14	44	0.828	1934.41	4	0.988	47.27	110	0.564	4.252
威海市	85.95	17	0.936	100.00	1	1.000	88.74	31	0.880	866.04	36	0.860	26.96	230	0.084	3.760
长沙市	33.76	104	0.588	100.00	1	1.000	81.40	73	0.712	1427.40	10	0.964	106.32	4	0.988	4.252
天津市	21.63	201	0.200	94.30	110	0.564	80.10	80	0.684	804.71	40	0.844	34.41	185	0.264	2.556
绍兴市	53.34	39	0.848	100.00	1	1.000	75.93	104	0.588	715.76	52	0.796	32.26	199	0.208	3.440
舟山市	25.94	166	0.340	92.73	120	0.524	70.54	129	0.488	585.47	84	0.668	32.93	193	0.232	2.252
呼和浩特市	22.26	196	0.220	95.20	99	0.608	73.80	116	0.540	585.91	83	0.672	20.47	262	-0.044	1.996
佛山市	22.82	191	0.240	95.47	97	0.616	68.83	138	0.452	1176.11	17	0.936	86.4	13	0.952	3.196

二级指标	居民生活环境水平子系统															
三级指标	人均绿地面积			生活垃圾无害化处理率			生活污水处理率			人均生活用电量			人均生活用水量			分值小计
	数值（平方米）	排序	分值	数值	排序	分值	数值	排序	分值	数值	排序	分值	数值（吨/人）	排序	分值	
金华市	28.19	147	0.416	98.97	80	0.684	61.71	161	0.360	561.18	88	0.652	36.71	167	0.336	2.448
东营市	66.37	25	0.904	98.39	84	0.668	76.15	102	0.596	338.77	197	0.216	38.19	157	0.376	2.760
成都市	30.95	127	0.496	83.63	163	0.352	78.78	88	0.652	710.77	53	0.792	103.31	5	0.984	3.276
银川市	56.67	34	0.868	100.00	1	1.000	90.93	15	0.944	691.69	59	0.768	42.28	136	0.460	4.040
湖州市	30.90	128	0.492	100.00	1	1.000	83.08	59	0.768	563.31	87	0.656	45.93	114	0.548	3.464
武汉市	29.64	136	0.460	77.95	183	0.272	89.80	22	0.916	940.75	29	0.888	65.79	43	0.832	3.368
太原市	27.01	158	0.372	94.80	107	0.576	70.00	130	0.484	557.76	89	0.648	44.93	119	0.528	2.608
郑州市	36.14	93	0.632	86.78	150	0.404	97.20	2	0.996	948.70	27	0.896	28.35	223	0.112	3.040
马鞍山市	76.39	20	0.924	100.00	1	1.000	69.80	133	0.472	481.86	122	0.516	60.89	57	0.776	3.688
沈阳市	50.75	46	0.820	100.00	1	1.000	78.00	93	0.632	697.38	56	0.780	35.87	172	0.316	3.548
济南市	31.49	122	0.516	77.68	184	0.268	78.21	92	0.636	753.41	46	0.820	47.93	106	0.580	2.820
烟台市	50.40	48	0.812	92.69	121	0.520	89.10	27	0.896	547.65	94	0.628	23.63	249	0.008	2.864
东莞市	156.68	8	0.972	28.79	252	-0.004	67.07	145	0.424	3053.98	2	0.996	64.09	47	0.816	3.204
包头市	49.78	51	0.800	92.00	123	0.512	82.01	70	0.724	639.31	66	0.740	19.25	264	-0.052	2.724
芜湖市	47.46	53	0.792	98.90	82	0.676	67.98	142	0.436	499.62	113	0.552	43.76	124	0.508	2.964
台州市	33.32	111	0.560	95.90	95	0.624	72.05	123	0.512	695.83	57	0.776	51.86	89	0.648	3.120
福州市	40.68	76	0.700	98.20	86	0.660	72.76	120	0.524	1696.50	5	0.984	56.32	74	0.708	3.576
南通市	18.00	224	0.108	100.00	1	1.000	82.90	63	0.752	508.91	109	0.568	90.4	9	0.968	3.396

第五部分 城市排行榜及部分城市数据

173

居民生活环境水平子系统

二级指标																分值小计
三级指标	人均绿地面积			生活垃圾无害化处理率			生活污水处理率			人均生活用电量			人均生活用水量			
	数值（平方米）	排序	分值	数值	排序	分值	数值	排序	分值	数值	排序	分值	数值（吨/人）	排序	分值	
扬州市	28.03	148	0.412	100.00	1	1.000	66.47	149	0.408	616.37	74	0.708	41.75	140	0.444	2.972
铜陵市	103.34	13	0.952	83.08	164	0.348	71.70	126	0.500	410.43	158	0.372	25.1	241	0.040	2.212
乌海市	19.91	220	0.124	81.53	174	0.308	68.86	137	0.456	360.34	182	0.276	72.19	33	0.872	2.036
昆明市	40.11	79	0.688	78.94	179	0.288	79.94	82	0.676	1401.14	11	0.960	42.14	139	0.448	3.060
淄博市	52.82	41	0.840	100.00	1	1.000	88.87	29	0.888	488.23	119	0.528	37.48	161	0.360	3.616
温州市	23.61	184	0.268	61.56	205	0.184	59.18	171	0.320	1301.26	12	0.956	8.4	286	-0.140	1.588
秦皇岛市	49.97	49	0.808	96.93	91	0.640	89.20	26	0.900	832.70	38	0.852	31.12	204	0.188	3.388

3. 城市居民就业水平子系统

居民就业水平子系统

二级指标				城镇化对就业的影响				城镇登记失业率					分值小计
三级指标	本年度失业人数（人）	去年失业人数（人）	本年度非农业人口（万人）	上年度非农业人口（万人）	数值	排名	分值	年末城镇就业人数（万人）	年末城镇登记失业人数（万人）	数值	排名	分值	
厦门市	29700	29200	142.0086	118.58	0.849318	33	0.872	194.80	3.0000	0.015167	17	0.936	1.808
宁波市	59183	58036	202.0400	198.49	1.001846	123	0.512	263.30	5.9000	0.021917	52	0.796	1.308
苏州市	47572	47905	/	368.43	/	241	0.040	318.70	4.8000	0.014838	15	0.944	0.984

二级指标	居民就业水平子系统												
三级指标	城镇化对就业的影响							城镇登记失业率					
	本年度失业人数（人）	去年失业业人数（人）	本年度非农业人口（万人）	上年度非农业人口（万人）	数值	排名	分值	年末城镇就业人数（万人）	年末城镇登记失业人数（万人）	数值	排名	分值	分值小计
杭州市	56489	54514	354.4800	340.76	0.996122	119	0.528	383.90	5.7000	0.014630	14	0.948	1.476
常州市	30811	32777	178.3100	177.73	0.936961	65	0.744	165.30	3.1000	0.018409	34	0.868	1.612
珠海市	12903	13181	102.6500	99.48	0.948679	80	0.684	84.90	1.3000	0.015081	16	0.940	1.624
深圳市	33988	28182	245.9600	228.07	1.118298	194	0.228	454.00	3.4000	0.007433	2	0.996	1.224
北京市	81550	103250	973.3234	950.71	0.77148	25	0.904	619.30	8.2000	0.013068	11	0.960	1.864
中山市	9500	9295	78.4300	77.26	1.006808	126	0.500	120.20	0.9506	0.007846	4	0.988	1.488
无锡市	47268	50473	/	325.15	/	241	0.040	209.20	4.7000	0.021973	53	0.792	0.832
上海市	278700	266000	1236.1586	1216.56	1.031133	155	0.384	385.40	27.9000	0.067505	272	-0.084	0.300
嘉兴市	27006	27034	139.9200	130.14	0.92914	59	0.768	165.10	2.7000	0.016091	25	0.904	1.672
广州市	278752	76453	714.0000	704.17	3.59586	239	0.048	375.30	7.7000	0.020104	42	0.836	0.884
大连市	67206	52533	357.9000	347.83	1.243315	223	0.112	243.30	6.7000	0.026800	89	0.648	0.760
鄂尔多斯市	9061	11621	47.5400	46.89	0.769048	24	0.908	31.10	0.9400	0.029938	111	0.560	1.468
镇江市	15999	16671	120.5900	120.50	0.958974	85	0.664	70.30	1.6000	0.022253	58	0.772	1.436
南京市	59401	64641	/	517.22	/	241	0.040	261.20	5.9000	0.022089	56	0.780	0.820
青岛市	59396	61912	/	/	/	241	0.040	226.80	5.9000	0.025355	83	0.672	0.712
威海市	7692	7598	/	/	/	241	0.040	61.80	0.8000	0.012780	10	0.964	1.004

二级指标		城镇化对就业的影响					居民就业水平子系统		城镇登记失业率			分值小计
三级指标	本年度失业人数（人）	去年失业人数（人）	本年度非农业人口（万人）	上年度非农业人口（万人）	数值	排名	分值	年末城镇就业人数（万人）	年末城镇登记失业人数（万人）	数值	排名	分值
长沙市	46067	43939	234.7616	234.45	1.047039	168	0.332	163.20	4.7000	0.027993	102	0.596	0.928
天津市	150000	129900	599.6991	588.27	1.132727	201	0.200	505.80	15.0000	0.028802	107	0.576	0.776
绍兴市	34174	30980	143.4600	139.97	1.076263	175	0.304	118.30	3.4000	0.027938	101	0.600	0.904
舟山市	7298	7729	36.1000	35.79	0.036128	64	0.748	30.30	0.7298	0.023519	68	0.732	1.480
呼和浩特市	26885	25555	108.0100	105.50	1.027597	149	0.408	65.20	2.7000	0.039764	192	0.236	0.644
佛山市	18818	19309	367.6300	364.34	0.96585	93	0.632	172.00	1.9000	0.010926	7	0.976	1.608
金华市	26920	25721	107.0600	105.31	1.029508	153	0.392	173.20	2.7000	0.015350	21	0.920	1.312
东营市	9913	9804	/	/	/	241	0.040	50.50	1.0000	0.019417	37	0.856	0.896
成都市	67400	69453	629.4000	612.08	0.943736	73	0.712	363.00	6.7000	0.018123	31	0.880	1.592
银川市	19403	20734	113.7133	98.13	0.872563	27	0.896	58.70	1.9000	0.031353	134	0.468	1.364
湖州市	12128	12295	81.8400	80.75	0.973279	98	0.612	77.70	1.2000	0.015209	18	0.932	1.544
武汉市	111200	111900	541.0100	537.24	0.98582	111	0.560	217.20	11.1000	0.048620	241	0.040	0.600
太原市	43032	40261	275.8298	260.65	1.010005	131	0.480	118.00	4.3000	0.035159	167	0.336	0.816
郑州市	39200	49410	312.3000	301.77	0.766511	23	0.912	219.40	3.9000	0.017465	30	0.884	1.796
马鞍山市	7702	8831	64.0949	63.06	0.858073	38	0.852	26.30	0.7702	0.028452	105	0.584	1.436
沈阳市	77492	75542	464.2000	460.49	1.017615	141	0.440	185.70	7.7000	0.039814	193	0.232	0.672

| 二级指标 | 居民就业水平子系统 | | | | | | | | | | | | |
| 三级指标 | 城镇化对就业的影响 | | | | | | | 城镇登记失业率 | | | | | 分值小计 |
	本年度失业人数（人）	去年失业人数（人）	本年度非农业人口（万人）	上年度非农业人口（万人）	数值	排名	分值	年末城镇就业人数（万人）	年末城镇登记失业人数（万人）	数值	排名	分值	
济南市	60163	52973	/	/	/	241	0.040	177.60	6.0000	0.032680	143	0.432	0.472
烟台市	47641	50063	/	/	/	241	0.040	142.40	4.8000	0.032609	142	0.436	0.476
东莞市	7674	7630	80.9600	76.80	0.954087	82	0.676	96.50	0.7674	0.007890	5	0.984	1.660
包头市	41924	35739	136.0700	135.58	1.168836	214	0.148	76.20	3.7000	0.046308	232	0.076	0.224
芜湖市	20539	21279	113.0972	113.72	0.970539	97	0.616	56.60	2.1000	0.035775	168	0.332	0.948
台州市	26790	26310	104.3900	103.35	1.0081	128	0.492	121.10	2.7000	0.021809	51	0.800	1.292
福州市	35935	35739	373.6274	262.91	0.707528	20	0.924	150.90	3.6000	0.023301	67	0.736	1.660
南通市	34850	37194	357.6500	321.60	0.842535	31	0.880	117.00	3.5000	0.029046	109	0.568	1.448
扬州市	31337	26912	/	217.03	/	241	0.040	110.50	3.1000	0.027289	97	0.616	0.656
铜陵市	10959	10177	43.4767	43.47	1.076674	176	0.300	26.50	1.1000	0.039855	194	0.228	0.528
乌海市	8186	8000	45.8600	44.53	0.993574	116	0.540	17.00	0.8300	0.046551	234	0.068	0.608
昆明市	34700	34700	257.4000	222.37	0.863908	41	0.840	94.00	12.0000	0.113208	286	-0.140	0.700
淄博市	27484	27651	/	/	/	241	0.040	85.60	2.7000	0.030578	126	0.500	0.540
温州市	30975	30912	167.1200	164.44	0.985969	109	0.568	242.00	3.1000	0.012648	9	0.968	1.536
秦皇岛市	18539	19976	120.2400	120.10	0.926983	58	0.772	55.30	1.9000	0.033217	146	0.420	1.192

4. 城市居民消费水平子系统

二级指标	居民消费水平子系统																			
三级指标	食品支出总额（元）	城镇居民人均生活消费性支出总额（元）	城镇居民恩格尔系数			人均年末储蓄余额			人均住宅建筑面积			居住支出占消费支出比重			人均社会消费品零售额			分值小计
			数值	排序	分值	数值	排序	分值	数值（平方米）	排名	分值	数值（%）	排序	分值	数值（元）	排序	分值	
厦门市	6879	17990	0.382	156	0.380	45956.333	12	0.956	30.77	120	0.524	10.79	182	0.276	22465.179	17	0.936	3.072
宁波市	6130	17621	0.348	91	0.640	42085.038	16	0.940	29.72	156	0.380	8.91	90	0.644	20734.953	20	0.924	3.528
苏州市	5919	17121	0.346	86	0.660	42201.608	15	0.944	33.11	74	0.708	9.89	146	0.420	21632.323	19	0.928	3.660
杭州市	6728	17952	0.375	143	0.432	54527.078	9	0.968	30.85	118	0.532	11.01	189	0.248	22957.648	14	0.948	3.128
常州市	5375	15693	0.343	82	0.676	39450.110	20	0.924	32.90	83	0.672	6.75	15	0.944	20026.605	24	0.908	4.124
珠海市	6747	17948	0.376	144	0.428	55528.574	8	0.972	29.25	167	0.336	10.19	163	0.352	27122.881	4	0.988	3.076
深圳市	7535	21526	0.350	99	0.608	64223.152	5	0.984	26.64	227	0.096	11.03	191	0.240	28813.478	3	0.992	2.920
北京市	5936	17893	0.332	61	0.760	82996.492	1	1.000	28.81	185	0.264	7.21	24	0.908	30255.766	2	0.996	3.928
中山市	6881	17415	0.395	180	0.284	48500.552	10	0.964	33.55	64	0.748	9.07	97	0.616	21838.464	18	0.932	3.544
无锡市	5717	15619	0.366	124	0.508	43587.486	14	0.948	34.70	46	0.820	11.53	208	0.172	24899.379	7	0.976	3.424
上海市	7345	20992	0.350	98	0.612	74728.052	3	0.992	34.00	56	0.780	9.11	103	0.592	26925.451	5	0.984	3.960
嘉兴市	5178	15361	0.337	70	0.724	33101.393	31	0.880	30.99	112	0.556	11.84	218	0.132	16586.144	34	0.868	3.160
广州市	7571	22821	0.332	62	0.756	79483.381	2	0.996	27.11	215	0.144	9.30	112	0.556	34987.329	1	1.000	3.452
大连市	5821	15330	0.380	154	0.388	47498.358	11	0.960	25.10	252	-0.004	9.35	113	0.552	22637.736	15	0.944	2.840
鄂尔多斯市	4823	18333	0.263	4	0.988	28596.038	52	0.796	36.77	31	0.880	9.56	125	0.504	19749.342	26	0.900	4.068

二级指标	城镇居民恩格尔系数					居民消费水平子系统												
三级指标	食品支出总额(元)	人均生活消费性支出总额(元)	数值	排序	分值	人均年末储蓄余额 数值	排序	分值	人均住宅建筑面积 数值(平方米)	排名	分值	居住支出占消费支出比重 数值(%)	排序	分值	人均社会消费品零售额 数值(元)	排序	分值	分值小计
镇江市	4731	12197	0.388	166	0.340	27615.814	54	0.788	34.12	53	0.792	9.59	128	0.492	15499.378	40	0.844	3.256
南京市	5679	15873	0.358	110	0.564	39625.424	19	0.928	27.04	218	0.132	6.55	11	0.960	25093.585	6	0.980	3.564
青岛市	6189	16080	0.385	160	0.364	29774.627	45	0.824	26.71	224	0.108	8.92	91	0.640	20379.542	23	0.912	2.848
威海市	4110	14442	0.285	8	0.972	29344.800	47	0.816	43.27	12	0.956	10.39	173	0.312	20453.677	22	0.916	3.972
长沙市	4859	15020	0.324	49	0.808	28323.787	53	0.792	29.03	170	0.324	10.83	185	0.264	22957.892	13	0.952	3.140
天津市	5405	14801	0.365	121	0.520	40491.874	17	0.936	29.89	152	0.396	10.17	161	0.360	19792.451	25	0.904	3.116
绍兴市	6173	16607	0.372	139	0.448	37262.746	22	0.916	29.11	169	0.328	11.06	192	0.236	15671.343	39	0.848	2.776
舟山市	5606	15236	0.368	128	0.492	34430.957	28	0.892	30.15	142	0.436	13.12	250	0.004	17554.203	30	0.884	2.708
呼和浩特市	4356	14752	0.295	13	0.952	28646.469	49	0.808	29.99	147	0.416	10.15	159	0.368	23674.089	11	0.960	3.504
佛山市	6679	19296	0.346	89	0.648	65785.174	4	0.988	38.70	25	0.904	9.19	107	0.576	23492.139	12	0.956	4.072
金华市	5063	15849	0.319	42	0.836	33690.425	29	0.888	34.06	54	0.788	7.42	30	0.884	15313.602	41	0.840	4.236
东营市	4084	13599	0.300	21	0.920	31728.387	37	0.856	33.04	75	0.704	8.89	89	0.648	16042.586	36	0.860	3.988
成都市	5132	13143	0.390	171	0.320	32906.194	33	0.872	28.88	179	0.288	7.43	31	0.880	15155.805	44	0.828	3.188
银川市	4027	12272	0.328	56	0.780	30520.096	41	0.840	28.94	176	0.300	10.32	171	0.320	10898.540	72	0.716	2.956
湖州市	5249	14561	0.360	113	0.552	24583.086	66	0.740	31.50	105	0.584	12.35	236	0.060	15806.071	38	0.852	2.788

二级指标						居民消费水平子系统															
三级指标	城镇居民恩格尔系数					人均年末储蓄余额			人均住宅建筑面积			居民支出占消费支出比重			人均社会消费品零售额			分值小计
	食品支出总额(元)	人均生活消费性支出总额(元)	数值	排序	分值	数值	排序	分值	数值(平方米)	排名	分值	数值(%)	排序	分值	数值(元)	排序	分值	
武汉市	5110	12710	0.402	199	0.208	33078.144	32	0.876	26.00	238	0.052	9.05	95	0.624	23781.179	10	0.964	2.724
太原市	3764	11708	0.321	46	0.820	59540.856	7	0.976	19.28	285	-0.136	11.87	221	0.120	20609.349	21	0.920	2.700
郑州市	3761	10804	0.348	92	0.636	33393.198	30	0.884	27.32	213	0.152	9.60	129	0.488	19079.274	28	0.892	3.052
马鞍山市	4979	12739	0.391	172	0.316	23536.977	73	0.712	26.83	222	0.116	8.78	84	0.668	9747.884	91	0.640	2.452
沈阳市	5745	16111	0.357	109	0.568	375513.252	21	0.920	30.23	141	0.440	9.46	118	0.532	22628.318	16	0.940	3.400
济南市	4837	14764	0.328	53	0.792	28622.206	51	0.800	29.40	162	0.356	10.14	158	0.372	23892.355	9	0.968	3.288
烟台市	5233	14537	0.360	112	0.556	26693.008	55	0.784	28.89	178	0.292	10.11	154	0.388	17521.768	31	0.880	2.900
东莞市	7972	24270	0.328	57	0.776	45741.260	13	0.952	53.75	2	0.996	9.20	109	0.568	15103.507	46	0.820	4.112
包头市	5985	18950	0.316	39	0.848	26670.985	56	0.780	30.60	122	0.516	8.32	59	0.768	24016.006	8	0.972	3.884
芜湖市	4735	11786	0.402	196	0.220	17699.087	102	0.596	29.37	163	0.352	11.43	203	0.192	10500.313	82	0.676	2.036
台州市	5578	16390	0.340	75	0.704	25282.848	63	0.752	39.88	20	0.924	7.62	35	0.864	14263.662	49	0.808	4.052
福州市	5675	14105	0.402	200	0.204	29814.737	44	0.828	27.05	217	0.136	8.53	72	0.716	19485.367	27	0.896	2.780
南通市	4336	11908	0.364	120	0.524	31793.469	36	0.860	32.25	93	0.632	7.15	22	0.916	15142.508	45	0.824	3.756
扬州市	4274	11439	0.374	141	0.440	24364.616	67	0.736	33.50	67	0.736	8.60	75	0.704	13626.653	54	0.788	3.404
铜陵市	4299	10114	0.425	237	0.056	22850.351	78	0.692	26.01	237	0.056	9.28	111	0.560	11327.311	69	0.728	2.092

二级指标							居民消费水平子系统									
三级指标	城镇居民恩格尔系数			人均年末储蓄余额			人均住宅建筑面积			居住支出占消费支出比重			人均社会消费品零售额			分值小计
	食品支出总额（元）	人均生活消费性支出总额（元）	数值	排序	分值	数值	排序	分值	数值（平方米）	排名	分值	数值（%）	排序	分值	数值（元）	排序	分值
乌海市	4211	14962	0.281	6	0.980	34941.797	25	0.904	30.30	139	0.448	7.14	21	0.920	12493.642	62	0.756	4.008
昆明市	4834	11396	0.424	236	0.060	30619.745	39	0.848	22.49	272	-0.084	7.65	37	0.856	13767.680	52	0.796	2.476
淄博市	3781	12685	0.298	16	0.940	23211.598	76	0.700	32.54	88	0.652	13.46	259	-0.032	16857.155	32	0.876	3.136
温州市	6478	17825	0.363	118	0.532	34840.859	26	0.900	30.93	116	0.540	8.53	72	0.716	16007.122	37	0.856	3.544
秦皇岛市	3453	8691	0.397	182	0.276	24876.733	64	0.748	26.93	220	0.124	9.44	117	0.536	9511.501	100	0.604	2.288

5. 城市居民安全水平子系统
（暂缺）

6. 城市居民实际享有水平母系统

一级指标	城市居民实际享有水平母系统															
二级指标	居民收入水平子系统			居民生活环境水平子系统			居民就业水平子系统			居民消费水平子系统			居民安全水平子系统			分值合计
	数值	排序	分值	数值	排序	分值	数值	排序	分值	数值	排序	分值	数值	排序	分值	
厦门市	2.276	71	0.720	4.276	3	0.992	1.808	5	0.984	3.072	43	0.832			0	3.528
宁波市	3.200	8	0.972	3.984	9	0.968	1.308	64	0.748	3.528	19	0.928			0	3.616
苏州市	2.904	28	0.892	4.208	6	0.980	0.984	108	0.572	3.660	14	0.948			0	3.392
杭州市	3.164	12	0.956	4.424	1	1.000	1.476	38	0.852	3.128	39	0.848			0	3.656
常州市	3.496	2	0.996	3.636	17	0.936	1.612	25	0.904	4.124	2	0.996			0	3.832
珠海市	2.584	49	0.808	3.480	27	0.896	1.624	23	0.912	3.076	42	0.836			0	3.452
深圳市	3.188	11	0.960	3.672	16	0.940	1.224	79	0.688	2.920	51	0.800			0	3.388
北京市	3.084	16	0.940	3.448	30	0.884	1.864	3	0.992	3.928	11	0.960			0	3.776
中山市	3.236	6	0.980	3.280	44	0.828	1.488	36	0.860	3.544	17	0.936			0	3.604
无锡市	2.908	27	0.896	4.424	1	1.000	0.832	148	0.412	3.424	24	0.908			0	3.216
上海市	3.084	16	0.940	3.480	27	0.896	0.300	251	0.000	3.960	10	0.964			0	2.800
嘉兴市	3.104	14	0.948	3.408	35	0.864	1.672	14	0.948	3.160	35	0.864			0	3.624
广州市	3.024	19	0.928	2.788	88	0.652	0.884	133	0.472	3.452	23	0.912			0	2.964
大连市	3.100	15	0.944	2.996	72	0.716	0.760	163	0.352	2.840	60	0.764			0	2.776
鄂尔多斯市	2.904	28	0.892	2.796	87	0.656	1.468	39	0.848	4.068	5	0.984			0	3.380
镇江市	3.436	3	0.992	3.580	21	0.920	1.436	44	0.828	3.256	30	0.884			0	3.624

一级指标	城市居民实际享有水平母系统															分值合计
二级指标	居民收入水平子系统			居民生活环境水平子系统			居民就业水平子系统			居民消费水平子系统			居民安全水平子系统			
	数值	排序	分值	数值	排序	分值	数值	排序	分值	数值	排序	分值	数值	排序	分值	
南京市	2.524	55	0.784	3.076	62	0.756	0.820	152	0.396	3.564	16	0.940			0	2.876
青岛市	2.532	52	0.796	4.252	4	0.988	0.712	171	0.320	2.848	59	0.768			0	2.872
威海市	2.648	46	0.820	3.760	14	0.948	1.004	104	0.588	3.972	9	0.968			0	3.324
长沙市	3.544	1	1.000	4.252	4	0.988	0.928	119	0.528	3.140	36	0.860			0	3.376
天津市	3.288	5	0.984	2.556	110	0.564	0.776	159	0.368	3.116	40	0.844			0	2.760
绍兴市	3.128	13	0.952	3.440	32	0.876	0.904	123	0.512	2.776	67	0.736			0	3.076
舟山市	3.320	4	0.988	2.252	137	0.456	1.480	37	0.856	2.708	72	0.716			0	3.016
呼和浩特市	2.524	55	0.784	1.996	165	0.344	0.644	188	0.252	3.504	21	0.920			0	2.300
佛山市	3.220	7	0.976	3.196	52	0.796	1.608	26	0.900	4.072	4	0.988			0	3.660
金华市	2.700	41	0.840	2.448	119	0.528	1.312	63	0.752	4.236	1	1.000			0	3.120
东营市	1.948	117	0.536	2.760	89	0.648	0.896	125	0.504	3.988	8	0.972			0	2.660
成都市	2.840	35	0.864	3.276	46	0.820	1.592	27	0.896	3.188	34	0.868			0	3.448
银川市	1.412	187	0.256	4.040	7	0.976	1.364	51	0.800	2.956	49	0.808			0	2.840
湖州市	3.200	8	0.972	3.464	29	0.888	1.544	31	0.880	2.788	64	0.748			0	3.488
武汉市	2.792	38	0.852	3.368	39	0.848	0.600	194	0.228	2.724	68	0.732			0	2.660
太原市	2.252	75	0.704	2.608	103	0.592	0.816	153	0.392	2.700	73	0.712			0	2.400
郑州市	2.804	37	0.856	3.040	67	0.736	1.796	8	0.972	3.052	44	0.828			0	3.392

一级指标	城市居民实际享有水平母系统															
二级指标	居民收入水平子系统			居民生活环境水平子系统			居民就业水平子系统			居民消费水平子系统			居民安全水平子系统			分值合计
	数值	排序	分值	数值	排序	分值	数值	排序	分值	数值	排序	分值	数值	排序	分值	分值合计
马鞍山市	2.972	23	0.912	3.688	15	0.944	1.436	44	0.828	2.452	106	0.580			0	3.264
沈阳市	3.084	16	0.940	3.548	24	0.908	0.672	179	0.288	3.400	26	0.900			0	3.036
济南市	2.024	104	0.588	2.820	85	0.664	0.472	221	0.120	3.288	29	0.888			0	2.260
烟台市	2.456	60	0.764	2.864	81	0.680	0.476	220	0.124	2.900	53	0.792			0	2.360
东莞市	2.828	36	0.860	3.204	50	0.804	1.660	18	0.932	4.112	3	0.992			0	3.588
包头市	2.752	40	0.844	2.724	95	0.624	0.224	267	-0.064	3.884	12	0.956			0	2.360
芜湖市	2.972	23	0.912	2.964	76	0.700	0.948	116	0.540	2.036	151	0.400			0	2.552
台州市	2.900	31	0.880	3.120	56	0.780	1.292	67	0.736	4.052	6	0.980			0	3.376
福州市	2.248	78	0.692	3.576	22	0.916	1.660	18	0.932	2.780	66	0.740			0	3.280
南通市	2.696	42	0.836	3.396	36	0.860	1.448	43	0.832	3.756	13	0.952			0	3.480
扬州市	2.572	50	0.804	2.972	74	0.708	0.656	183	0.272	3.404	25	0.904			0	2.688
铜陵市	2.600	48	0.812	2.212	141	0.440	0.528	205	0.184	2.092	144	0.428			0	1.864
乌海市	2.692	43	0.832	2.036	159	0.368	0.608	192	0.236	4.008	7	0.976			0	2.412
昆明市	1.296	201	0.200	3.060	64	0.748	0.700	174	0.308	2.476	102	0.596			0	1.852
淄博市	2.432	61	0.760	3.616	18	0.932	0.540	201	0.200	3.136	37	0.856			0	2.748
温州市	2.864	32	0.876	1.588	200	0.204	1.536	33	0.872	3.544	17	0.936			0	2.888
秦皇岛市	2.312	69	0.728	3.388	38	0.852	1.192	84	0.668	2.288	126	0.500			0	2.748

四、E&G 综合体系

母系统	定量分析系统									E&G 综合指数	
	城市经济发展水平系统			城市公共服务水平系统			城市居民实际享有水平系统				
	合计	排序	分值	合计	排序	分值	合计	排序	分值	分值总计	总排名
厦门市	3.196	9	0.968	2.948	2	0.996	3.528	10	0.964	2.928	1
宁波市	3.380	3	0.992	2.772	12	0.956	3.616	7	0.976	2.924	2
苏州市	3.628	1	1.000	2.776	11	0.960	3.392	16	0.940	2.900	3
杭州市	2.976	20	0.924	2.856	6	0.980	3.656	4	0.988	2.892	4
常州市	3.272	6	0.980	2.436	31	0.880	3.832	1	1.000	2.860	5
珠海市	2.956	22	0.916	2.888	5	0.984	3.452	13	0.952	2.852	6
深圳市	2.892	29	0.888	2.936	3	0.992	3.388	18	0.932	2.812	7
北京市	2.592	48	0.812	2.964	1	1.000	3.776	2	0.996	2.808	8
中山市	3.176	10	0.964	2.312	39	0.848	3.604	8	0.972	2.784	9
无锡市	3.120	11	0.960	2.572	23	0.912	3.216	27	0.896	2.768	10
上海市	3.116	12	0.956	2.912	4	0.988	2.800	46	0.820	2.764	11
嘉兴市	3.260	7	0.976	2.076	64	0.748	3.624	5	0.984	2.708	12
广州市	2.792	36	0.860	2.828	7	0.976	2.964	35	0.864	2.700	13
大连市	2.804	34	0.868	2.804	9	0.968	2.776	49	0.808	2.644	14
鄂尔多斯市	2.580	49	0.808	2.524	26	0.900	3.380	19	0.928	2.636	15
镇江市	3.052	16	0.940	1.960	74	0.708	3.624	5	0.984	2.632	16

母系统	定量分析系统									E&G综合指数	
	城市经济发展水平系统			城市公共服务水平系统			城市居民实际享有水平系统				
	合计	排序	分值	合计	排序	分值	合计	排序	分值	分值总计	总排名
南京市	2.780	37	0.856	2.692	18	0.932	2.876	42	0.836	2.624	17
青岛市	3.112	14	0.948	2.280	42	0.836	2.872	43	0.832	2.616	18
威海市	2.560	50	0.804	2.488	27	0.896	3.324	23	0.912	2.612	19
长沙市	2.624	47	0.816	2.408	33	0.872	3.376	20	0.924	2.612	19
天津市	2.724	39	0.848	2.796	10	0.964	2.760	52	0.796	2.608	21
绍兴市	2.948	23	0.912	2.208	51	0.800	3.076	31	0.880	2.592	22
舟山市	2.636	45	0.824	2.468	28	0.892	3.016	34	0.868	2.584	23
呼和浩特市	3.116	12	0.956	2.648	19	0.928	2.300	79	0.688	2.572	24
佛山市	2.380	73	0.712	2.300	40	0.844	3.660	3	0.992	2.548	25
金华市	3.232	8	0.972	1.876	82	0.676	3.120	28	0.892	2.540	26
东营市	3.364	5	0.984	2.168	55	0.784	2.660	58	0.772	2.540	26
成都市	2.552	51	0.800	2.148	57	0.776	3.448	14	0.948	2.524	28
银川市	2.456	63	0.752	2.740	15	0.944	2.840	44	0.828	2.524	28
湖州市	2.948	23	0.912	1.756	96	0.620	3.488	11	0.960	2.492	30
武汉市	2.492	59	0.768	2.768	13	0.952	2.660	58	0.772	2.492	30
太原市	2.644	42	0.836	2.592	22	0.916	2.400	69	0.728	2.480	32
郑州市	2.352	75	0.704	2.272	43	0.832	3.392	16	0.940	2.476	33

母系统	城市经济发展水平系统			定量分析系统 城市公共服务水平系统			城市居民实际享有水平系统			E&G 综合指数	
子系统	合计	排序	分值	合计	排序	分值	合计	排序	分值	分值总计	总排名
马鞍山市	2.448	65	0.744	2.248	46	0.820	3.264	26	0.900	2.464	34
沈阳市	2.172	89	0.648	2.732	16	0.940	3.036	33	0.872	2.460	35
济南市	2.900	28	0.892	2.300	40	0.844	2.260	83	0.672	2.408	36
烟台市	2.972	21	0.920	2.096	61	0.760	2.360	72	0.716	2.396	37
东莞市	2.500	58	0.772	1.804	88	0.652	3.588	9	0.968	2.392	38
包头市	2.408	70	0.724	2.760	14	0.948	2.360	72	0.716	2.388	39
芜湖市	2.552	51	0.800	2.192	52	0.796	2.552	61	0.760	2.356	40
台州市	3.376	4	0.988	1.220	146	0.420	3.376	20	0.924	2.332	41
福州市	2.352	75	0.704	1.964	72	0.716	3.280	25	0.904	2.324	42
南通市	2.836	32	0.876	1.360	129	0.488	3.480	12	0.956	2.320	43
扬州市	3.532	2	0.996	1.568	116	0.540	2.688	57	0.776	2.312	44
铜陵市	2.832	33	0.872	2.540	25	0.904	1.864	120	0.524	2.300	45
乌海市	2.140	96	0.620	2.724	17	0.936	2.412	67	0.736	2.292	46
昆明市	2.948	23	0.912	2.372	36	0.860	1.852	122	0.516	2.288	47
淄博市	2.544	55	0.784	1.864	83	0.672	2.748	53	0.792	2.248	48
温州市	2.376	74	0.708	1.856	84	0.668	2.888	41	0.840	2.216	49
秦皇岛市	2.416	68	0.732	1.908	81	0.680	2.748	53	0.792	2.204	50

第五节 全部城市排名分布区域

一、西南地区城市排名分布表

重庆市

城市	总排名
重庆市	136

四川省

城市	总排名
成都市	28
自贡市	191
攀枝花市	81
泸州市	239
德阳市	132
绵阳市	147
广元市	230
遂宁市	250
内江市	207
乐山市	223
南充市	272
眉山市	219
宜宾市	130
广安市	225
达州市	171
雅安市	170
巴中市	267
资阳市	275

西藏自治区

城市	总排名
拉萨市	249

贵州省

城市	总排名
贵阳市	65
六盘水市	260
遵义市	240
安顺市	273

云南省

城市	总排名
昆明市	47
曲靖市	177
玉溪市	69
保山市	264
昭通市	286
丽江市	240
普洱市	253
临沧市	262

二、西北地区城市排名分布表

陕西省

城市	总排名
西安市	66
铜川市	136
宝鸡市	121
咸阳市	180
渭南市	208
延安市	99
汉中市	193
榆林市	116
安康市	265
商洛市	247

甘肃省

城市	总排名
兰州市	71
嘉峪关市	57
金昌市	142
白银市	234
天水市	254
武威市	279
张掖市	185
平凉市	254
酒泉市	133
庆阳市	229
定西市	285
陇南市	284

青海省

城市	总排名
西宁市	187

宁夏回族自治区

城市	总排名
银川市	28
石嘴山市	112
吴忠市	232
固原市	270
中卫市	245

新疆维吾尔自治区

城市	总排名
乌鲁木齐市	104
克拉玛依市	59

三、华南地区城市排名分布表

福建省

城市	总排名
福州市	42
厦门市	1
莆田市	164
三明市	86
泉州市	55
漳州市	107
南平市	169
龙岩市	75
宁德市	181

海南省

城市	总排名
海口市	107
三亚市	72

广东省（1）

城市	总排名
广州市	13
韶关市	120
深圳市	7
珠海市	6
汕头市	158
佛山市	25
江门市	66
湛江市	190
茂名市	226
肇庆市	127
惠州市	89
梅州市	131
汕尾市	201
河源市	228
阳江市	173
清远市	162
东莞市	38

广东省（2）

城市	总排名
中山市	9
潮州市	139
揭阳市	242
云浮市	160

广西省

城市	总排名
南宁市	125
柳州市	129
桂林市	149
梧州市	261
北海市	203
防城港市	232
钦州市	287
贵港市	283
玉林市	268
百色市	266
贺州市	259
河池市	194
来宾市	254
崇左市	220

四、华北地区城市排名分布表

北京市

城市	总排名
北京市	8

天津市

城市	总排名
天津市	21

河北省

城市	总排名
石家庄市	58
唐山市	94
秦皇岛市	50
邯郸市	123
邢台市	121
保定市	214
张家口市	106
承德市	93
沧州市	156
廊坊市	69
衡水市	112

山西省

城市	总排名
太原市	32
大同市	145
阳泉市	85
长治市	61
晋城市	51
朔州市	79
晋中市	75
运城市	168
忻州市	176
临汾市	144
吕梁市	147

内蒙古自治区

城市	总排名
呼和浩特市	24
包头市	39
乌海市	46
赤峰市	201
通辽市	165
鄂尔多斯市	15
呼伦贝尔市	88
巴彦淖尔市	199
乌兰察布市	154

五、华中地区城市排名分布表

河南省

城市	总排名
郑州市	33
开封市	276
洛阳市	99
平顶山市	124
安阳市	157
鹤壁市	172
新乡市	152
焦作市	119
濮阳市	181
许昌市	109
漯河市	221
三门峡市	83
南阳市	186
商丘市	278
信阳市	263
周口市	274
驻马店市	245

湖北省

城市	总排名
武汉市	30
黄石市	118
十堰市	160
宜昌市	75
襄樊市	198
鄂州市	167
荆门市	155
孝感市	227
荆州市	281
黄冈市	183
咸宁市	254
随州市	178

湖南省

城市	总排名
长沙市	19
株洲市	128
湘潭市	96
衡阳市	197
邵阳市	268
岳阳市	78
常德市	174
张家界市	258
益阳市	235
郴州市	195
永州市	277
怀化市	250
娄底市	218

安徽省

城市	总排名
合肥市	54
芜湖市	40
蚌埠市	208
淮南市	203
马鞍山市	34
淮北市	221
铜陵市	45
安庆市	206
黄山市	110
滁州市	250
阜阳市	282
宿州市	280
巢湖市	216
六安市	243
亳州市	271
池州市	224
宣城市	145

江西省

城市	总排名
南昌市	74
景德镇市	115
萍乡市	150
九江市	175
新余市	68
鹰潭市	53
赣州市	248
吉安市	208
宜春市	165
抚州市	243
上饶市	189

六、华东地区城市排名分布表

上海市

城市	总排名
上海市	11

江苏省

城市	总排名
南京市	17
无锡市	10
徐州市	73
常州市	5
苏州市	3
南通市	43
连云港市	91
淮安市	110
盐城市	80
扬州市	44
镇江市	16
泰州市	62
宿迁市	159

浙江省

城市	总排名
杭州市	4
宁波市	2
温州市	49
嘉兴市	12
湖州市	30
绍兴市	22
金华市	26
衢州市	52
舟山市	23
台州市	41
丽水市	56

山东省

城市	总排名
济南市	36
青岛市	18
淄博市	48
枣庄市	134
东营市	26
烟台市	37
潍坊市	64
济宁市	102
泰安市	102
威海市	19
日照市	163
莱芜市	63
临沂市	134
德州市	140
聊城市	116
滨州市	97
菏泽市	237

七、东北地区城市排名分布表

辽宁省

城市	总排名
沈阳市	35
大连市	14
鞍山市	82
抚顺市	126
本溪市	98
丹东市	143
锦州市	90
营口市	101
阜新市	183
辽阳市	105
盘锦市	60
铁岭市	141
朝阳市	196
葫芦岛市	152

吉林省

城市	总排名
长春市	95
吉林市	87
四平市	200
辽源市	188
通化市	114
白山市	151
松原市	212
白城市	236

黑龙江省

城市	总排名
哈尔滨市	83
齐齐哈尔市	205
鸡西市	215
鹤岗市	238
双鸭山市	179
大庆市	91
伊春市	217
佳木斯市	211
七台河市	192
牡丹江市	138
黑河市	230
绥化市	213

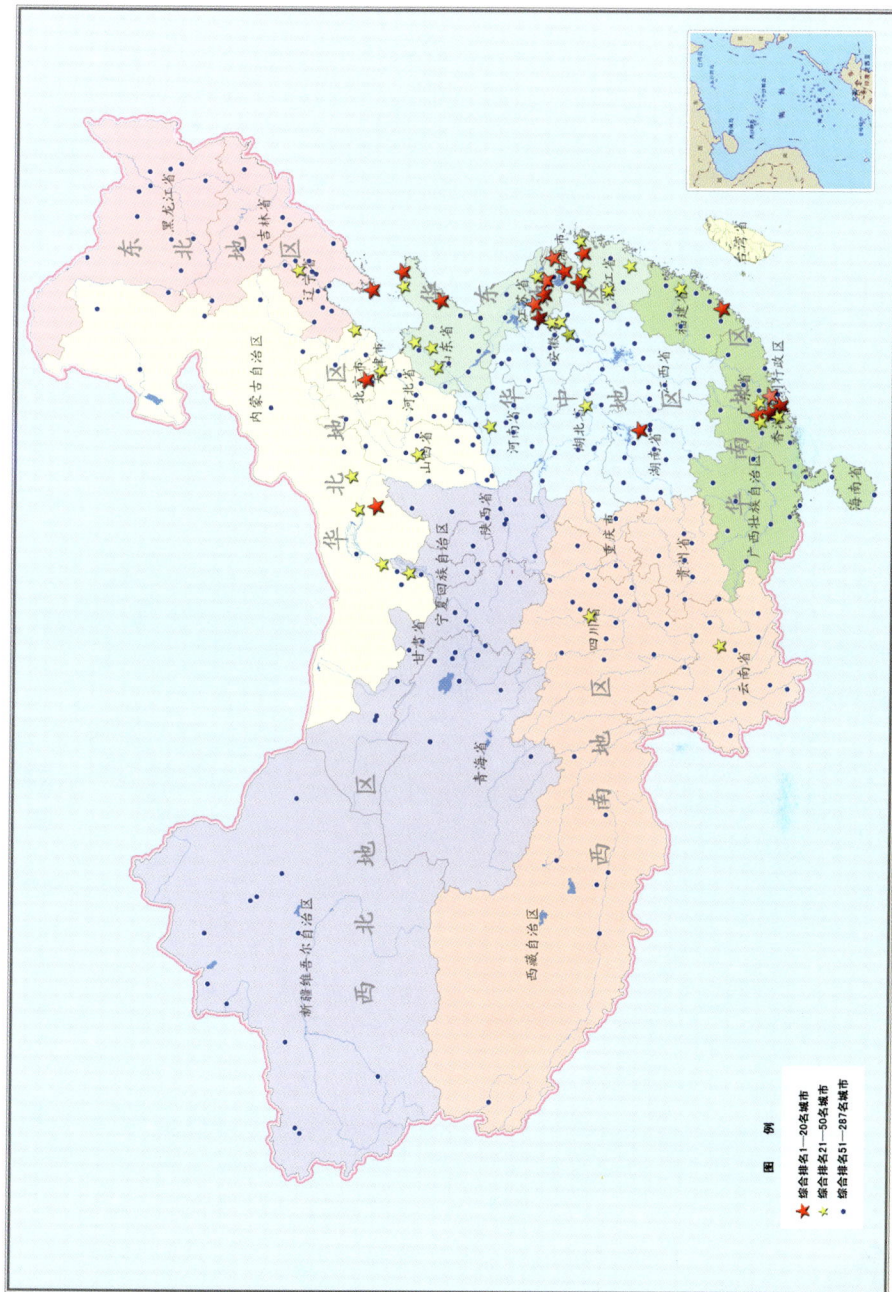

全国城市排名分布图

西南地区城市综合排名位置图

四川省
云南省
贵州省
重庆市
西藏自治区

广元市230
巴中市171
达州市267
南充市260
广安市225
遂宁市272
绵阳市147
重庆市138
黔江市275
内江市207
德阳市132
成都市8
眉山市219
自贡市239
泸州市239
雅安市170
乐山市223
宜宾市130
昭通市286
遵义市240
贵阳市240
铜仁市273
安顺市273
六盘水市2
曲靖市172
昆明市47
攀枝花市
丽江市240
保山市264
玉溪市59
临沧市262
普洱市253

拉萨市249

西北地区城市综合排名位置图

榆林市116

延安市99

陕

西

石嘴山市112
银川市28
吴忠市232

咸阳市180 铜川市136
咸阳市121
西安市208
渭南市254
西安市247
商洛市265
安康市285

中卫市99

固原市70
固原市71

宝鸡市285
汉中市193

甘

白银市234
兰州市254
定西市285
天水市646
陇南市284

嘉峪关市57
酒泉市133

武威市279
金昌市142
张掖市165

西宁市187

青

肃

海

省

省

省

乌鲁木齐市104

克拉玛依市59

新疆维吾尔自治区

华南地区城市综合排名位置图

福建省
广东省
广西壮族自治区
海南省

宁德市81
福州市4
南平市189
莆田市164
三明市86
泉州市55
龙岩市75
漳州市107 厦门市6
梅州市131
潮州市139
汕头市158
揭阳市242
汕尾市230
河源市228
惠州市38 东莞市89
深圳市9
广州省13
佛山市66 中山市26
清远市102
江门市66 珠海市6
肇庆市127
云浮市160
阳江市173
韶关市120
梧州市26
贺州市259
茂名市226
湛江市190
桂林市149
贵港市283
玉林市268
海口市107
柳州市254
来宾市254
北海市261
三亚市72
河池市194
南宁市125
钦州市287
防城港市233
崇左市220
百色市266

华北地区城市综合排名位置图

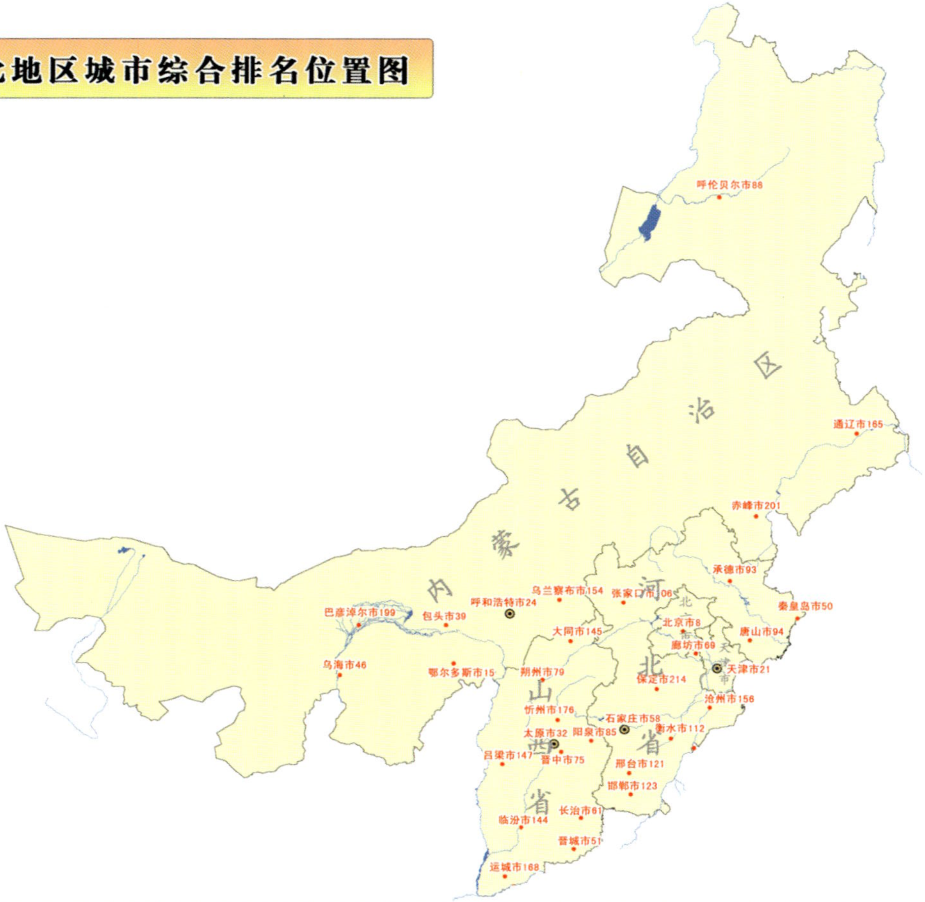

通辽市165

呼伦贝尔市88

区治自

赤峰市201

秦皇岛市50

承德市93

唐山市94

天津市21

沧州市156

张家口市66

北京市8

廊坊市69

保定市214

乌兰察布市154

大同市145

石家庄市58

衡水市112

古蒙内

呼和浩特市24

朔州市79

阳泉市65

邢台市121

忻州市176

晋中市75

邯郸市123

太原市32

包头市30

吕梁市147

长治市86

临汾市144

运城市168

晋城市51

鄂尔多斯市15

巴彦淖尔市169

乌海市46

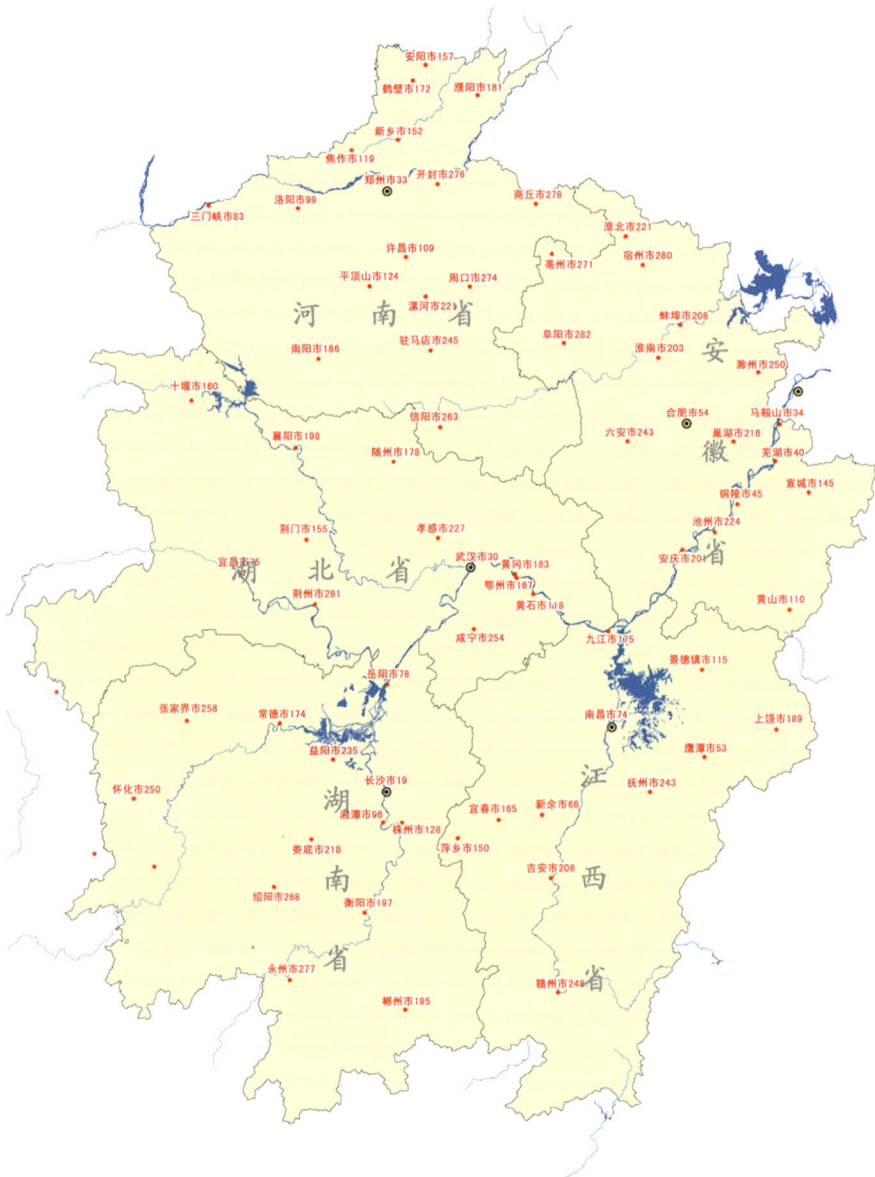

华中地区城市综合排名位置图

安阳市157
鹤壁市172　濮阳市181
新乡市152
焦作市119　开封市276
郑州市33
三门峡市83　洛阳市99　　　　　商丘市278
许昌市109　　　　　　淮北市221
平顶山市124　周口市274　亳州市271　宿州市280
河　南　省　漯河市223
　　　　　　　　　　阜阳市282　　蚌埠市208
南阳市186　驻马店市245　　　　　　淮南市203　安
　　　　　　　　　　　　　　　　滁州市250
十堰市160　　　　　信阳市263　　　　合肥市54　马鞍山市34
襄阳市198　　　　　　　　六安市243　巢湖市216　芜湖市40
随州市178　　　　　　　　　　　　　　宜城市145
徽　铜陵市45
荆门市155　孝感市227　　　　　　池州市224
宜昌市　　　　　　武汉市30　黄冈市183　安庆市20　省
荆州市281　　湖　北　省　鄂州市167　　　　黄山市110
　　　　　　　　　黄石市118
　　　　　咸宁市254　九江市175
岳阳市78　　　　　　　景德镇市115
张家界市258　常德市174　　　南昌市74　上饶市189
益阳市235　　　　　　　　　鹰潭市53
怀化市250　　　　　　　　　抚州市243
湖　长沙市19
湘潭市96　宜春市165　新余市68
娄底市218　株洲市128　江
南　萍乡市150　吉安市208　西
邵阳市268　衡阳市197　　　　　省
省
永州市277　　　　　赣州市248
郴州市195

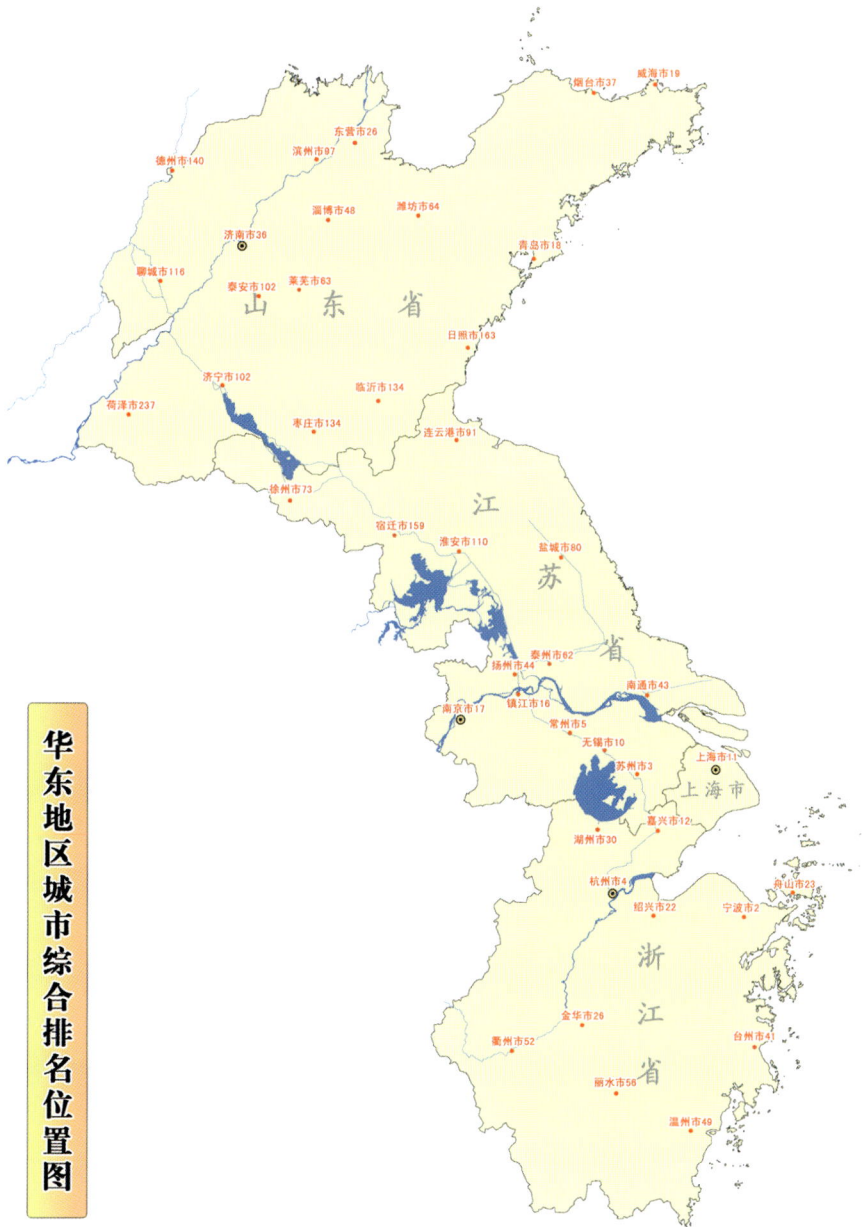

华东地区城市综合排名位置图

威海市19
烟台市37
东营市26
滨州市87
德州市140
潍坊市84
淄博市48
济南市36
青岛市18
聊城市116
莱芜市63
泰安市102
山 东 省
日照市163
济宁市102
临沂市134
荷泽市237
枣庄市134
连云港市91
徐州市73
宿迁市159
江
淮安市110
盐城市80
苏
泰州市62
省
扬州市44
南通市43
镇江市16
南京市17
常州市5
无锡市10
上海市11
苏州市3
上海市
嘉兴市12
湖州市30
杭州市4
舟山市23
绍兴市22
宁波市2
浙 江 省
金华市26
衢州市52
台州市41
丽水市58
温州市49

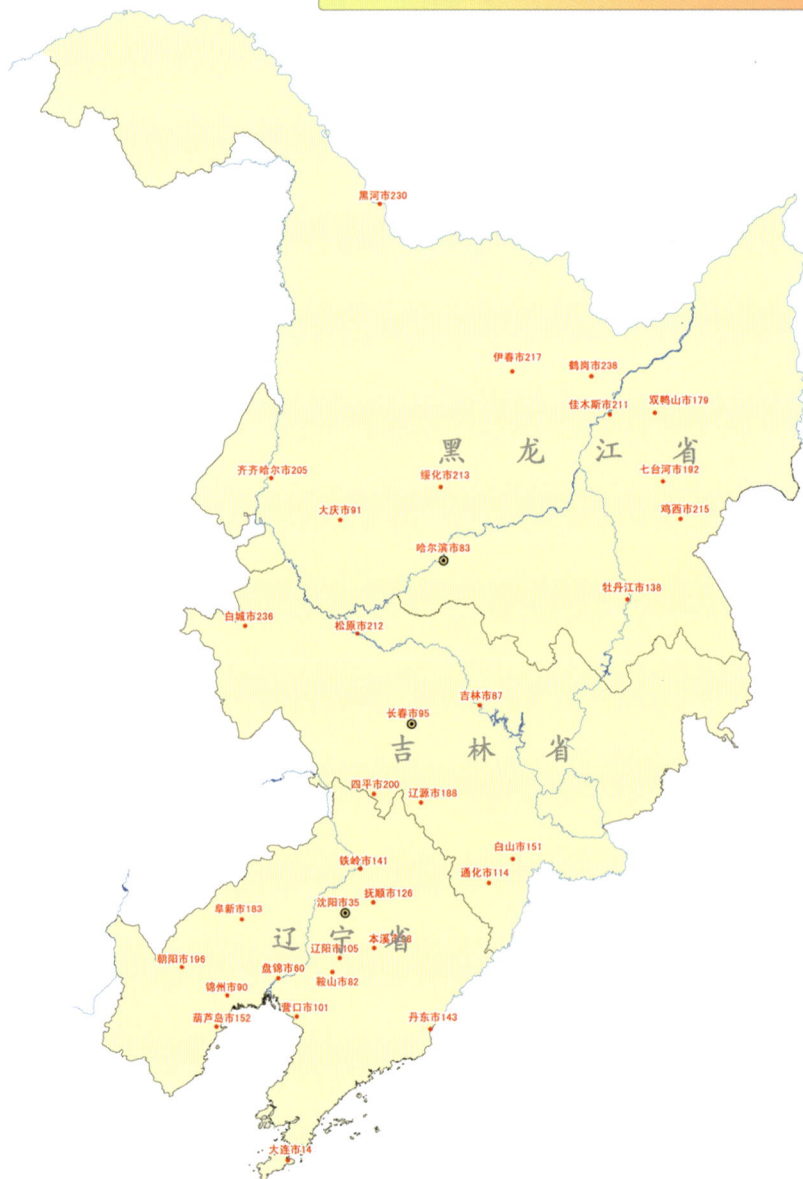

东北地区城市综合排名位置图

黑河市230

伊春市217　鹤岗市238

佳木斯市211　双鸭山市179

黑　龙　江　省

齐齐哈尔市205　绥化市213　七台河市192

大庆市91　　鸡西市215

哈尔滨市83

牡丹江市138

白城市236　松原市212

吉林市87

长春市95

吉　林　省

四平市200　辽源市188

白山市151

铁岭市141

通化市114

阜新市183　抚顺市126

朝阳市196　沈阳市35

辽　宁　省

辽阳市105　本溪市88

盘锦市60

锦州市90　鞍山市82

葫芦岛市152　营口市101

丹东市143

大连市14

中　山　市

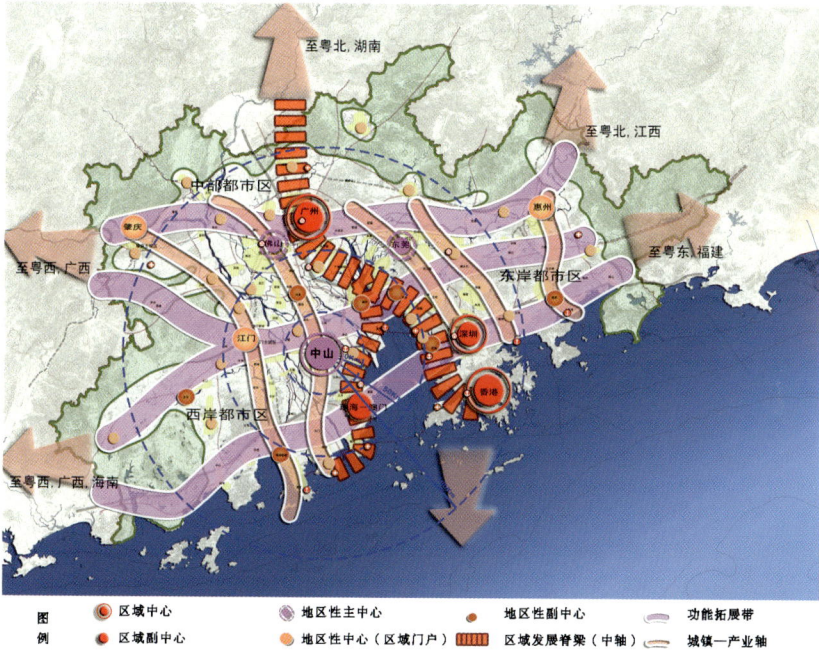

图例：
🔴 区域中心　　🟣 地区性主中心　　🟤 地区性副中心　　功能拓展带
🔴 区域副中心　　🟠 地区性中心（区域门户）　▥ 区域发展脊梁（中轴）　城镇—产业轴

中山市是珠江口西岸地区性中心城市，是珠江口西岸重要的先进制造业和现代服务业基地，是珠三角三大经济圈的重要交通枢纽。

中山市"十二五"规划提出加快建设"适宜创业、适宜创新、适宜居住"的幸福和美新型城市。图为市委书记、市人大常委会主任薛晓峰（左四），市委副书记、市长陈茂辉（左二）等领导一起谋划发展蓝图。

中山市打造碧水蓝天绿地花鸟城，积极创建幸福和美家园。图为获得美国景观设计奖、中国建筑艺术奖等多项荣誉的工业生态主题公园——中山市岐江公园。

镇 江 市

南徐新城："城市山林"气势磅礴，一座现代气息与悠久文化交相辉映的新城拔地而起

镇江市委书记　许津荣

镇江市长　刘捍东

万达广场：商贸巨舰，璀璨起航。

第六部分　城市成果推介

中山市：贯彻落实科学发展观　建设幸福和美中山

广东省中山市，古称香山，因"多神仙花卉"而得名，因诞生了孙中山先生而更闻名世界，是中国唯一以伟人命名的城市。中山位于珠江三角洲中南部，珠江口西岸，北连广州，毗邻港澳，总面积1800平方公里，常住人口312万，旅居世界90多个国家地区的华侨和港澳台乡亲80多万人。中山是一个社会和谐、经济兴旺、环境优美、民生幸福的现代化城市，以广东省1%土地、3%人口连续多年创造了全省第五的经济总量。2010年全市实现生产总值1826亿元，人均生产总值5.85万元。城镇化率为87.8%，达到发达国家地区水平。拥有国家级产业基地27个，省级专业镇15个，国家和省名牌名标410个，落户中山世界500强企业26家。获得联合国人居奖、全国文明城市、国家历史文化名城、全国生态市、全国园林城市、中国优秀旅游城市、全国环保模范城市、中国最具幸福感城市等多项荣誉。贯彻落实科学发展观，中山努力构筑经济发达、社会和谐、法治进步、文化繁荣、环境优美、人民安康、城乡一体的和美家园，加快建设适宜创业、适宜创新、适宜居住的全面协调可持续发展的新型城市。

中山是一座发展之城。中山市委市政府坚持以科学发展为主题，以加快转变发展方式为主线，率先加快转型升级，建设幸福和美家园。把结构调整作为主攻方向；把自主创新作为重要支撑；把民生改善作为本质要求；把生态环保作为重要保障；把改革开放作为工作动力，不断提升发展水平。注重强化发展内生动力，推动经济发展由外向带动为主向内外需协调拉动转变，由产业价值链低端向高端延伸转变，由要素驱动向创新驱动转变。建设"一个平台两大基地"，整合孙中山故里资源，建设"翠亨新区"，打造全省推进海峡两岸更紧密合作实践区、全球华人共同精神家园建设先行区、珠三角新一代城镇群建设试验区、创新社会管理与文化建设示范区；推动风电装备基地和电动汽车产业基地跨越发展，打造新能源产业集聚区。注重发展的人均水平、资源承载和环境效益，推进绿色发展，增强可持续发展能力。与 2008 年相比，全市生产总值增长 25.3%，全员劳动生产率增长 20%，污染物总量减排考核连续三年居广东省第一。

中山是一座畅通之城。中山地处珠三角圆心，北连广州，东望深圳，毗邻港澳，区位优势十分突出。中山是珠江口西岸重要交通节点，全市拥有"五纵六横七高速九加密"交通路网，随着广珠城轨开通，以及港珠澳大桥、深中通道、西部沿海铁路规划建设，中将成为香港澳门深圳连接粤西乃至我国大西南的黄金走廊。90 公里半径内有五大机场和四大外轮深水港，港口集装箱吞吐量全国居前。全市实现"市域半小时生活圈、镇区 15 分钟上高速、村村通公路公交"，连续 6 次评为全国畅通工程"一等管理水平"先进城市，成为全国唯一"六连冠"地级市。实施"交通先行"和"以路为纲"战略，"十二五"时期组织投入 343 亿元发展交通，力争 2015 年公路密度达 125 公里/百平方公里，跻身全省前列。

中山是一座繁荣之城。中山是珠三角重要的先进制造业城市和现代服务业基地，是国家特色产业集群创新基地和广东省产业集群升级创新试点城市。全市有经济主体 20 多万家，拥有装备制造、电子信息、灯饰光源、家用电器等 10 大产业集群，18 项产业集群联盟标准，15 家上市企业，中船、中铁、中海油、中机钢构等大批央企进驻中山。拥有珠江口西岸唯一的保税物流中心、三大中心商务区、四大集聚商圈，现代服务业加快发展。今年上半年，全市经济平稳较快发展，实现生产总值 1026.3 亿元，增长 14.5%。1—8 月，规模以上工业总产值增长 18.3%，固定资产投资增长 27.4%，财政一般预算收入增长 43.1%，社会消费品零售总额增长 17%，进出口贸易总值增长 11.8%。上半年财政一般预算收入、固定资产投资增速均居广东省第一，规模以上工业增加值、生产总值增速均排全省第三，增幅与广东省排名都创中山近年上半年最好成绩。力争"十二五"期末经济总量保持全省前列，全市人均生产总值达 10 万元。

中山是一座和美之城。中山是《珠江三角洲地区改革发展规划纲要》明确的统筹城乡综合改革试点市，近年来市财政六成投入发展城乡公共服务，建立起城乡一体化的促进就业、社会保险、教育文化、医疗卫生、住房保障等社会保障体系，努力让市民"老有所养、病有所医、贫有所助、幼有所教"。全市实现基本养老保险、住院和门诊基本医疗保险全覆盖。城乡居民收入比为 1.7：1，城乡收入差距广东省最小。实现教育资源均衡布局，成为广东省教育强市，所有镇区成为省教育强镇，高等教育毛入学率达54.5%，进入普及化阶段，人均受教育年限达13.5年，这些指标都达到或接近中等发达国家地区水平。村村建有卫生站，全部镇区成为国家或省级卫生镇。今年积极办好交通畅行、平安建设、综合治水、"菜篮子"工程、绿色环境、文化卫生、社会保险、住房保障、社会救助、富农强农十件民生实事，社会大局和谐稳定，人民群众生活质量不断提升。

中山是一座宜居之城。中山坚持"既要金山银山，也要绿水青山"的科学发展理念，以新加坡、香港特制行政区等发达国家和地区为对标，结合自身实际，创造了具有中山特色的宜居城市建设模式。全市24个镇区全部建有生活污水处理厂，城镇生活污水处理率达87.5%，中山城区生活垃圾无害化处理率达100%，全市森林覆盖率近20%，人均公园绿地面积达到12平方米。获得中国和谐之城、中国十佳和谐可持续发展城市、中国十佳休闲宜居生态城市、中国人居环境范例奖等殊荣。实施绿地碧水工程，组织投入15亿元植树造林，组织投入60亿元实施母亲河——岐江河综合治理，建设"碧水蓝天绿地花鸟城"。

中山是一座人文之城。中山人杰地灵，名人辈出，不仅诞生了一代伟人孙中山先生，还走出了中国第一位驻外大使郑藻如，中国空军之父杨仙逸，中国近代留学生之父容闳，中国近代著名改良主义思想家实业家郑观应，中国"为共和革命牺牲者之第一人"陆皓东，四大百货公司永安、先施、新新、大新公司的创建人，四角号码发明者王云五等一大批影响中国影响世界的英才俊杰。中山近五年投入100多亿元建设孙中山文化、历史文化、民俗文化、博爱文化、生态文化等"八大文化工程"，城市文化实力大幅提升。在广东省率先实现农家书屋、农村社区文化室全覆盖，所有镇区文化站达到省特级标准，成为"全国公共文化服务示范项目"，今年3月被国务院授予"国家历史文化名城"称号。弘扬"博爱、创新、包容、和谐"新时期中山人精神，连续24年举办"慈善万人行"，获得"全国精神文明建设创新奖"、"全国十大公益品牌奖"、全国公益领域最高政府奖——"中华慈善奖"，被誉为"中华民族慈善文化的一面旗帜"。纪念辛亥革命100周年，中山市积极开展孙中山文化节、央视"心连心"艺术团慰问演出、翠亨论坛、"中山杯"华侨华人文学奖等一系列重大文化活动，大力弘扬孙中山文化，全面展示伟人故里形象。

中山是一座创新之城。积极实施"十大技术创新工程"，连续四届获评"全国科技进步考核先进市"，高新技术产品产值占工业总产值35%，成为国家知识产权试点城市、广东省教育部产学研结合示范基地。有国家、省、市级工程技术中心 560 家。建成国家灯具质量监测检验中心和两家国家级示范生产力促进中心。积极创新社会建设管理，形成具有中山特色的"一个理念，两个突破，三个共享"社会建设管理模式，坚持包容增长理念，有效破解城市人与农村人、本地人与外地人双重二元结构，实现经济发展成果、基本公共服务、平等发展机遇三个全民共享。建立流动人口积分管理制度、构建和谐劳动关系等工作走在全国前列，社区管理"2＋8＋N"模式获评"全国农村社区建设实验全覆盖示范单位"。积极推进城市发展创新，构建结构合理、功能完备、环境优美、辐射力强的现代化城市发展新格局，不断提升主城区首位度，提升城乡一体化发展水平，增强人民群众幸福感。

镇江市：坚持科学发展　推进跨越发展

镇江，位于长江下游南岸，总面积 3847 平方公里，人口 311 万。现辖丹阳、句容、扬中 3 个市，丹徒、京口、润州 3 个区和镇江新区。近年来，镇江市委、市政府坚持以科学发展观为统领，突出"人才引领、创新驱动、绿色增长、和谐共享"，经济社会发展呈现明显而深刻的变化，各项主要经济指标增幅持续在江苏或苏南领先。2010 年，实现地区生产总值 1988 亿元，是"十五"末的 2.25 倍；固定资产投资累计完成 4123 亿元，是前五年的 3.2 倍；财政一般预算收入年均增长 23.5%、连续 16 个月增幅列苏南第一。先后获得中国十大最关爱民生城市、中国十佳和谐可持续发展城市、人民满意城市、国家创新型试点城市、国家知识产权工作示范城市、全国社会治安综合治理优秀地市、全国双拥模范城等称号。

一、加快转型升级，跑出科学发展"加速度"

2008 年以来，镇江把跨越发展作为主旋律，并明确提出这一跨越不是片面追求速度、拼资源、拼环境的跨越，而是发展方式、发展质量的新跨越，以科技创新为支撑、提升核心竞争力的新跨越。

——突出人才引领、创新驱动。着眼于构筑镇江发展的新优势，明确提出"招才引智"全天候（不受时间、批次限制）、不封顶（财政扶持资金不受限制）、求实效（带动新兴产业发展），让高端人才向镇江"流动"，引领产业创新。实施人才引进"331"计划，引进 125 个人才（团队），其中国家"千人计划"12人，64人进入省"双创"计划。碳纤维、光伏、光学膜、合金材料等产业，依靠高层次人才和科技创新，站了行业前沿。加大各类创新投入，全社会研发投入占GDP比重2%，今年可超过2.2%。不断推出政产学研"创新联盟"，新增科技孵化器100万平方米、国家级高新技术企业51家、企业院士工作站5家、省级以上研发机构和检测中心11家。高新技术产业产值占规模工业比重43.04%，位居江苏第二。

——狠抓产业结构调整。促进新兴产业爆发式增长。制定"5＋X"发展规划，建立专项扶持资金，强化政策、资金、公共平台和载体支持。2010年，新兴产业投资、销售分别增长106.1%和45%，培育并形成新区航空零部件、丹阳特种纤维、丹徒二重核电装备、扬中工程电器、润州船用动力等5个省级特色产业基地。启动"云神工程"，组建国家级云计算研究院，大力发展云计算产业。加快主导产业优化发展。建立规模企业梯次培育机制，6家企业销售超百亿，新增上市公司10家。三年来五大主导产业占规模工业比重提高7.6个百分点，装备制造业跻身千亿级产业。推动现代服务业快速发展。服务业增加值五年翻一番、占GDP比重40%。镇江港迈入亿吨大港行列。八佰伴、红星美凯龙、万达广场等一批新型商贸业态和城市综合体相继开业，城市更具现代商业气息。软件与信息服务业营业收入五年增长6.8倍。文化产业投资增长102.6%、是2006年的3.8倍。

——强化政策引导扶持。树立鲜明政策导向，先后出台科学发展综合评价体系和"千百亿"工程实施意见，文化产业、旅游业、创业创新人才引进等三年行动计划，以及转型升级"八大工程"实施意见，强化以科学发展论政绩的鲜明导向。实施联姻央企战略，抢抓央企新一轮扩张和转移机遇，主动加强对接，推进战略合作，已有总投资1364亿元的38个央企项目落户，成为近年来江苏与央企合作最多的城市。发挥金融助推作用，先后引进华夏、民生、浦发、中信等6家银行分支机构入驻，成立农村小额贷款公司24家、村镇银行4家，在江苏率先组建科技支行和科技小额贷款公司，使金融成为科技创新和转型升级的"推进器"。

二、坚持绿色增长，建设"山水花园城市"

以对历史和子孙后代负责的态度，把绿色增长作为发展的鲜明导向，加大生态修复，涵养生态资源，打造生态品牌，努力形成节约能源资源、修复和保护生态环境的增长方式。

——优化生态空间，为可持续发展"做储蓄"。发展中坚持"不涂鸦，多留白"，为未来发展留出空间，最大限度放大山水资源优势，进行保护性开发、可持续开发。完善主城区功能，确定"一核四区"的城市功能新格局：以南山为绿核，老城区为长江最美城市港湾，南徐新城为行政、商务和文化体育中心，丁卯—官塘为城市低碳生活示范区和科技新城，丹徒新区为生态宜居新城。明确中心城区、辖市城区、新市镇的功能定位和产业布局。构建城市大生态系统，让拥有8平方公里水面的金山湖重现"水漫金山"的美景，成为"城市之肾"；延绵起伏、生态优美的南山已建成森林公园，成为"城市之肺"。

——狠抓生态市创建，"铁腕"节能减排。出台生态市创建《问责办法》，动真碰硬抓创建。3个辖市和丹徒区通过生态市省级考核，80%的镇建成全国环境优美乡镇，实现污水处理厂乡镇全覆盖，通过国家环保模范城市省级复核。下决心做"减法"，调轻产业结构，淘汰落后产能，累计关停并转"五小"企业611家，实施重点节能项目180多个、污染减排项目226个，超额完成"十一五"节能降耗污染减排任务。加快实施老城区雨污分流工程，城市污水处理率90%以上，今年9月底前地表水全面达标。加强城市绿化建设，全市林木覆盖率、建成区绿化覆盖率分别提高到22.6%、42.1%，城市人均绿地15.9平方米，环境空气质量良好以上天数比例90.7%，公众对城市环保满意度91.2%。

——展露"青山绿水"，彰显文化底蕴。为充分彰显"城市山林、大江风貌"特色，让更多百姓享受"生态福利"，2009年启动实施"青山绿水"两年行动计划，对老城区范围内的11座山体、3条通江河道进行综合整治，新添12个开放式市民公园，市民出门500米就能见到绿地。下决心整治市区9条黑臭河流，今年全面达标。现在，镇江市区已由"显山露水"走向"青山绿水"，生态价值、旅游价值全面提升。去年接待国内外游客突破3000万人次，旅游综合收入增长21.7%、列江苏第三。作为全国历史文化名城，在城市建设中坚持以"文化"领航，传承历史文脉，重点推进西津渡历史文化街区、金山湖文化旅游圈等保护性开发建设，让历史文化和现代城市相辅相成、相得益彰。2009年，"西津渡历史文化街区保护更新工程"被国家住建部授予"中国人居环境范例奖"。

三、加快城乡融合，推进公共服务"均等化"

顺应人民群众热切期盼，注重城乡协调同步发展，开工建设一批重大基础设施项目，开启了镇江城乡建设的"黄金期"。累计完成城乡建设投资 1270 亿元，是"十五"时期的 2.6 倍。

——推进城乡融合。在全省率先推行新市镇、新园区、新农村"三新"建设和"万顷良田"建设试点，制定《关于加快推进新市镇建设的意见》和土地、金融、户籍等 8 个配套文件，选择 11 个镇先行试点，已开工建设 104 个农民集中居住点、建成面积 429 万平方米。同时强化产业支撑，因地制宜规划建设高效农业园区、新兴工业集中区、商贸集聚区，为农民提供更多的创业机会和就业岗位，并切实配套养老保险、医疗保险等各种社会保障，真正让"新市民"过上幸福美好的生活。

——做新做美城市。新城区重点推进"南山北水"建设，总投资近 700 亿元。如今，南徐新城拔地而起，展现出现代城市气息，钟灵毓秀的南山更显新城魅力；怀抱长江的北部滨水区尽展古城神韵，"三山、一湖、一渡"成为镇江人引为自豪的标志性景区，湖光山色、游人如织。总投资 600 亿元的 14 个城市综合体建设不断推进，万达广场、九润商业广场已开业，常发广场、东方伟业、碧桂园等也已经封顶。旧城区大力推进改造"翻新"，完成老小区改造 250 万平方米，开工建设安置房 458 万平方米。

——致力推进公共服务均等化。积极推进以工扶农、以城带乡，着力建设一个让农民有家业、能就业、有收入、有保障、有好的居住环境、文化物质生活不断改善的美好家园，把城市的文明、舒适带给农村。城乡道路、供水、供电、供气、电信网络等基础设施实现"无缝对接"，全市区域供水普及率达到 95%，城乡污水管网铺设突破 400 公里，农村公路总里程突破 6000 公里。大力推进被征地农民养老保险城乡接轨，目前各类保障在镇江基本上实现了广覆盖，城镇养老、医疗、失业保险参保率和农村新型合作医疗参合率均保持 98% 以上，新型农村养老保险超过 70%。

四、坚持和谐共享，建设可观可感的"民生幸福"

坚持发展依靠人民、发展为了人民，公共财政向民生倾斜，多做惠及群众的好事、实事，让"幸福感"从百姓心里流出来，绽放在笑容可掬的脸庞上。2008 年以来用于改善民生的支出 218 亿元，年均增幅高于一般预算支出 5.7 个百分点。

——推进全民创业和充分就业。制定出台扶持政策，从创业培训、载体建设、融资服务等方面打出"组合拳"，让更多的劳动者成为创业者。2009 年荣获首批"中国创业之城"称号。去年新建创业孵化基地 200 万平方米，新增私个注册资本、私营企业户、个体工商户三项指标增幅均位居江苏省第一。积极调整财政支出结构，实施一系列促进、稳定和扩大就业的政策措施，让每一个有就业能力和愿望的人，都能早就业、就好业。连续五年城镇登记失业率控制在 3.5% 以内，累计新增城镇就业 32.7 万人，建成"充分就业市"。

——加快推进民生"五有"。在五个方面积极探索和提高居民实际享有水平："学有优教"，坚持教育优先发展，办人民满意教育，2009 年实施教育基本现代化高中阶段毛入学率 104.5%，人均受教育年限达到 14.5 年。"劳有多得"，积极推进工资协商制度，提高最低工资标准，增加一线工人收入，有效保障劳动者合法权益。"病有良医"，医改试点全国领先，成立两大医疗集团，与社区卫生服务中心信息联网，实现"诊疗信息化、小病在社区、大病进医院、康复回社区"；建立城乡一体化的医疗保障体系，城郊 30 多万农民享受医保"同城同待遇"。"住有宜居"，大幅增加保障性住房供给，建立"租赁补贴为主、实物配租和租金核减为辅"的组合型住房保障模式，市区和农村人均住房面积分别达到 34.2 平方米、48.5 平方米。"老有善养"，在实现社会保障广覆盖、上水平的同时，大幅度提高退休人员养老金、居民医保住院费报销比例，构建起"三基本两补充"的社会养老保障体系。

——繁荣文化事业。积极满足广大人民群众日益增长的精神文化需求，提供公益、便利、均等的公共文化服务，让镇江成为一座弥漫着文化幸福的风尚之城。引入市场机制，将文化活动项目化、产业化，实现公益文化事业的可持续发展。一批文化产业重点项目加快推进，文化产业增加值占 GDP 比重今年有望比全省提前一年实现 5%。连续多年推进"文心公益行动"，"文化嘉年华"连续举行三届，成为引领文化潮流、培育文化消费的强力载体，使古城迸放出崭新的活力和魅力。

——建设大爱镇江。连续举办三届"大爱镇江"新闻人物颁奖典礼，在全国打响了"大爱镇江"品牌，提升了城市的人文高度。"满城尽飘黄丝带"、"社会妈妈"、"生命志愿者"等"爱"的故事不断涌现。为确保贫困家庭不因物价上涨而降低生活水平，去年市财政投入 1000 万元，5 万多人享受补贴。为环卫工人提供公共租赁房 144 套（间），在江苏是首创。完善慈善救助机制，慈善资金总规模已近 10 亿元，在江苏省名列前茅，近年来 33400 人次获得慈善救助。

今天，拥有 3000 年文明史的镇江，科学发展的旗帜更加鲜明，跨越发展的步伐愈发铿锵。这座充满生机与活力的城市，正以昂扬奋进的姿态，向着率先基本实现现代化的目标阔步前行！

Copyright Statement of *Comprehensive Evaluation and Grading System (E&G) Design of China Urban Scientific Development*

2011 *Comprehensive Evaluation and Grading Report of China Urban Scientific Development*
Editorial Organizations

Editorial Board

Editorial Department

Table of Contents

Foreword

We have successively invited more than ten professional scholars and experts to hold about ten Seminars since March of 2011. We have fully discussed and studied such aspects as theme, framework, methodologies and module dividing. We changed the draft for several times and it took another four months to finish data analysis, questionnaire survey and commission authors to write on given topics, thus finally 2011 *Comprehensive Evaluation and Grading Report of China Urban Scientific Development* (*Report* for short)., What's different from before, is its basic framework. What's more, there is a specific theme—"city and people" for this year's *Report*. We re-regulated the perspective of evaluation. The focus is diverted to the clear and distinct point that cities should be developed for people, which is closely related to people's well-being.

Editorial Department

October 10, 2011

Preface

About Cities

(*Sun Jiazheng, vice chairman of the National Committee of the Eleventh Chinese People's Political Consultative Conference*)

With the development of economy and the progress of technology, the urbanization is obviously quickened. Currently the number and scale of cities are increased. The city population in the world is quickly rising after surpassing agricultural population. The global "city era" has approached.

The development of city civilization is the progress of history and influences people's lifestyle and social psychology extensively and profoundly. Urban development brings more comfort, convenience and opportunities for people as well as some new troubles and problems. Our city home on which we rely is faced with such problems as memory disappearance, convergent appearance, traffic jam and environmental degradation with different degrees. Urban development keeps meeting and stimulating people's physical demands but spiritual and psychological comfort and expectations are gradually lost.

City is the residence and spiritual home of urban dwellers. The principle of people-oriented should be adhered to while building the city. The planning, construction, management and services of the city should meet demands of the most extensive common people and meanwhile demands of different people groups should be satisfied. It is people's common with and requirement to create an ecological environment where people and Nature can live on friendly terms with each other. Faced with quick and convenient changes of modern life and the intense competition of market economy, people's physical demands have to be constantly satisfied but their psychological confusions and troubles should also be addressed. The process of the change and development of city cultural forms should be the process of people's spiritual demands being met, people's quality improved and all-round development of people. City construction and management call deep love and care of humanity. The spirit, environment and atmosphere of love and care of humanity should be an important yardstick for evaluating the city construction level and management quality.

People created tangible cities which in turn cultivate and shape people in an intangible way. Factors such as values, thinking, morality and social morals of urban dwellers are the comprehensive reflection of city cultural construction and the process in which city cultural construction plays its role. Both tangible city appearance and intangible city spirit are caused by certain culture. The building and evolution of cities due to culture have unconscious impact on the life and behaviors of city dwellers. The city is the container of culture. Streets, square, buildings, sculpture, equipment, afforestation and sketch in cities constitute cities' tangible and exterior physical system and influence our vision, listening, smell, touch and soul; meanwhile, they again carry human activities happening in cities. It is just these different, vivid and interesting activities that make cities popular and full of vitality.

Convergence should be refused and prevented while building cities; instead individuality and uniqueness should be protected and demonstrated. Modernization and internationalization is undoubtedly a double-edged sword. It is an indisputable fact that internationalization strikes traditions and modernization obliterates individuality. Only when cities' historical traditions, regional appearance and ethnic features are respected and cherished can the unique cultural charms of a city can be kept and demonstrated. A city is a history. We cannot sever the history. It is people's psychological needs and the responsibility that people should bear for ancestors and grandchildren to carefully protect historical and cultural heritage, maintain historical thread and keep historical memory.

In terms of urban construction, constant creation and upgrading should be made in order to be adapt to the development of era and lifestyle while traditions being inherited. A successful city must be a city with innovation while keeping its own cultural traditions. Historical traditions and cultural innovation in line with the era are the soul and vitality of urban development. It entails steadfast confidence and inclusive mind to make internal cultural innovation in city construction. It is China's basic state policy to open to the outside world. Harmony but not sameness is China's philosophical thinking. Pursuit of harmony is the value orientation of Chinese people.

City is never an isolated existence. It is found by hard and thorough research that it is village, agriculture and farmers that breed and nurse cities. This is especially true in China's urbanization process. It is the priority of urban development to repay the village, be kind to farmers and promote urban-rural harmonious development. It is a moral necessity as well as an essential condition for the city's own sustainable development.

Comprehensive evaluation and grading of China cities according to Scientific Outlook on Development is able to promote healthy development of society and economy of China cities. It is also a summary and confirmation of city culture. I sincerely hope that *Comprehensive Evaluation and Grading Report of China Urban Scientific Development* can be a success and make its unique contribution to China urban development.

Part One   2011 General Report of China Urban Development

City: how to develop for people and how to make people happy

The sixth population census data shows that up to the end of 2010 our country's urbanization rate had reached 49. 68%. The statistics is mainly based on practical permanent resident population of cities and towns. However, compared with data of management of registered permanent residence and social security system, the number is a little bit higher; compared with the current situation of employment, that is, the number of people who make a living in cities and towns, the number is far lower than that in reality. Therefore we can note that our management of registered permanent residence and population statistics based on it do not necessarily reflect the actual situation of changes of our country's economic population. China's economic development is sure to enter the peak time of urbanization in future. Immediate interest of each person will be taken into consideration in urban development.

I. Well-being oriented and evaluate urban development and its policy system

It has been people's common feeling that "city develops for people" and "city makes life better", which has been agreed by people from all walks of life in society. China City Development Academy has studied and come up with a set of new city evaluation system and conducted comprehensive classification and e-valuation of cities (or higher level) by using annual statistical indicators data since 2008. New attempt has been made for evaluation urban development from the perspective of Scientific Outlook on Development. In 2011 we further opti-mize the classification system on the basis of the original classification and summarize the evaluation system which can reflect relations between city and people from the perspective of indicator logic.

Current urban statistical indicators cover such fields as economy, society and culture and they are divided into three categories: the first one is economic development level indicator which belongs to national economy productivity indicator; the second one is public service level indicator which reflects the scale and scope of urban social public service and belongs to the indicator of fortunes shared by society; the third one is personal fortune level indicator which belongs to residents' personal benefits indicator. In addition to evaluating each city's performance in those categories, the focus is the evaluation and analysis of relations among those three categories. Its logic relation is: abilities reflected by the first indicator determines the scale and level of the second indicator; the scale and level reflected by the second and third indicator is determined by certain distribution system and technical ways. If the ranking of three indicators of a city is close on the list, it means that the achievements actually shared by residents are consistent with the urban development level. Otherwise there are problems. Attempt to use the method, that is, from the perspective of the final benefits that residents gain, to evaluate comprehensive development of cities.

II. The general tendency of China urban development in current stage

1. Common problems and challenges

Incompatibility always exists in urban development whether it is in the world or in a country. The thing is that the incompatibility has different expressions and forms in different stages. In China, incompatibility of urban development in current stage is a quite complicated topic which involves physical geography, history and humanity and policy system. In terms of its form of expression, it can be reduced to the following aspects:

(1) Modern market economy system is imperfect. Blindness in investment and low level expansion leads to constant and deep contradictions of excessive rapidness of economic growth and low quality.

(2) The functional orientation of the subject is unclear. Production factors cannot circulate freely and reasonably and be allocated with optimization. There is great imbalance between regional development and the gap is being enlarged.

(3) The development of social public cause obviously lags behind the eco-

nomic development. Public service resources are unreasonably allocated and the social security system is to be improved.

(4) The expansion of economic aggregate is accompanied by the quick promotion of industrialization and urbanization; however extensive economy growth pattern spells the fast growth of cost. The ecological economic model which makes people, resources, environment, economy and society develop in harmony is still in exploration stage.

2. Corresponding measures taken by the country and achievements

(1) Economic strength and comprehensive national strength are dramatically increased. Our country's GDP was RMB 34,050.7 billion in 2009, an increase of 84.12% with an annual increase of 12.98% compared with the number of RMB 18,493.7 billion planned in "the eleventh five-year plan" (from 2006 to 2010) in 2005. Given the time limit of actual statistics data, our dynamic analysis is made according to data from 2005 to 2009.

Gross Domestic Product

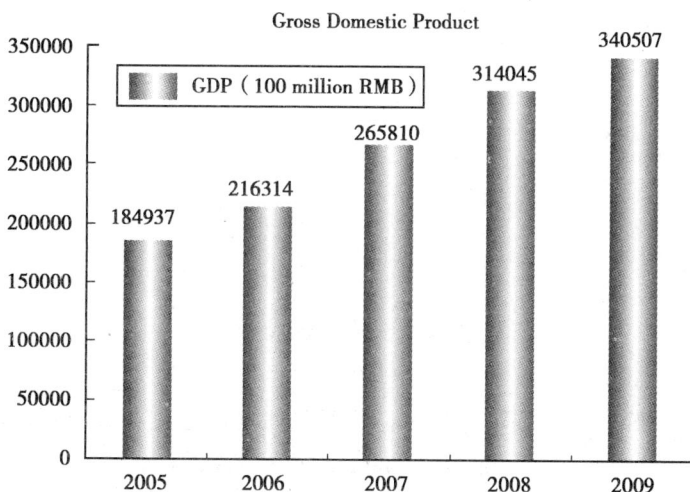

(2) People's living standard is obviously improved. The urban dwellers' average disposable income per capita was increased to RMB 17,175 in 2009 from RMB 10,493 in 2005, an increase of 63.68% with an annual increase of 10.36%; farmers' average net income per capita was increased to RMB 5,153 from RMB 3,255, an increase of 58.31% with an annual increase of 9.62%. Other well-being indicators such as average green land area per capita, average residence area per capita, average urban road area per capita and number of bus per million people are gradually increasing year by year.

Growth Trend of Citizens' Income

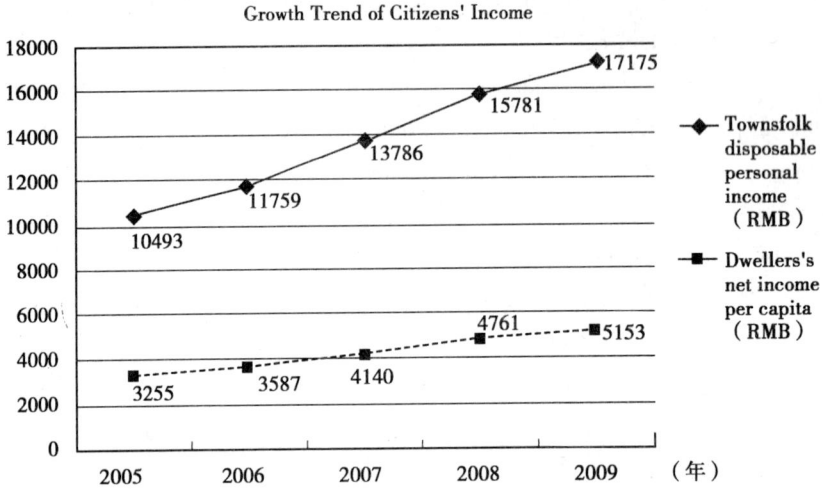

Growth Trend of Citizens' Income

- 10493, 11759, 13786, 15781, 17175 — Townsfolk disposable personal income (RMB)
- 3255, 3587, 4140, 4761, 5153 — Dwellers's net income per capita (RMB)

2005 2006 2007 2008 2009 (年)

Other Index of People's Well-being Growth

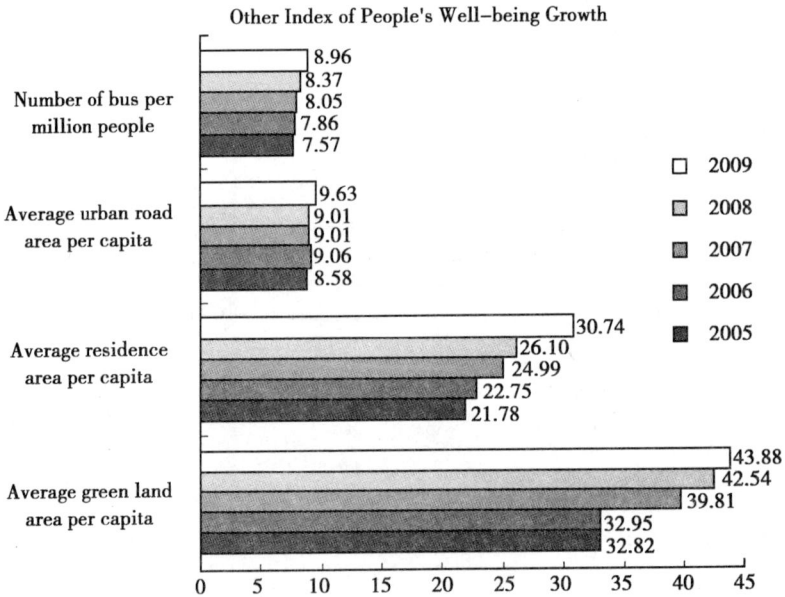

Number of bus per million people: 8.96, 8.37, 8.05, 7.86, 7.57

Average urban road area per capita: 9.63, 9.01, 9.01, 9.06, 8.58

Average residence area per capita: 30.74, 26.10, 24.99, 22.75, 21.78

Average green land area per capita: 43.88, 42.54, 39.81, 32.95, 32.82

□ 2009
▨ 2008
▨ 2007
▨ 2006
■ 2005

(3) With the powerful driving of a series of regional development strategies and policies, Central China, western part of China and northeast part of China develops rapidly and primary effects have been achieved in regional harmonious development. The annual growth rate of average GDP in East China, Central China, the west part of China and Northeast part of China is respectively 12.34%, 13.65%, 14.87% and 12.64%. The growth in Central China, western part of China and northeast part of China is higher than that in East China

with the west part of China in particular; other indicators such as per capita
GDP, average disposable income of urban dwellers per capita and net income of
farmers are also increasing with the same tendency.

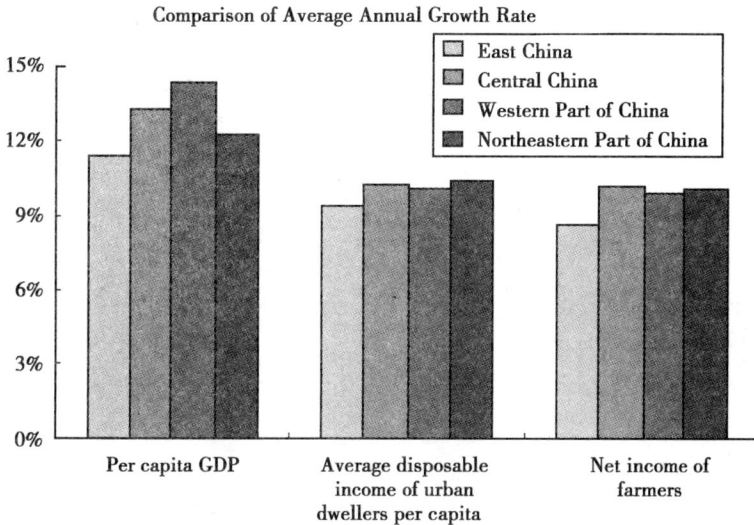

Comparison of Average Annual Growth Rate

(4) Usage efficiency of development elements is constantly increasing. Output rate of unit land area keeps increasing. It had increased to RMB 1, 315, 600, 000 in 2009 from RMB 858, 670, 000 in 2005, an increase of 53. 21% with an annual increase of 8. 91%; the total energy consumption volume keeps growing. It had increased to 3, 066, 470, 000 tons of standard coal from 2, 359, 970, 000 tons of standard coal in 2005, an increase of 29. 94%. However GDP consumption per RMB 10, 000 decreases. It had decreased to 0. 9 ton from 1. 28 tons in 2005, a decrease of 29. 69%.

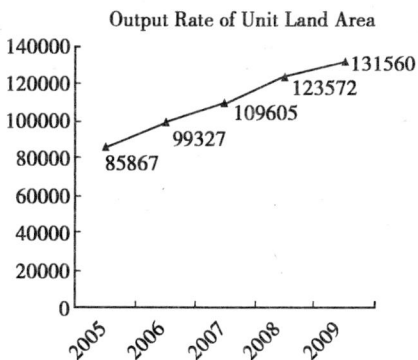

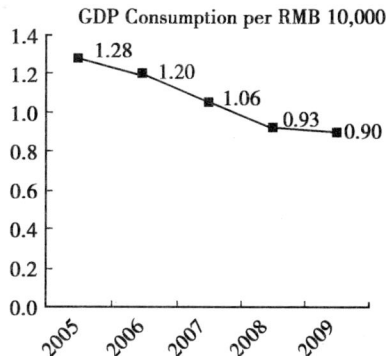

(5) Social situation is generally harmonious and stable. The national social situation generally maintains a stable and orderly development tendency after going through the attack and influences of a series of significant events. Social contradictions tend to be mitigated. The occurrences of traffic accidents, casualty and direct property loss are being reduced. The fire accident statistics data shows the same feature.

Situation of Traffic Accidents Occurence

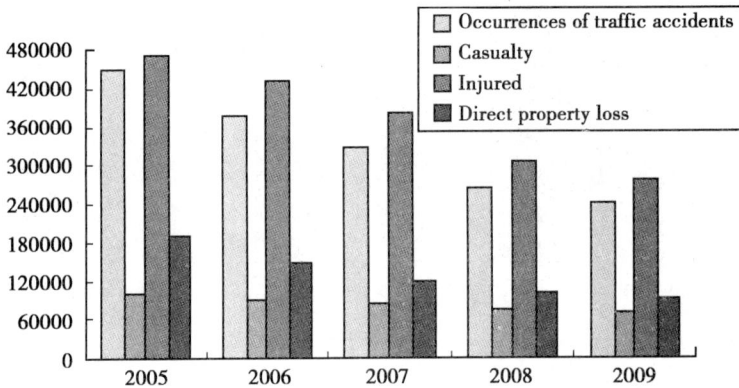

Data of Fire Accidents

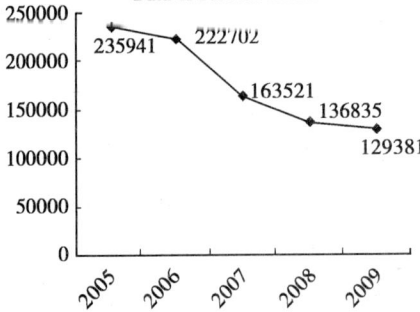

Number of Death Toll and Injured Peoplein Fire Accidents

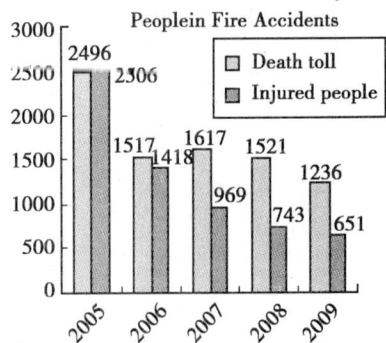

III. Judgment of economic development stage of China cities

Per capita GDP is an important indicator and the main basis to judge the stage of economic and social development. According to the development stage theory of scholars including Chenery and the indicator system put forward by World Bank, the process of structural transformation with growth of income growth per capita is divided into three stages (see the table).

Chenery's income per capita stages (per capita GDP) (unit: U. S. dollars)

	The initiation stage of industrialization	The implementation stage of industrialization			Post-industrialization stage
		Initial stage	mid stage	later stage	
Per capita GDP (1970)	140 – 280	280 – 560	560 – 1120	1120 – 2100	2100 above
Per capita GDP (1996)	620 – 1240	1240 – 2480	2480 – 4960	4960 – 9300	9300 above
Per capita GDP (2007)	748 – 1495	1495 – 2990	2990 – 5981	5981 – 12000	12000 above

Determine city zones first according to our country's urban statistics data in 2009 and choose some typical cities to conduct detailed data processing and analysis in order to help understand features of development in each stage.

(I) Development features when per capita GDP is over $ 3,000

It is an important turning period of economic development when per capita GDP reaches over $ 3,000. The economic development and urbanization enter the key stage of dynamism and fast development. It is also the crucial stage of economic restructuring. There are 108 cities with GDP per capita from $ 3,000 to $ 6,000 in our country which account for 38% of the total cities or cities with higher level. We choose super big cities such as Jiangmen, Nanchang, Zhuzhou and Changchun as references while considering geographical distribution and city types. With a population of 2 million to 5 million, they are among top 50, top 100 and top 150 in the comprehensive rank.

The urban development features of the stage are as follows:

1. The economy maintains a stable and fast development; urban-rural dwellers' income increases stably

2. Regard industry as the leading role; environment pollution limits economic development; industrial structure of part of cities changes

3. Consumer spending is quickly increased; basic consumption occupies a lower ratio while service consumption a higher ratio

4. Social security level is improved stably. There is still development imbalance among regions

(II) Development features when per capita GDP is over $ 6,000

International experience shows that when per capita GDP reaches over $ 6,000, urbanization process and national economy begins to develop quickly, which brings not only growth of the economic aggregate but also daily diversification of social economic sectors, distribution forms and organization forms.

Per capita GDP in some big developed cities in East China has successively sur-
passed $ 5,000 in recent years. Calculated on the basis of permanent popula-
tion, per capita GDP of metropolis whose annual economic aggregate ranking the
front 23rd is over or close to $ 6,000 in 2009. Per capita GDP in Beijing,
Shanghai, Foshan, Dalian and Ningbo is from $ 10,000 to $ 12,000 and that
of Tianjin, Hangzhou, Qingdao, Shenyang, Nanjing, Dongguan and Changsha
is from $ 8,000 to $ 9,000, as well as that of Wuhan, Tangshan, Yantai, Ji-
nan, Zhengzhou is from $ 6,000 to $ 8,000. The development features of the
stage are:

1. The economy maintains a rapid growth. The income growth is inconsistent
with the economy.

2. The industry and employment structure are modernized with the guide of
technology.

3. The usage rate of development elements is increased; economic management has features of intensification, efficiency and low pollution.

4. Attach great importance to social public service system construction.

5. Residents' living standard is quickly increased.

(III) Development features when per capita GDP is over $ 12,000

It is a developed status when per capita GDP is over $ 12,000. The eco-
nomic growth tends to be driven by efficiency and innovation instead of elements. In 2009 Erdos, Suzhou, Wuxi, Dongying, Shenzhen, Guangzhou, Kara-
may and Baotou reached the standard. per capita GDP of Erdos and Suzhou is up
to $ 20,000 and that of other cities is from $ 12,000 to $ 16,000.

1. Per capita GDP increases quickly and the gap between urban and rural
income tend to be narrowed.

2. It is post-industrialization stage; industry structure is advanced.

3. Pressure of resources and environment restrain economic development
and become main constraints.

4. The consumption structure is obviously optimized and enters sharing consumption stage.

5. Urban public service expenses are gradually stabilized and the urban and
rural public services are integrated daily.

It can be noted that there is imbalance in economic development of our cities which are in different stages mentioned above through the statistics analysis

and comparison of cities (or higher level) in our country. Therefore in addition to establishing a consistent evaluation system, it is necessary to further divide regions and make classifications during the analysis.

IV. Analysis and judgment of this year's city evaluation system ranking

1. There are still distinct differences in urban development with different development speed in different regions

Among 287 cities (or higher level), there are 101 cities in East China, which accounts for 35. 2% ; there are 101 cities in Central China, which accounts for 35. 2% ; there are 85 cities in the west part of China, which accounts for 29. 6% .

According to the comprehensive ranking of three indicator categories, top 50 cities include 35 cities in East China, accounting for 70% , 8 cities in Central China, accounting for 16% and 7 cities in the west part of China, accounting for 14% . The general development level of different regions is demonstrated in different cities.

According to ranking of economic development, top 50 cities include 36 in East China, accounting for 72% , 8 in Central China, accounting for 16% and 6 in the west part of China, accounting for 12% .

According to ranking of investment in public service, top 50 cities include 28 in East China, accounting for 56% , 9 in Central China, accounting for 18% and 13 in the west part of China, accounting for 26% .

According to ranking of residents' sharing level, top 50 cities include 40 in East China, accounting for 80% , 5 in Central China and 5 in the west part of China, both accounting for 10% .

It can be noted that through comprehensive and specific indicator ranking of top 50 cities, comprehensive development of cities in East China is clearly better than that of cities in Central China and the west part of China. There is little gap between Central China and west part of China; The gap among cities in East China, Central China and the west part of China is larger than that among regions.

The development level and competitiveness of East China, especially coastal areas, have been dramatically enhanced with the help of geographical advantage and international market since the reform and opening-up. However due to influences of long-term extensive economic growth pattern, excessive dependence on external market, ignorance of the upgrading of one's own industry structure and transformation of independent innovation ability, East China has always been at the end of the industry chain in international division of labor and singly relied on low-cost labor force and land element to maintain the quick growth of the economy.

Thus the situation is: firstly the development of East China is greatly influenced by international economy. Its ability to resist risks is relatively low although its economy develops quickly. Environment and resources cost is irreversibly increasing in economic development; secondly, although Central China and the west part of China have rich labor force and land resources, but they lack reasonable division of labor. A development pattern where East China, Central China and the west part of China can interact well has not been shaped so labor intensive and resource processing industries in East China cannot be reasonably diverted to Central China and the west part of China, which in turn limits the development progress of Central China and western part of China. Take GDP and per capita GDP for example, we can see clearly the differentiation in urban development in the following illustration.

We still use the division pattern of East China, Central China and the west part of China for written report for the convenience of assessing the regional differentiation of urban development. However while managing regional data, we have to adopt the division of East China, Central China, the west part of China and northeastern part of China according to obtained statistics. The division difference won't influence our comprehensive evaluation.

In next stage how to guide Central China and the west part of China to develop in a good and fast way and constantly narrow the gap between Central China, the west part of China and East China will be dealt with. Cities in East China and western part of China are still faced with arduous tasks.

2. Generally speaking, the economic and social development among cities is inharmonious

In order to evaluate degree of coordination among three indicators, we first rank 287 cities according to comprehensive scores. Then we orderly regard each 50 cities as one zone. If the three indicators of a city can be in the same zone,

GDP in different region

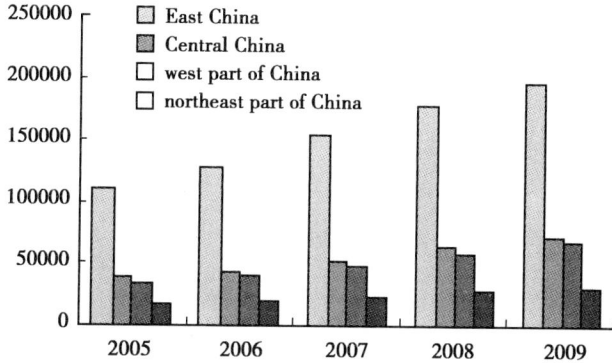

per capita GDP

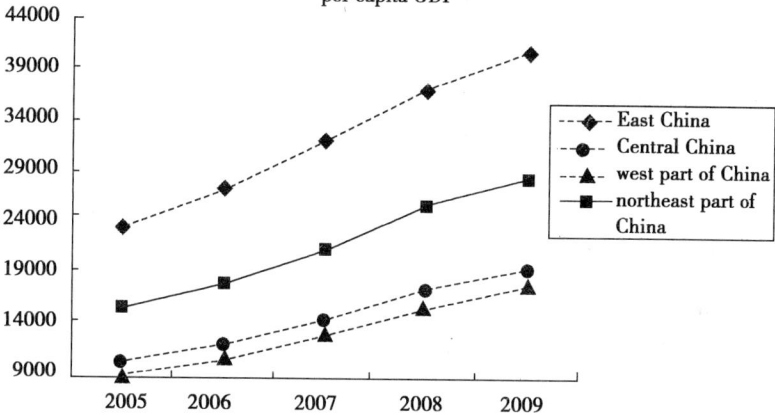

then it is a relatively harmonious city.

Among top 50 cities in terms of comprehensive level, there are 18 cities whose three indicators are in the same zone, accounting for 36%; 4 cities ranking from 51 to 100, accounting for 8%; 4 cities ranking from 101 – 150, accounting for 8%; 3 cities ranking from 151 – 200, accounting for 6%; 4 cities ranking from 201 – 250, accounting for 8%; 2 cities ranking from 251 – 287, accounting for 2%. Except the first zone, the degree of coordination of other zones is less than 8%. Cities which are harmonious only account for 11.5%. Generally speaking, it is extremely inharmonious.

Among 18 cities out of 50 cities with good coordination among three indicators, in addition to Beijing and Shanghai, there is only one city, Changsha, in Central China and one city, Erdos, in the west part of China, 4 in Jiangsu, 3 in

Zhejiang, 4 in Guangdong, 1 in Fujian, 1 in Shandong and 1 in Liaoning which are almost distributed in coastal developed areas.

It can be noted that there is little correlation among three indicators of 287 cities. The high level of economic development does not correspondingly bring the high level of urban public service and residents' actual sharing of achievements. Public service and residents' sharing of achievements in most cities, especially in some cities with fast development, obviously lag behind local economic development. The second and third indicator level of cities with low level of economic development is higher than economic development level on the surface. However their public service and residents' sharing level are quite low. They are supported by national financial transfer as well as local economic development. So the conclusion mentioned above won't be affected.

City ranking coordination Relatively harmonious cities

1 – 50	Suzhou, Ningbo, Changzhou, Xiamen, Zhongshan, Wuxi, Shanghai, Qingdao, Hangzhou, Zhuhai, Shenzhen, Dalian, Nanjing, Guangzhou, Zhoushan, Changsha, Erdos and Beijing
51 – 100	Wuhu, Zibo, Qinhuangdao and Hefei
101 – 150	Jiaozuo, Huangshan, Shaoguan and Zhuzhou
151 – 200	Nanping and Hebi
201 – 250	Chizhou, Chuzhou, Fuzhou and Ganzhou
251 – 287	Shangqiu and Qinzhou

Note: Cities in the table are not listed by ranking

3. Municipality, provincial capitals and municipalities with independent planning status still demonstrate comprehensive strength

Take comprehensive indicator ranking for example, there are 26 municipalities and provincial capitals in top 100 cities which account for 84% of the total 31 cities. There are 17 in top 50 cities, accounting for 55%; 5 municipalities with independent planning status are all listed.

Measured by economic development, there are 20 municipalities and provincial capitals in top 100 cities, accounting for 64.5% of the total 31 cities of which 12 cities are among top 50, accounting for 38.7% and 5 municipalities with independent planning status are all listed.

Measured by investment in public services, there are 26 municipalities and provincial capitals in top 100 cities, accounting for 84% of the total 31 cities of which 18 cities are among top 50, accounting for 58% and 5 municipalities with independent planning status are all listed.

Measured by residents' sharing level, there are 26 municipalities and provincial capitals in top 100 cities, accounting for 84% of the total 31 cities of which 12 cities are among top 50, accounting for 38.7% and 5 municipalities with independent planning status are all listed.

We can see that municipalities, provincial capitals and municipalities with independent planning status enjoy absolute superiority in gathering resources of economic development and public investment. It also means that currently China cities' economic and social development level is to a great extent determined by administrative rank and power.

Comparison between Municipality, provincial capitals and municipalities with independent planning status

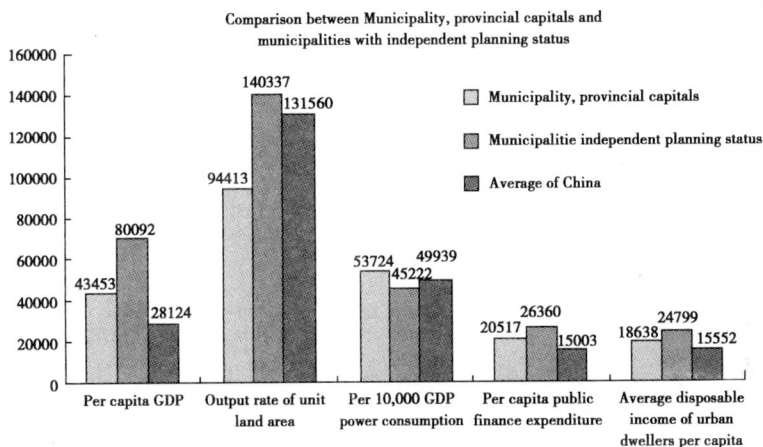

Comparison between Municipality, provincial capitals and municipalities with independent planning status

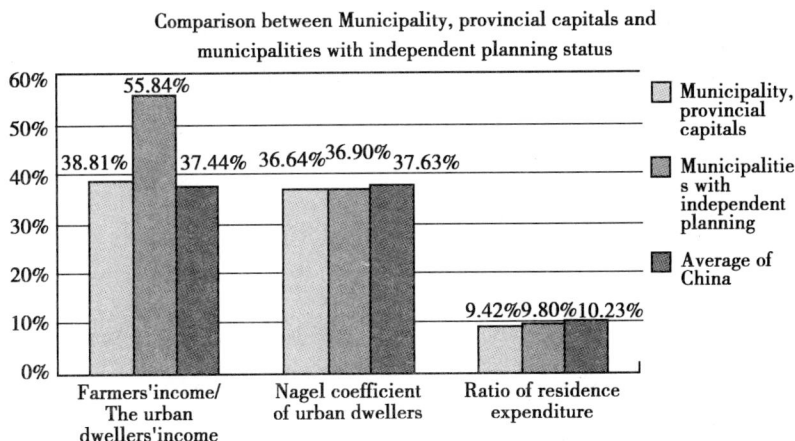

4. No obvious effects have been made in economic transformation

In terms of economic development indicator system, we regard usage rate of land, water, labor and energy, investment in science and technology and external environmental effects as benchmarks for evaluating quality of development. Among top 50 cities in terms of economic development level, 22 are listed for usage rate of elements, accounting for 44%; 18 are listed for good external environmental effects, accounting for 36%; 23 are listed for investment in technology, accounting for 46%. Not a single city's three subsystems mentioned above can be listed among top 50 at the same time. Many cities, municipalities and provincial capitals in particular, enlarge investment in technology in the process of economic development transformation. 25 cities, 80% of the total, are among top 50 in terms of investment in technology. However, they do not have prominent achievements in usage rate of elements and reduction of environment pollution at present.

Take a further look at top 10 cities in terms of economic growth efficiency, only Suzhou and Yulin are among top 10 in terms of usage rate. None of top 10 cities in terms of economic growth efficiency is listed top 10 cities in terms of external environmental effects. The growth with high speed but low efficiency will bring great pressure on resources and environment. Although cities with high efficient economic growth will keep such macro-economic development strength in a long time, "Bottlenecks" of resources and environment have become more basic and new constraints. Diversion of growth towards needs of resources and environment marks the fundamental change in growth pattern.

5. Incoordination between economic development level and residents' sharing level

Public investment is not consistent with economic development level on the whole. Only 7 cities are listed among top 50 both in terms of economic development level and public financial investment, accounting for 17%, a little bit over 1/3.

The immediate influence of urban development on residents is that whether income is synchronous with GDP growth. Through comparison of urban per capita GDP and per capita income growth, we can see that 28 cities are among top 50 both in terms of economic development level and good synchronicity, accounting for 56%, just over a half.

Among top 50 cities in terms of economic development level, 24 cities are listed both in terms of individual benefits projects and coverage of social security and level, accounting for 48%; 20 are listed in terms of residents' living environment, accounting for 40%; 14 are listed in terms of residents' employment level, accounting for 28%. The percentage of all three indicators is less than a half.

Likewise, among top 50 in terms of economic development level, 28 are listed in top 50 in terms of sharing projects in public services, accounting for 56%; 23 municipalities and provincial capitals are among top 50, accounting for 74% of municipalities and provincial capitals.

It is thus clear that in urban social service field, public sharing projects are developed relatively well among various well-being projects organized by the government while residents' individual benefits projects are not so well conducted.

V. Learn actual opinions of urban dwellers through urban questionnaire survey and judge whether differences exist between urban public investment, system adjustment, system construction and actual demands of urban dwellers

Currently there are many studies on urban evaluation and grading, which usually regard statistics calculation as their objective indicators and ignore residents as the subject of urban life. We will try to learn urban residents' subjective feelings of their cities, lay a foundation for further regulating and improving indicator systems and include it in future evaluation system from this year on in order to make the analysis and evaluation of cities more pragmatic on the basis of being scientific, rigorous, comprehensive and practical and truly put in place the "people-oriented" Scientific Outlook on Development. In 2011 we choose Beijing and Shenzhen which are characteristic and typical in such aspects as population and its composition, geographic location, development pattern and speed, management models and history as pilot places for investigation. We have got 1,629 effective questionnaires through systematic sampling and random sampling. The analysis result shows:

1. What residents are most satisfied with is individual consumption and service provided by cities. What they are most disappointed at is housing price, commodity price and social justice. What they are most longing for is increase of

income, stabilization of commodity price, housing, enhancement of government management level, social justice and more opportunities for individual development. This means that employment, income and opportunities for individual development are emphasized for urban attraction instead of the richness of commodities and services. This provides a research basis for setting and examination of related indicators in future indicator system.

2. Different people groups with local registered permanent residence and nonlocal registered permanent residence are not equal in income, residence, social security, employment, opportunities for individual development, education and medical treatment, so they have different satisfaction degrees and senses of belonging. This means that the problem of social injustice is getting severer. Therefore justice indicator in various aspects of urban life should be an importance for future evaluation system.

3. It tests the administrative wisdom and management ability of each urban administrator to retain the reasonable function of registered permanent residence system in current system, weaken its unreasonable functions, arrange transition with replaceable system and break the hedge of registered permanent residence system which leads to social inequity. It will become a part of future urban evaluation system whether the urban administrator can make corresponding policies, institution adjustment and institution construction to deal with problems of identity barriers and social inequity. The analysis of the two cities' residents feelings and evaluation, links and differences among survey objectives and cities helps us grasp the relation between "urban development" and "people's live" in a more comprehensive and precise way on the basis of objective data.

VI. Final analysis

It is easy to come to a conclusion through results of comprehensive evaluation and grading and situation demonstrated by questionnaire survey: the most prominent problem that China's cities are faced with is that economic development level, financial expenses and public investment and residents' actual sharing have not been developed in a coordinated and interdependent way. In other words, the economic development of cities does not necessarily efficiently improve people's well-being and people's life quality.

We try to discuss the reasons from the perspective of two questions:

1. What on earth do people need?

Social development theory shows that there are different stages for development. There are different focuses, development models and ideas in different stages. It is true for economy and society as well as people's demands.

The quick development of economy has primarily met people's demands of materials and fortune since the reform and opening-up, but as the material demands are gradually met, people begin to pay more attention to spiritual and cultural demands so as to get more and richer senses of happiness, satisfaction and achievements. This kind of demand is more complicated. People with different income, education backgrounds and even sexes have different degree of demands. It is a huge project that cannot be solved by relying on economic methods only. At present, none of so many topics on urban development has thoroughly and completely studied on this. The current statistics of the country only focuses on material results or materialized numbers.

Therefore we cannot precisely and comprehensively learn the situation of urban development and further analyze and study it. National policy makers and urban management executors have no way of knowing what people really need and what they are not satisfied. Given the unidirectional and blind development and construction, how to timely adjust development thinking and planning? How to realize the goal of "people-oriented"?

2. Why aren't fruits of economic development directly changed into residents' benefits?

The most fundamental reason is that institutionalization and normalization of urban management are yet to be realized.

Plenty of data and examples show that currently the development pattern with GDP as its core in China cities is not essentially changed. Well-being projects are not the leading factor in development. Most of them are just conducted for emergency, by force or out of petty favors. There is a lack of initiative and pertinence. When it comes to contradictions in development or management, residents' interests (transportation, vegetable stop, store and rural migrant worker school) will be infringed.

The "people-oriented" strategy is forced to adapt to development requirements and goals of the central government due to lack of institutional security. Relying on finance leads to two kinds of extremes in improving well-being: they can be the leading ones such as medical treatment at public expense in Shenmu, Shaanxi; they can be backward. For example, in this year's ranking, Tai' an ranks 23rd in terms of economic level, 167th in terms of public services and 143rd in terms of residents' sharing level; Shuozhou ranks respectively 27th, 110th and 135th while Yibin ranks respectively 50th, 171st and 164th. There are obvious deviations between the government's guide, development planning and residents' demands. The government makes too many arrangements without knowing practical details and demands. The institution brings imbalance in sharing public service projects. It will be a great hidden danger for social stability.

The urban development should be people oriented. Normal development of cities, and scientific and institutional management should be promoted as soon as possible. Residents' right to share fruits of urban development should be secured. Firstly, residents' right to speak should be institutionally guaranteed so as to be convenient for residents and city administrators to conduct exchange and dialogue. More residents can participate in the city's development, play the role of experiencing, promoting and supervising and finally enjoy the fruits of urban development. Meanwhile, detail well-being demands fields, frequency and development tendency and make city plans with purpose, planning and targets; distribute reasonably residents' sharing projects and coordinate the relation between efficiency and justice; establish a set of reasonable coordination system in sharing projects and deal with relation between convenience of common people and commercial profits. All this will gradually become an important part of our future study.

Part Two   Analysis Report of Urban Questionnaire Survey

I. Survey design

- ### Survey purpose

The main basis of common urban grading is only objective indicators such as per capita resource calculated by statistics, but the evaluation made by the subject (residents) of the city is ignored. City exists due to people. We try to embed dweller's evaluation in the system in order to make the urban grading more scientific and practical and provide research foundation for formulating improved and scientific urban grading indicator system in future.

- ### Survey content

The survey tries to learn urban residents' subjective evaluation of cities. Contents cover 12 aspects including individual consumption and service, residence, employment and enterprise establishing, education, medical treatment, social security, transportation, environment, social order, social equity, social trust and respect, government management and public service.

- ### Survey places

Beijing and Shenzhen are selected. They are both mature metropolis with more 2/3 migration population. It is easy to learn people's role transition and identity changes in the process of urbanization. Beijing is an ancient and traditional city. Shenzhen is a newly emerging city with migrants.

- ### Survey methods

The method of combination of self-made questionnaire and interview is adopted for the survey. Sampling survey is conducted for residents in Beijing and Shenzhen. System sampling is carried out in the two cities according to research purpose and their detailed situation. Then random sampling is conducted in each section. Firstly, check out population of Beijing and Shenzhen through statistics and determine number of people in each city for sampling; select five positions of east, south, west, north and center in a district for choosing survey places (areas) (see illustration 1 for details) according to distribution of different people groups (white collar, worker, commercial personnel and rural migrant workers) and the geographical position of areas; after research areas being determined, go to public places where all groups will go to for encounter sampling and at the same time given different people groups (for example, old people in the park and young people in Mcdonald's and KFC) in different public places, achieve balance in selection of public places. Therefore we selected such public places as Hutong/old town, community, urban village, park, fast-food restaurant and bank halls. Some people seldom go to public places, so we also selected some enterprises and administrative institutions and did some household surveys to ensure the representativeness of the sampling.

- Sample introduction

820 questionnaires were made in Beijing for the survey and 814 effective questionnaires were retrieved. The survey areas cover six main districts including Chaoyang, Xicheng (original Xuanwu District included), Dongcheng (original Chongwen District included), Fengtai, Haidian and Shijingshan (see table 1 for detailed samples); 820 questionnaires were made in Shenzhen and 815 effective questionnaires were retrieved. The survey areas cover six main districts including Bao'an (New Guangming District governed by Bao'an District), Futian, Longgang (New Pingshan District belonged to Longgang District), Luohu, Nanshan and Yantian (see table 1 for detailed samples).

Table 1 Distribution of interviewees in districts of Beijing and Shenzhen

	Chaoyang	Xicheng	Dongcheng	Fengtai	Haidian	Shijingshan	Total
Beijign	101	209	194	74	172	64	814
	Bao'an	Futian	Longgang	Luohu	Nanshan	Yantian	Total
Shenzhen	88	179	111	268	102	67	815

II. Overview of interviewees

Among Beijing's interviewees, male interviewees account for 48.5% while female interviewees account for 51.5%; people of the city's registered permanent residence account for 45.3% while people of non-local registered permanent residence 54. 7%; people of non-agriculture registered permanent residence 69. 4% while people of agriculture registered permanent residence 30. 6%. Their age ranges from 14 years old to 84 years old. The main tadget pait is young people and middle-aged people with education background from primary school student to post graduate. They are the people with intermediate and advanced education. Among Shenzhen's interviewees, male interviewees 47. 2% while female ones 52. 8%; people of the city's registered permanent residence account for 32. 5% while people of non-local registered permanent residence 67. 5%; people of non-agriculture registered permanent residence 63. 7% while people of agriculture registered permanent residence 36. 3%. Their age ranges from 18 years old to 64 years old. The main part is young people and middle-aged people with education background from primary school student to post graduate. They are the people with intermediate and advanced education (see table 2 for details).

Table 2   **Basic features of interviewees**

Content		Beijing		Shenzhen		Beijing and Shenzhen Total	
		Number of people	Percentage	Number of People	Percentage	Number of People	Percentage
Sex	Male	395	48. 5%	385	47. 2%	780	47. 9%
	Female	419	51. 5%	430	52. 8%	849	52. 1%
Age	18 years old or below	16	2. 0%	13	1. 6%	29	1. 8%
	19 – 35 years old	495	60. 8%	604	74. 3%	1099	67. 5%
	36 – 55 years old	236	29. 0%	184	22. 6%	420	25. 8%
	56 years old or above	67	8. 2%	12	1. 5%	79	4. 9%
Nature of registered permanent residence	Non-agriculture registered permanent residence	564	69. 4%	517	63. 7%	1081	66. 5%
	Agriculture registered permanent residence	249	30. 6%	295	36. 3%	544	33. 5%
Location of registered permanent residence	Local	367	45. 3%	261	32. 5%	628	38. 9%
	Non-local	444	54. 7%	541	67. 5%	985	61. 1%
	Of which: big cities	97	12. 0%	92	11. 5%	189	11. 7%
	Mid-sized and small cities	174	21. 5%	195	24. 3%	369	22. 9%
	Villages and towns	173	21. 3%	254	31. 7%	427	26. 5%

Content		Beijing		Shenzhen		Beijing and Shenzhen Total	
		Number of people	Percentage	Number of People	Percentage	Number of People	Percentage
Education Background	Below primary school	5	0. 6%	2	0. 2%	7	0. 4%
	Primary school	21	2. 6%	12	1. 5%	33	2. 0%
	Junior high school	124	15. 3%	94	11. 6%	218	13. 4%
	Senior high school	136	16. 7%	165	20. 4%	301	18. 6%
	Technical college	66	8. 1%	125	15. 5%	191	11. 8%
	Junior college	136	16. 7%	202	25. 0%	338	20. 8%
	Undergraduate	271	33. 3%	187	23. 1%	458	28. 2%
	Postgraudate	54	6. 6%	22	2. 7%	76	4. 7%

Table 3   Current (or past) occupations of interviewees

Occupation type	Beijing		Shenzhen		Beijing and Shenzhen total	
	Number of people	Percentage	Number of people	Percentage	Number of people	Percentage
Worker	64	7. 9%	56	7. 0%	120	7. 4%
Farmer	3	0. 4%	3	0. 4%	6	0. 4%
Self-employed entrepreneur	124	15. 3%	41	5. 1%	165	10. 2%
Personnel in commercial undertaking	76	9. 3%	74	9. 2%	150	9. 3%
Personnel in service industry	86	10. 6%	107	13. 3%	193	12. 0%
Salesman	46	5. 7%	57	7. 1%	103	6. 4%
White collar	107	13. 2%	185	23. 1%	292	18. 1%
People engaged in finance	22	2. 7%	21	2. 6%	43	2. 7%
Educator	49	6. 0%	24	3. 0%	73	4. 5%
Researchers and teacher in college	11	1. 4%	0	0. 0%	11	0. 7%
Lawyer	2	0. 2%	28	3. 5%	30	1. 9%
Medical worker	18	2. 2%	30	3. 7%	48	3. 0%
Engineers and technicians	37	4. 6%	35	4. 4%	72	4. 5%
Personnel in administrative institutions	69	8. 5%	50	6. 2%	119	7. 4%
Unemployed	11	1. 4%	16	2. 0%	27	1. 7%
People in charge from small private enterprises	13	1. 6%	33	4. 1%	46	2. 8%
Senior executive in medium-sized and large private enterprise	1	0. 1%	4	0. 5%	5	0. 3%

Occupation type	Beijing		Shenzhen		Beijing and Shenzhen total	
	Number of people	Percentage	Number of people	Percentage	Number of people	Percentage
Undergraduate	40	4. 9%	8	1. 0%	48	3. 0%
People in charge from the government, Party organization and institutions	0	0. 0%	3	0. 4%	3	0. 2%
Soldier	6	0. 7%	0	0. 0%	6	0. 4%
Freelancer	28	3. 4%	27	3. 4%	55	3. 4%

Table 4   Nature of current (or past) companies of interviewees

Nature of current (or past) companies	Beijing		Shenzhen		Beijing and Shenzhen Total	
	Number of people	Percentage	Number of people	Percentage	Number of people	Percentage
State-owned enterprise	157	20. 2%	109	13. 8%	266	17. 0%
Collective enterprise	47	6. 0%	53	6. 7%	100	6. 4%
Private enterprise	211	27. 2%	331	42. 0%	542	34. 6%
Foreign-owned enterprise	59	7. 6%	34	4. 3%	93	5. 9%
Self-employed entrepreneur	153	19. 7%	124	15. 7%	277	17. 7%
Joint venture	20	2. 6%	30	3. 8%	50	3. 2%
Public institution	81	10. 4%	52	6. 6%	133	8. 5%
Party and government offices	30	3. 9%	14	1. 8%	44	2. 8%
Others	19	2. 4%	42	5. 3%	61	3. 9%

Table 5   Annual income of interviewees' families

Annual income of families	Beijing		Shenzhen		Beijing and Shenzhen Total	
	Number of people	Percentage	Number of people	Percentage	Number of people	Percentage
RMB 30,000 and below	121	14. 9%	236	29. 0%	357	21. 9%
RMB 30,000 – 50,000	178	21. 9%	176	21. 6%	354	21. 7%
RMB 50,000 – 70,000	138	17. 0%	100	12. 3%	238	14. 6%
RMB 70,000 – 100,000	148	18. 2%	120	14. 7%	268	16. 5%
RMB 100,000 – 150,000	82	10. 1%	75	9. 2%	157	9. 6%
RMB 150,000 – 200,000	65	8. 0%	42	5. 2%	107	6. 6%
RMB 200,000 – 300,000	40	4. 9%	31	3. 8%	71	4. 4%
RMB 300,000 – 500,000	28	3. 4%	21	2. 6%	49	3. 0%
RMB 500,000 – 1 million	8	1. 0%	12	1. 5%	20	1. 2%
Over RMB 1 million	6	0. 7%	2	0. 2%	8	0. 5%

Table 6   Average annual income of interviewees' families

City	Beijing	Shenzhen	Total
Average value	2. 59	2. 08	2. 33

Note: Grading codes of income interzone are as follows: $0 = (0-3)$, $1 = (3-5)$, $2 = (5-7)$, $3 = (7-10)$, $4 = (10-15)$, $5 = (15-20)$, $6 = (20-30)$, $7 = (30-50)$, $8 = (50-100)$, $9 = (100+)$; unit: RMB 10,000. The average value is a average number of grading codes of each income interzone instead of number of currency.

III. General evaluation of cities

3.1   General satisfaction degree with residents' cities

Table 7   Interviewees' general satisfaction degree with their cities

City	Very satisfied	Relatively Satisfied	So so	Not so satisfied	Unsatisfied	Average value
Beijing	14. 8%	48. 2%	28. 9%	5. 5%	2. 6%	3. 67
Shenzhen	11. 2%	50. 7%	31. 0%	5. 0%	2. 1%	3. 64
Total	13. 0%	49. 4%	30. 0%	5. 3%	2. 3%	3. 65

Note: Very satisfied = 5, relatively satisfied = 4, so so = 3, not so satisfied = 2, unsatisfied = 1. Distinctiveness $P = 0.457$, which means there is no distinct difference in terms of residents' evaluation in the two cities.

According to the five-level grading, the average value is 3; the average value of all interviewees is 3.65 which is more than 3.5, which means people are relatively satisfied with cities where they live.

There is no distinct difference in terms of the question answered by interviewees in Beijing and Shenzhen. What's more, actually as the result of data processing shows, its difference is of no obvious significance whether it is classified according to age, occupation, nature of companies, income, nature of registered permanent residence (agriculture registered permanent residence and non-agriculture registered permanent residence), areas of registered permanent residence (local or non-local), location of registered permanent residence (local and non-local; small, medium-sized and large cities; villages and towns) and number of years of living in the cities, or according to combination of these factors. Differences exist only among people groups with different education backgrounds. The more educated people are, the lower their evaluation of the cities. See table 8.

Table 8   **General satisfaction degree with cities of residents**

with different education backgrounds

Degree of education	Number of people?	Average value
Primary education (primary school and below, and junior high school)	258	3. 77
Intermediate education (senior high school, technical secondary school and vocational school)	491	3. 69
Advanced education (junior college, undergraduate and post graduate)	869	3. 59

This means that residents in Beijing and Shenzhen have almost the same satisfaction degree with cities no matter how different their age, occupation and identity are. The degree is between so so and relatively satisfied with a tendency of being relatively satisfied. The negative correlation between education background and satisfaction degree possibly reflects the negative correlation between expectation value and satisfaction degree.

3. 2   Reasons why there is no distinct difference among people groups: attraction of large cities

In our survey samples, the ratio of local registered permanent residence and non-local registered permanent residence is 38. 9% and 61. 1% (generally consistent with population statistics). More than 60% are non-local people. Given the fact that some non-local people just got local registered permanent residence in recent years, the percentage is supposed to have been higher. We divided people with local registered permanent residence into two categories according to the number of years of living in cities: new local people living for less than 11 years; old local people living for 11 years and above. See table 9 for number of people and percentage.

Table 9   **Ratio of old local people, new local people and**

non-local people among interviewees

Identity	Number of people	Percentage
Old local people (living in the city for 11 years and above)	462	28. 7%
New local people (living in the city for less than 11 years)	160	10. 0%
Non-local people	985	61. 3%

Old local people account for almost 30%; new local people and non-local ones account for 70%. Non-local people live and work in the city due to its attraction and charms. Otherwise they won't leave their home so easily. Therefore it seems reasonable that residents commonly speak highly of the city and there is no distinct difference in their evaluation.

However if we detail and classify evaluation contents, there will be great disparity in terms of satisfaction degree. Later we will see that. First let's see what people are most satisfied, most unsatisfied and most longing for.

IV. Comprehensive evaluation and expectation of cities

Table 10   **What interviewees are most satisfied**

Most satisfied	Rank	Number of people	Percentage
Life convenience	1	805	50. 00%
Transportation	2	643	40. 00%
Environment	3	590	36. 70%
Opportunity for personal development	4	549	34. 10%
Social order	5	398	24. 70%
Public service	6	380	23. 60%
Social security	7	336	20. 90%
Medical treatment	8	287	17. 80%
Education	9	266	16. 50%
Employment	10	194	12. 10%
Commodity price	11	96	6. 00%
Justice	12	52	3. 20%
Housing price	13	23	1. 40%

Table 11   **What interviewees are most unsatisfied**

Most unsatisfied	Rank	Number of people	Percentage
Housing price	1	1216	75. 40%
Commodity price	2	1019	63. 20%
Transportation	3	461	28. 60%
?Justice	4	401	24. 90%
Social order	5	334	20. 70%
Medical treatment	6	328	20. 30%
Social security	7	246	15. 30%
Employment	8	241	14. 90%
Education	9	226	14. 00%
Environment	10	168	10. 40%
Opportunity for personal development	11	160	9. 90%
Public service	12	116	7. 20%
Life convenience	13	70	4. 30%

Table 12   **What interviewees are most longing for**

Most longing for	Rank	Number of people	Percentage
Increasing residents' income	1	916	56. 40%
Stabilizing commodity price	2	832	51. 20%
Solving housing problem	3	794	48. 90%
Enhancing government management level	4	413	25. 40%
Solving social justice problem	5	395	24. 30%
More development opportunities	6	301	18. 50%
Solving household register problem	7	284	17. 50%
Solving medical treatment problem	8	270	16. 60%
Solving social security problem	9	269	16. 60%
Solving unemployment problem	10	246	15. 10%
Solving social safety problem	11	235	14. 50%
Solving environment problem	12	178	11. 00%
Being understood and respected	13	148	9. 10%

From the percentage, what interviewees are the most satisfied are life convenience, transportation, environment, opportunity for personal development whose percentage is above 30% while percentage of house price, justice and commodity price is 10% with distinct difference than other choices; what interviewees are the most unsatisfied are house price and commodity price with a percentage of 60% while percentage of others is less than 30% and the percentage of life convenience, public service and opportunity for personal development is below 10%.

It can be noted that what people are the most satisfied are unique strengths that big cities own such as life convenience and opportunity for personal development. This serves as a footnote for the fact above that people generally speak highly of the city and there is no distinct difference among different people groups.

What people are the most unsatisfied are house price, commodity price and justice with the two former ones in particular. The number of people who choose them goes so far to 1,216 and 1,019, respectively accounting for 75. 40% and 63. 20%, with a great gap between other respects (transportation ranking 3rd accounting for 28. 60% only). Correspondingly what people are the most longing for are increasing residents' income, stabilizing commodity price, solving housing problems, enhancing government management level and solving social justice problem. There is great difference between these five factors and other factors with the three former ones in particular.

V. Identity, occupation and income

Increasing income ranks first among residents' expectations (more than 916 people choosing it), thus its importance. Then how different people groups' income is?

5.1 Registered permanent residence and income

5.1.1 Areas and nature of registered permanent residence and income

Divided by registered permanent residence, average value of income of local people is higher than that of non-local people while average value of income of people with non-agriculture registered permanent residence is higher than that of people with agriculture registered permanent residence. There is great gap between their incomes. Combing two kinds of registered permanent residence, income of local people with non-agriculture registered permanent residence is higher than that of local people with agriculture registered permanent residence while income of local people with agriculture registered permanent residence is higher than that of non-local people with non-agriculture registered permanent residence; income of non-local people with non-agriculture registered permanent residence is higher than that of non-local people with agriculture registered permanent residence. It is a progressive relation. See table 13.

Table 13   Average annual family income divided by areas of registered permanent residence and nature of registered permanent residence

Identity		Number of people	Average value of family income	Distinctiveness
Areas of registered permanent residence	Local people	628	3.12	0.000
	Non-local people	985	1.83	
Nature of registered permanent residence	People with non-agriculture registered permanent residence	1081	2.77	0.000
	People with agriculture registered permanent residence	544	1.47	
Areas of registered permanent residence + Nature of registered permanent residence	Local people with non-agriculture registered permanent residence	594	3.13	0.000
	Local people with agriculture registered permanent residence	33	2.94	
	Non-people with non-agriculture registered permanent residence	480	2.31	
	Non-local people with agriculture registered permanent residence	504	1.37	

5. 1. 2   Areas of registered permanent residence, number of years of living and income

With further detailed division, income of new local people is higher than that of old local people whose income is higher than that of non-local people. There is distinct disparity. See table 14.

Table 14   Average annual family income divided by areas of registered permanent residence and number of years of living

Identity	Number of people	Average value of annual family income
New local people	160	3. 35
Old local people	462	3. 05
Non-local people	985	1. 83

Distinctiveness P = 0. 000

5.2   Occupation and Income

5. 2. 1   Occupation type and income

We divided 21 occupations into seven categories including worker, personnel in commercial undertaking and service industry (including personnel in commercial undertaking and service industry), self-employed entrepreneur and unemployed, (there are only 27 unemployed people in all samples and in reality there are few people of the right age who do not work and earn money so they are classified as self-employed entrepreneur; there are only 6 farmers so they are also included in this category), business owner and people in charge of enterprises (including people in charge of small private enterprises and senior executive in medium-sized and large enterprises), white collar (including white collar, salesman, people engaged in finance, engineers and technicians, freelancers and undergraduate), professional people (including educator, researcher and college teacher, lawyer and medical worker) and personnel in administrative institutions (including personnel in administrative institutions, people in charge of the government, Party organization and public institutions and soldier) for the sake of analysis. See table 15 for annual family income of different occupaiton groups.

Table 15   **Annual family income divided by occupation**

Occupation	Number of people	Average value of annual family income
Business owner and people in charge from enterprises	51	4. 53
Professional people	210	3. 26
Personnel in administrative institutions	128	2. 43
Self-employed entrepreneurs and unemployed	198	2. 40
White collar	565	2. 34
Personnel in commercial undertaking and service industry	343	1. 64
Worker	120	1. 55

Distinctiveness P = 0. 000

Business owners and people in charge from enterprises take the lead and next are professional people. Personnel in administrative institutions, self-employed entrepreneur and unemployed and white collar are in the middle. Personnel in commercial undertaking and service industry and worker lag behind with great gap with groups mentioned above.

Then what kind of people are engaged in occupation with higher income? What kind of people are engaged in occupation with lower income? See table 16.

Table 16   **Occupation distribution of different people groups**

Identity	Business owner	Professional peopl	Personnel in administrative institutions	self-employed entrepreneur and unemployed	white collar	personnel in commercial undertaking and service industry	worker
Old local people	2. 4%	17. 7%	10. 0%	8. 7%	33. 6%	14. 2%	13. 3%
New local people	5. 0%	22. 6%	11. 3%	6. 3%	40. 3%	10. 1%	4. 4%
Non-local people	3. 1%	9. 1%	6. 6%	15. 1%	34. 6%	26. 4%	5. 1%

17. 7% and 22. 6% of old local people and new local people are engaged in professional jobs while only 9. 1% of non-local people do the same job. The percentage of two former ones who work in administrative institutions is more than 10% and that of the latter is only 6. 6%; the percentages of the two former ones who are engaged in commercial undertaking and service industry are 14. 2% and 10. 1% and the percentage of the latter is 26. 4%. The percentage of unemployed is higher than that of self-employed entrepreneur. As to workers, the percentage of old local people is the highest; for white collar, the percentage

of old local people and non-local people is almost the same while the percentage of new local people is the highest. Therefore there is a certain relation between registered permanent residence and occupation.

5. 2. 2 Nature of companies and income

Seen from the nature of interviewees' work unit, the ranking of average value of income is: offices and institutions (including Party and government offices and public institutions), foreign-owned enterprise and joint venture, state-owned enterprise, collective enterprise, private enterprise and self-employed entrepreneur. There is great gap. See table 17.

Table 17　　Annual family income divided by nature of companies

Nature of companies	Number of people	Average value of annual family income
Offices and institutions	177	3. 23
Foreign-owned enterprise and joint venture	143	2. 94
State-owned enterprise	266	2. 67
Collective enterprise	100	2. 08
Private enterprise	542	1. 97
Self-employed entrepreneur	277	1. 71

Distinctiveness P = 0. 000

So what kind of people work in companies with high payment? What kind of people work in companies with low payment? We can see from table 18 that 22. 6% of old local people work in offices and institutions while only 5. 6% of non-local people do the same job; 32. 2% of old local people work in state-owned enterprise and only 9. 5% of non-local people do the same job; only 6. 7% of old local people are self-employed entrepreneurs while up to 25. 5% of non-local people are. It is noted that there is a close relation between registered permanent residence and nature of companies.

Table 18　　Companies distribution of different people groups

Identity	Offices and institutions	Foreign-owned enterprise and joint venture	State-owned enterprise	Collective enterprise	Private enterprise	Self-employed entrepreneur
Old local people	22. 6%	9. 1%	32. 2%	8. 7%	20. 7%	6. 7%
New local people	20. 6%	8. 5%	28. 4%	7. 8%	27. 0%	7. 8%
Non-local people	5. 6%	9. 7%	9. 5%	5. 6%	44. 2%	25. 5%

5.3 Registered permanent residence, occupation and income

We combine registered permanent residence and occupation to see their relation with income. We divided seven kinds of occupations into relatively high-end occupation (personnel in administrative institutions, professional people, white collar, business owner and people in charge from enterprises) and relatively low-end occupations (worker, personnel in commercial undertaking and service industry, self-employed entrepreneur and unemployed) according to economic status and social position. We can see from table 19 that the average income of new and old local people are both higher than that of non-local people who do relatively high-end jobs. That of the latter is again higher than that of non-local people who do relatively low-end jobs. The difference is equally obvious.

Table 19 Annual family income divided by areas of registered permanent residence and occupation

Identity	Number of people	Average value of annual family income
New local people	160	3.35
Old local people	462	3.05
Non-local people with high-end occupations	521	2.04
Non-local people with low-end occupations	455	1.60

Distinctiveness P = 0.000

5.4 Education and income

5.4.1 Education background and income

Another factor that influences the income level is education. Table 20 shows the relation between personal education degree and family income. The higher the education is, the higher the income is. There is great gap.

Table 20 Annual family income of people with different educated

Education	Number of people	Average value of annual family income
Primary education	258	1.28
Intermediate education	492	1.71
Advanced education	872	2.99

Distinctiveness P = 0.000

5.4.2 Education background and identity

The education background is in proportion to income. This has been much different than that in the initial stage of reform and opening-up. Different incomes of people are related with their education background. We can see from table 21 that 67. 0% of local people received higher education while only 20. 7% of non-local people did; 68. 2% of people with non-agriculture registered permanent residence while 25. 3% of people with agriculture registered permanent residence; as to primary education, only 8. 8% of local people received that; 20. 7% of non-local people; only 6. 7% of people with non-agriculture registered permanent residence while there are 34. 1% of people with agriculture registered permanent residence. We can see the clear difference through average values of education background of different people groups.

Table 21   Education background of people with different areas of registered permanent residence and nature of registered permanent residence

Identity		Primary education	Intermediate education	Advanced education	Average value	Distinctiveness
Areas of registered permanent residence	Local people	8. 8%	24. 2%	67. 0%	5. 11	0. 000
	Non-local people	20. 7%	33. 9%	45. 4%	4. 47	
Nature of registered permanent residence	People with non-agriculture registered permanent residence	6. 7%	25. 1%	68. 2%	5. 13	0. 000
	Local people with non-agriculture registered permanent residence	34. 1%	40. 6%	25. 3%	3. 93	
Areas of registered permanent residence + Nature of registered permanent residence	Local people with non-agriculture registered permanent residence	7. 8%	23. 9%	68. 3%	5. 17	0. 000
	Local people with agriculture registered permanent residence	27. 3%	27. 3%	45. 5%	4. 18	
	Non-local people with non-agriculture registered permanent residence	5. 5%	26. 5%	68. 1%	5. 08	
	Non-local people with agriculture registered permanent residence	35. 1%	41. 0%	23. 9%	3. 90	

Note: below primary school = 1, primary school = 2, junior high school = 3, senior high school and technical secondary school/technical school = 4, junior college = 5, undergraduate = 6, postgraduate = 7.

As information mentioned above, new local people's income is higher than that of old local people because education background of new local people is higher. As shown by table 22, 61.0% of old local people received higher education while 85.0% of new local people did; there are 32.5% of old non-local people and 47.3% of new non-local people. Among people who received primary education only, there are 1.3% of new local people, 11.1% of old local people, 29.8% of old non-local people and 19.4% of new non-local people. This means that in recent decade, compared with before, non-local residents who come to big cities have higher education background. However the outstanding average value of education background of new local people makes them have higher income and have higher expectations and demands of urban life. They have relatively negative opinions about some aspects.

Table 22   Education background of people with different areas of registered permanent residence and number of years of living

Identity	Primary education	Intermediate education	Advanced education	Average value of education background
Old local people	11.1%	28.0%	61.0%	4.92
New local people	1.3%	13.8%	85.0%	5.69
Old non-local people (living in the city for 11 years and above)	29.8%	37.7%	32.5%	4.12
New non-local people (living in the city for less than 11 years)	19.4%	33.4%	47.3%	4.53

Distinctiveness P = 0.000

Likewise, the education of non-local people with high-end occupations is far higher than that of non-local people with low-end occupations. The percentages are respectively 60.8% and 27.8%; as to primary education, the percentages are respectively 10.6% and 32.4%. See table 23.

Table 23   Education background of people with different areas of registered permanent residence and occupation

Identity	Primary education	Intermediate education	Advanced education	Average value of education background
Old local people	11.1%	28.0%	61.0%	4.92
New local people	1.3%	13.8%	85.0%	5.69
Non-local people with high-end occupations	10.6%	28.7%	60.8%	4.87
Non-local people with low-end occupations	32.4%	39.8%	27.8%	4.02

Distinctiveness P = 0.000

34

There is significant difference for education background of different people groups. There is a direct correlation between education background and income level. However a person's opportunity for education is inseparable from his/her identity. This will be proven in Part Ten.

5.4.3 Education, age and income

Generally, the relation between age and income is invert U. The age of interviewees is in proportion to income because there are few youngsters and old people in the survey. We can see from table 24 that the ranking (higher to lower) of average income value is old people, middle-aged people, youth and youngsters. We know from information mentioned above that the average income of new local people is higher than that of old local people and the average age of new local people is about 10 years old junior than that of old local people. See table 25. This indicates that the impact of education background on income is great.

Table 24   **Annual family income of people with different ages**

Age	Number of people	Average value of annual family income
Youngsters (18 years old and below)	29	1. 90
Youth (19-35 years old)	1099	2. 20
Middle-aged people (36-55 years old)	420	2. 62
Old people (56 years old and above)	79	2. 76

Distinctiveness P = 0. 001

Table 25   **Average age of old local people, new local people and non-local people**

Identity	Number of people	Average age value	Mid-value of age
Old local people	462	40. 16	40. 00
New local people	160	30. 27	30. 00
Non-local people	983	29. 44	27. 00

Distinctiveness P = 0. 000

To sum up, people have different identities due to areas of registered permanent residence, nature of registered permanent residence, occupation and nature of companies. It is an important factor which influences income. Generally speaking, having local registered permanent residence is quite crucial. In the following we will learn identity's influences over residents' urban life. Identity is a key factor that influences people's evaluation of cities.

It is worth noting that average income value of new local people is higher than that of old local people and non-local people. Later we will learn that new local people's evaluation of many aspects is lower than other people due to their higher education. Therefore they have higher expectations.

VI. Residence

According to table 11, 12 and 13, in terms of satisfaction degree, housing price ranks last (23 people choose it); in terms of unsatisfaction degree, housing price ranks first (1, 216 people choose it); in terms of longing, solving housing problem ranks third (794 people choose it) following increasing income and stabilizing commodity price with far higher percentage than others. This shows that people are most concerned with housing.

6.1 Residence overview

Average residence area value of all interviewees is 65.00 square meters; per capita residence area is 27.20 square meters; average annual rent of tenants is RMB 1,430.98.

6.1.1 Residence of different people groups

Seen from table 26, the higher the income is, the larger the residence area is. It is reasonable.

Table 26   **Residence area of people with different income**

levels (unit: square meter)

Income groups	Residence area of whole family		Per capita residence area		Distinctiveness	
	Number of people	Average value	Number of people	Average value	Whole family	Per capita
Low income (less than RMB 30,000)	339	37.53	338	18.72		
Low and middle income (RMB 30,000 – 50,000)	345	43.29	344	20.34		
Medium income (RMB 50,000 – 100,000)	493	62.15	492	27.59	0.000	0.000
Medium and high income (RMB 100,000 – 200,000)	260	78.64	260	29.52		
High income (more than RMB 200,000)	147	164.59	147	57.32		

6.1.2 Residence of different people groups

In terms of residence area, that of local people is larger than that of non-local people; that of people with non-agriculture registered permanent residence is larger than that of people with agriculture registered permanent residence. The gap is great. Although average income of new local people is higher than that of old local people, their number of living in the city is fewer. Their average age is 10 years old junior than that of old local people. They have fewer fortune accumulations so their residence area is less than that of old local people. However even so, its average value is still higher than that of non-local people with high-end occupations. Non-local people with low-end occupations rank last. If divided according to buying of houses, residence area of non-local people who have bought houses is far larger that of new local people who are almost the same with old local people. Non-local people who do not buy houses lag behind. See table 27.

Table 27   Residence area of different people groups (unit: square meter)

Identity		Average residence area value of whole family	Per capita residence area value of family	Distinctiveness	
				Whole family	Per capita area of whole family
Areas of registered permanent residence	Local people	99. 70	32. 67	0. 000	0. 000
	Non-local people	42. 47	23. 51		
Nature of registered permanent residence	People with non-agriculture registered permanent residence	75. 97	31. 02	0. 000	0. 000
	People with agriculture registered permanent residence	42. 83	19. 37		
Areas of registered permanent residence + Number of years of living in the city	Old local people	109. 94	33. 51	0. 000	0. 000
	New local people	69. 80	30. 33		
	Non-local people	42. 47	23. 51		
Areas of registered permanent residence + Number of years of living in the city + Occupation	Old local people	109. 94	33. 51	0. 000	0. 000
	New local people	69. 80	30. 33		
	Non-local people with high-end occupations	47. 30	26. 63		
	Non-local people with low-end occupations 36. 9420. 05	36. 94	20. 05		
Areas of registered permanent residence + Number of years of living in the city + Buying houses	Old local people	109. 94	33. 51	0. 000	0. 000
	New local people	69. 80	30. 33		
	Non-local people who bought houses	98. 41	43. 87		
	Non-local people who haven't bought houses	33. 79	20. 32		

In terms of residence ways, 63.4% of local people have their own house property and 13.0% of non-local people, 9.7% of local people live in public house while there is only 0.7% of non-local people live in public house. 15.6% of local people rent houses and 65.5% of non-local people rent houses. The percentage is opposite in terms of self-owned property and houses rent. The relation between people with non-agriculture registered permanent residence and people with agriculture registered permanent residence is almost similar. The percentage of new local people's self-owned property is higher than that of non-local people, but it is still lower than that of old local people. The percentages of their living in their own houses and renting houses are both about 40%. See table 28.

Table 28   **Residence ways of different people groups**

Identity		Buy/inherit	Public house	Rented house	Collective dorm	Working house	Self-built houses	Construction work shed
Areas of registered permanent residence	Local people	63.4%	9.7%	15.6%	4.0%	2.7%	4.5%	0.0%
	Non-local people	13.0%	0.7%	65.5%	16.6%	2.7%	0.9%	0.5%
Nature of registered permanent residence	People with non-agriculture registered permanent residence	45.0%	6.0%	37.1%	6.7%	2.7%	2.2%	0.2%
	People with agriculture registered permanent residence	7.6%	0.6%	64.2%	21.8%	2.8%	2.4%	0.6%
Areas of registered permanent residence + Number of years of living in the city + Occupation	Old local people	70.0%	11.7%	7.8%	2.0%	2.6%	5.9%	–
	New local people	43.5%	3.9%	39.6%	9.7%	3.2%	–	–
	Non-local people with high-end occupations	16.6%	0.8%	63.5%	15.8%	2.0%	1.2%	0.2%
	Non-local people with low-end occupations	8.6%	0.7%	68.0%	17.7%	3.5%	0.7%	0.9%

In terms of residence area, the percentage of local people and people with non-agriculture registered permanent residence living in communities is far higher than that of non-local people and people with agriculture registered permanent residence. However the fact is opposite for people living in urban villages. There are only 7.6% of local people and 12.1% of people with non-agriculture registered permanent residence; there are up to 23.7% of non-local people and 28.3% of people with agriculture registered permanent residence. See table 29.

Table 29   **Residence areas of different people groups**

Identity		Hutong/old town	Common community	High-end community	Urban village	Industrial park
Areas of registered permanent residence	Local people	7.8%	77.0%	7.0%	7.6%	0.6%
	Non-local people	10.2%	58.2%	4.2%	23.7%	3.7%
Nature of registered permanent residence	People with non-agriculture registered permanent residence	7.3%	70.7%	7.7%	12.1%	2.2%
	People with agriculture registered permanent residence	13.0%	54.8%	0.4%	28.3%	3.5%

6.1.3   Residence overview of different people groups

Seen from residence areas of people with different occupations, business owners and people in charge of enterprises take the lead; the following are professional people; personnel in public institutions and white collar are in the middle; self-employed entrepreneurs and unemployed, workers and personnel in commercial undertaking and service industry lag behind. See table 30.

Table 30   **Residence area of different people groups**

(unit: **square meter**)

Occupation	Average residence area value of whole family	Per capita residence area value	Distinctiveness	
			Whole family	Per capita value of whole family
Business owners and people in charge of enterprises	147.00	61.05		
Professional people	76.64	31.74		
Personnel in administrative institutions	69.21	27.71		
White collar	65.28	27.66	0.000	0.000
Self-employed entrepreneurs and unemployed	60.10	21.50		
Worker	55.51	22.44		
Personnel in commercial undertaking and service industry	46.89	23.34		

Seen from nature of companies, people who work in offices and institutions have the largest area followed by state-owned enterprise, collective enterprise and foreign-owned enterprise and joint venture, private enterprise and self-employed entrepreneur. See table 31.

Table 31   Residence area divided by nature of companies

(unit: square meter)

Nature of companies	Average residence area value of whole family	Per capita residence area value	Distinctiveness	
			whole family	Per capita value of whole family
Offices and institutions	89. 72	34. 42		
State-owned enterprise	79. 87	31. 59		
Collective enterprise	72. 25	25. 78		
Foreign-owned enterprise and joint venture	68. 11	32. 09	0. 000	0. 000
Private enterprise	54. 08	26. 06		
self-employed entrepreneur	43. 57	18. 84		

To sum up, people with different identities and occupations have great differences in residence. Local people and people with relatively high-end occupations have great superiority be it residence area, residence ways and residence zones. On the surface it is related to income level; however, according to last chapter's analysis, the more profound reason is identity.

6.2 Satisfaction degree with residence

Table 32   Interviewees' satisfaction degree with current residence

Very satisfied	Relatively satisfied	So so	Not so satisfied	Very unsatisfied	Average value
6. 5%	29. 4%	34. 9%	19. 4%	9. 8%	3. 04

Note: very satisfied = 5, relatively satisfied = 4, so so = 3, not so satisfied = 2, very unsatisfied = 1.

The average value is close to 3, which means that people are basically satisfied with their residence.

6.3 Satisfaction degree with residence of different people groups

6. 3. 1   Income and satisfaction degree with residence

Income is in proportion to residence satisfaction. The higher one's income, the more one is satisfied with residence. Satisfaction values of people who have low income and low and middle income are both less than 3. See table 33.

Table 33   **Satisfaction degree with residence of people with different income levels**

Income group	Number of people	Average value of Satisfaction degree with residence
Low income	313	2. 75
Low and middle income	322	2. 85
Medium income	444	3. 10
Medium and high income	233	3. 17
High income	139	3. 65

Distinctiveness P = 0. 000

6.3.2   Identity and satisfaction degree with residence

The satisfaction degree of local people is higher than that of non-local people and that of people with non-agriculture registered permanent residence is higher than that of people with agriculture registered permanent residence. Average evaluation values of both non-local people and people with agriculture registered permanent residence are less than 3. This is consistent with number of houses they have. Therefore old local people are most satisfied. The satisfaction degree of new local people is lower than that of old local people and old non-local people and even new non-local people, which fully demonstrates their high expectations. In terms of its combination with occupations, average evaluation values of new local people and non-local people with low-end occupations are the same, both less than 3. The average evaluation value of non-local people who have bought houses is the highest. See table 34.

Table 34   Satisfaction degree with residence of different people groups

Identity		Number of people	Average residence satisfaction value	Distincti-veness
Areas of registered permanent residence	Local people	577	3. 15	0. 001
	Non-local people	862	2. 96	
Nature of registered permanent residence	People with non-agriculture registered permanent residence	964	3. 11	0. 000
	People with agriculture registered permanent residence	484	2. 89	
Areas of registered permanent residence + Number of years of living in the city	Old local people	432	3. 23	0. 000
	New local people	142	2. 91	
	Old non-local people	102	3. 01	
	New non-local people	755	2. 95	

Identity		Number of people	Average residence satisfaction value	Distincti-veness
Areas of registered permanent residence + Number of years of living in the city + Occupation	Old local people	432	3. 23	0. 000
	New local people	142	2. 91	
	Non-local people with high-end occupations	456	3. 01	
	Non-local people with low-end occupations	399	2. 89	
Areas of registered permanent residence + Number of years of living in the city + Buying houses	Old local people	432	3. 23	0. 000
	New local people	142	2. 91	
	Non-local people who have bought houses	114	3. 48	
	Non-local people who haven't bought houses	747	2. 88	

6.3.3 Occupation and satisfaction degree with residence

Professional people, business owners and people in charge of enterprises, and personnel in administrative institutions take the lead. White collar, self-employed entrepreneur and unemployed are in the middle while evaluation value of the latter, personnel in commercial undertaking and service industry, and worker is less than 3. See table 35.

Table 35   Satisfaction degree with residence of different people groups

Occupation	Number of people	Average residence satisfaction degree
Professional people	177	3. 31
Business owners and people in charge of enterprises	47	3. 30
Personnel in administrative institutions	109	3. 29
White collar	518	3. 03
Self-employed entrepreneur and unemployed	182	2. 98
Personnel in commercial undertaking and service industry	305	2. 88
Worker	101	2. 68

Distinctiveness P = 0. 000

In terms of nature of companies, offices and institutions take the lead. The average value of foreign-owned enterprises and joint venture is more than 3. That of state-owned and private enterprises and self-employed entrepreneurs is less than 3. See table 36.

Table 36   Satisfaction degree with residence divided by nature of companies

Nature of companies	Number of people	Average residence satisfaction value
Offices and institutions	146	3.41
Foreign-owned enterprise and joint venture	126	3.11
Collective enterprise	91	3.10
State-owned enterprise	243	2.97
Private enterprise	479	2.96
Self-employed entrepreneur	252	2.93

Distinctiveness P = 0.000

To sum up, housing is the most basic life security for people living in cities. The residence situation of non-local people, new local people, and people with agriculture registered permanent residence, people with low income and low social position is not so good. The satisfaction degree is negative and contrasts vividly with other people.

VII. Social security

Social security ranks 7th in both satisfaction and unsatisfaction, 336 people are satisfied and 246 are not. In terms of the most longing for, it ranks 9th. 269 people choose it.

7.1   Social security overview

Table 37 shows all interviewees' insurance participation. There is no distinction of places of insurance, including new rural insurance and new rural co-operative medical care.

Table 37   Interviewees' insurance participation

Insurance type	Number of people	Percentage
Endowment insurance	1031	63.8%
Medical insurance	1163	71.9%
Unemployment insurance	553	34.2%
Insurance against injury at work	526	32.5%
Maternity insurance	307	19.0%
Medical insurance at public expense	157	9.7%
Commercial insurance	250	15.5%
Housing fund	506	31.3%
Without any insurance	269	16.6%

See table 38 for classification according to different natures of insurances. 79.1% of interviewees have social insurance and 15.5% have commercial insurance, which account for only 1.8% of those who have medical insurance at public expense. 16.6% of interviewees do not have any insurance. Note: Being without any insurance has a very broad meaning, that is, as long as one have any of table 37 social insurances (even insurance against injury at work only or maternity insurance), he/she is counted as having social insurance.

Table 38   Interviewees' insurance divided by natures of insurances

Nature of insurances	Number of people	Percentage
Only social insurance	1070	66.2%
Both social insurance and commercial insurance	208	12.9%
Only commercial insurance	42	2.6%
Only medical insurance at public expense	29	1.8%
Without any insurance	268	16.6%
Total	1617	100.0%

Note: only medical insurance at public expense refers to people without any other insurance but medical insurance at public expense. People who have both medical insurance at public expense and social insurance and commercial insurance have been included in corresponding social insurance and commercial insurance category.

7.1.1   Insurance participation of different people groups

There is a great gap between local people and non-local people, people with non-agriculture registered permanent residence and people with agriculture registered permanent residence in terms of insurance participation percentage. More than 30% of people from villages and towns have no insurance in terms of location of registered permanent residence. See table 39.

Table 39   Insurance participation of different people groups

Identity		Only social insurance	Social insuranc + commercial insurance	Only commercial insurance	Only medical insurance at public expense	Without any insurance
Identity of registered permanent residence	Local people	69.6%	20.1%	1.9%	2.7%	5.6%
	Non-local people	64.3%	8.4%	3.0%	1.1%	23.3%
Nature of registered permanent residence	People with non-agriculture registered permanent residence	68.3%	17.2%	2.1%	2.0%	10.2%
	People with agriculture registered permanent residence	61.8%	4.3%	3.5%	1.3%	29.1%
Location of registered permanent residence	Local city	69.6%	20.1%	1.9%	2.7%	5.6%
	Other big cities	65.1%	14.8%	5.8%	0.5%	13.8%
	Other medium and small cities	65.4%	10.6%	2.7%	1.9%	19.3%
	Other villages and towns	63.0%	3.5%	1.9%	0.7%	30.9%

We can see from table 40 that there is certain gap between people with high-end occupations and people with low-end occupations. The percentage of non-local people who have bought houses and have no insurances is less than that of old local people. The percentage of new local people is the lowest.

Table 40   Insurance participation of different people groups with different occupations and people who bought and haven't bought houses

Identity		Only social insurance	Social insurance + commercial insurance	Only commercial insurance	Only medical insurance at public expense	Without any insurance
Areas of registered permanent residence + Occupationf	Local people	69.6%	20.1%	1.9%	2.7%	5.6%
	Non-local people with high-end occupations	66.9%	9.8%	2.9%	1.3%	19.1%
	Non-local people with low-end occupations	61.3%	6.9%	3.1%	0.9%	27.9%
Areas of registered permanent residence + Number of years of living in the city + Buying houses	Old local people	69.6%	19.3%	1.7%	3.5%	5.9%
	New local people	69.9%	21.8%	2.6%	0.6%	5.1%
	Non-local people who have bought houses	66.7%	21.4%	6.3%	–	5.6%
	Non-local people who haven't bought houses	63.9%	6.4%	2.5%	1.3%	25.9%

7.1.2   Insurance participation of people with different occupations

The insurance difference is very obvious for people with different occupations. 88.3% of personnel in administrative institutions have social insurance while only 64.6% of self-employed entrepreneurs and unemployed (there are 27 unemployed in total in this survey) did; only 7.8% of the former have no insurance while 26.8% of the latter have no insurance. See table 41

Table 41   Insurance participation of people with different occupations

Occupation	Only social insurance	Social insurance + commercial insurance	Only commercial insurance	Only medical insurance at public expense	Without any insurance
Personnel in administrative institutions	78.1%	10.2%	0.8%	3.1%	7.8%
Professional people	71.2%	11.5%	3.8%	4.8%	8.7%
Workers	78.3%	4.2%	–	2.5%	15.0%

Occupation	Only social insurance	Social insurance + commercial insurance	Only commercial insurance	Only medical insurance at public expense	Without any insurance
White collar	66. 5%	15. 7%	1. 8%	0. 9%	15. 2%
Business owners and people in charge of enterprises	36. 0%	38. 0%	8. 0%	–	18. 0%
Personnel in commercial undertaking and service industry	66. 7%	9. 7%	1. 5%	1. 2%	20. 9%
Self-employed entrepreneurs and unem-ployed	51. 5%	13. 1%	7. 1%	1. 5%	26. 8%

Seen from companies, 91. 4% of people who work in state-owned companies have social insurance and only 5. 3% of them have no insurance at all. The
two percentages of self-employed entrepreneurs are respectively 55. 3% and
37. 4%. They are quite distinct from each other. That is to say, almost 40% of
self-employed entrepreneurs have no insurance at all. See table 42.

Table 42   Insurance participation divided by nature of companies

Nature of organization	Only social insurance	Social insurance + commercial insurance	Only commercial insurance	Only medical insurance at public expense	Without any insurance
State-owned enterprise	75. 6%	15. 8%	1. 9%	1. 5%	5. 3%
Foreign-owned enterprise and joint venture	70. 6%	22. 4%	1. 4%	–	5. 6%
Offices and institutions	71. 6%	14. 2%	1. 7%	6. 8%	5. 7%
Collective enterprise	74. 0%	13. 0%	2. 0%	1. 0%	10. 0%
Private enterprise	68. 5%	11. 0%	1. 3%	0. 7%	18. 4%
Self-employed entrepreneur	48. 0%	7. 3%	6. 2%	1. 1%	37. 4%

7. 2 Evaluation of social security

**Table 43   Interviewees' evaluation of social
security in cities that they live**

Very good	Relatively good	So so	Bad	Very bad	Average value
5. 9%	31. 4%	49. 8%	10. 1%	2. 8%	3. 27

Note: very good = 5, relatively good = 4, so so = 3, bad = 2, very bad = 1.

7.3 Evaluation of social security of different people groups

7.3.1 Identity and evaluation of social security

Evaluation of different people groups is consistent with their insurance participation. The evaluation of local people and people with non-agriculture registered permanent residence is obviously higher than that of non-local people and people with agriculture registered permanent residence. In terms of location of registered permanent residence, the ranking (from higher to lower) of evaluation is people from local city, other big cities, other medium and small cities, and villages and towns. The higher the insurance participation degree is, the higher the evaluation is. Vice versa. See table 44.

Table 44   Evaluation of social security of different people groups

Identity		Number of people	Average evaluation value of social security	Distinctiveness
Areas of registered permanent residence	Local people	628	3. 46	0. 000
	Non-local people	982	3. 17	
Nature of registered permanent residence	People with non-agriculture registered permanent residence	1081	3. 35	0. 000
	People with agriculture registered permanent residence	541	3. 13	
Location of registered permanent residence	Local city	628	3. 46	0. 000
	Other big cities	189	3. 28	
	Other medium and small cities	369	3. 20	
	Other villages and towns	424	3. 09	

7.3.2 Identity, occupation, house property and evaluation of social security

Table 45 indicates that evaluations of non-local people with high-end occupations and non-local people with low-end occupations are almost the same and lower than that of local people. In terms of social security, the influence of identity is greater than occupation. Average evaluation value of non-local people who have bought houses is almost the same with that new local people. It is a very significant phenomenon. Later we will see the group's evaluations of many aspects. "People who have fixed asset are persistent". Even they lack a local registered permanent residence, non-local people who have bought houses speak equally highly of the city with local people.

Table 45   Insurance participation of different people groups with different occupations and people who bought and haven't bought houses

Identity		Number of people	Average evaluation value of social security	Distinctiveness
Areas of registered permanent residence + Occupation	Local people	627	3. 45	0. 000
	Non-local people with high-end occupations	521	3. 18	
	Non-local people with low-end occupations	452	3. 15	
Areas of registered permanent residence + Number of years of living in the city + Buying houses	Old local people	462	3. 52	0. 000
	New local people	160	3. 27	
	Non-local people who have bought houses	127	3. 26	
	Non-local people who haven't bought houses	854	3. 15	

To sum up, just like housing, social security is the basic guarantee for people living in cities. There is great disparity whether in current status or evaluation due to different identities and occupations. The percentage of local people, people with non-agriculture registered permanent residence, people with high-end occupations is higher than that of the opposite groups. However the percentage is inverted in terms of people without any insurance. This means that there is great injustice in social security.

VIII. Employment and business establishment

As mentioned before, comprehensive evaluation of the city, employment evaluation and expectation of solving employment problem separately rank 8th, 9th and 10th in the 13 options (number of people who choose it are respectively 194, 241 and 246) in satisfaction side, unsatisfaction side and most longing for. There are more people who are unsatisfied with it, which means employment is still what people are concerned with but not the most urgent one.

8.1   Satisfaction degree with current job

Table 46   Interviewees' satisfaction degree with their current (or past) jobs

Very satisfied	Relatively satisfied	So so	Not so satisfied	Very unsatisfied	Average value
9. 3%	35. 8%	40. 4%	12. 2%	2. 2%	3. 38

Note: very satisfied = 5, relatively satisfied = 4, so so = 3, not so satisfied = 2, very unsatisfied = 1.

Average value of people's satisfaction with jobs is more than 3, a medium between so so and relatively satisfied.

8.2 What they are unsatisfied

Table 47   **What interviewees are unsatisfied**

unsatisfying aspect	Frequency	Percentage
Income	857	57. 70%
Well-being	402	27. 10%
Opportunity for development	337	22. 70%
Work time	324	21. 80%
Labor intensity	320	21. 50%
Social position	304	20. 50%
Work stability	177	11. 90%
Work environment	164	11. 00%
Interpersonal relation	141	9. 50%
Others	20	1. 30%

Table 47 shows that what they are most unsatisfied is income, followed by well-being and opportunity for development. This means that income level is the most important factor that determines satisfaction with jobs. Opportunity for development closely follows income and well-being.

8.3 Satisfaction degree with jobs of different people groups

8. 3. 1   Income and satisfaction degree with jobs

The higher the income is, the higher the satisfaction degree with jobs is. See table 48.

Table 48   **Satisfaction degree with jobs of different income levels**

Income group	Number of people	Average satisfaction value of jobs
Low income	304	3. 10
Middle and low income	311	3. 31
Medium income	429	3. 45
Medium and high income	219	3. 48
High income	129	3. 78

Distinctiveness P = 0. 000

8. 3. 2   Identity and satisfaction value with jobs

We can see from table 49 that the satisfaction degree of local people is higher than that of non-local people and people with non-agriculture registered permanent residence than people with registered permanent residence. However in terms of old and new local people, the satisfaction degree of new local people is the lowest, even lower than that of non-local people. This again proves new local people's high expectations.

Table 49   Satisfaction degree with jobs of different people groups

Identity		Number of people	Average satisfaction value of jobs	Distinctiveness
Areas of registered permanent residence	Local people	545	3. 44	0. 033
	Non-local people	835	3. 34	
Nature of registered permanent residence	People with non-agriculture registered permanent residence	919	3. 44	0. 001
	People with agriculture registered permanent residence	470	3. 26	
Areas of registered permanent residence + Number of years of living in the city	Old local people	405	3. 50	0. 004
	New local people	137	3. 26	
	Non-local people	835	3. 34	

8.3.3　Occupation and satisfaction degree with jobs

The ranking of satisfaction degree with jobs according to occupations: business owners and people in charge of enterprises, personnel in administrative institutions, professional people, white collar, worker, personnel in commercial undertaking and service industry and self-employed entrepreneurs. See table 50; according to nature of companies, the ranking is: offices and institutions, state-owned enterprises, foreign-owned enterprise and joint venture, collective enterprise, private enterprise and self-employed entrepreneurs. See table 51.

Table 50   Satisfaction degree with jobs of people with different occupations

Occupation	Number of people	Average satisfaction value of jobs
Business owner and people in charge from enterprises	47	3. 68
Personnel in administrative institutions	107	3. 57
Professional people	140	3. 47
White collar	516	3. 37
Worker	100	3. 36
Personnel in commercial undertaking and service industry	305	3. 32
Self-employed entrepreneur and unemployed	166	3. 28

Distinctiveness P = 0. 016

Table 51   Satisfaction degree with jobs divided by nature of companies

Nature of companies	Number of people	Average satisfaction value of jobs
Offices and institutions	141	3.65
State-owned enterprises	243	3.51
Foreign-owned enterprise and joint venture	125	3.46
Collective enterprise	91	3.43
Private enterprise	476	3.32
Self-employed entrepreneur	249	3.24

Distinctiveness $P = 0.000$

8.3.4   Identity, occupation and satisfaction degree with jobs

According to areas of registered permanent residence and occupation, the ranking is: old local people, non-local people with high-end occupations, non-local people with low-end occupations and new local people. The average income value of new local people is the highest but their satisfaction degree is even lower than that of so-called migrant boy and girl workers. See table 52.

Table 52   Satisfaction degree with different position people and occupations

Identity + occupation	Number of people	Average satisfaction value of jobs
Old local people	405	3.50
New local people	137	3.26
Non-local people with high-end occupations	438	3.38
Non-local people with low-end occupations	391	3.29

Distinctiveness $P = 0.004$

8.4   Ways of looking for jobs

We can see from table 53 that 25.5% of local people get jobs arranged by the government and there is only 2.0% of non-local people; there is 28.4% of non-local people who look for jobs on their own and there is only 17.5% of local people looking for jobs on their own; 17.1% of non-local people look for jobs online while only 11.1% of local people look for jobs; 16.7% of non-local people do businesses on their own and there is only 8.9% of local people do the same. Non-local people who are not favored by identity have stronger initiative spirit than local people do.

Table 53   Ways of looking for jobs of different people groups

Identity	government Arrangement	government Job fair	Job fair	Job agency	Adverti- sement	family nd friends Introduce	Go to employer	Find job on line	Self owned enterprise
Local people	25. 5%	2. 0%	12. 5%	1. 4%	5. 5%	23. 2%	17. 5%	11. 1%	8. 9%
Non-local people	2. 0%	1. 1%	14. 9%	4. 0%	8. 2%	27. 1%	28. 4%	17. 1%	16. 7%

8.5   Opportunity for employment and business establishment

Table 54   Interviewees' evaluation of looking for jobs and business establishment in cities where they live

Object of evaluation	Very hard	Relatively hard	So so	Relatively easy	Very easy	Average
Do you think it is difficult to look for jobs here	12. 7%	29. 2%	37. 4%	16. 2%	4. 6%	3. 29
Do you think it is difficult to establish businesses here	30. 6%	40. 6%	22. 6%	5. 2%	0. 9%	3. 95

Note: very hard = 5, relatively hard = 4, so so = 3, relatively easy = 2, very easy = 1.

The average value is more than 3. It is negative evaluation. The average value of business establishment is close to 4. The evaluation of employment difficulty is between so so and relatively hard. The evaluation of business establishment difficulty is close to relatively hard.

8. 6   Evaluation of opportunity for employment of different people groups

8.6.1   Income and evaluation of opportunity for employment

Table 55 shows that the higher the income is, the more difficult getting a job is, that is to say, people with high income feel more difficult to find jobs than people with low income.

Table 55   Evaluation of employment difficulty of people with different income levels

Income group	Number of people	Average value of employment difficulty
Low income	356	3. 51
Low and middle income	354	3. 32
Medium income	505	3. 26
Medium and high income	263	3. 14
High income	148	3. 11

Distinctiveness P = 0. 000

8.6.2 Identity and evaluation of opportunity for employment

Table56 indicates that local people who have more opportunities for employment than non-local people do feel more difficult to find jobs. New local people with highest average income value feel it is hardest for them to find jobs.

Table 56   Evaluation of employment difficulty of different people groups

Identity	Number of people	Average value of employment difficulty
Old local people	461	3. 39
New local people	160	3. 42
Non-local people	983	3. 23

Distinctiveness P = 0. 005

8.6.3 Occupation and evaluation of opportunity for employment

We can see from table 57 that people who work in companies that are universally acknowledged as good ones such as offices and institutins and state-owned enterprises feel quite difficult to find jobs while people who work in companies that are universally acknowledged as bad ones such as private enterprises and collective enterprises feel not so difficult to find jobs.

Table 57   Evaluation of employment difficulty divided by nature of companies

Nature of companies	Number of people	Average value of employment difficulty
Offices and institutions	177	3. 47
State-owned enterprises	266	3. 33
Self-employed entrepreneurs	277	3. 30
Private enterprises	540	3. 25
Collective enterprises	100	3. 24
Foreign-owned enterprises and joint venture	143	3. 05

Distinctiveness P = 0. 012

Data mentioned above shows that different people have different demands of employment. People who have higher income, better identity and companies is more demanding for employment than other people do. Different standards lead to different evaluation. This again illustrates that personal expectation is in inverse to personal evaluation. The higher the expectation is, the lower the valuation. Besides, universally acknowledged good jobs cannot meet needs of people. There are too many competitors. This is one of reasons.

To sum up, employment is still not the most urgent problem for people. But it is worth noting that employment channels for non-local people are fewer than that of local people. Meanwhile pay attention to classifying job demands of different people groups and that of people with high income and high education background who are very important for urban development.

IX. Personal development opportunity

Personal development opportunity ranks 4th (549 people choose it) in people's most satisfaction side among those 13 options and ranks 11th (160 people choose it) in people's most unsatisfaction side. This means that people are relatively satisfied with personal development opportunity in big cities. However it ranks 6th (301 people choose it) in most longing side, which shows people's longing for more development opportunities.

9.1 Evaluation of personal development opportunity

Table 58   **Interviewees' evaluation of personal development opportunity in cities where they live**

Cities	Many	Relatively numerous	So so	Relatively few	Rare	Average value
Total	14.6%	42.9%	29.7%	9.5%	3.4%	3.56

Note: many = 5, relatively numerous = 4, so so = 3, relatively few = 2, rare = 1.

Evaluation of development opportunity is quite delighting, which is between so so and relatively numerous.

9.2   Evaluation of personal development opportunity of different people groups

9.2.1   Income and evaluation of personal development opportunity

The higher the income is, the higher the evaluation of personal development opportunity. It is in inverse to great difference. See table 59.

Table 59   **Evaluation of personal development opportunity of different people with different income levels**

Income group	Number of people	Average value of personal development opportunity
Low income	356	3.20
Low and middle income	354	3.45
Medium income	506	3.71
Medium and high income	264	3.74
High income	148	3.83

Distinctiveness P = 0.000

9.2.2　Evaluation of Individual development opportunity in different position

In terms of areas of registered permanent residence, there is no significant difference by comparing evaluations of local people with that of non-local people. Combined with occupation, non-local people with high-end occupations have the highest evaluation of the city's development opportunity while non-local people with low-end occupations have the lowest evaluation. Local people are in the middle but with little difference. In terms of nature of registered permanent residence, evaluation of people with non-agriculture registered permanent residence is much higher than that of people with agriculture registered permanent residence. In terms of location of registered permanent residence, the ranking is: other big cities, other medium and small cities, the city and other villages and towns. See table 60. This means that the influence of areas of registered permanent residence on evaluation of personal development opportunity is very little while nature of registered permanent residence and location of registered permanent residence are very influential. People with non-agriculture registered permanent residence and non-local people have higher evaluation. People with agriculture registered permanent residence and people from other villages and towns have lower evaluation. Local people are in the middle. This reflects different people groups' difference in terms of seeking personal development, own conditions, adaptability and initiative. Local people who enjoy exceptional advantages have medium evaluation. It is a phenomenon that is worth thinking about. Non-local people with low-end occupations and people from other villages and towns have relatively low evaluation. It may be limited by own conditions. Non-local people with high-end occupations and people from other cities have relatively higher evaluation. In addition to better own conditions and adaptability, the initiative spirit of getting somewhere in big cities and trying to achieve something may be a factor.

Table 60　Evaluation of personal development opportunity of different people groups

	Identity	Number of people	Average value	Distinctiveness
Areas of registered permanent residence + Occupation	Local people	627	3. 56	0. 033
	Non-local people with high-end occupations	521	3. 64	

	Identity	Number of people	Average value	Distinctiveness
Nature of registered permanent residence	Non-local people with low-end occupations	454	3. 47	0. 000
	People with non-agriculture registered permanent residence	1081	3. 64	
Location of registered permanent residence	People with agriculture registered permanent residence	543	3. 39	0. 000
	This city	628	3. 56	
	Other big cities	189	3. 83	
	Other medium and small cities	369	3. 64	
	Other villages and towns	426	3. 36	

9.2.3   Occupation and evaluation of personal development opportunity

Table 61 shows that the evaluation of professional people takes the lead, followed by self-employed, business owners and people in charge of enterprises, white collar. There is no obvious disparity. Personnel in administrative institutions, commercial undertaking and service industry and worker lag behind. Self-entrepreneurs who are not protected by companies and struggle on their own have relatively high evaluation. It is a phenomenon that is worth pondering over.

Table 61   Evaluation of personal development opportunity of people with different occupations

Occupation	Number of people	Average value of personal development opportunity
Professional people	210	3. 77
Self-employed entrepreneurs and unemployed	198	3. 64
Business owners and people in charge of enterprises	51	3. 63
White collar	565	3. 59
Personnel in administrative institutions	128	3. 44
Personnel in commercial undertaking and service industry	342	3. 43
Worker	120	3. 42

Distinctiveness P = 0. 001

9.2.4   Education and evaluation of personal development opportunity

The higher the education background, the higher the evaluation. They are in proportion with obvious disparity. See table 62. Apparently, own condition is a crucial factor for obtaining and discovering more personal development opportunities.

Table 62　　　Evaluation of personal development opportunity of
people with different education background

Education background	Number of people	Average value of personal development opportunity
Primary education	258	3. 27
Intermediate education	491	3. 47
Advanced education	872	3. 69

Distinctiveness P = 0. 000

In conclusion, different people groups are different in grasping and discovering personal development opportunity. This results from such own conditions as education background, experience and adaptability. Expectation value and initiative are e-qually important factors. Local people with exceptional advantages are in the middle. Self-employed entrepreneurs who are not protected by companies have higher evaluation. It is worth thinking about. On the whole, having more development opportunities in cities is the common with of all interviewees. In last chapter, development opportunity takes the lead in unsatisfaction side, which proves this.

X. Education

Education ranks 9th in both satisfaction and unsatisfaction side among 13 options. 266 people are satisfied while 226 are unsatisfied. This means people are relatively satisfied with education in cities where they live.

10. 1　Family members' schooling in cities where they live

Education has great influences over people's income and social position. Children's education becomes the priority of families at present. Therefore we did survey. Among 1,617 interviewees, 534 people have children studying in the city, which accounts for 33. 0% . Among 534 people, local people account for 60. 5% while non-local people account for 39. 5% . See table 63 for basic information.

Table 63　　　Students' schooling information in the city

Content		Number of people	Percentage
Nature of companies	State-run school	395	74. 8%
	Non-governmental school	114	21. 6%
	Noble/international school	4	0. 8%
	School for children of migrant workers	15	2. 8%

Content		Number of people	Percentage
What kind of schooling	Kindergarten	115	21. 7%
	Primary school	120	22. 6%
	Junior high school	67	12. 6%
	Senior high school	44	8. 3%
	Technical secondary school/technical school	17	3. 2%
	Junior college	38	7. 2%
	Undergraduate	108	20. 4%
	Postgraduate	21	4. 0%

Most of them study in state-run schools. We can see from table 64 that most of students in primary school and senior high school, undergraduate and post-graduate study in state-run schools. Students of technical secondary schools, technical schools and junior college study in non-governmental schools. Most of kindergartens are run by private people. There are few students in school for children of migrant workers who are in kindergarten stage. Table 65 shows that a-mong students in state-run school, 31. 3% (percentage in column) is non-local people; table 66 shows that even in senior high school, 11. 6% (percentage in column) is non-local people. This means that the barrier of registered permanent residence has been overcome in state-run schools including primary school and senior high school. The percentages in rows of table 65 show that 85. 2% of local people study in state-run schools and only 59. 4% of non-local people do. Colum percentage shows that the percentage of local people is two times bigger than that of non-local people in state-run schools. The fact is opposite in non-governmental schools. This may prove that it is more difficult for non-local people to study in state-run schools of the city than local people.

Table 64   Relation between study stage and nature of schools

What kind of schooling	Nature			
	State-run schools	Non-governmental schools	Noble/international school	School for children of migrant workers
Kindergarten	39. 3%	50. 9%	1. 8%	8. 0%
Primary school	80. 0%	17. 5%	–	2. 5%
Junior high school	87. 9%	10. 6%	–	1. 5%
Senior high school	86. 0%	11. 6%	2. 3%	–

continued

What kind of schooling	Nature			
	State-run schools	Non-governmental schools	Noble/international school	School for children of migrant workers
Technical secondary school/ technical school	62. 5%	37. 5%	–	–
Junior college	75. 0%	25. 0%	–	–
Undergraduate	91. 6%	7. 5%	0. 9%	–
Postgraduate	95. 2%	4. 8%	–	–
Total	74. 9%	21. 9%	0. 8%	2. 5%

Table 65   Nature of schools of local people and non-local people

Areas and nature of registered permanent residence		Nature of companies			
		State-run schools	Non-governmental schools	Noble/ international school	School for children of migrant workers
Local people	Percentage in row	85. 2%	12. 6%	0. 9%	1. 3%
	Percentage in column	68. 7%	35. 1%	75. 0%	30. 8%
Non-local people	Percentage in row	59. 4%	35. 7%	0. 5%	4. 3%
	Percentage in column	31. 3%	64. 9%	25. 0%	69. 2%

Table 66   Study stage distribution of local people and non-local people

Areas and nature of registered permanent residence		What kind of schooling							
		Kinderg-arten	Primary school	Junior high school	Senior high school	Technical secondary school/technical school	Junior college	Underg-raduate	Postgr-aduate
Local people	Percentage in row	19. 2%	20. 5%	12. 9%	12. 0%	1. 9%	6. 9%	22. 7%	3. 8%
	Percentage in column	53. 0%	54. 2%	62. 1%	88. 4%	37. 5%	59. 5%	67. 3%	57. 1%
Non-local people	Percentage in row	26. 0%	26. 4%	12. 0%	2. 4%	4. 8%	7. 2%	16. 8%	4. 3%
	Percentage in column	47. 0%	45. 8%	37. 9%	11. 6%	62. 5%	40. 5%	32. 7%	42. 9%

10. 2   Tuition and sponsoring fee

In our survey, 352 people out of 534 have handed over tuition fee and 50 people submitted plenty of sponsoring fee. It is normal to give tuition and sponsoring fee if studying in non-governmental schools. If students study in state-run primary and junior high schools they should not give any tuition. Sponsoring fee should not be asked in any stage of study in state-run schools. Tuition is not needed during the nine-year compulsory education. Sponsoring fee for entrance to state-run school is forbidden, which is explicityly stipulated by the country.

We can see from table 67 that students who are in kindergarten and senior high school occupy a higher percentage but there is still 35.8% and 31.8% of students in primary and junior high school where tuition is exempted who give tuition. Then how many of them study in state-run schools? Table 68 shows that among 120 students who are in primary school, 96 are in state-run schools and 22 of them give tuition, accounting for 22.9% among whom there are 9 local people, accounting for 15.3% of local people who study in state-run schools. There are 11 non-local people, accounting for 35.1% of non-local people who study in state-run schools. 58 out of 67 who are in junior high school study in state-run schools among whom 14 people give tuition fee, accounting for 24.1%. 8 are local people, accounting for 21.1% of local people who study in state-run junior high school. 4 are non-local people, accounting for 30.0% of non-local people who study in state-run junior high school. This means in compulsory education stage, many schools still ask tuition. The percentage of non-local students who give tuition is much higher than that of local students.

Table 67 **Relation between study stage and paying**
of tuition and sponsoring fee

Study stage		Pay tuition		Pay sponsoring fee	
		No	Yes	No	Yes
Kindergarten	Percentage in row	6.1%	93.9%	80.0%	20.0%
	Percentage in column	4.0%	30.8%	19.3%	46.0%
Primary school	Percentage in row	64.2%	35.8%	87.5%	12.5%
	Percentage in column	44.0%	12.3%	22.1%	30.0%
Junior high school	Percentage in row	68.2%	31.8%	92.4%	7.6%
	Percentage in column	25.7%	6.0%	12.8%	10.0%
Senior high school	Percentage in row	34.9%	65.1%	90.7%	9.3%
	Percentage in column	8.6%	8.0%	8.2%	8.0%
Technical secondary school/ technical school	Percentage in row	–	100.0%	93.8%	6.3%
	Percentage in column	–	4.6%	3.2%	2.0%
Junior college	Percentage in row	18.9%	81.1%	97.3%	2.7%
	Percentage in column	4.0%	8.5%	7.6%	2.0%
Undergraduate	Percentage in row	15.7%	84.3%	99.1%	0.9%
	Percentage in column	9.7%	25.9%	22.5%	2.0%
Postgraduate	Percentage in row	33.3%	66.7%	100.0%	–
	Percentage in column	4.0%	4.0%	4.4%	–
Total		33.3%	66.7%	90.5%	9.5%

Table 68   Tuition payment information in state-run primary
and junior high schools

state-run schools	Identity		No tuition payment	Tuition payment	Total
Primary school	Local people	Number of people	50	9	59
		Percentage	84.7%	15.3%	100.0%
	Non-local people	Number of people	24	13	37
		Percentage	64.9%	35.1%	100.0%
	Total	Number of people	74	22	96
		Percentage	77.1%	22.9%	100.0%
Junior high school	Local people	Number of people	30	8	38
		Percentage	78.9%	21.1%	100.0%
	Non-local people	Number of people	14	6	20
		Percentage	70.0%	30.0%	100.0%
	Total	Number of people	44	14	58
		Percentage	75.9%	24.1%	100.0%

It is worse with sponsoring fee. Table 67 shows that sponsoring fee is necessary expense from kindergarten to undergraduate except postgraduate. The ranking of paying percentage is: kindergarten, primary school, senior high school, junior high school, technical secondary school/technical school, junior college, undergraduate and postgraduate. Table 69 shows that much sponsoring fee is paid to state-run schools. Among all people who pay sponsoring fee, 83.7% give it to state-run schools (percentage in column) while 10.4% of students who study in state-run schools pay sponsoring fee (percentage in row). This means even though entrance sponsoring fee is forbidden in the country's repeated orders, schools still ignore it and receive that.

Table 69   Relation between nature of schools and paying of
tuition and sponsoring fee paying

Nature of schools		Pay tuition		Pay sponsoring fee	
		No	Yes	No	Yes
State-run schools	Percentage in row	42.9%	57.1%	89.6%	10.4%
	Percentage in column	94.9%	64.8%	74.2%	83.7%
Non-governmental schools	Percentage in row	5.3%	94.7%	93.9%	6.1%
	Percentage in column	3.4%	31.1%	22.5%	14.3%
Noble/international school	Percentage in row	25.0%	75.0%	75.0%	25.0%
	Percentage in column	0.6%	0.9%	0.6%	2.0%
School for children of migrant workers	Percentage in row	15.4%	84.6%	100.0%	0.0%
	Percentage in column	1.1%	3.2%	2.7%	0.0%
Total		33.9%	66.1%	90.7%	9.3%

See table 70 for average sum of sponsoring fee and annual tuition. The data in the table is not limited to state-run schools and other types of schools which receive tuition and sponsoring fee are included.

Table 70 Average annual tuition and entrance sponsoring fee of families who have paid tuition and sponsoring fee in the city

	Beijing	Shenzhen	Total	Distinctiveness
Average value of annual tuition	7612. 35	9715. 32	8442. 78	0. 000
Average value of entrance sponsoring fee	17861. 11	4025. 00	15647. 33	0. 020

10. 3 Evaluation of education quality and education policy

Table 71 Evaluation of education quality of people whose children study in the city

Best	Better	So so	Bad	Worst	Average value
11. 9%	38. 1%	42. 5%	5. 8%	1. 7%	3. 54

Note: best = 5, better = 4, so so = 3, bad = 2, worst = 1.

Table 72 Interviewees' satisfaction degree with education policy in the city where they live

Very satisfied	Relatively satisfied	So so	Not so satisfied	Very unsatisfied	Average value
5. 9%	26. 6%	40. 0%	20. 5%	7. 0%	3. 01

Note: very satisfied = 5, relatively satisfied = 4, so so = 3, not so satisfied = 2, very unsatisfied = 1.

The average value of education quality is more than 3. 5. It is positive between so so and better. The satisfaction degree with education policy is around the median.

10. 4 Education opportunity and justice in primary and high schools

It is the core in the training and education of children to have them study in ideal schools. We especially asked such a question: do you think you are able to send your children to ideal primary and high schools for study? See table 73 for interviewees' answers.

Table 73 Interviewees' self affirmation of their own abilities to send children to ideal primary and high schools for study

Surely	Probably	So so	Possible	Surely not	Average value
14. 8%	25. 2%	22. 8%	24. 1%	13. 1%	3. 05

Note: surely = 5, probably = 4, so so = 3, possible = 2, surely not = 1.

The average value is 3. 05, a median. Is there any difference among confidence of different people groups? Who are more confident?

10. 4. 1   Income and education opportunity

Table 74 shows that the higher the interviewees' annual family income, the more confident they are. There is great disparity among different groups. The average value of both low income group and low and middle income group is less than 3 while that of high income group reaches up to 4. 06. This means that economic ability plays a great role.

**Tabale 74   Self affirmation of abilities of people with different income
levels to send children to ideal primary and high schools for study**

Income group	Number of people	Average value of self affirmation of abilities
Low income	356	2. 45
Low and middle income	347	2. 82
Medium income	501	3. 11
Medium and high income	262	3. 46
High income	146	4. 06

Distinctiveness P = 0. 000

10. 4. 2   Identity and education opportunity

Economic ability is an important factor, but interviewees' identity and social relation are also important. We can see from table 75 that in terms of confidence in this, local people are more confident than non-local people and people with non-agriculture registered permanent residence than people with agriculture registered permanent residence. There is great difference. The average value of the two latter ones is less than 3.

The number of years of living the city is a crucial factor for accumulating contacts. Combined with identity of registered permanent residence, old local people are superior over new local people who are superior over old non-local people. Old non-local people are superior over new non-local people with vivid contrasts. There are two quite interesting points: as long as one has local registered permanent residence, new local people are more confident than old non-local people even though they do not live that long in the city; new local people whose average income value is higher than that of old local people are less confident than old local people.

Urban life experience is an important foundation for establishing social relations. The environment where people grow up is equally and subconsciously important for people's confidence in this. In terms of location of registered permanent residence, people in the city are more confident than people from other big cities, followed by people from medium and small cities and villages and towns. The average value of the two latter ones is less than 3.

Table 75   Self affirmation of abilities of different people groups to send children to ideal primary and high schools for study

Identity		Number of people	Average value of self affirmation of abilities	Distinctiveness
Areas of registered permanent residence	Local people	621	3.31	0.000
	Non-local people	975	2.88	
Nature of registered permanent residence	People with non-agriculture registered permanent residence	1070	3.18	0.000
	People with agriculture registered permanent residence	538	2.78	
Areas of registered permanent residence + Number of years of living in the city	Old local people	456	3.38	0.000
	New local people	159	3.08	
	Old non-local people	113	2.96	
	New non-local people	854	2.87	
Location of registered permanent residence	This city	621	3.31	0.000
	Other big cities	186	3.29	
	Other medium and small cities	369	2.87	
	Other villages and towns	420	2.70	

10.4.3   Occupation, identity and education opportunity

Occupation is the source of income as well as social relations. Combining identity and occupation, table 76 shows that the average value of local people is higher than that of non-local people with high-end occupations whose value is higher than non-local people with low-end occupations. Even if occupation factor is added, the average value of self affirmation of people with high-end occupations is still less than 3. However in terms of nature of companies, the confidence ranking is: people in offices and institutions, state-owned enterprises, foreign-owned enterprises and joint venture, collective enterprises, private enterprises and self-employed entrepreneurs. The average value of the two latter ones is less than 3. Therefore identity of registered permanent residence is quite influential.

Table 76　　**Self affirmation of abilities of people with different occupations and identities to send children to ideal primary and high schools for study**

	Occupation and identity	Number of people	Average value of self affirmation of abilities	Distinctiveness
Areas of registered permanent residence + Occupation	Local people	620	3. 30	0. 000
	Non-local people with high-end occupations	516	2. 97	
	Non-local people with low-end occupations	450	2. 78	
Nature of companies	Offices and institutions	176	3. 40	0. 000
	State-owned enterprises	264	3. 24	
	Foreign-owned enterprises and joint venture	141	3. 18	
	Collective enterprises	100	3. 13	
	Private enterprises	535	2. 89	
	Self-employed entrepreneurs	273	2. 78	

According to the above analysis, whether one has the ability to send children to ideal primary and high schools for study mainly depends on economic ability, identity and position and social relation. Owning local registered permanent residence is of prime importance.

To sum up, children's education is what almost every resident is concerned with. Many families spare no effort to let their children receive better education. However in current system, in terms of primary and high schools, there is severe injustice among families with different identities and income levels whether it is about entrance, choice of schools or tuition and sponsoring fee.

XI. Individual consumption and service

Life convenience ranks respectively 1st and the last in interviewees' most satisfied side and most unsatisfied side among 13 options (805 satisfied and 70 unsatisfied). So people are very satisfied with life in big cities.

11. 1　Satisfaction degree with individual consumption and services

Table 77　**Interviewees' satisfaction degree with individual consumption and services in cities where they live**

Very satisfied	Relatively satisfied	So so	Not so satisfied	Very unsatisfied	Average value
6. 8%	34. 6%	36. 9%	16. 3%	5. 4%	3. 21

Note: very satisfied = 5, relatively satisfied = 4, so so = 3, not so satisfied = 2, very unsatisfied = 1.

The average value is more than 3. It is positive.

11. 2　Satisfied and unsatisfied aspects of individual consumption and services

What interviewees are most satisfied is shopping and most unsatisfied is financial service. See table 78 and table 79.

Table 78　**Interviewees' satisfied aspects of individual consumption and service in cities where they live**

Satisfied aspects of individual consumption and service	rank	Number of people	Percentage
Shopping	1	723	46. 10%
Entertainment	2	435	27. 70%
Communications service	3	421	26. 80%
Daily life service	4	352	22. 40%
Culture and sports	5	238	15. 20%
Finacial service	6	229	14. 60%

Table 79　**Interviewees' unsatisfied aspects of individual consumption and service in cities where they live**

Unsatisfied aspects of individual consumption and service	rank	Number of people	Percentage
Financial service	1	454	29. 80%
Daily life service	2	400	26. 30%
Communications service	3	371	24. 40%
Shopping	4	358	23. 50%
Culture and sports	5	296	19. 40%
Entertainment	6	247 ·	16. 20%

11. 3　Satisfaction degree with individual consumption and service of different people groups

There is no distinct difference between local people and non-local people, which means they feel almost the same with individual consumption and service. The satisfaction degree of people with non-agriculture registered permanent residence is higher than that of people with agriculture registered permanent residence. This is related with their income, residence conditions and environment. The satisfaction degree of non-local people who have bought houses is much higher than that of local people and non-local people who haven't bought houses. There is 43.5% new local people who are less satisfied but with high expectations and have their own house property as it is with people who haven't bought houses. See table 80.

Table 80   **Satisfaction degree with individual consumption and service of different people groups**

Identity		Number of people	Average satisfaction value of individual consumption and service	Distinctiveness
Nature of registered permanent residence	People with non-agriculture registered permanent residence	1080	3.28	0.000
	People with agriculture registered permanent residence	544	3.07	
Areas of registered permanent residence + Number of years of living in the city + Buying houses	Old local people	432	3.23	0.003
	New local people	142	2.91	
	Non-local people who have bought houses	114	3.48	
	Non-local people who haven't bought houses	747	2.88	

In the past the biggest attraction of cities was richness of commodities and service and life convenience. With immense development of social economy and homogenization of urban construction, individual consumption and service are what people are relatively satisfied with in current urban life. This indicates that its weight in urban attractions is decreasing.

XII. Medical treatment

About comprehensive evaluation of the city, medical treatment ranks 8th (287 people choose it) in interviewees' satisfaction side and ranks 6th (328 choose it) in unsatisfaction side. It ranks 8th (270 people choose it) among things that are most longed for. Among 13 satisfied options, the position of medical treatment is in the less middle.

12. 1 Medical resources in cities: seeing doctors

According to the survey, the average value of time spent on seeing doctors is 2. 9 hours.

Table 81 Interviewees' evaluation of seeing doctors in cities where they live

Very convenient	Relatively convenient	So so	Not so convenient	Very inconvenient	Average value
10. 7%	28. 2%	25. 4%	22. 4%	13. 2%	3. 01

Note: very convenient = 5, relatively convenient = 4, so so = 3, not so convenient = 2, very inconvenient = 1.

Average evaluation value of seeing doctors is moderate. It is a neutral evaluation.

12. 2 Evaluation of medical treatment level and medical treatment policy

Table 82 Interviewees' evaluation of medical treatment level in cities where they live

Very satisfied	Relatively satisfied	So so	Not so satisfied	Very unsatisfied	Average value
15. 3%	42. 5%	33. 7%	5. 5%	3. 1%	3. 61

Note: best = 5, better = 4, so so = 3, bad = 2, worst = 1.

The average evaluation value is above 3. 5 which is between so so and better, more close to better.

Table 83 Interviewees' satisfaction degree with medical treatment policy in cities where they live

Very satisfied	Relatively satisfied	So so	Not so satisfied	Very unsatisfied	Average value
5. 7%	28. 5%	41. 8%	18. 5%	5. 5%	3. 10

Note: very satisfied = 5, relatively satisfied = 4, so so = 3, not so satisfied = 2, very unsatisfied = 1.

The average value is more than 3. It is positive evaluation.

12. 3 Satisfaction degree with medical treatment policy of different people groups

12. 3. 1 Identity and satisfaction degree with medical treatment policy

The satisfaction degree of new local people is the lowest. There is great gap compared with that old local people and even non-local people who haven't bought houses. The satisfaction degree of non-local people who have bought houses is between that of new and old local people. See table 84.

Table 84   **Satisfaction degree with medical treatment**

policy of different people groups

Identity	Number of people	Average satisfaction value of medical treatment policy
Old local people	459	3. 27
New local people	160	2. 98
Non-local people who have bought houses	127	3. 10
Non-local people who haven't bought houses	846	3. 04

Distinctiveness P = 0. 000

12. 3. 2   Occupation and satisfaction degree with medical treatment policy

Offices and institutions and state-owned enterprises take the lead. Self-employed entrepreneurs and private enterprises are at the bottom. The average evaluation value of the latter is below than 3. See table 85.

Table 85   **Satisfaction degree with medical treatment**

policy divided by nature of companies

Identity	Number of people	Average satisfaction value of medical treatment policy
Offices and institutions	177	3. 26
State-owned enterprises	265	3. 24
Collective enterprises	97	3. 18
Foreign-owned enterprises and joint venture	142	3. 11
Self-employed entrepreneurs	274	3. 09
Private enterprises	537	2. 99

Distinctiveness P = 0. 003

To sum up, medical treatment resource is not a problem in big cities. The problem is justice in medical services. The problem of justice will be mainly discussed in Part Sixteen.

XIII. Transportation

Transportation ranks 2nd in interviewees' satisfaction side and ranks 3rd in unsatisfaction side. 643 people are satisfied and 461 are not.

13. 1   Urban transportation

According to our survey, the average single journey time spent on going to work is 39. 03 minutes. See table 86 for commonly used transportation vehicles.

Table 86   Interviewees' most commonly used transportation vehicles

Private cars	taxi	bus/metro	motorbike/electrombile bicycle	bicycle
18. 9%	3. 1%	68. 6%	3. 2%	6. 2%

13. 2   Evaluation of urban transportation

Table 87   Interviewees' evaluation of public transportation convenience in cities where they live

Very convenient	Relatively convenient	So so	Not so convenient	Very inconvenient	Average value
21. 6%	48. 5%	19. 6%	7. 8%	2. 6%	3. 79

Note: very convenient = 5, relatively convenient = 4, so so = 3, not so convenient = 2, very inconvenient = 1.

The average evaluation value is above 3. 5. it is quite positive with a tendency of being relatively convenient.

Table 88   Interviewees' satisfaction degree with transportation in cities where they live

Very satisfied	Relatively satisfied	So so	Not so satisfied	Very unsatisfied	Average value
7. 6%	24. 7%	27. 1%	26. 7%	14. 0%	2. 85

Note: very satisfied = 5, relatively satisfied = 4, so so = 3, not so satisfied = 2, very unsatisfied = 1.

The average satisfaction value of transportation is less than 3. It is negative evaluation.

Any big city is faced with the problem of traffic jam. This is also what urban administrators are commonly concerned with.

XIV. Environment

Environment ranks the 3rd in satisfaction side with 590 people choosing it and ranks 10th in unsatisfaction side with 168 people choosing it. The former is far more than the latter. It ranks 12th (last but one) in things that are most longed for with 178 choosing it. This means in interviewees' opinion environment problem is not an urgent one.

Table 89   Interviewees' satisfaction degree with environment in cities where they live

Content	Very satisfied	Relatively satisfied	So so	Not so satisfied	Very unsatisfied	Average value
Urban afforestation	15.2%	43.5%	32.6%	6.5%	2.2%	3.63
Urban air quality	4.6%	22.0%	42.7%	23.3%	7.5%	2.93
Urban environment hygiene	5.5%	32.7%	40.0%	16.3%	5.5%	3.16

Note: very satisfied = 5, relatively satisfied = 4, so so = 3, not so satisfied = 2, very unsatisfied = 1.

From table 89 we can see that the average satisfaction value of air quality is less than 3. It is negative evaluation. It is positive evaluation for both urban afforestation and hygiene. The average evaluation value of afforestation is quite high, close to 4.

As well-known metropolises, Beijing and Shenzhen have in recent years spent painstaking efforts in improving environment and urban afforestation, interviewees are relatively satisfied with it. However urban air quality is still a severe problem. It is still negative evaluation even though interviewees are not concerned with it. (It is almost the last one among things most longed for.)

XV. Social order

Social order ranks 5th in both satisfaction side and unsatisfaction side. 398 people are satisfied and 334 are not. There is a little gap. It ranks 11th among things that are most longed for. 225 choose it. This means the problem of social order is not so prominent in interviewees' mind.

15.1 Urban social order

30% of people or families and friends have been cheated, and almost 40% of people or families and friends have been robbed in recent three years. See table 90.

Table 90   Interviewees' experiences of being swindled, stolen or robbed

Content	Yes	No
Have you or your families and friends been swindled in the city in recent three years	30.3%	69.7%
Have you or your families and friends been robbed or stolen in the city in recent three years	39.0%	61.0%

The percentage of non-local people who have worse residence and environment being robbed is higher than that of local people. See table 91.

Table 91   Experiences of being swindled, stolen or robbed of different people groups or their families and friends in recent three years

Identity	Yes	No
Local people	36. 6%	63. 4%
Non-local people	40. 4%	59. 6%

15. 2   Evaluation of urban social order

Table 92   Interviewees' satisfaction degree with social order in cities where they live

Very satisfied	Relatively satisfied	So so	Not so satisfied	Very unsatisfied	Average value
9. 4%	39. 3%	34. 8%	11. 8%	4. 8%	3. 37

Note: very satisfied = 5, relatively satisfied = 4, so so = 3, not so satisfied = 2, very unsatisfied = 1.

The average value is more than 3. It is positive evaluation.

In these survey cities, social order is mostly concerned by interviewees. They are relatively satisfied with it.

XVI. Social equity

People are more concerned with social equity. Justice is the last but one in people's satisfaction side with only 52 people and ranks 4th in unsatisfaction side with over 401 people. It ranks 5th among things most longed for with 395 people.

16. 1   General evaluation of social equity

Table 93   Interviewees' evaluation of social equity in cities where they live

Very fair	Relatively fair	So so	Not so fair	Very unfair	Average value
2. 5%	23. 8%	39. 4%	25. 4%	8. 9%	2. 85

Note: very fair = 5, relatively fair = 4, so so = 3, not so fair = 2, very unfair = 1.

The average value is less than 3. It is negative evaluation. It means most of people think it is not fair enough.

16. 2　Detailed evaluation of social equity

Table 94　　　　　**Interviewees' detailed evaluation of**
social equity in cities where they live

Content	Very satisfied	Relatively satisfied	So so	Not so satisfied	Very unsatisfied	Average value
Satisfaction degree with fairness in income distribution	1. 5%	17. 2%	33. 8%	32. 6%	14. 8%	2. 58
Satisfaction degree with fairness in job opportunity	3. 5%	22. 4%	43. 0%	22. 7%	8. 5%	2. 90
Satisfaction degree with fairness in housing system	1. 6%	10. 3%	35. 3%	33. 4%	19. 4%	2. 41
Satisfaction degree with fairness in education opportunity	3. 3%	19. 3%	39. 5%	25. 4%	12. 6%	2. 75
Satisfaction degree with fairness in medical system	3. 0%	20. 9%	45. 3%	21. 3%	9. 5%	2. 87

Note: very satisfied = 5, relatively satisfied = 4, so so = 3, not so satisfied = 2, very unsatisfied = 1.

The satisfaction degree with housing system is the lowest, followed by income distribution; the satisfaction degree with job opportunity is the highest, followed by medical system; the satisfaction degree with education opportunity is in the middle. But there is no exception that the average satisfaction value of five aspects is less than 3. It is negative evaluation. The value of housing system is less than 2.

16. 3　Satisfaction degree with social equity of different people groups

There is no significant disparity in terms of general evaluation of social equity whether it is classified by areas of registered permanent residence, nature of registered permanent residence and location of registered permanent residence or by age, number of years of living in the city, education background or nature of companies except by occupation and income. This demonstrates that people have common idea of social equity. Most of them think it is not fair. It is true for more detailed aspects of society. People have different evaluations of some aspects. Here take medical system for example. See table 95. The evaluation of local people is higher than that of non-local people. If new local people is included, the evaluation is even lower than that of non-local people.

Table 95   **Satisfaction degree with medical system**

fairness of different people groups

Identity		Number of people	Average satisfaction value of medical system	Distinctiveness
Areas of registered permanent residence	Local people	627	2. 99	0. 000
	Non-local people	983	2. 79	
Areas of registered permanent residence + Number of years of living in the city	Old local people	461	3. 10	0. 000
	New local people	160	2. 67	
	Non-local people	983	2. 79	

In terms of occupation, professional people, business owners and people in charge of enterprises have the highest evaluation while white collar and worker have the lowest evaluation. Other 3 occupations are almost the same in evaluation. In addition to that of professional people, business owners and people in charge of enterprises, the evaluation of people engaged in other five occupations is negative. See table 96.

Table 96   **Satisfaction degree with medical system**

of people with different occupations

Occupation	Number of people	Average satisfaction value of medical system
Professional people	210	3. 06
Business owners and people in charge from enterprises	51	3. 04
Personnel in commercial undertaking and service industry	343	2. 92
Personnel in administrative institutions	128	2. 91
Self-employed entrepreneurs and unemployed	197	2. 90
Worker	120	2. 80
White collar	563	2. 74

Distinctiveness $P = 0. 001$

In terms of nature of companies, people who work in offices and institutions have the highest evaluation, followed by people in state-owned enterprises whose average value is close. People in private enterprises lag behind. In addition to the first, evaluation of others is negative. People who work in universally acknowledged good companies have relatively high evaluation. See table 97.

Table 97 Satisfaction degree with medical system
divided by nature of companies

Nature of companies	Number of people	Average satisfaction value of medical system
Offices and institutions	177	3. 02
State-owned enterprises	266	2. 98
Self-employed entrepreneurs	276	2. 89
Collective enterprises	100	2. 88
Foreign-owned enterprises and joint venture	143	2. 82
Private enterprises	540	2. 76

Distinctiveness P = 0. 005

Social equity is one of issues that people are most concerned with as well as one of core issues in urban management. It is not only related with social harmony and stability but also urban attraction and sustainable development. The evaluation of social equity is generally less satisfying in the survey. Evaluation of most of people is negative no matter how they are classified. It is worth our attention.

XVII. Social trust and respect

Being understood and respected is the last one among the questionnaire, which is most longed for city. But still 148 people choose it.

17. 1 Evaluation of social trust and respect

Table 98 Interviewees' evaluation of social trust in cities where they live

Content	Very trustful	Relatively trustful	So so	Not so trustful	Very trustless	Average value
Trust in government	7. 2%	27. 5%	37. 5%	17. 8%	10. 0%	3. 04
Trust in broadcast, TV and newspaper	3. 9%	22. 6%	44. 6%	22. 2%	6. 7%	2. 95
Trust in internet contents	1. 4%	10. 9%	45. 6%	33. 0%	9. 1%	2. 63
Trust among people in society	0. 9%	13. 6%	49. 0%	29. 2%	7. 4%	2. 71

Note: very trustful = 5, relatively trustful = 4, so so = 3, not so trustful = 2, very trustless = 1.

Table 98 shows that in addition to trust in government, evaluation of others is negative. The evaluation of trust among people is the lowest. This demonstrates profound influences generated by lack of social integrity over the past years. Correspondingly the evaluation of internet contents is equally low.

However evaluation of social mutual respect is relatively high. It is positive. See table 99.

Table 99   **Interviewees' evaluation of mutual respect among people in cities where they live**

Very respectful	Relatively respectful	So so	Not so respectful	Very Rude	Average value of mutual respect among people
3.2%	31.8%	50.4%	12.2%	2.5%	3.21

Note: very respectful = 5, relatively respectful = 4, so so = 3, not so respectful = 2, very rude = 1.

17.2 Evaluation of social trust of different people groups

There is no significant difference in the four aspects mentioned above in terms of people's evaluation except evaluation of government trust.

17.2.1 Identity and trust in government

People with agriculture registered permanent residence has greater trust in government than people with non-agriculture registered permanent residence do while non-local people with low-end occupations than old local people, non-local people with high-end occupations, new local people has the lowest trust. The two latter ones' evaluation is negative one. See table 100.

Table 100   **Different people groups' trust in government in cities where they live**

Identity		Number of people	Average value of trust in government	Distinctiveness
Nature of registered permanent residence	People with non-agriculture registered permanent residence	1076	2.99	0.007
	People with agriculture registered permanent residence	540	3.14	
Areas of registered permanent residence + Number of years of living in the city + Occupation	Old local people	460	3.08	0.004
	New local people	160	2.79	
	Local People with high-end occupations	517	2.99	
	Local People with low-end occupations	452	3.12	

17.2.2 Occupation and trust in government

Personnel in administrative institutions have greatest trust in government, followed by self-employed entrepreneurs and unemployed, personnel in commercial undertaking and service industry and professional people. Their evaluation value is more than 3. It is positive one. Business owners and people in charge of enterprises have the weakest trust. Their evaluation and that of worker and white collar is negative. See table 101.

Table 101   Trust degree of government of people with different jobs

Occupation	Number of people	Average value of trust in government
Personnel in administrative institutions	128	3. 36
Self-employed entrepreneurs and unemployed	197	3. 28
Personnel in commercial undertaking and service industry	341	3. 09
Professional people	208	3. 04
White collar	562	2. 91
Worker	119	2. 88
Business owners and people in charge of enterprises	51	2. 82

Distinctiveness P = 0. 000

17. 2. 3   Education background and trust in government

The higher the education background, the lower the evaluation of trust in government. It is very apparent. Table 102.

Table 102   Trust degree of local government of people with different education backgrounds

Education background	Number of people	Average trust value of government
Primary education	255	3. 27
Intermediate education	491	3. 05
Advanced education	867	2. 96

Distinctiveness P = 0. 000

To sum up, education background, knowledge and experience have impact on people's trust in government. Among people with various occupations, business owners and people in charge of enterprises have weakest trust in government. It is quite interesting.

XVIII. Urban management and public service

Public service ranks 6th in satisfaction side with 380 people choosing it and ranks 12th in unsatisfaction side with 116 people choosing it. Improving government management level ranks 4th among things most longed for with 413 people choosing it. It is noted that interviewees are relatively satisfied with public service and they are looking forward to improving government management level.

18. 1　Evaluation of urban management and public service

18. 1. 1　Evaluation of administrative institutions' efficiency and management level

Table 103　Interviewees' evaluation of administrative institutions' efficiency and management level in cities where they live

Content	Very high	Relatively high	So so	Relatively low	Very low	Average value
Evaluation of efficiency of the city's administrative institutions	2. 3%	16. 2%	46. 6%	24. 1%	10. 8%	2. 75
Evaluation of management level of the city's administrative institutions	2. 7%	17. 4%	51. 9%	18. 6%	9. 4%	2. 85

Note: very high = 5, relatively high = 4, so so = 3, relatively low = 2, very low = 1.

The average value is less than 3. It is negative. The evaluation of efficiency is lower. It means that most of interviewees are not satisfied with administrative institutions' management level and efficiency, especially the latter.

18. 1. 2　Evaluation of attitude of administrative institutions

Table 104　Interviewees' evaluation of attitude of administrative institutions in cities where they live

Best	Better	So so	Bad	Worst	Average value
3. 1%	23. 4%	44. 4%	19. 4%	9. 7%	2. 91

Note: best = 5, better = 4, so so = 3, bad = 2, worst = 1.

It is negative evaluation but close to median. This means that most of people think the attitude of administrative institutions so so. There are more people are unsatisfied than people who are satisfied.

18. 1. 3 Evaluation of incorruptness of personnel in government bodies and law enforcement officials

Table 105　Interviewees' evaluation of incorruptness of personnel in government bodies and law enforcement officials

Very honest	Relatively honest	So so	Not so honest	Very corrupt	Average value
2. 2%	10. 6%	39. 1%	29. 6%	18. 5%	2. 48

Note: very honest = 5, relatively honest = 4, so so = 3, not so honest = 2, very corrupt = 1.

It is strong negative evaluation that the average value is less than 2. 5. It is worth mentioning, there is no significant difference in evaluation of incorruptness in different ways to different people groups. This means negative evaluation of incorruptness is the society's common view. There is no great gap among evaluations of different people groups.

18. 2　Different people groups' evaluation of urban management and public service

18. 2. 1　Identity and evaluation of management level of administrative institutions

The evaluation of non-local people is higher than that local people and that of people with agriculture registered permanent residence than people with non-agriculture registered permanent residence. There is great disparity. In terms of location of registered permanent residence, the ranking is: other villages and towns, other medium and small cities, other big cities and this city. See table 106.

Table 106　Evaluation of management level of administrative institutions of people with different identities

Identity		Number of people	Average evaluation value of management level of administrative institutions	Distinctiveness
Areas of registered permanent residence	Local people	625	2. 73	0. 000
	Non-local people	981	2. 92	
Nature of registered permanent residence	People with non-agriculture registered permanent residence	1080	3. 28	0. 001
	People with agriculture registered permanent residence	544	3. 07	
Location of registered permanent residence	This city	625	2. 73	0. 000
	Other big cities	189	2. 84	
	Other medium and small cities	367	2. 90	
	Other villages and towns	425	2. 98	

Combined with such factors as number of years of living, occupation and house buying, non-local people with low-end occupations and non-local people who haven't bought houses have the highest evaluation. The average value of non-local people who have bought houses and non-local people with high-end occupations is the same, lowest evaluation by new local people and old local people . See table 107.

Table 107 Evaluation of management level of administrative institutions divided by registered permanent residence, number of years of living, occupation and house property

Identity		Number of people	Average evaluation value of management level of administrative institutions	Distinctiveness
Areas of registered permanent residence + Number of years of living in the city + Occupation	Old local people	459	2. 71	
	New local people	160	2. 78	
	Non-local people with high-end occupations	518	2. 90	0. 000
	Non-local people with low-end occupations	454	2. 94	
Areas of registered permanent residence + Number of years of living in the city + Buying houses	Old local people	459	2. 71	
	New local people	160	2. 78	
	Non-local people who have bought houses	127	2. 90	0. 000
	Non-local people who haven't bought houses	853	2. 92	

18. 2. 2   Education background and evaluation of management level of administrative institutions

As is with trust in government, the higher the education background, the lower the evaluation. See table 108.

Table 108   Evaluation of management level of administrative institutions of people with different education backgrounds

Education background	Number of people	Average evaluation value of management level of administrative institutions
Primary education	258	3. 02
Intermediate education	488	2. 89
Advanced education	869	2. 78

Distinctiveness P = 0. 001

18. 3 Evaluation of urban infrastructure

Table 109   Table Interviewees' evaluation of urban infrastructure

Best	Better	So so	Bad	Worst	Average value
9. 0%	43. 8%	35. 1%	8. 0%	4. 1%	3. 46

Note: best = 5, better = 4, so so = 3, bad = 2, worst = 1.

The average value is much above 3. It means interviewees are relatively satisfied with construction of urban infrastructure.

In conclusion, interviewees are relatively satisfied with construction of urban infrastructure, which demonstrates the superiority of big cities. However it is negative evaluation in terms of management level of administrative institutions, efficiency, attitude and incorruptness. In terms of different people groups, the evaluation of non-local people, people with agriculture registered permanent residence, people from villages, people with low income and low education background is relatively higher, which again shows the influence of education background, knowledge and experience over people's interest in public affairs.

XIX. Urban life pressure

The above analysis touches upon various aspects of urban life. It all comes down to one point that urban residents are faced with life pressure. The final pressure is burdened on each interviewee whether it is about income, housing, employment or social security, education and medical treatment.

19. 1 Evaluation of urban life pressure

Table 110   Interviewees' evaluation of urban life pressure

Very heavy	Relatively heavy	So so	Relatively low	Very low	Average value
29. 4%	43. 0%	21. 6%	4. 4%	1. 7%	3. 94

Note: very heavy = 5, relatively heavy = 4, so so = 3, relatively low = 2, very low = 1.

The average value is close 4. Interviewees feel the urban pressure is quite heavy.

19. 2 Different people groups' evaluation of urban life pressure

19. 2. 1 Identity and evaluation of life pressure

Life pressure of non-local people is greater than that of old local people while new local people feel the heaviest life pressure with an average value of over 4. There is great disparity. Non-local people who have bought houses feel much less pressure than non-local people who haven't bought houses and even old local people. This tells the importance of housing in urban residents' life.

Table 111 Evaluation of life pressure of people with different identities

Identity		Number of people	Average evaluation value of life pressure	Distinctiveness
Areas of registered permanent residence + Number of years of living in the city	Old local people	461	3. 86	0. 016
	New local people	160	4. 09	
	Non-local people	981	3. 95	
Areas of registered permanent residence + Number of years of living in the city + Buying houses	Old local people	461	3. 86	0. 000
	New local people	160	4. 09	
	Non-local people who have bought houses	127	3. 72	
	Non-local people who haven't bought houses	853	3. 99	

19. 2. 2 Occupation and evaluation of life pressure

There is no significant difference among people with different occupations

In terms of nature of companies, people in private enterprises and self-employed entrepreneurs feel the heaviest pressure with an average value of over 4; people in collective enterprises and administrative institutions feel the lowest pressure with an average value of over 3. 5; people in state-owned enterprises and foreign-owned enterprises and joint venture feel medium pressure. See table 112.

Table 112 Evaluation of life pressure divided by nature of companies

Nature of companies	Number of people	Average evaluation value of life pressure
Private enterprises	540	4. 02
Self-employed enterprises	276	4. 00
State-owned enterprises	265	3. 93
Foreign-owned enterprises and joint venture	143	3. 90
Offices and institutions	176	3. 79
Collective enterprises	100	3. 68

Distinctiveness $P = 0. 002$

To sum up, generally most of interviewees feel life pressure is great. Housing is the main reason for life pressure. With housing problem solved, people will have sense of basic security. Without it, they feel lack of security. Non-local people who have bought houses feel less pressure than other people groups and even new and old local people.

It is understandable that interviewees put housing price before anything else in most unsatisfied side. Solving housing problem ranks 3rd in things most longed for; it is understandable that new local people who have strengths of identity and income level are more unsatisfied than other people groups.

XX. Sense of belonging and urban attraction

City is where people live together. City and people coexist and thrive together. It is the core of urban development to enable residents to feel sense of belonging and attract people.

20. 1   Sense of belonging

We asked all interviewees the same question: do you feel homey in Beijing/Shenzhen? See table 11 for answers.

Table 113   **Interviewees' sense of belonging**

City	Very great	Great	So so	Not so great	Totally no	Average value
Beijing	29. 7%	29. 6%	19. 0%	13. 9%	7. 7%	3. 60
Shenzhen	7. 4%	29. 7%	28. 7%	22. 9%	11. 3%	2. 99
Total	18. 6%	29. 6%	23. 9%	18. 4%	9. 5%	3. 29

Note: very great = 5, great = 4, so so = 3, not so great = 2, totally no = 1.

The average value is more than 3 which means most people have a certain sense of belonging. It is understandable that the average value of Beijing is higher than that of Shenzhen because the latter is a newly emerging emigrant city out of a fishing village. Its age is only 31 years old. Genuine indigenous people are rare.

In the two cities where non-local people occupy a percentage of 2/3, it is not easy to have such a high average value. This shows that the governments of the two cities have made great efforts in making the city home to all people.

20. 2   Different people groups' sense of belonging

What kind of people are identified with the city where they live and have sense of belonging in current system?

20. 2. 1   Identity and sense of belonging

There is obvious difference in terms of sense of belonging among people with different identities. That of local people is greater than non-local people while people with non-agriculture registered permanent residence than people with agriculture registered permanent residence. Among non-local people, that of people from big cities than people from medium and small cities while the latter than people from villages and towns. The average value among all people groups is so different. The average value of non-local people and people with agriculture registered permanent residence is less than 3 and that of local people is close to 4. See table 114.

Table 114 Sense of belonging of people with different identities

Identity		Number of people	Average value of sense of belonging	Distinctiveness
Areas of registered permanent residence	Local people	627	3. 95	0. 000
	Non-local people	983	2. 87	
Nature of registered permanent residence	People with non-agriculture registered permanent residence	1079	3. 50	0. 000
	People with agriculture registered permanent residence	543	2. 87	
	This city	627	3. 95	
Location of registered permanent residence	Other big cities	189	3. 10	0. 000
	Other medium and small cities	368	2. 89	
	Other villages and towns	426	2. 76	

20. 2. 2 Number of years of living and sense of belonging

Undoubtedly the number of years of living plays an important role in forming people's sense of belonging. See table 115. The longer people live in the city, the stronger people's sense of belonging. People who live for more than 18 years have an average value of over 4. Although new local people have local registered permanent residence, their average value is much lower than that of old local people and even old non-local people.

Table 115 Sense of belonging divided by number of years of living in the city

Number of years of living in the city & Areas of registered permanent residence		Number of people	Average value of sense of belonging	Distinctiveness
Number of years of living in the city	Less than 2 years	302	2. 64	0. 000
	2 – 7 years	503	2. 89	
	8 – 17 years	373	3. 27	
	More than 18	433	4. 24	

continued

Number of years of living in the city & Areas of registered permanent residence		Number of people	Average value of sense of belonging	Distinctiveness
Areas of registered permanent residence + Number of years of living in the city	Old local people	461	4. 24	0. 000
	New local people	160	3. 11	
	Old non-local people	114	3. 34	
	New non-local people	861	2. 81	

20. 2. 3   Identity, occupation, house property and sense of belonging

Table 116 shows that the average value of non-local people with high-end occupations and non-local people with low-end occupations is almost the same but lower than that new and old local people. This means the limited influence of occupation over sense of belonging. Influence of registered permanent residence is greater while that of buying houses is greatest. Non-local people who have bought houses have higher average value than new local people do. This again proves that "people who have fixed property are persistent".

Table 116   Sense of belonging of people with different identities

Identity		Number of people	Average value of sense of belonging	Distinctiveness
areas of registered permanent residence + Number of years of living in the city + occupation	Old local people	461	4. 24	0. 000
	New local people	160	3. 11	
	Non-local people with high-end occupations	520	2. 87	
	Non-local people with low-end occupations	454	2. 88	
Areas of registered permanent residence + Number of years of living in the city + Buying houses	Old local people	461	4. 24	0. 000
	New local people	160	3. 11	
	Non-local people who have bought houses	127	3. 57	
	Non-local people who haven't bought houses	855	2. 77	

20. 2. 4   Nature of companies and sense of belonging

The influence of occupation is not obvious but the nature of companies has great influence. People who work in offices and institutions and state-owned enterprises take the lead in sense of belonging, followed by people in collective enterprises, foreign-owned enterprises and joint venture, self-employed entrepreneurs and people in private enterprises. This means tthat ownership and identity of organization still have powerful influence in current planning system since the reform and opening-up.

Table 117   Sense of belonging divided by nature of companies

Nature of company	Number of people	Average value of sense of belonging
Offices and institutions	176	3. 79
State-owned enterprises	266	3. 69
Collective enterprises	100	3. 45
Foreign-owned enterprises and joint venture	143	3. 34
Self-employed entrepreneurs	276	3. 08
Private enterprises	541	3. 00

Distinctiveness P = 0. 000

To sum up, system of registered permanent residence and system of ownership and administrative institutions still influence people's sense of belonging in current system. The system of registered permanent residence limits and puts off the forming of people's sense of belonging. The barriers set by the government while conducting micro-regulation (for example limited buying of houses) and urban management (for example automobile buying) undoubtedly increase the impact of the system of registered permanent residence.

XXI. Conclusion: people and city

21. 1   People are the subject of city and city exists for people. We build the city not for the sake of building the city but for people to live a better life.

21. 2   The core competitiveness of city is people. Only when people in the city live and work in peace and contentment, perform their own duties, improve their qualities and are introduced and kept the city be vigorous and develops in a sustainable way. Then the city must be attractive and enable people living in the city have strong sense of belonging.

21. 3   Urban attraction first comes from more opportunities for employment, income increase and personal development. Survey data shows that people have highest evaluation of urban individual consumption and services and life convenience is the last among things that people most long for. What people most

long for are income increase and more development opportunities. This means that changes have taken place compared with that before reform and opening-up. People flock to big metropolises no longer for prosperity but for more opportunities for employment and personal development.

21. 4　Urban attraction more comes from social equity. Increasing opportunities is one thing and creating equal opportunities is another. This is the two sides of a coin. If too many discriminating policies exist in a city, this does not only prevent people from doing their best, but also cause great waste of human resources as well as damaging its attraction and sense of belonging and sustainable development.

The system of registered permanent residence has greatly affected social equity and equal opportunities by setting barriers for people's residence, employment, social security, medical treatment and children's education, thus severe inequity.

21. 5　The process of urbanization is the process of system reforms. The social structure changes so the system needs change. The original systems of the city should be correspondingly adjusted when migrant population increases. In fact it is true. For example, in Beijing, people who do not have local permanent residence were not allowed to study in senior high schools many years ago. Now the hedge is broken. Urban administrators should follow the example and discuss how to increase equity degree in primary and high school education, employment, housing, medical treatment and social security. Discriminating policies should be avoided in order to create a system space where there are more opportunities for personal development.

21. 6　The process of urbanization is equally an integration process for local people and non-local ones. In the process all people need to change their roles and identities. This is not only about non-local people but also about local people. Urban administrators should make the city home to all people by adjustment of systems and publicity and guidance.

21. 7　New local people and Must locals are worth great attention in urban development. The former ones with high education background have high expectations but they live in the city for only a short time. As the survey data shows, most of them haven't bought houses and they have negative opinions and evaluation of society while feeling unsatisfied. The latter ones have their own houses in

the city. They have high income. Although they do not have local registered permanent residence, they have strong sense of belonging.

21. 8　　Finally, a few suggestions for improving the city's evaluation indicator system:

1. The richness of commodities and services is occupying a lower percentage in urban attractions which more comes from more opportunities for employment, income and personal development. This provides research foundation for the setting of related indicators and measurement in future indicator system.

2. Obvious inequity exists in terms of income, housing, social security, employment, opportunity for personal development, education and medical treatment among people with local registered permanent residence and non-local people so there are obvious differences in terms of satisfaction degree and sense of belonging. This indicates that the problem of social equity is getting severe. Therefore indicators of equity in various aspects of urban life should be considered as important in future evaluation system.

3. It tests the administrative wisdom and management ability of each urban administrator to retain the reasonable function of registered permanent residence system in current system, weaken its unreasonable functions, arrange transition with replaceable system and break the hedge of registered permanent residence system which leads to social inequity. It will become a part of future urban evaluation system whether the urban administrator can make corresponding policies, institution adjustment and institution construction to deal with problems of identity barriers and social inequity.

Part Three Overview of China Designated Town Development

I. The significance of evaluation of designated town development

1. Development of designated town is "beachhead" of our country's urban and rural integration development "Urban and Rural Planning Law of the People's Republic of China", implemented on January 1, 2008, marks a brand new stage of an all-round development of our urbanization.

Designated town is part of urban and rural planning and plays an important role in coordinated urban-rural development. Seen from our country's new town system, designated town is a satellite distribution center of residence and industry on which a city can rely on and excessive centralization of population. The administrative regions it governs are part of the city district. Therefore the urban development is inseparable from coordinated planning and development of designated town.

2. There are historical reasons for formation of designated town. According to its functions, it can be divided into: administrative center (political center in certain administrative regions, the place where county government and town government are located), industrial town, fishery town, mine town, tourism town, transportation town, trading town, port town and famous historical and cultural town. It will become an important task of our urbanization to protect the historical appearance of designated town, strengthen its functions and make it serve urban development according to historical reasons of designated town.

3. Designated town is an administrative concept and it has the same administrative functions with sub-district of cities. Therefore designated town has an administrative function of community management from the perspective of management. Its principles are:

- All places where county-level government offices are located (or Chengguan Town);

- Places and villages where village governments are located with a population of below 20,000 people and a population of more than 2,000 people with non-agriculture registered permanent residence;

- Places and villages where village governments are located with a population of below 20,000 people. Its people with non- agriculture registered permanent residence occupies 10% of the total population in the village;

- Or areas inhabited by ethnic minorities, under populated remote areas, mountain areas and small industrial and mining areas, little port, tourist areas and frontier ports with less than 2,000 people with non-agriculture registered permanent residence but it is necessary to set up towns.

II. Guidelines of evaluation and analysis of designated town

It is necessary to re-illustrate the meaning of urbanization in order to better evaluate and analyze the development of designated town.

1. Concepts of city and town

Currently there is confusion between "city" and "town" in our country:

(1) The meaning of city in a narrow sense: only cities; towns are not included.

(2) The meaning of city in a broad sense: both cities and towns included.

(3) The meaning of town in a narrow sense: both cities and designated towns included.

(4) The meaning of town in a broad sense: cities, designated towns and market towns.

We analyze and evaluate designated town on the basis of city in a broad sense and town in a narrow sense, and try to study the urbanization process with relation between designated town and city.

2. Concepts of "Chengshihua" and "Chengzhenhua"

There are concepts of "Chengshihua" and "Chengzhenhua" due to confusion of concepts of city and town and in English both of them are called "Urbanization". Besides, there is a saying of "Dushihua" but we regard super huge cities as metropolises. Therefore the saying of "Dushihua" is rare. "Lose no time to implement Chengzhenhua strategy", which was put forward in the "Outline of the Tenth Five-year Plan for National Economy and Social Development of the People's Republic of China", published in 2001.

We re-illustrate the concept in order to demonstrate our guidelines of evaluation designated towns. "Chengshihua" tends to cause such misunderstandings as large scale, centralization, commercialization and industrialization. As a result we think "Chengzhenhua" is more suitable for the original intention of our argumentation from the perspective of urban and rural coordination. In doing so we can avoid the "extinction" of designated town and blindness in pursuing "largeness and completeness".

Besides, we can understand it from the perspective of planning of town development:

(1) Chengshihua is a kind of development based on centralization of people. It provides relatively concentrated conditions including production and manufacturing, circulated trading and transportation distribution in industrialization period. Although cost effects of centralization are generated, great burden is on city resources; Chengzhenhua is a kind of measure taken against decentralization of people and relieving the burden of city resources in order to solve "city diseases" in post-industrial period.

(2) Chengshihua causes great gap between urban and rural areas, imbalance of distribution of social resources and great disparity among urban and rural areas and regions; Chengzhenhua promotes coordinated urban-rural development, guides villages to urbanization, commercialization and deep processing of agricultural products. Traditional little towns will become important support for urban development.

(3) For Chengshihua, its type of operation basis is industry, commerce, finance and transportation. It is the distribution center of manufacturing and circulation of materials. Apposition is easy to take shape and isolation of cities and competition among cities will be caused; Chengzhenhua more focuses on changing the development pattern so as to form a multi-function pattern. Adjust measures to local conditions for the construction of little towns with goals of serving life, harmonizing people and nature, protecting history and make environment suitable for people's residence.

3. Defining of territorial scope of towns

How to define territorial scope of towns? There are three ways: defining by built areas, functional areas of towns and administrative areas.

Although defining territorial scope of towns by administrative areas cannot totally reflect the status quo of urbanization, this is the only adoptable data for comprehensive evaluation. Therefore we think:

(1) It is our country's relatively mature management and statistics system. We can figure out necessary rules through comparison and analysis of consecutive data.

(2) Its territorial scope is equally its space resources. Space scale is undoubtedly an objective foundation for development of designated town from the perspective of resource reserves.

(3) Current indicators of designated town are not complete. New data is needed through calculation and maths deduction so other consistent statistics materials are necessary. Our statistics materials are obtained through requirements of administrative divisions.

(4) Town planners are usually limited to planning of detailed lands and hope "the red line" is clear but administrators and social workers focus on development of regional space and its development conditions.

(5) Now that designated town is governed by city, our evaluation and analysis of designated town is necessary supplement of evaluation of urban development.

(6) The development of Chengzhenhua represents economic development. Economic development is inseparable from agriculture. According to administrative divisions, it includes agriculture, forestry and grassland farming. This is the support for coordinated urban-rural development.

(7) The science is developing and creating in itself from the perspective of ekistics. It has been a fact that the city will develop from planning extension to regional planning. This has been practiced and proven in developed countries.

III. Methods of evaluation and analysis of designated town

1. Primiple of establishing indicators

The development of Chengzhenhua is not determined by a single factor but influenced by numerous factors such as geographic location, geographical features, environment, local resources and transportation. Its development speed is surely influenced by economic development level of venues, cities and counties. This determines that multi-indicator analysis methods must be adopted when analyzing and evaluating the development of designated town. Meanwhile the situation of governed cities and districts must be considered, that is to say, regard the development of designated town as an important part of urban harmonious development.

In addition to indicator of development, comparison has to be made among conditions of Chengzhenhua, including municipal administration conditions, social service, public safety and social hygiene.

2. Design framework of indicator system

(1) Internal indicators, that is, designated town's own conditions which are the result of its historical development as well as unchangeable objective and supporting factors in future development.

- Population structure indicators include: age, occupation and circulating structure;
- Land resource indicators include: downtown proportion, arable land proportion, mountain forest and population density;
- Financial revenues and expense indicators include: total revenues and expenses, per capita revenues and expenses and balance of per capita revenues;
- Economic growth indicators include: GDP, per capita revenue, corporate profits and residents' income.

(2) External indicators, that is, influences of economic development of governing cities, including circulation of population (if population inflow is greater than outflow, it means urbanization of the designated town quickens; the town is attractive to people); circulation of materials (when inflow is greater than outflow, it means the living standard of the region is high with high added value of local products); transportation (including passenger flow, waterway and land transportation). Factors mentioned above determine the possibility of inflow of capital.

- Indicators of governing cities: number of designated towns and classified analysis; average level of public infrastructure, road network and road coverage; urban planning and influences of related control and regulations;

- Circulation of population indicators include: age structure of inflow population, outflow population and floating population;

- Transportation indicators include: density of highway and railway networks, number of waterway ports and throughput per hour;

- Capital inflow indicators include: number of fixed asset investment, number of foreign enterprises, number of economic contracts and sum, and increase of bank deposits.

(3) Town indicators (status quo indicators), that is, depict the urbanization level of designated towns to reflect its social service functions.

- Municipal administration indicators include: running water supply, power supply, gas supply, bus and capacity;

- Social service indicators include: education, culture and sports equipment and commercial network and centers;

- Social safety indicators include: public security organizations and safety facility;

- Public hygiene indicators include: city appearance and environmental hygiene, medical facility and epidemic prevention.

Systematic analysis according to above ideas cannot be totally made due to incomplete statistics of designated town. Only initial comparison is made with available materials.

3. Methods of evaluation and analysis

Our country has a vast territory with great gap in economic development of different regions. Any objective explanation is not possible only by general comparison and sequencing and it is hard to be convincing. Designated town is a basic administrative unit, so its power is limited and equally its available conditions are limited. There is a lot of work to do if comparing 19,322 designated towns and it is impossible to bring about encouraging effects. As a result, we adopt a comprehensive comparison method of classified regions and use corresponding indicators (per capita indicators, proportion structure and density) to compare and make comparisons of geographical factors according to available geographical differences.

Besides, in evaluation and analysis of urbanization, dealing with arable land is a topic worth discussing. Agriculture is always the foundation of economic development. Mechanization, modernization of agriculture, deep processing, commercialization of agricultural products and high added value of subsidiary agricultural products can be opportunity for urbanizations and strategic resources. Therefore as land resources, we still regard arable land as an important indicator for comparison.

IV. Primary result of evaluation and analysis of designated town

(I) Comparison of internal indicators

1. Data comparison according to provincial divisions

(1) Population density

Number	Place	Population density (person/sq km)	Number	Place	Population density (person/sq km)
1	Shanghai	1966.87	17	Guangxi	249.98
2	Jiangsu	763.96	18	Guizhou	241.11
3	Henan	580.25	19	Hainan	217.83
4	Shandong	525.47	20*	Shanxi	217.41
5	Tianjin	479.03	21	Liaoning	194.25
6	Zhejiang	460.76	22	Shaanxi	173.71
7	Anhui	458.05	23	Yunnan	139.84
8	Chongqing	434.66	24	Ningxia	102.51
9	Guangdong	423.54	25	Jilin	98.35
10	Hebei	409.65	26	Heilongjiang	77.73
11	Sichuan	400.54	27	Gansu	66.11
12	Beijing	382.74	28	Sinkiang	26.85
13	Hunan	357.65	29	Inner Mongolia	21.91
14	Fujian	320.28	30	Qinghai	9.17
15	Jiangxi	276.81	31	Tibet	4.32
16	Hubei	261.92			

(2) Percentage of population of employment

Number	Place	Percentage of population of employment (%)	Number	Place	Percentage of population of employment (%)
1	Zhejiang	67.28%	17	Ningxia	51.05%
2	Henan	57.86%	18	Hebei	49.82%
3	Shandong	56.48%	19	Tibet	49.80%
4	Hunan	55.15%	20	Gansu	49.80%
5	Anhui	54.62%	21	Liaoning	49.76%
6	Guizhou	53.97%	22	Jiangxi	49.46%
7	Jiangsu	53.97%	23	Inner Mongolia	49.11%
8	Chongqing	53.94%	24	Heilongjiang	47.76%
9	Beijing	53.85%	25	Hubei	47.13%
10	Guangxi	53.53%	26	Qinghai	46.08%
11	Yunnan	53.49%	27	Hainan	45.06%
12	Shaanxi	52.78%	28	Tianjin	44.81%
13	Sichuan	52.64%	29	Jilin	44.43%
14	Shanghai	52.29%	30	Shanxi	43.27%
15	Guangdong	51.97%	31	Sinkiang	38.38%
16	Fujian.	51.76%			

(3) Per capita financial revenues

Number	Place	Per capita financial revenues	Number	Place	Per capita financial revenues
1	Shanghai	5322.39	17	Guangxi	316.45
2	Zhejiang	3225.77	18	Jilin	309.31
3	Jiangsu	2674.64	19	Sichuan	305.04
4	Beijing	2040.16	20	Sinkiang	296.80
5	Tianjin	1551.34	21	Anhui	280.19
6	Hebei	958.54	22	Guizhou	267.37
7	Guangdong	908.48	23	Hunan	266.22
8	Liaoning	844.20	24	Ningxia	253.88
9	Shanxi	842.45	25	Hainan	253.18
10	Shandong	816.86	26	Hubei	219.81
11	Fujian	778.60	27	Heilongjiang	216.19
12	Inner Mongolia	673.30	28	Shaanxi	183.20
13	Jiangxi	415.11	29	Gansu	138.10
14	Yunnan	392.97	30	Qinghai	108.70
15	Henan	344.26	31	Tibet	97.11
16	Chongqing	327.23			

(4) Per capita education investment

Number	Place	Per capita education investment	Number	Place	Per capita education investment
1	Shanghai	267. 24	17	Hubei	42. 88
2	Zhejiang	253. 96	18	Chongqing	36. 79
3	Tianjin	252. 84	19	Shaanxi	33. 74
4	Jiangsu	207. 40	20	Guizhou	32. 24
5	Guangdong	157. 50	21	Hunan	29. 35
6	Liaoning	120. 49	22	Henan	28. 51
7	Beijing	117. 41	23	Qinghai	26. 47
8	Shandong	108. 04	24	Hainan	25. 87
9	Jiangxi	95. 43	25	Jilin	25. 58
10	Shanxi	86. 66	26	Anhui	25. 16
11	Hebei	74. 22	27	Gansu	24. 30
12	Sinkiang	61. 21	28	Fujian	20. 46
13	Guangxi	57. 96	29	Ningxia	15. 26
14	Yunnan	57. 72	30	Heilongjiang	6. 34
15	Sichuan	57. 59	31	Tibet	4. 03
16	Inner Mongolia	57. 08			

(5) Per capita investment in science and technology

Number	Place	Per capita investment in science and technology	Number	Place	Per capita investment in science and technology
1	Shanghai	20. 88	17	Ningxia	3. 08
2	Beijing	15. 81	18	Jiangxi	2. 97
3	Zhejiang	14. 30	19	Anhui	2. 53
4	Guangdong	11. 34	20	Guangxi	2. 35
5	Jiangsu	9. 26	21	Yunnan	2. 30
6	Sinkiang	9. 07	22	Guizhou	2. 15
7	Hebei	7. 66	23	Jilin	1. 78
8	Inner Mongolia	6. 68	24	Gansu	1. 74
9	Shandong	6. 40	25	Chongqing	1. 54
10	Hunan	4. 97	26	Tianjin	1. 26
11	Liaoning	4. 17	27	Sichuan	1. 10
12	Hubei	4. 08	28	Hainan	0. 81
13	Shanxi	4. 08	29	Heilongjiang	0. 67
14	Fujian	3. 97	30	Tibet	0. 14
15	Henan	3. 93	31	Qinghai	0. 10
16	Shaanxi	3. 25			

(6) Per capita social general investment

Number	Place	Per capita general investment	Number	Place	Per capita general investment
1	Jiangsu	11470. 70	17	Ningxia	2285. 61
2	Shandong	9302. 06	18	Jiangxi	2039. 61
3	Zhejiang	7974. 59	19	Qinghai	1789. 35
4	Shanghai	7839. 90	20	Shanxi	1728. 32
5	Tianjin	7353. 15	21	Hubei	1676. 15
6	Hebei	6513. 26	22	Shaanxi	1665. 79
7	Beijing	5948. 73	23	Hunan	1636. 25
8	Inner Mongolia	5921. 57	24	Sinkiang	1406. 26
9	Henan	5627. 91	25	Gansu	1195. 21
10	Chongqing	4611. 87	26	Yunnan	1004. 36
11	Fujian	4513. 17	27	Guizhou	818. 60
12	Jilin	4440. 50	28	Heilongjiang	720. 74
13	Guangdong	4348. 44	29	Liaoning	581. 72
14	Guangxi	2537. 35	30	Hainan	442. 93
15	Sichuan	2326. 56	31	Tibet	148. 74
16	Anhui	2292. 14			

(7) Per capita asset

Number	Place	Per capita property	Number	Place	Per capita property
1	Shanghai	3062. 31	17	Sichuan	268. 57
2	Beijing	2199. 72	18	Inner	254. 49
3	Guangdong	1634. 08	19	Hebei	232. 44
4	Jiangsu	1133. 80	20	Shanxi	224. 11
5	Zhejiang	862. 82	21	Hainan	216. 81
6	Tianjin	708. 97	22	Jiangxi	213. 65
7	Henan	635. 29	23	Jilin	208. 75
8	Shandong	594. 94	24	Ningxia	184. 79
9	Hubei	538. 78	25	Guizhou	162. 38
10	Yunnan	493. 96	26	Heilongjiang	157. 23
11	Liaoning	487. 73	27	Shaanxi	128. 20
12	Hunan	474. 32	28	Qinghai	126. 28
13	Anhui	359. 09	29	Guangxi	125. 82
14	Chongqing	339. 61	30	Gansu	122. 66
15	Fujian	313. 55	31	Tibet	112. 78
16	Sinkiang	291. 41			

(8) Percentage of arable land area

Number	Place	Percentage of arable land	Number	Place	Percentage of arable land
1	Jiangsu	45.20%	17	Sichuan	17.73%
2	Tianjin	43.95%	18	Shaanxi	15.79%
3	Henan	43.34%	19	Beijing	15.72%
4	Shandong	40.94%	20	Guangxi	14.01%
5	Shanghai	36.67%	21	Jiangxi	13.94%
6	Hebei	36.12%	22	Hainan	13.48%
7	Anhui	32.35%	23	Guangdong	11.69%
8	Heilongjiang	26.96%	24	Guizhou	11.22%
9	Liaoning	25.93%	25	Fujian	9.66%
10	Shanxi	22.55%	26	Gansu	8.26%
11	Jilin	22.33%	27	Yunnan	7.86%
12	Chongqing	19.18%	28	Inner	7.26%
13	Hunan	18.04%	29	Sinkiang	4.27%
14	Hubei	17.84%	30	Qinghai	0.94%
15	Zhejiang	17.83%	31	Tibet	0.43%
16	Ningxia	17.75%			

We can see from above information: the top provinces are located in East China. Although they have high population density, their per capita indicators take the lead, which is determined by economic foundation and historical conditions. Relatively centralized population not only provides production labor force but also forms great consumption group. The centralization of population must be moderate. It is quite necessary to effectively control town scale. Besides, East China and Central China are still regions with high percentage of arable land. It is proven that agriculture does not go against urbanization. They supplement each other and develop in harmony.

2. We conduct comprehensive analysis and comparison according to regions in order to learn different features of different regions in a more visualized way:

(1) We intended to use GDP indicator for areas with different population density but available statistics does not allow this. So we replace it with per capita financial revenues.

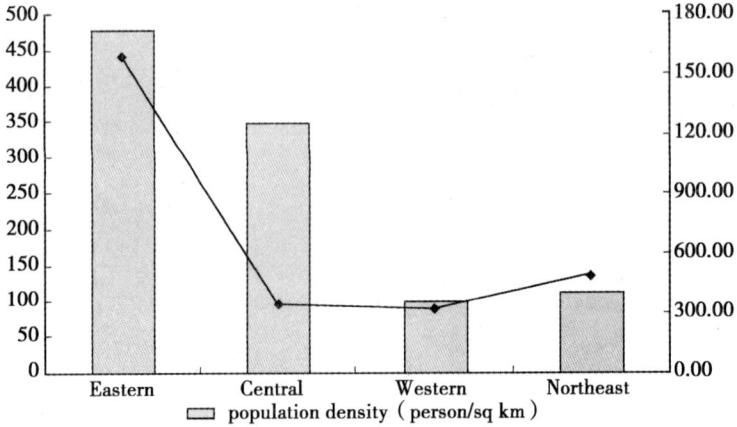

population density（person/sq km）

The illustration above shows that revenues are in positive proportion to population density. Population density in East China and Central China is the greatest and more obvious than that in west part of China and northeast part of China. The per capita revenues in East China are quite high. This is related with export processing industry of coastal areas of East China since the reform and opening-up.

This issue can be theorectically analyzed through statistics data of employment population of designated towns.

（2）Regional employment structure

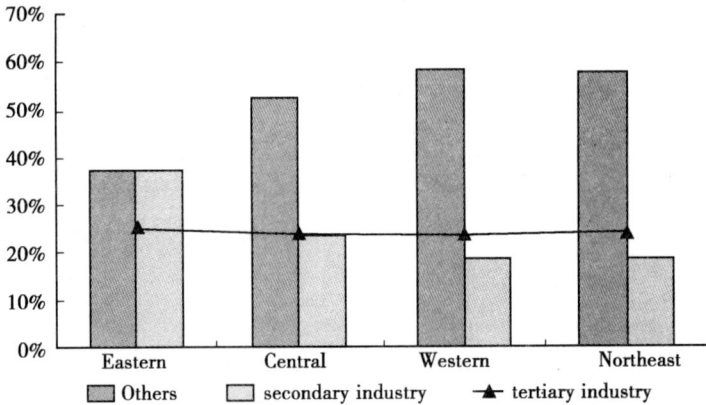

Others   secondary industry   tertiary industry

The employment percentage in tertiary industry in four regions is almost the same. The difference lies in second industry. "Others" means redundant labor force released from agriculture. So we made further analysis according to statistics explanations:

Employment population include: local general population of employment + inflow population;

Employment population in second industry and tertiary industry is actual local employment population;

Analyze and deduct outflow migrant population: local migrant population = local general population of employment + population without local registered permanent residence-employment population in first, second and tertiary industry;

Among employment population, the second and tertiary industry in designated towns should belong to local employment structure. Employment population beyond second and tertiary industry is not clearly included in agriculture population. However it is impossible for employment in agriculture to have such a high percentage. So we can refer that this part of employment population is actually redundant migrant population.

Workers in East China actually are transferring in this area and part of them go to cities. However labor force in Central China and west part of China including northeast part seek work opportunities in other parts of the country, that is, flock to cities. It is imaginable that outflow of employment population shows that local economy develops very slowly and there is little opportunity for employment. Meanwhile, outflow of people further influences local consumption and production which leads to slower development of economy and economic differences among regions.

(3) There is no GDP indicator in current materials so indicators of per capita surplus in the budget and per capita tax payment are temporarily used. Local financial revenues may be the necessary capital of local urbanization.

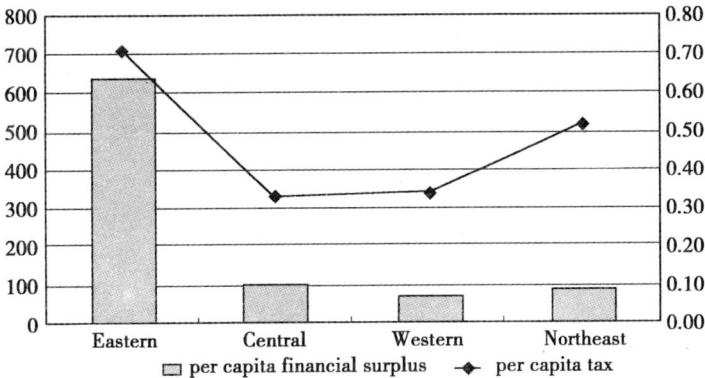

per capita financial surplus ☐   per capita tax ◆

(4) Investment in science and technology and its percentage

In terms of per capita, East China is far superior than Central China and west part of China whether it is about education investment or investment in sci-

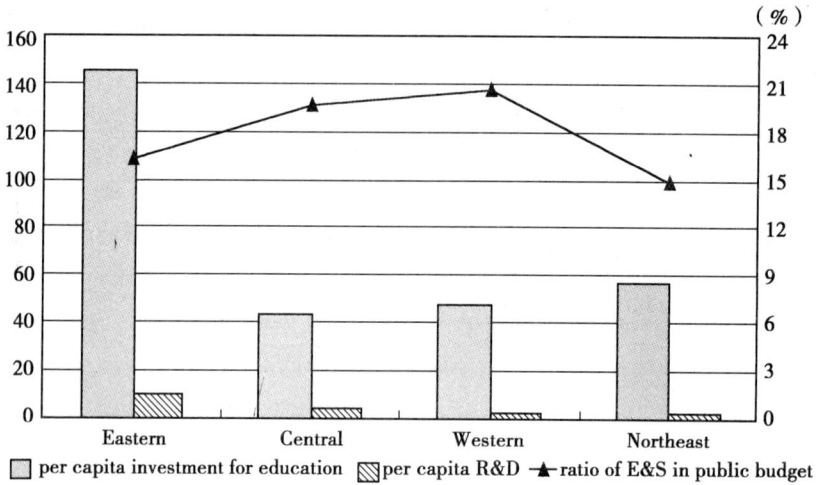

| | per capita investment for education | per capita R&D | ratio of E&S in public budget |

ence and technology, followed by the northeast part of China. However in terms of financial expenses, Central China and the west part of China surpasses East China and the northeast part of China. This demonstrates different local financial situations led by economic development disparity. Meanwhile, education of remote region more depends on local financial strength, without education resources of cities around it. More financial expenses are necessary.

(5) Per capita investment and new property formula: newly increased asset = accomplished fixed asset investment sum-finished investment sum of unsettled projects. Data in the previous year cannot be obtained due to lack of consecutive data of designated town. So the formula cannot be used and per capita sum is temporarily used for comparison.

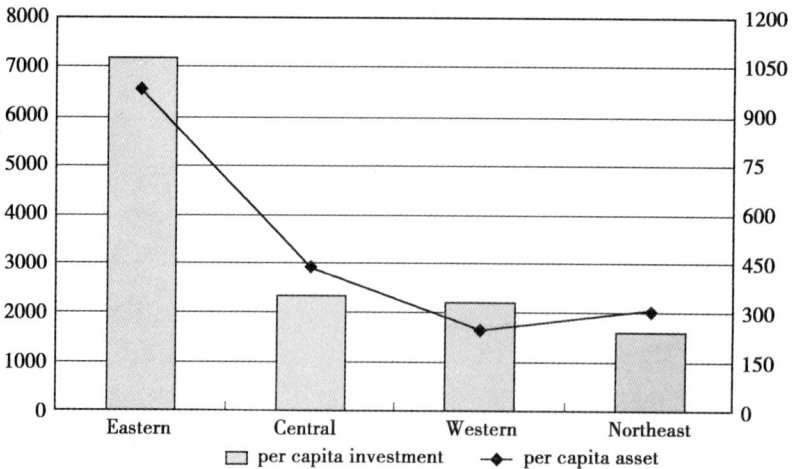

| | per capita investment | per capita asset |

As a result, Central China, the west part and the northeast part, and East China still contrast with each other.

In addition, total investment volume in fixed asset include newly built, expanded and transformed one. Newly built and expanded ones belong to increased ones while transformed ones belong to compensation ones. So they are consistent in asset sum. We just made a comparison using asset investment proportion.

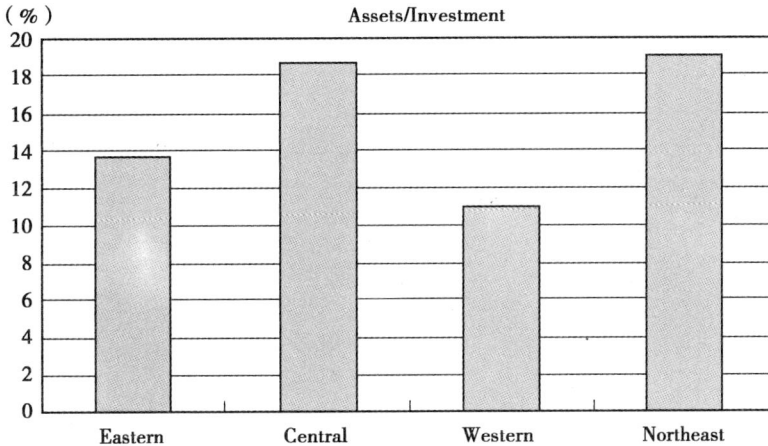

Factors that influence asset investment are asset sum and finished investment in fixed asset. The ratio actually reflects the scale of fixed asset investment in designated towns and asset reserves in designated towns. Finished investment scale is in negative proportion to indicators. The lower the asset investment, the greater the local investment; on the contrary, asset scale is in positive proportion to indicators. The higher the asset investment, the greater local asset reserves. There is no standard for a reasonable ration. However if the median 26. 13% is adopted, such seven provinces as Shanghai, Beijing, Guangdong, Hubei, Hunan, Heilongjiang and Sinkiang are in the middle in terms of investment while investment in Liaoning, Tibet, Yunnan and Hainan is little and investment in other provinces are relatively great. Although investment ratio is moderate in Shanghai, Beijing and Guangdong, their actual asset base is large. Their investment sum is not little. This means designated towns in these cities and provinces have certain asset strength.

Average value of total designated towns is only 15. 63%. This means that designated towns are in the stage of great investment and accumulation of local assets. Plenty of external investment is needed and actual funds are gradually used for designated towns. This is inevitable for urban development. Built district of city is either expanded like making pancakes, or connected like satellite town. Social surplus capital is guided to designated towns in the process of urbanization.

(6) Comparison of arable lands in different regions

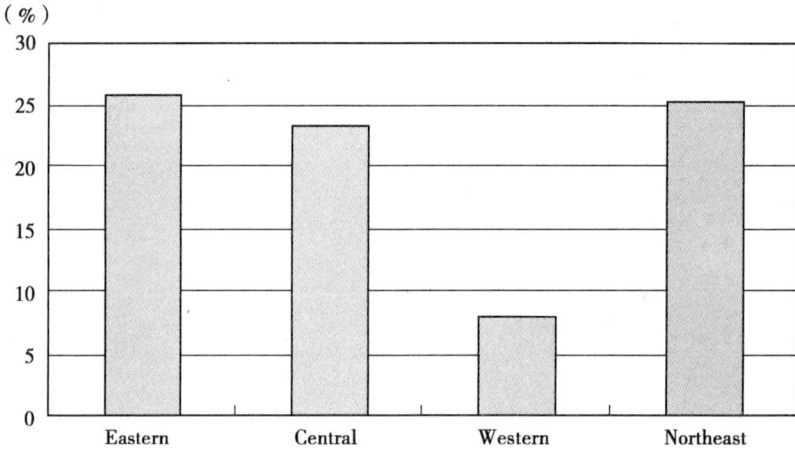

(%)

In addition to west part, percentage of arable lands in different regions is almost the same. It is because west part is huge. Analysis of arable lands around the country:

Percentage of plowland among four divisions in town areas

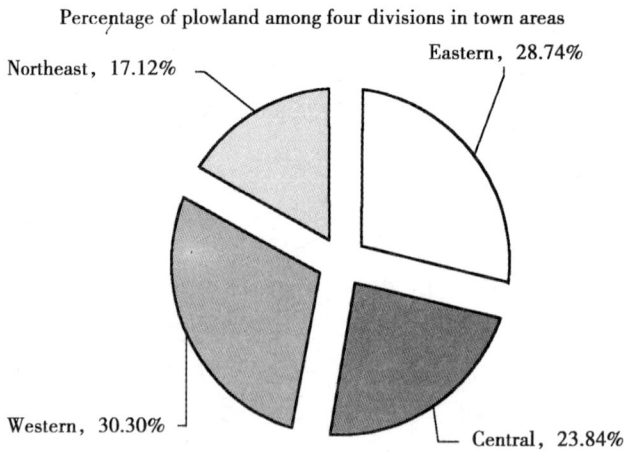

Northeast, 17.12%
Eastern, 28.74%
Western, 30.30%
Central, 23.84%

West part occupies 57% of the total area, there are obviously less arable lands. This is mainly determined by geographical features of west part.

Compare relation between seeding area and arable land area:

Crop areas/plowland

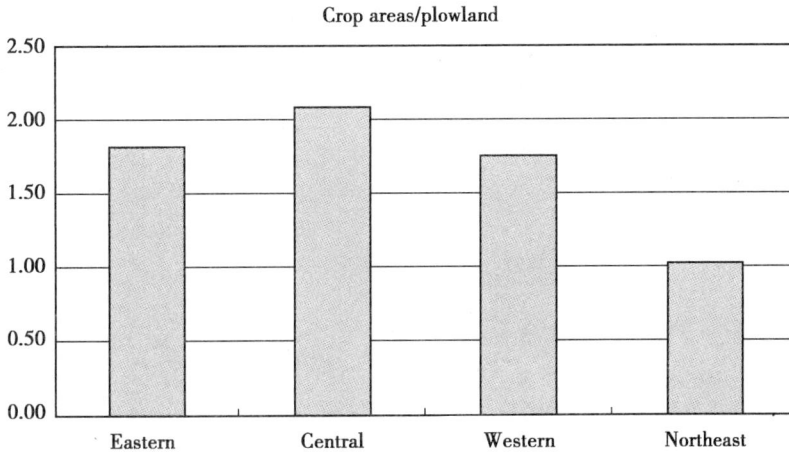

If the ratio between arable land and administrative regions reflect arable land resource scale of designated towns, the ratio between seeding land and arable land reflects the usage of arable land. The seeding area percentage is relatively high because west part includes three provinces in southwest. According to seeding area of the country, the percentages of four regions are:

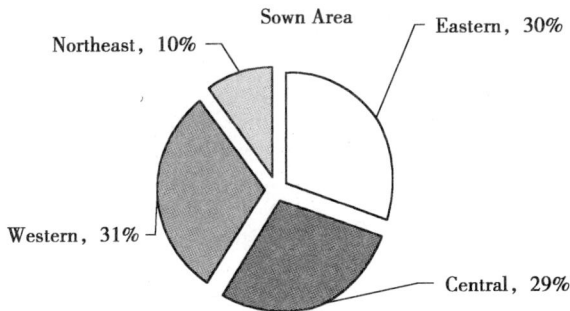

Sown Area
Northeast, 10%
Eastern, 30%
Western, 31%
Central, 29%

3. We made comparison among different geographical locations in addition to division of four regions:

(1) Population density divided by geographical locations

Geograghic Comparison of Population Density

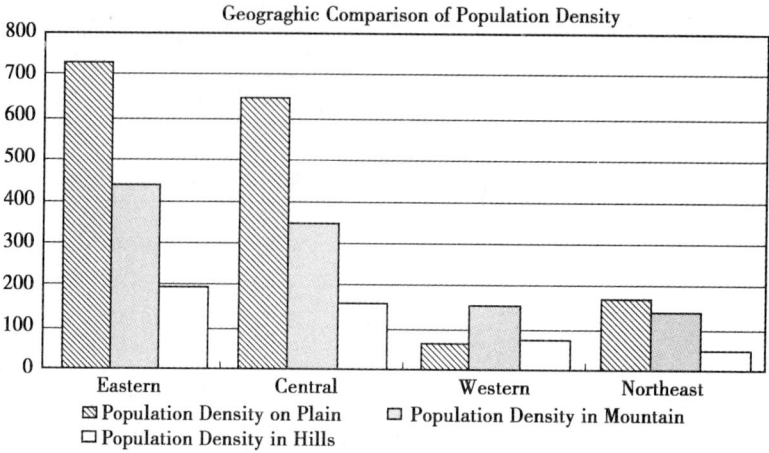

☒ Population Density on Plain　　☐ Population Density in Mountain
☐ Population Density in Hills

(2) Per capita financial revenues divided by geographical locations

Per capita Financial Revenues

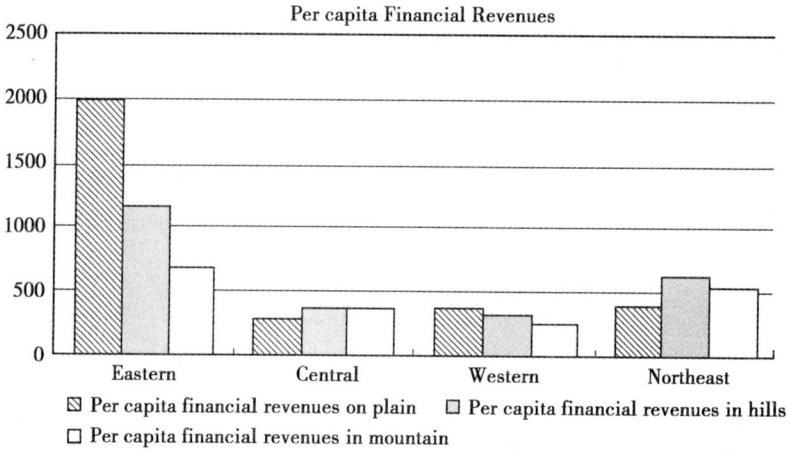

☒ Per capita financial revenues on plain　☐ Per capita financial revenues in hills
☐ Per capita financial revenues in mountain

Compare by combining the two indicators:

Comparison of Population Density and per capita Financial Revenues

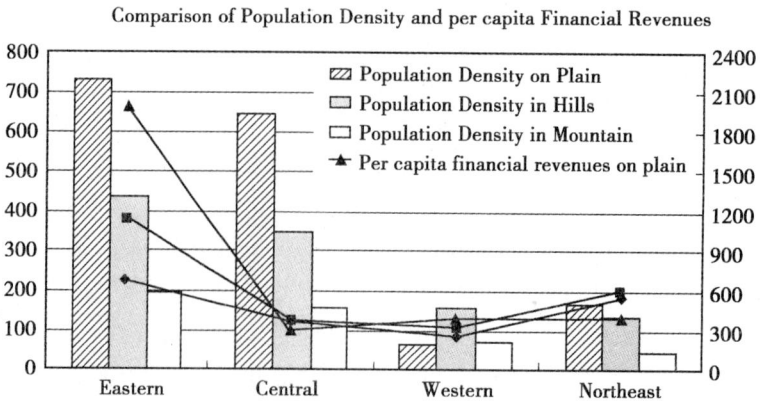

☑ Population Density on Plain
☐ Population Density in Hills
☐ Population Density in Mountain
▲ Per capita financial revenues on plain

We can see that according to population density of geographical locations, plain is superior over hills, hills over mountain areas (it is hill area in west part of China with high population density). However in terms of per capita financial revenues, per capita revenues is relatively high in Central China, west part and northeast part and hill areas. Reasons are further analyzed according to division of population percentage and financial revenues in different regions and geographical locations:

A   Population percentage in different regions and geographical locations

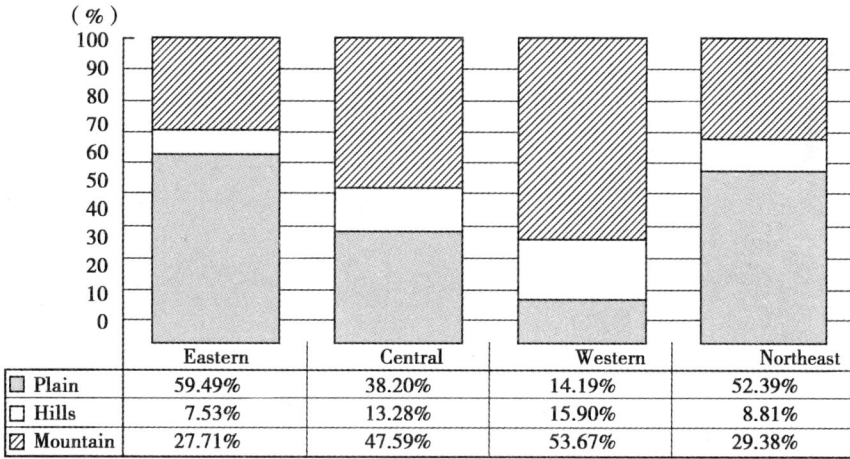

	Eastern	Central	Western	Northeast
☐ Plain	59.49%	38.20%	14.19%	52.39%
☐ Hills	7.53%	13.28%	15.90%	8.81%
☒ Mountain	27.71%	47.59%	53.67%	29.38%

B   Financial revenues percentage in different regions and geographical locations

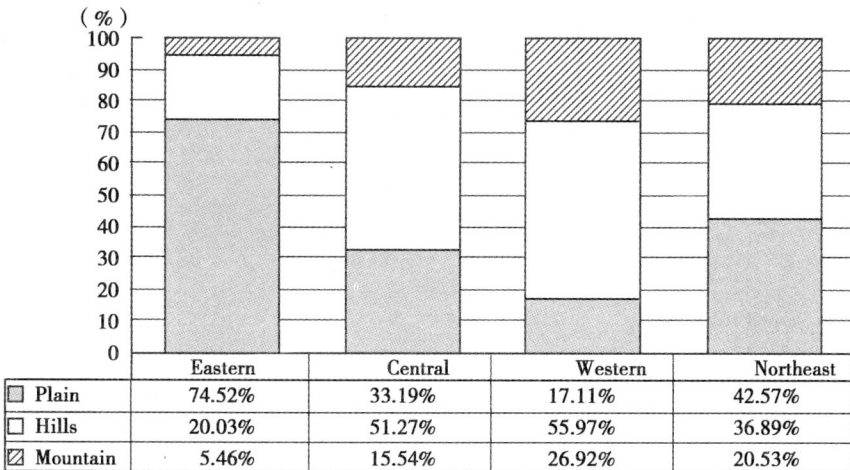

	Eastern	Central	Western	Northeast
☐ Plain	74.52%	33.19%	17.11%	42.57%
☐ Hills	20.03%	51.27%	55.97%	36.89%
☒ Mountain	5.46%	15.54%	26.92%	20.53%

We can see through data comparison that there is less population in hill area but with high percentage of financial revenues. This may be a problem of financial policy, or related with exploit of resources, for example, local development of forestry and mining industry.

(II) Compared analysis of external indicators

(20, 000 designated towns have to be returned to their governing cities one by one due to relation of external indicators with their governing city. It takes a lot of efforts so it is omitted temporarily.)

(III) Compared analysis of urbanization indicators

1. Data comparison divided by provinces

(1) Comparison of towns

Number	Place	Town percentage (%)	Number	Place	Town percentage (%)
1	Shanghai	10. 69%	17	Shaanxi	2. 26%
2	Tianjin	7. 95%	18	Chongqing	2. 25%
3	Hebei	7. 14%	19	Guizhou	2. 20%
4	Zhejiang	6. 55%	20	Hubei	2. 09%
5	Beijing	6. 42%	21	Yunnan	1. 71%
6	Jiangsu	6. 41%	22	Hainan	1. 62%
7	Henan	4. 81%	23	Jilin	1. 44%
8	Shandong	4. 26%	24	Ningxia	1. 43%
9	Guangdong	3. 84%	25	Shanxi	1. 43%
10	Anhui	3. 28%	26	Heilongjiang	1. 40%
11	Liaoning	3. 24%	27	Guangxi	1. 37%
12	Tibet	3. 13%	28	Sinkiang	1. 13%
13	Hunan	3. 12%	29	Gansu	0. 76%
14	Fujian	2. 57%	30	Inner Mongolia	0. 59%
15	Sichuan	2. 43%	31	Qinghai	0. 24%
16	Jiangxi	2. 32%			

(2) Comparison of town population

Number	Place	Percentage of town population (%)	Number	Place	Percentage of town population (%)
1	Tibet	57.90%	17	Fujian	25.29%
2	Shanghai	34.59%	18	Tianjin	24.87%
3	Jiangsu	33.59%	19	Hunan	24.45%
4	Heilongjiang	33.10%	20	Jiangxi	24.02%
5	Zhejiang	31.78%	21	Guangdong	24.01%
6	Hebei	31.70%	22	Sichuan	23.60%
7	Sinkiang	30.09%	23	Chongqing	23.57%
8	Shanxi	28.74%	24	Qinghai	23.06%
9	Inner Mongolia	28.37%	25	Yunnan	21.36%
10	Beijing	28.00%	26	Hubei	21.10%
11	Jilin	27.68%	27	Shandong	20.71%
12	Henan	27.11%	28	Guizhou	19.41%
13	Ningxia	26.74%	29	Shaanxi	19.33%
14	Gansu	26.48%	30	Anhui	17.61%
15	Hainan	26.47%	31	Guangxi	16.80%
16	Liaoning	26.44%			

(3) Afforestation rate in towns

Number	Place	Affforestation rate in towns (%)	Number	Place	Affforestation rate in towns (%)
1	Jiangsu	10.79%	17	Guangxi	3.30%
2	Shanghai	9.41%	18	Sichuan	3.14%
3	Shandong	7.38%	19	Zhejiang	3.03%
4	Beijing	7.32%	20	Ningxia	2.90%
5	Hunan	5.98%	21	Guizhou	2.81%
6	Chongqing	5.17%	22	Inner Mongolia	2.74%
7	Guangdong	4.98%	23	Yunnan	2.67%
8	Hubei	4.95%	24	Gansu	2.24%
9	Sinkiang	4.68%	25	Shaanxi	1.84%
10	Jiangxi	4.49%	26	Hebei	1.70%
11	Anhui	4.39%	27	Jilin	1.66%
12	Hainan	4.06%	28	Heilongjiang	1.51%
13	Shanxi	4.01%	29	Tianjin	0.90%
14	Henan	3.69%	30	Qinghai	0.44%
15	Fujian	3.67%	31	Tibet	0.04%
16	Liaoning	3.34%			

(4) Per capita annual power consumption (KW)

Number	Place	Per capita power consumption	Number	Place	Per capita power consumption
1	Zhejiang	3064. 67	17	Ningxia	245. 56
2	Jiangsu	2310. 59	18	Hunan	234. 06
3	Guangdong	1788. 69	19	Anhui	221. 84
4	Shanghai	1718. 36	20	Hubei	221. 19
5	Tianjin	1405. 22	21	Jiangxi	202. 81
6	Beijing	1323. 32	22	Heilongjiang	199. 44
7	Fujian	1117. 71	23	Sichuan	182. 34
8	Liaoning	1007. 95	24	Chongqing	181. 06
9	Hebei	856. 98	25	Guizhou	166. 66
10	Shandong	844. 67	26	Gansu	152. 88
11	Sinkiang	517. 74	27	Shaanxi	144. 24
12	Henan	513. 77	28	Tibet①	140. 53
13	Inner	365. 49	29	Hainan	138. 30
14	Jilin	314. 07	30	Guangxi	115. 71
15	Shanxi	305. 29	31	Qinghai	89. 37
16	Yunnan	288. 78			

(5) Road network density (kilometer/square kilometer)

Number	Place	Road network density	Number	Place	Road network density
1	Sichuan	1. 57	17	Jiangxi	0. 51
2	Jiangsu	1. 55	18	Shanxi	0. 50
3	Shanghai	1. 44	19	Shaanxi	0. 50
4	Henan	1. 18	20	Yunnan	0. 48
5	Beijing	1. 10	21	Liaoning	0. 44
6	Shandong	1. 06	22	Hainan	0. 39
7	Hubei	0. 90	23	Guangxi	0. 32
8	Zhejiang	0. 85	24	Jilin	0. 26
9	Anhui	0. 82	25	Ningxia	0. 22
10	Tianjin	0. 81	26	Heilongjiang	0. 19
11	Hebei	0. 79	27	Gansu	0. 15
12	Hunan	0. 69	28	Inner	0. 08
13	Chongqing	0. 67	29	Sinkiang	0. 06
14	Guizhou	0. 63	30	Qinghai	0. 03
15	Fujian	0. 57	31	Tibet	0. 01
16	Guangdong	0. 56			

① Mistaken data; adjustment made.

The rule of road network density sequencing is related with population density and economic development.

(6) Education

① Percentage of pupils (sequenced by hill area)

Number	Place	Percentage of pupils (%)			Number	Place	Percentage of pupils (%)		
		Plain	Hill	area			Plain	Hill	area
1	Ningxia	11.26%	16.87%	11.75%	16	Sichuan	7.61%	7.38%	11.73%
2	Tibet	15.34%	14.25%	13.61%	17	Fujian	7.64%	6.91%	6.45%
3	Hainan	11.62%	11.85%	10.50%	18	Hunan	6.30%	6.42%	6.43%
4	Guizhou		11.65%	11.61%	19	Chongqing	5.10%	6.39%	9.06%
5	Gansu	10.34%	10.49%	11.76%	20	Liaoning	6.17%	6.30%	5.66%
6	Guangdong	10.28%	10.18%	9.69%	21	Hubei	5.65%	6.20%	6.16%
7	Yunnan	10.04%	9.92%	10.66%	22	Jilin	6.36%	6.09%	5.10%
8	Guangxi	10.78%	9.78%	8.58%	23	Zhejiang	7.17%	6.05%	6.57%
9	Jiangxi	8.60%	9.73%	8.89%	24	Inner Mongolia	6.06%	5.82%	5.14%
10	Shanxi	9.35%	8.63%	8.98%	25	Jiangsu	6.06%	5.59%	4.12%
11	Henan	10.32%	8.32%	8.73%	26	Heilongjiang	5.28%	5.31%	5.82%
12	Shaanxi	9.00%	8.31%	9.10%	27	Shandong	6.73%	5.28%	5.88%
13	Hebei	6.80%	7.68%	7.69%	28	Tianjin	6.88%	4.86%	6.32%
14	Anhui	9.51%	7.58%	6.67%	29	Beijing	4.11%	4.30%	5.10%
15	Sinkiang	10.36%	7.46%	7.68%	30	Shanghai	3.02%		

② Teachers in primary schools (sequenced by hill area)

Number	Place	Number of teachers per			Number	Place	Number of teachers per		
		Plain	Hill area	Mountain			Plain	Plain	Hill area
1	Beijing	9.41	11.73	15.61	17	Henan	5.24	5.93	6.31
2	Jilin	9.72	11.52	13.24	18	Hainan	5.32	5.92	6.35
3	Inner Mongolia	9.23	10.31	11.30	19	Chongqing	8.95	5.87	5.33
4	Tianjin	8.36	9.96	8.35	20	Gansu	5.47	5.35	5.15
5	Heilongjiang	9.35	8.78	9.29	21	Zhejiang	5.02	5.35	5.95
6	Sinkiang	6.97	8.68	9.01	22	Yunnan	5.28	5.32	5.13
7	Shandong	6.86	7.80	7.36	23	Guangxi	5.33	5.23	6.37
8	Liaoning	7.35	7.61	8.70	24	Anhui	4.49	5.11	6.33
9	Jiangsu	6.49	7.32	8.66	25	Jiangxi	5.24	5.02	5.32
10	Shanxi	6.16	7.21	7.09	26	Sichuan	5.27	4.96	5.48
11	Hebei	7.69	7.09	7.17	27	Guizhou		4.52	4.48
12	Shaanxi	6.18	6.67	6.39	28	Guangdong	4.06	4.47	5.19
13	Fujian	5.44	6.53	8.24	29	Ningxia	5.33	3.29	4.97
14	Tibet	6.58	6.16	5.95	30	Shanghai	7.37		
15	Hubei	5.86	6.05	6.13	31	Qinghai	6.02		5.91
16	Hunan	6.67	6.04	7.16					

③ Percentage of high school students (sequenced by hill area)

Number	Place	Percentage of high school students (%)			Number	Place	Percentage of high school students (%)		
		Plain	Hill area	Mountain			Plain	Hill area	Mountain
1	Sinkiang	7.90%	8.13%	5.82%	17	Hubei	5.16%	5.20%	4.97%
2	Ningxia	7.09%	7.78%	6.55%	18	Guangdong	5.45%	5.15%	5.50%
3	Shaanxi	7.28%	7.47%	7.31%	19	Jiangsu	5.47%	5.11%	2.94%
4	Hainan	6.72%	6.44%	4.65%	20	Chongqing	2.61%	5.06%	6.67%
5	Henan	6.53%	6.42%	4.61%	21	Guangxi	6.93%	4.86%	4.92%
6	Gansu	6.21%	6.35%	6.90%	22	Inner Mong	4.72%	4.83%	4.28%
7	Fujian	6.18%	6.12%	5.81%	23	Zhejiang	5.25%	4.81%	4.56%
8	Yunnan	6.49%	6.11%	5.72%	24	Liaoning	4.43%	4.77%	3.78%
9	Sichuan	10.17%	6.06%	12.45%	25	Hunan	4.76%	4.55%	5.20%
10	Guizhou		5.76%	5.97%	26	Shandong	4.50%	4.09%	3.31%
11	Tianjin	4.61%	5.71%	5.62%	27	Jilin	3.99%	3.66%	3.47%
12	Anhui	5.47%	5.67%	6.15%	28	Beijing	2.86%	3.40%	3.68%
13	Tibet	10.08%	5.55%	8.74%	29	Heilongji	4.04%	3.32%	4.70%
14	Jiangxi	6.04%	5.40%	5.02%	30	Shanghai	2.57%		
15	Shanxi	7.39%	5.28%	5.66%	31	Qinghai	6.81%		6.75%
16	Hebei	5.61%	5.27%	6.89%					

④ Teachers in high schools (sequenced by hill area)

Number	Place	Teachers per hundred students in high schools			Number	Place	Teachers per hundred students in high schools		
		Plain	Hill area	Mountain			Plain	Hill area	Mountain
1	Sinkiang	13.54	12.64	14.96	17	Hebei	6.33	6.69	7.25
2	Fujian	9.14	9.66	11.00	18	Chongqing	6.40	6.44	6.73
3	Shanxi	8.86	9.63	9.48	19	Inner Mongolia	8.55	6.37	5.60
4	Henan	8.46	9.53	10.12	20	Hubei	6.37	6.27	6.60
5	Qinghai	8.30	9.17	9.33	21	Anhui	4.93	6.13	6.36
6	Ningxia	8.99	8.79	10.42	22	Guangxi	5.78	6.09	5.78
7	Yunnan	8.22	8.27	8.81	23	Jilin	6.45	6.03	6.59
8	Shaanxi	6.98	7.97	7.39	24	Zhejiang	6.68	5.96	6.68
9	Guizhou	7.22	7.95	8.85	25	Beijing	6.77	5.93	5.91
10	Guangdong	8.26	7.75	7.63	26	Liaoning		5.86	5.63
11	Gansu	7.92	7.51	8.54	27	Jiangsu	5.53	5.73	5.87
12	Hainan	7.28	7.22	7.98	28	Shanghai	6.41	5.53	7.09
13	Tibet	6.84	7.06	7.89	29	Shandong	6.68	5.05	5.95
14	Tianjin	6.82	6.98	6.99	30	Sichuan	10.02		
15	Jiangxi	5.97	6.87	7.18	31	Heilongjiang	7.55		7.30
16	Hunan	6.25	6.78	6.24					

(7) Social security (sequenced by hill area)

① Number of gerocomium per 10,000 people

Number	Place	Number of gerocomium per 10,000 people			Number	Place	Number of gerocomium per 10,000 people		
		Plain	Hill area	Mountain			Plain	Hill area	Mountain
1	Guangxi	0.54	0.61	0.63	17	Shandong	0.24	0.25	0.25
2	Beijing	0.28	0.45	0.65	18	Shanxi	0.21	0.24	0.25
3	Jiangsu	0.27	0.43	0.42	19	Shaanxi	0.13	0.24	0.40
4	Chongqing	0.97	0.42	0.49	20	Guangdong	0.16	0.24	0.32
5	Liaoning	0.50	0.40	0.41	21	Sinkiang	0.28	0.22	0.37
6	Jiangxi	0.31	0.37	0.50	22	Hunan	0.28	0.22	0.31
7	Jilin	0.30	0.36	0.52	23	Heilongjiang	0.27	0.22	0.26
8	Hubei	0.26	0.36	0.54	24	Gansu	0.26	0.20	0.18
9	Sichuan	0.15	0.35	0.25	25	Guizhou		0.20	0.21
10	Inner Mongolia	0.26	0.34	0.31	26	Fujian	0.08	0.17	0.30
11	Hainan	0.21	0.34	0.33	27	Yunnan	0.15	0.17	0.17
12	Henan	0.27	0.33	0.39	28	Ningxia	0.20	0.12	0.18
13	Zhejiang	0.22	0.33	0.41	29	Tibet	1.45	0.00	0.56
14	Anhui	0.24	0.33	0.42	30	Shanghai	0.21		
15	Tianjin	0.28	0.30	0.54	31	Qinghai	0.26		0.16
16	Hebei	0.21	0.28	0.31					

② Number of adopted people per 10,000

Number	Place	Number of adopted people per 10,000 people			Number	Place	Number of adopted people per 10,000 people		
		Plain	Hill area	Mountain			Plain	Hill area	Mountain
1	Hubei	19.67	21.79	92.11	17	Sinkiang	7.92	6.91	20.67
2	Jilin	12.68	20.90	47.71	18	Guangxi	6.57	6.90	23.68
3	Jiangsu	12.60	17.08	48.28	19	Hebei	5.69	4.84	18.61
4	Jiangxi	9.36	17.06	71.22	20	Guangdong	5.21	4.80	22.73
5	Beijing	20.13	15.70	48.72	21	Tianjin	6.48	4.07	21.36
6	Zhejiang	11.43	14.70	45.04	22	Hainan	1.35	4.02	9.59
7	Liaoning	15.64	14.44	63.35	23	Shaanxi	1.52	3.64	24.93
8	Shandong	11.93	13.20	48.60	24	Shanxi	2.00	2.70	9.12
9	Hunan	10.19	11.87	30.22	25	Yunnan	1.98	2.59	7.41
10	Henan	10.04	11.40	48.59	26	Guizhou		1.93	8.40
11	Chongqing	39.81	11.19	27.90	27	Fujian	1.68	1.74	12.64
12	Sichuan	6.40	10.06	19.40	28	Gansu	4.02	1.65	7.18
13	Heilongjiang	12.06	8.57	22.78	29	Tibet	16.97	0.00	30.10
14	Inner Mongolia	6.20	8.46	24.32	30	Shanghai	21.63		
15	Ningxia	6.35	8.23	15.99	31	Qinghai	5.01		13.94
16	Anhui	6.16	7.75	22.25					

(8) Entertainment and sports facility (sequenced by hill area)

① Number of museum and culture stops per 10,000 (people in towns only)

Number	Place	Number of museum and culture stops per 10,000 people			Number	Place	Number of museum and culture stops per 10,000 people		
		Plain	Hill area	Mountain			Plain	Hill area	Mountain
1	Beijing	0.76	1.35	1.74	17	Hubei	0.86	1.04	1.26
2	Tianjin	1.30	4.17	1.83	18	Hunan	0.98	1.11	1.46
3	Hebei	1.55	3.64	1.91	19	Guangdong	0.56	1.02	1.72
4	Shanxi	2.18	2.68	2.61	20	Guangxi	0.80	1.42	1.65
5	Inner Mongolia	1.86	1.48	0.91	21	Hainan	1.13	1.67	1.74
6	Liaoning	2.10	3.37	2.02	22	Chongqing	7.69	1.05	1.31
7	Jilin	1.15	1.37	1.42	23	Sichuan	0.39	1.75	0.82
8	Heilongjiang	1.03	0.87	0.72	24	Guizhou		1.05	1.43
9	Shanghai	0.48			25	Yunnan	0.94	1.16	1.59
10	Jiangsu	0.91	1.42	1.18	26	Tibet	1.93	0.18	1.87
11	Zhejiang	1.28	1.65	1.87	27	Shaanxi	1.98	1.82	2.38
12	Anhui	1.07	1.40	2.41	28	Gansu	2.56	1.86	2.19
13	Fujian	1.00	1.05	1.51	29	Qinghai	0.49		1.71
14	Jiangxi	1.34	1.21	1.88	30	Ningxia	1.42	0.00	1.63
15	Shandong	1.80	2.12	1.69	31	Sinkiang	2.20	2.98	1.78
16	Henan	1.26	1.80	1.43					

② Number of theaters per 10,000 people (people in towns only)

Number	Place	Number of theaters per 10,000 people			Number	Place	Number of theaters per 10,000 people		
		Plain	Hill area	Mountain			Plain	Hill area	Mountain
1	Sinkiang	0.47	1.07	0.43	17	Hunan	0.36	0.27	0.34
2	Beijing	0.48	1.06	0.91	18	Liaoning	0.16	0.25	0.16
3	Shanxi	0.25	0.45	0.37	19	Henan	0.16	0.21	0.30
4	Hubei	0.45	0.42	0.26	20	Guizhou		0.18	0.12
5	Shaanxi	0.40	0.41	0.26	21	Hebei	0.13	0.18	0.13
6	Gansu	0.60	0.39	0.27	22	Chongqin	0.00	0.17	0.07
7	Zhejiang	0.38	0.39	0.49	23	Inner Mo	0.15	0.16	0.07
8	Yunnan	0.26	0.35	0.28	24	Sichuan	0.12	0.12	0.24
9	Jiangsu	0.39	0.35	1.18	25	Jilin	0.14	0.09	0.21
10	Shandong	0.24	0.33	0.20	26	Heilongj	0.08	0.07	0.07
11	Guangdong	0.29	0.32	0.42	27	Tianjin	0.12	0.00	0.00
12	Fujian	0.24	0.32	0.50	28	Tibet	0.00	0.00	0.00
13	Anhui	0.21	0.32	0.33	29	Ningxia	0.26	0.00	0.18
14	Hainan	0.33	0.30	0.13	30	Shanghai	0.25		
15	Guangxi	0.25	0.30	0.22	31	Qinghai	0.49		0.25
16	Jiangxi	0.26	0.28	0.53					

③ Number of stadiums per 10,000 people (people in towns only)

Number	Place	Number of stadiums per 10,000 people			Number	Place	Number of stadiums per 10,000 people		
		Plain	Hill area	Mountain			Plain	Hill area	Mountain
1	Sinkiang	1.01	1.07	0.57	17	Hunan	0.10	0.27	0.21
2	Beijing	0.18	1.06	0.30	18	Liaoning	0.44	0.25	0.24
3	Shanxi	0.79	0.45	1.03	19	Henan	0.41	0.21	0.50
4	Hubei	0.11	0.42	0.14	20	Guizhou		0.18	0.13
5	Shaanxi	0.40	0.41	0.33	21	Hebei	0.16	0.18	0.21
6	Gansu	0.54	0.39	0.30	22	Chongqing	0.00	0.17	0.07
7	Zhejiang	0.38	0.39	0.56	23	Inner Mongolia	0.15	0.16	0.37
8	Yunnan	0.23	0.35	0.27	24	Sichuan	0.17	0.12	0.46
9	Jiangsu	0.36	0.35	1.78	25	Jilin	0.08	0.09	0.16
10	Shandong	0.39	0.33	0.29	26	Heilongjiang	0.27	0.07	0.27
11	Guangdong	0.82	0.32	0.38	27	Tianjin	0.17	0.00	0.00
12	Fujian	0.27	0.32	0.30	28	Tibet	0.18	0.00	0.00
13	Anhui	0.35	0.32	0.63	29	Ningxia	0.35	0.00	0.05
14	Hainan	0.38	0.30	0.13	30	Shanghai	0.21		
15	Guangxi	0.46	0.30	0.31	31	Qinghai	0.49		0.36
16	Jiangxi	0.30	0.28	0.69					

As we see, According to the sequencing based on hill area, there is still great gap among 8 indicators which reflect urbanization. Why?

We know that per capita indicators and density indicators are calculated by two corresponding limit indicators. Any indicator will influence changes of corresponding indicator value. Generally population is in negative proportion to per capita and town area is in inverse proportion to density and even not determined by total volume. China has a very unbalanced distribution of population. The natural environment is quite different in East China and west part of China. This explains the reason that those provinces that we subconsciously regard as backward areas take the lead while adopting corresponding indicators.

Besides, it is easier to allocate resources of little towns than big cities from the perspective of investment in urbanization. Potential demands are not so great, which guarantees less investment risk and quick recovery and greater investment benefits. It can motivate the maximum development of local economy with minimum efforts. This is an issue worth our future study.

2. We try to make a comprehensive comparison of regions and geography according to main indicators mentioned above in order to better learn differences

among indicators.

(1) Per capita power consumption according to geography and regions

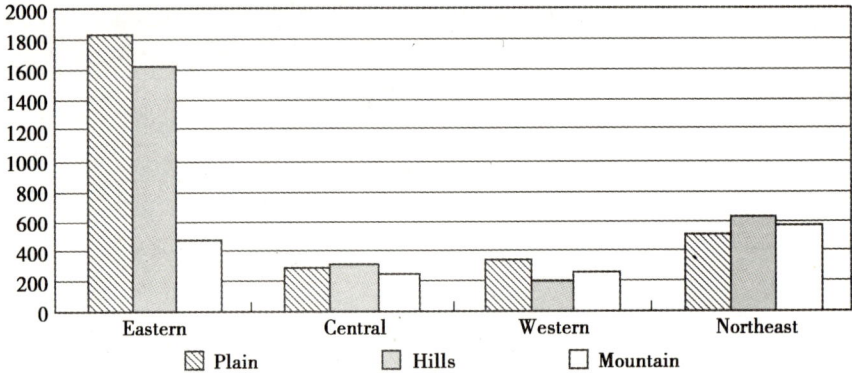

More power is used in remote hill areas and mountain in East China than in other regions. This is inevitable in East China. However higher relative percentage of per capita power consumption occurred in hill areas of Central China and northeast part of China and mountains in northeast part. This means there is a higher percentage of resource industry. It is consistent with analysis of financial revenues mentioned above.

(2) Road network density comparison according to geography and regions

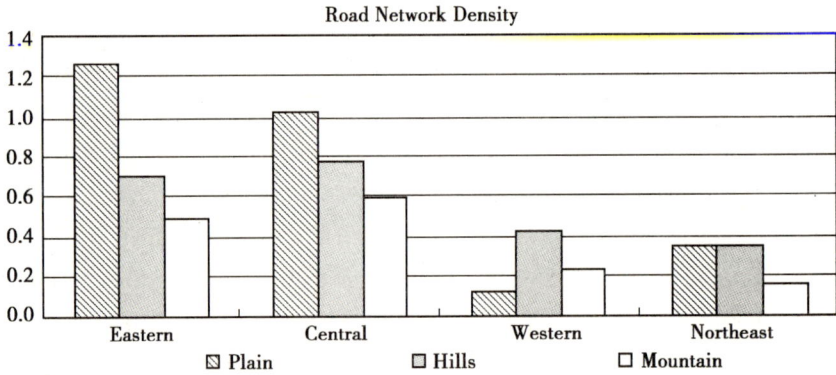

Road Network Density

The traffic in East China has been quite convenient since ancient times. It gathers businessmen and plenty of population. It has become more developed due to foreign trading through sea passageway since reform and opening-up. This is determined by its unique and favorable geographical location. Its road network is more developed just because of economic basis.

Therefore we have to make further analysis of size of designated towns:

116

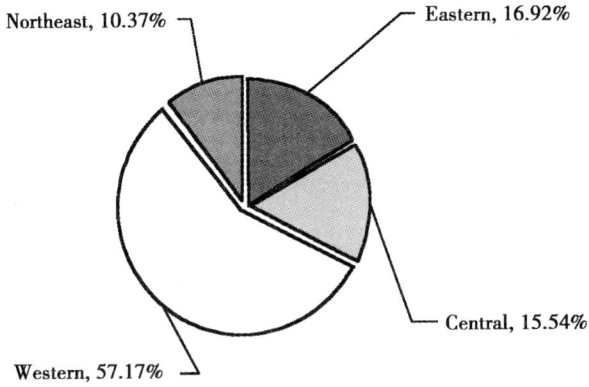

Northeast, 10.37% — Eastern, 16.92%

Central, 15.54%

Western, 57.17%

More than half designated towns are located in west part of China with large base number and low density.

Again compare village density:

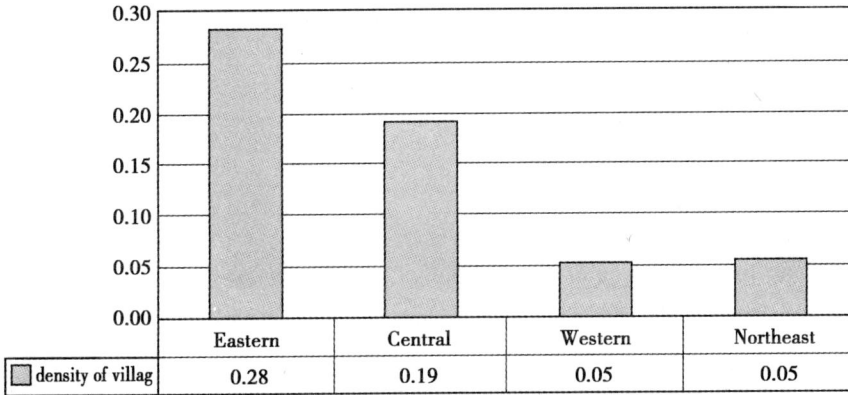

	Eastern	Central	Western	Northeast
density of villag	0.28	0.19	0.05	0.05

Obviously village density in provinces of east part of China is high while village density in provinces of west part of China is low.

Comparison of highway mileage of designated towns:

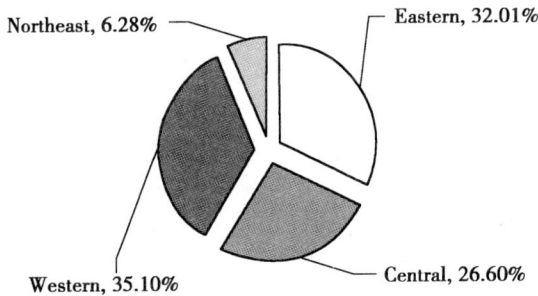

Northeast, 6.28% — Eastern, 32.01%

Western, 35.10%   Central, 26.60%

Theoretically if villages are scattered, longer highway is needed instead of dense road networks. It is a bit hard to recover investment by toll for highway construction in west part due to such factors as traffic flow and investment in single mileage. It is impossible to totally rely on limited local finance. It should be "be rich before building roads".

(3) Education comparison according to geography and regions

Number of Teachers per Hundred Pupils

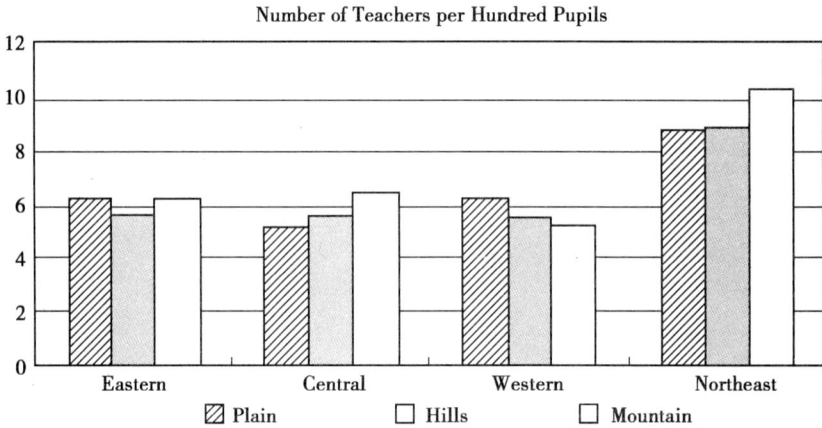

Percentage of Pupils

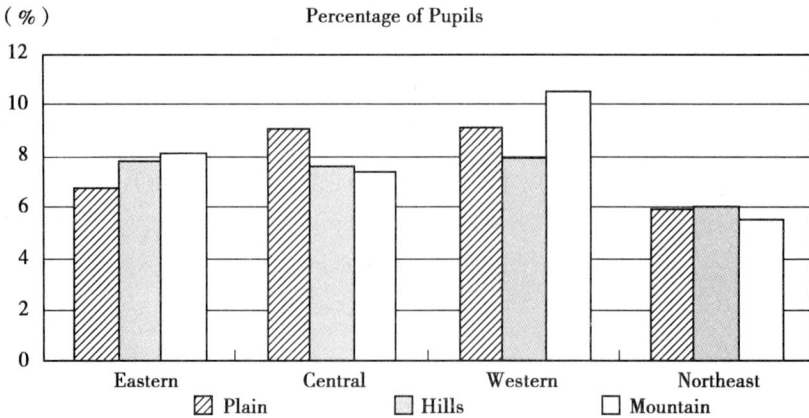

Compare teachers in primary schools and number of pupils, we can see that pupils in northeast part are decreasing so the percentage of teachers for hundred students is high.

(4) Comparison of social well-being and security according to geography and regions

Number of Gerocomium per 10,000 People

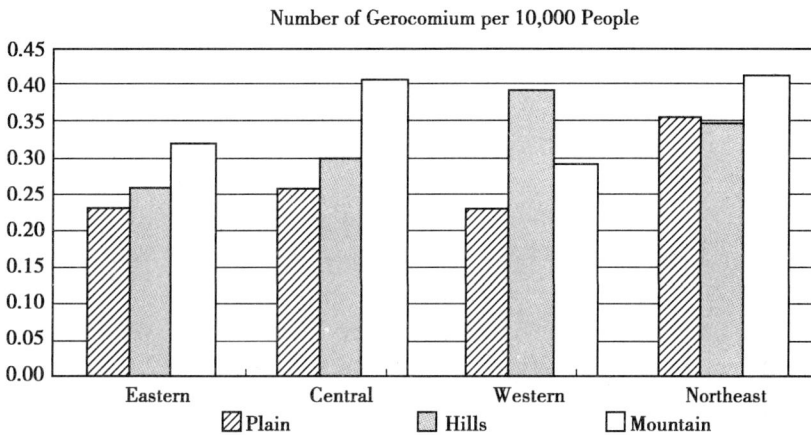

Eastern   Central   Western   Northeast

◨ Plain   ▨ Hills   ☐ Mountain

Number of Adopted People per 10,000 People

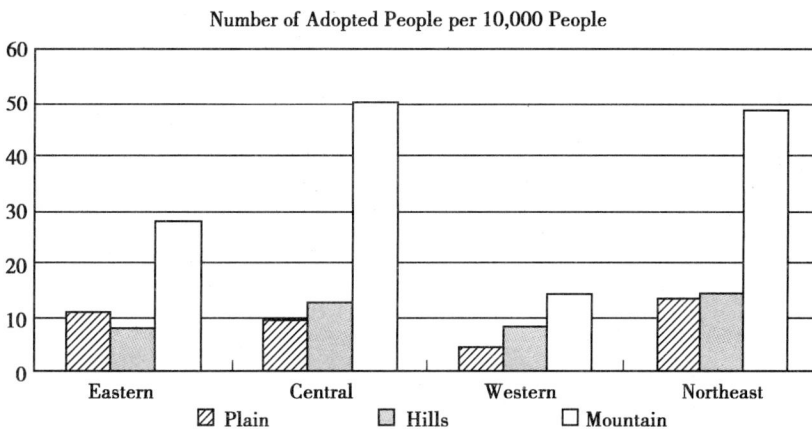

Eastern   Central   Western   Northeast

◨ Plain   ▨ Hills   ☐ Mountain

There are more gerocomiums and charity houses in hill area and mountains because of different social security systems between urban and rural areas. Well-being finance system and subsidiary financial supplement forms the social well-being system of cities while in villages families depend on family members and groups for support. Therefore the construction of gerocomiums in villages is earlier than that of cities. The adopted population in villages is greater than that of cities. So we can see that average family income is relatively high in richer places. The percentage of centralized adoption is low. This may be why the percentage in mountain areas is higher than that in plain areas.

We have entered an aging society. The development of urbanization will be surely faced with model design of providing for retired seniors. Materialize funds of social security in villages and establish rural social security system will be based on urban well-being finance system, but we should not ignore the construction of gerocomium of centralized adoption. In this sense, the city has to learn from villages. Establish high quality social well-being facility such as gerocomiums.

V. The conclusion obtained by the indicator analysis mentioned above is as follows

1. Scientific Outlook on Development should be adhered to for development of designated towns

We have a vast territory with great disparity. Being advanced or backward is not decided by people; neither can it be solved in a short time. Objective geographical environment, local customs and life features result in necessary result of historical evolution. Therefore local historical evolution factors should be fully analyzed for development of designated towns and its urbanization planning. Local custom features should be grasped; tap one's own potential and resource strengths; adjust measures to local conditions and make development planning. Apposition should be avoided as much as possible in our urban development. Besides it is an important principle for planning of designated town to protect local environment and historical heritage in future construction and development of urbanization. Plan and build designated towns from the perspective of inheriting and developing.

2. The direction of reform and opening-up should be abided by for the development of designated towns

In our country, "town" is established for the sake of administrative management and is formed with economic development. More attention is paid to jurisdiction and local development thinking is blocked by terms of responsibility and power. In western countries, town is a settlement with smaller size. It is usually located in villages or urban-rural combination places. More attention is paid to habitation. As a result, development and planning of designated towns have to be combined with construction and development of cities. A reasonable layout and supplement of resources among towns should be formed without blind self-devel-

Pictures of Excellent Model Cities

Xiamen

Xiamen Software Park

The first International Marathon in Xiamen

Ningbo

Hemudu Culture Relics of Ningbo

**Tianyi Pavilion the oldest private library in existence in China
and one of the three most ancient family libraries in the entire world.**

Suzhou

Suzhou Gardens

Suzhou Sports Center

Hangzhou

Thousand Island Lake

The Broken Bridge in West Lake

Changzhou

Yuanyang Temple in Mt. Maoshan

Changzhou Tianmu Lake

Zhuhai

Bird's Eye View of Zhuhai

Statue of Zhuhai Fishing Woman, located at beautiful Xianglu Bay in Zhuhai

Shenzhen

Shenzhen Cross – sea Bridge

Window of the World

Beijing

The Forbidden City

Fireworks in 2008 Olympic Games

Zhongshan

Zhongshan Comprehensive Garbage Treatment Base with disposal capacity of 3,100 tons per day

Triumph Wetland Park The first wetland park in Zhongshan

Wuxi

Liyuan, one of the main view spots in national key scenic area of Taihu Lake

Wu Cultural Festival, offering sacrifices to Wu Taibo

Shanghai

Expo 2010 Shanghai

Night View of the Bund

Jiaxing

Three Pagodas in Jiaxing

Ancient Watertown—Xitang in Jiaxing

Guangzhou

Canton Fair Venue

Watertown Festival

Dalian

Dalian Landscape

**The Largest and Most Influential International Fashion Culture and
Economy Pageant, Dalian International Fashion Festival**

Erdos

Erdos Theatre

Mongolian Wedding

Zhenjiang

Zhenjiang Jinshan Temple

Zhenjiang Museum

Nanjing

The Nanjing Yangtze River Bridge

Nanjing Landscape

Qingdao

Panorama of Qingdao

Qingdao Sailing Base of 2008 Olympic Games

Weihai

Weihai Wharf

Weihai Happiness Gate

Changsha

Yuelu Academy

Dufu Pavilion in scenery belt of Xiangjiang River

opment of industry; conditions suitable for habitation should be created. This is a kind of open thinking.

3. More opportunities for employment should be created during the development of designated towns

"Settlement" should become a basis for development of designated towns. A region's attraction should be the target of regional development. Population drain has become a prominent problem in designated towns, especially in needy towns. It has become shackles of local economic development. Our statistics analysis is not profound, detailed and accurate, but we can get a glimpse of it. The evaporation of population has occurred in almost all industrial countries. It is the reason why there is imbalance between urban and rural population. It is a severe social problem. We are facing such a challenge.

4. The development of designated towns should regard cities and county-level cities as the subject

As we see in above statistics analysis, the development of designated towns entails investment for construction of infrastructure. It is impossible to singly rely on town's finance. Correspondingly the development of designated towns should be part of urban planning and an indicator for urban development. Create deep processing bases of subsidiary agricultural products, production bases of little commodities and tourism bases from the perspective of serving cities so as to create more employment opportunities.

We made a general comparison of designated towns in 19 provinces and cities in East China, Central China and north part of China. 13,011 designated towns in these 19 provinces and cities occupy almost 70% of the country. In addition to designated towns in three municipalities directly under the Central Government, almost all designated towns in Hebei, Shanxi, Shandong, Liaoning, Guangdong, Jiangsu and Hubei are covered by province-level, cities and county-level cities. This means that China has entered a development period of all-round urbanization. The development and planning of designated towns is the responsibility of province-level, cities and county-level cities and should be assessment indicators for urban development. We can see from percentage that 64.74% of towns are governed by cities with 65.61% of town population and 77.73% of town territories. It actually provides wider space for urban development.

5. The principle of environment first should be adhered to for the development of designated towns

The environment of most of designated towns is superior over cities. This should be an advantage for development of designated towns. We cannot actually grasp the problem of environment pollution but we can get a glimpse of worries over environment damage from analysis of local finance. The old way of polluting before dealing with it in urban construction should be abandoned for the development of designated towns. Reasonable planning should be made to prevent pollution. Make orientations carefully according to features of resources. First plan and then build; first formulate measure and then implement them. This does not only include town planning but also planning of economic development. Therefore the country should support it by policies and capital. Promote it on the basis of pilot places and include the transformation of designated towns in outline of economic development and the five-year plan.

6. The principle of people oriented should be observed for the development of designated towns

Traditional urban planning focuses on functions of cities and demands of industrial and commercial development so as to form a huge city machine. Designated towns governed by cities should plan its construction from the perspective of habitation environment, especially the establishment of charity houses. Although the facility and service quality in villages cannot match the level of that in cities, villages has an earlier start with a long history. It is favored by number; what's more fresh air and peaceful environment are more suitable for seniors.

7. The core of development of designated towns should be management level

The development of designated towns is not only about space planning and material layout but also about management of social development. Town is a system. Town management is a science which needs knowledge integration of several sciences. Administrators should be trained and sense of scientific management and management level should be enhanced. A long-term and effective mechanism should be formed.

8. Local agriculture features should be relied on for the development of designated towns

Leeks and vegetables of Shouguang make its dehydrated vegetable industry.

Apples of north part of Shaanxi attract jam businessmen in Southeast Asia. Navel oranges of Ganzhou and dates of Hetian become the brand of towns. Developing towns does not mean ignorance of agriculture. The fundamental principle of development of designated towns should be coordination and integration of urban and rural areas. The development of agriculture should be combined. For example, pasture bases, breeding bases and dairy processing bases can be established in Inner Mongolia while planting grass to fix sand.

9. Integrate planning of designated towns from the perspective of regional planning

Regional planning is developed on the basis of urban planning and planning of industrial and mining areas. Strategies of national economy and social development have to be made for the entire planning; assign detailed key construction measures related with regional development and regulation to specific regions and conduct general layout of comprehensive coordination among department so as to provide basis for making middle and long-term department planning and urban planning. Regard regional planning as a middle step between economic planning and urban planning. Economic planning points out direction for regional planning which in turn provides basis for urban planning. As a result only when the thinking of regional planning is implemented can coordinated development of designated towns be possible, can blind development and apposition competition is prevented. Only in this way can urban planning break away from scope of built areas of cities and planning controlled areas, can designated town clusters be formed while considering coordinated development of economic regions.

Part Four   City Ranking List and Data of Part of Cities

Chapter One   Excellent Model Cities of China Urban Scientific Development

Ranking	City	Ranking	City
1	Xiamen	11	Shanghai
2	Ningbo	12	Jiaxing
3	Suzhou	13	Guangzhou
4	Hangzhou	14	Dalian
5	Changzhou	15	Erdos
6	Zhuhai	16	Zhenjiang
7	Shenzhen	17	Nanjing
7	Beijing	18	Qingdao
9	Zhongshan	19	Weihai
10	Wuxi	20	Changsha

Cities listed above are "Comprehensive Evaluation and Grading (E&G) System of China Urban Scientific Development" top 20 in terms of comprehensive ranking.

Chapter Two   Representative Cities of China Urban Scientific Development

I. Representative cities in terms of comprehensive strength

Ranking	City	Ranking	City
21	Tianjin	36	Jinan
22	Shaoxing	37	Yantai
23	Zhoushan	38	Dongguan
24	Huhehaote	39	Baotou
25	Foshan	40	Wuhu
26	Jinhua	41	Taizhou
26	Dongying	42	Fuzhou
28	Chengdu	43	Nantong
28	Yinchuan	44	Yangzhou
30	Huzhou	45	Tongling
30	Wuhan	46	Wuhai
32	Taiyuan	47	Kunming
33	Zhengzhou	48	Zibo
34	Ma' anshan	49	Wenzhou
35	Shenyang	50	Qinhuangdao

Cities listed above are "Comprehensive Evaluation and Grading (E&G) System of China Urban Scientific Development" top 21 – 50 in terms of compre-hensive ranking.

II. Representative cities in terms of system development (top 50 cities in terms of three parent systems)

Economic development level system

Ranking	City	Ranking	City
1	Suzhou	26	Tai'an
2	Yangzhou	27	Shuozhou
3	Ningbo	28	Jinan
4	Taizhou	29	Shenzhen
5	Dongying	30	Lianyungang
6	Changzhou	31	Taizhou
7	Jiaxing	32	Nantong
8	Jinhua	33	Tongling
9	Xiamen	34	Dalian
10	Zhongshan	35	Xuzhou
11	Wuxi	36	Guangzhou
12	Huhehaote	37	Nanjing
12	Shanghai	38	Yulin
14	Qingdao	39	Tianjin
15	Jincheng	40	Changzhi
16	Zhenjiang	41	Yan'an
17	Yancheng	42	Taiyuan
18	Weifang	42	Xinyu
19	Shijiazhuang	44	Yingtan
20	Hangzhou	45	Zhoushan
21	Yantai	46	Quanzhou
22	Zhuhai	47	Changsha
23	Huzhou	48	Beijing
23	Shaoxing	49	Erdos
23	Kunming	50	Weihai

Public service level system

Ranking	City	Ranking	City
1	Beijing	26	Erdos
2	Xiamen	27	Weihai
3	Shenzhen	28	Zhoushan
4	Shanghai	29	Hulun Buir
5	Zhuhai	30	Panjin
6	Hangzhou	31	Changzhou
7	Guangzhou	32	Changchun
7	Karamay	33	Anshan
9	Dalian	33	Changsha
10	Tianjin	35	Fushun
11	Suzhou	36	Kunming
12	Ningbo	37	Lanzhou
13	Wuhan	38	Daqing
14	Baotou	39	Zhongshan
15	Yinchuan	40	Jinan
16	Shenyang	40	Foshan
17	Wuhai	42	Qingdao
18	Nanjing	43	Zhengzhou
19	Huhehaote	44	Yangquan
20	Jiayuguan	45	Urumqi
21	Benxi	46	Ma' anshan
22	Taiyuan	47	Sanya
23	Wuxi	48	Yingkou
24	Panzhihua	48	Liaoyang
25	Tongling	50	Shizuishan

Residents' actual sharing level system

Ranking	City	Ranking	City
1	Changzhou	26	Ma' anshan
2	Beijing	27	Wuxi
3	Foshan	28	Jinhua
4	Hangzhou	29	Jiangmen
5	Zhenjiang	30	Karamay
5	Jiaxing	31	Shaoxing
7	Ningbo	32	Sanya
8	Zhongshan	33	Shenyang
9	Dongguan	34	Zhoushan
10	Xiamen	35	Quzhou
11	Huzhou	35	Guangzhou
12	Nantong	37	Yueyang
13	Zhuhai	38	Lishui
14	Chengdu	39	Langfang
15	Quanzhou	40	Yancheng
16	Suzhou	41	Wenzhou
16	Zhengzhou	42	Nanjing
18	Shenzhen	43	Qingdao
19	Erdos	44	Yinchuan
20	Taizhou	45	Suizhou
20	Changsha	46	Shanghai
20	Huizhou	47	Xuzhou
23	Weihai	48	Panjin
24	Jiayuguan	49	Dalian
25	Fuzhou	50	Longyan

Chapter Three   Superior Cities in terms of China Urban Characteristic Development

I. Superior cities in terms of economic growth efficiency

Top ten cities according to sub-system of general economic development:

City	City
Zhuhai	Shanghai
Dongguan	Yulin
Xiamen	Jiaxing
Hangzhou	Suzhou
Ningbo	Shaoxing

II. Superior cities in terms of residents' income planning

Top ten cities according to sub-system of residents' income level:

City	City
Changsha	Zhongshan
Changzhou	Foshan
Zhenjiang	Ningbo
Zhoushan	Huzhou
Tianjin	Anshan

III. Superior cities in terms of element usage efficiency

Top ten cities according to sub-system of element usage efficiency

City	City
Erdos	Jinhua
Yan' an	Yancheng
Yulin	Suzhou
Taizhou	Qingyang
Lüliang	Shaoxing

IV. Superior cities in terms of human settlement environment

Top ten cities according to sub-system of human settlement environment:

City	City
Wuxi	Suzhou
Hangzhou	Yinchuan
Xiamen	Yueyang
Qingdao	Ningbo
Changsha	Hefei

V. Superior cities in terms of externality regulation

Top ten cities according to sub-system of externality:

City	City
Yingtan	Neijiang
Tongling	Qujing
Kunming	Tongchuan
Rizhao	Huhehaote
Fuyang	Huainan
Huangshi	

VI. Superior cities in terms of development speed

Top ten cities according to development speed compared with that of 2008:

City	City
Yueyang	Shuozhou
Yibin	Suqian
Yancheng	Xinyu
Yingtan	Yulin
Zaozhuang	Jilin